Washington

COMMUNITY TREASURES

by William Faubion

a part of the Morgan & Chase Treasure Series
www.treasuresof.com

 MORGAN & CHASE PUBLISHING INC.

Published by:
Morgan & Chase Publishing, Inc.
531 Parsons Drive, Medford, Oregon 97501
(888) 557-9328
www.treasuresof.com

Printed by:
Taylor Specialty Books - Dallas TX

First edition 2006

ISBN: 1-933989-03-3

THE
TREASURE
SERIES

*I gratefully acknowledge the contributions
of the many people involved in the writing and production of this book.
Their tireless dedication to this endeavor has been inspirational.*
—Damon Neal, *Publisher*

Managing Editor:
David Smigelski

Senior Story Editor:
Mary Beth Lee

Senior Writer:
Gregory Scott

Proof Editors:
Avery Brown and Robyn Sutherland

Graphic Design:
C.S. Rowan, Jesse Gifford, Tamara Cornett, Jacob Kristof, Michael Frye

Photo Coordinators:
Wendy Gay and Donna Lindley

Website:
Casey Faubion, Molly Bermea, Ben Ford

Morgan & Chase Home Team
Cindy Tilley Faubion, Anita Fronek, Emily Wilkie, Cari Qualls, Anne Boydston,
Virginia Arias, Danielle Barkley, Shauna O'Callahan, Clarice Rodriguez, Terrie West

Contributing Writers:
Judi Bailey, Andre Osborne, Dusty Alexander, Mary Knepp, Paul Hadella, Arla Miller, Janice Ariza, Leslie Hansen, Malika Summer, Marie Sundquist,
Nancy Velando, Perianne Myers, Tara Harmon, Yvonne Rains, Amber Dusk, Candy Schrodek, CJ White, Claudia Van Dyke,
Kevin Monk, Larry George, Maggie McClellen, Rochelle Ford, Susan Vaughn, Tammy Volk

Special Recognition to:
Sarah Brown, Jolee Moody, Carolyn Courian, Kimberley Wallan,
Judy Stallcop, Mike Stallcop, Jennifer Strange, Nancy McClain

To the people of Washington.
Thank you for making this book possible.

Table of Contents

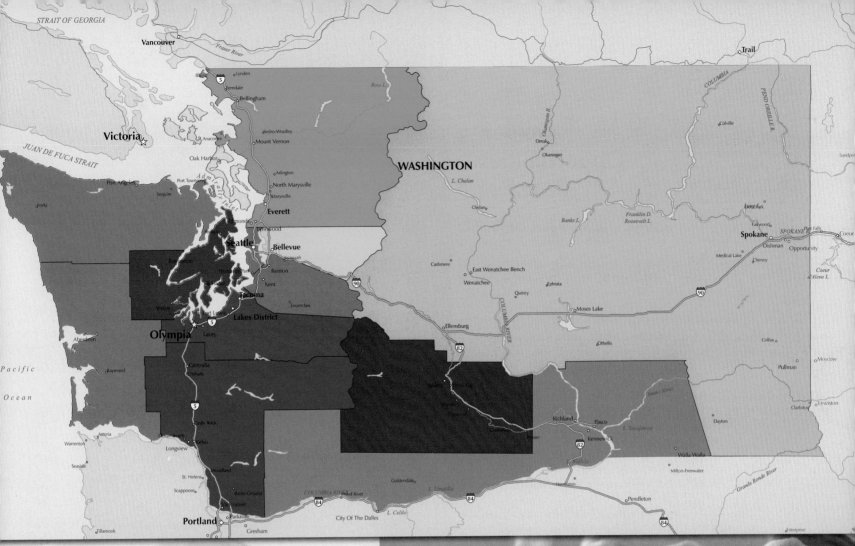

How to use this book

Washington Community Treasures is divided into 13 geographic regions: Seattle Metro, Eastside, The Valley, South Puget Sound, Vancouver-Mount St. Helens, Olympic Peninsula, Snohomish and Skagit, Kitsap Peninsula, The Coast, The Islands, Eastern Washington, Columbia Gorge/Tri-Cities and Yakima Valley.

The opening spreads for each region provide a quick geographical sketch of the area, including a list of the cities covered in that region. As you page through the regions, you'll find a short description of each city followed by a list of selected parks, attractions and events.

In the index, cities and Treasures are listed alphabetically.

We have provided contact information for each Treasure in the book, because these are places and businesses we have personally visited, and which we encourage you to visit on your travels through Washington.

Announcing Golden Opportunities to Travel

Receive Free Treasures Dollars

The Treasures featured in *Washington Community Treasures*, as well as the Treasures from all of the books in our Treasures Series, can be found on our interactive website: **TreasuresOf.com**.

You can find them easily by clicking on the corresponding area of the map found on our home page. This will lead you to a list of cities covered in each book. Within each city, Treasures are listed under headings such as accommodations, attractions, restaurants, etc.

Look for Treasures with a Treasure Chest next to their name. This means they have made a special offer, redeemable by presenting one of our Treasure Dollars. The offer may be substantial; anything from a free night's stay to a free meal or gift. Many offers can be worth $100 or more.

To get your three Free Treasure Dollars, send the receipt for the purchase of this book to:

Morgan & Chase Publishing
Treasure Dollar Division
PO Box 1148
Medford, OR 97501-0232

Please include your name and address. We will send the coins to you.

We hope you enjoy reading *Washington Community Treasures* as much as we enjoyed writing it. Happy travels from the staff at Morgan & Chase Publishing.

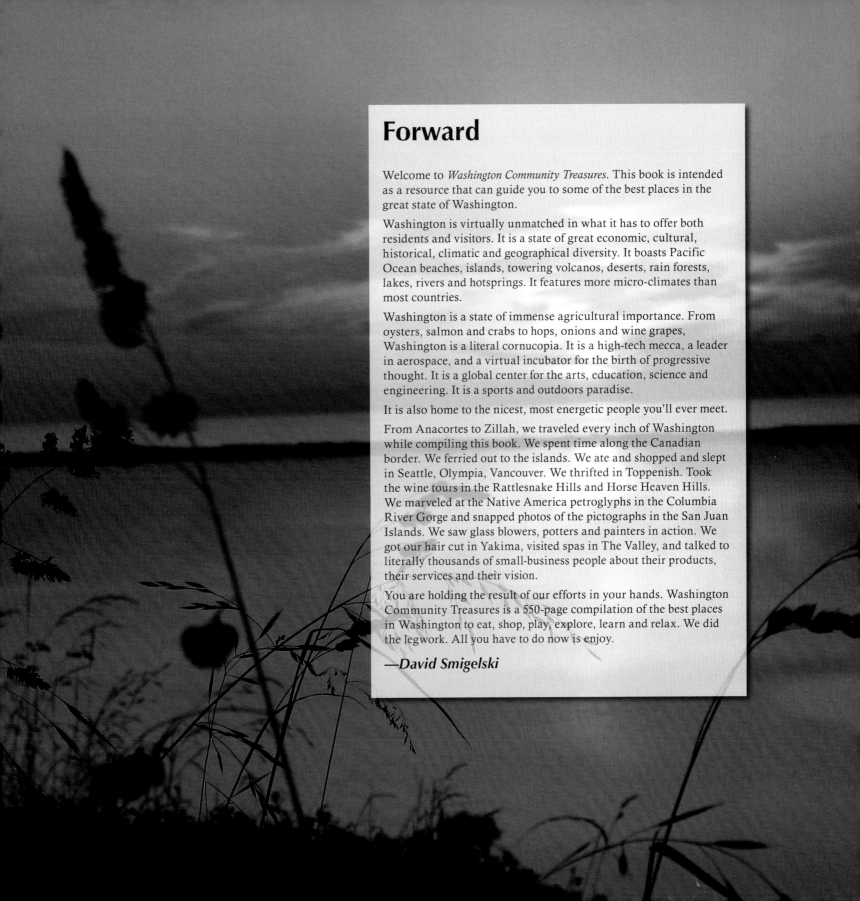

Forward

Welcome to *Washington Community Treasures*. This book is intended as a resource that can guide you to some of the best places in the great state of Washington.

Washington is virtually unmatched in what it has to offer both residents and visitors. It is a state of great economic, cultural, historical, climatic and geographical diversity. It boasts Pacific Ocean beaches, islands, towering volcanos, deserts, rain forests, lakes, rivers and hotsprings. It features more micro-climates than most countries.

Washington is a state of immense agricultural importance. From oysters, salmon and crabs to hops, onions and wine grapes, Washington is a literal cornucopia. It is a high-tech mecca, a leader in aerospace, and a virtual incubator for the birth of progressive thought. It is a global center for the arts, education, science and engineering. It is a sports and outdoors paradise.

It is also home to the nicest, most energetic people you'll ever meet.

From Anacortes to Zillah, we traveled every inch of Washington while compiling this book. We spent time along the Canadian border. We ferried out to the islands. We ate and shopped and slept in Seattle, Olympia, Vancouver. We thrifted in Toppenish. Took the wine tours in the Rattlesnake Hills and Horse Heaven Hills. We marveled at the Native America petroglyphs in the Columbia River Gorge and snapped photos of the pictographs in the San Juan Islands. We saw glass blowers, potters and painters in action. We got our hair cut in Yakima, visited spas in The Valley, and talked to literally thousands of small-business people about their products, their services and their vision.

You are holding the result of our efforts in your hands. Washington Community Treasures is a 550-page compilation of the best places in Washington to eat, shop, play, explore, learn and relax. We did the legwork. All you have to do now is enjoy.

—David Smigelski

Photo by Robert Badgley

Seattle Metro

Seattle Metro

SEATTLE, known as the Emerald City, is a place of green landscapes that sparkle with activities and wonders, both natural and human made. The region is defined by its proximity to water, and maritime industries have always been central to the city's identity. People even live on water here. Lake Union is the nation's largest floating community.

Seattle's innovation and creativity are represented by sights ranging from the Space Needle (built for the 1962 World Fair) to a three-story guitar sculpture (created for Paul Allen's Experience Music Project). Art is everywhere in Seattle. The Seattle Art Museum contains more than 21,000 objets d'art. Pike Place Market on the waterfront, one of the nation's oldest farmer's markets, bustles with the wares and talents of hundreds of craftspeople, merchants and street performers. Downtown, Pioneer Square is a testament to the city's tenacity, a brick-and-iron replacement for the wooden downtown destroyed in the Great Fire of 1889. Young people crowd the University of Washington, which sprawls over 700 acres. The Fremont neighborhood embodies the freer side of Seattle. Its landmark is a 53-foot Cold War-era rocket bearing the motto, De Libertas Quirkas (Freedom to be Peculiar).

Metro Seattle includes Seattle Southside, some of the closest-in suburbs. SeaTac is home to the Seattle-Tacoma airport, and Tukwila contains Westfield Southcenter, Puget Sound's largest shopping complex. Just north of Seattle lie Edmonds, with one of the best birding trails in America, and neighboring Lynnwood, once a checkerboard of chicken ranches, but now home to Lynnwood Ice Center.

Festivals and events, including the baseball Mariners, football Seahawks and basketball Supersonics, draw visitors to Seattle Metro every month of the year. The city celebrates the end of each lunar cycle with the world's tallest fireworks show, launched from the Space Needle on New Year's Eve.

Elliot Bay seen from the top of Pike Place Market

BURIEN

The first European inhabitants called the Burien area Sunnydale. When the first real town was established at the end of the 1900s, however, it was renamed after Gottlieb Van Boorian, a German immigrant and the town's founder. Early transportation was provided by the Mosquito Fleet, small steamboats that stopped en route from Seattle to Olympia. Today, Burien Town Square, a $130 million development, is reshaping the downtown into a plaza surrounded by a new city hall and library, along with condominiums, stores and offices.

PLACES TO GO

- Seahurst Art Gallery
  15210 10th Avenue SW
  (206) 244-7844

- Burien Community Center and Grounds
  425 SW 144th Street

- Moshier Park and Community Art Center
  430 S 156th Street

- Seahurst Park
  SW 140th Street

THINGS TO DO

June
- Burien Strawberry Festival
  (206) 433-2882

September
- Burien's Downtown Artwalk
  (206) 433-2882

- Van Boorian Days
  (206) 433-2882

2006 Fourth of July Parade, Burien
Photo by Eric Weaver

Glass Expressions

ARTS & CRAFTS:
Best stained glass art studio

Glass Expressions is a full-service stained-glass studio that makes custom windows, does repairs and teaches classes, while selling an abundance of arts and crafts supplies. You can find the shop just south of Seattle and directly west of the SeaTac Airport. Owned by Kathy Johnson and Lael Smidt, Glass Expressions offers good service and a friendly atmosphere. Kathy has been making beads for 10 years. Her specialty is horsehead beads, which evolved from a lifetime of drawing and sculpting. Glass Expressions has been in business since 1974. It was originally called Stained Glass Art and Supply. In 1980 Kathy sold her horse so she could buy the store, and she renamed it Glass Expressions. In 1988 Ray Crudo went into partnership with Kathy and they moved the store two blocks east to a larger storefront. A few years later, Ray retired. Lael, who was one of Kathy's students, quit her job at Boeing and became Kathy's partner. Kathy and Lael have created a small, friendly atmosphere. The shop is very low-key, with an art studio ambience. They carry a full line of tools and supplies for stained glass, fusing and glass bead making. Visit Glass Expressions to shop, or enroll in one of their classes and begin your journey of imagination.

648 SW 152nd Street, Burien WA
(206) 242-2860
www.glassexpressions.com

Market Place Salon & Day Spa

HEALTH & BEAUTY: *Best salon and day spa in Burien*

Market Place Salon & Day Spa in Burien offers relaxing and reviving day-spa services that cover a wide range of choices from skin-care treatments and massage to luxurious spa experiences designed to renew the spirit as well as the body. Owners Daniel and Melinda are justifiably proud of the warm and welcoming environment here where staff and clients always feel relaxed, comfortable and at home. Over the course of his impressive career, Daniel Keane has honed his skills in countless master classes with industry professionals and educators from all over the world. He has been a featured educator for Aveda and a member of the National Show and Education Team for Italy Hair Fashion, participating in shows and conducting seminars where he has developed an international reputation for his highly original and ground-breaking coloring techniques. He has also been a regular guest on regional television programs, creating makeovers and discussing the latest trends in hair fashion and personal grooming. Working together with their enthusiastic team of stylists and beauty professionals, Daniel and Melinda have created a spa and beauty oasis that, after more than 20 successful years, is one of the region's best.

15858 1st Avenue S, Burien WA (206) 224-8886 *marketplacesalonspa.com*

Bison Creek Pizza

RESTAURANTS & CAFÉS: *Best pizza in Burien*

Bison Creek Pizza is Burien's absolutely best pizza and party place. Owned by Mike Ramussen and Connie Salazar, Bison Creek Pizza has been serving great pizza and beer since 1977. Located on the western tip of downtown, the restaurant is just a short drive from any point in town. Bison Creek Pizza features 16 taps of microbrews from local and Northwest breweries. This family-oriented pizza parlor also has a kid's game room. Bison Creek makes their own delectable homemade pizza dough and ranch dressing from scratch. The name Bison Creek was derived from the name of a dude ranch in East Glacier Park, Montana. Mike and Connie love to be involved in the community. They support youth sports and aid regional fundraising for various civic groups. They attribute a lot of their success to the friends and family who have helped out over the years. In this same spirit of community, they provide a big-screen television where you can catch all of the big sporting events. If you check out their website, you can print out a coupon to use when you visit. So no more excuses, head to Bison Creek Pizza.

630 SW 153rd Street, Suite F, Burien WA
(206) 244-8825
bisoncreekpizza.com

EDMONDS

Edmonds is north of Seattle, right across the county line in Snohomish County. Founded in 1890, Edmonds has a fine view of Puget Sound, the Olympic Mountains and the Cascade Range. It has been called the friendliest town on Puget Sound.

PLACES TO GO

- Edmonds-South Snohomish County Historical Society Museum
  118 5th Avenue N (425) 774-0900

- Edmonds Center for the Arts
  410 4th Avenue N (425) 275-4485

- Yost Park
  9535 Bowdoin Way

- Edmonds Underwater Park
  Brackett's Landing

THINGS TO DO

April
- Edmonds in Bloom Spring Festival
  Anderson Center (425) 771-2631

May
- Edmonds Jazz Connection
  www.jazzconnection.org

- Edmonds Waterfront Festival
  (425) 771-1744

- Puget Sound Bird Fest
  (425) 771-0227

June
- Edmonds Arts Festival
  Anderson Center (425) 771-6412

August
- A Taste of Edmonds
  (425) 670-9112

Sunset over Puget Sound
Photo by Liz Lawley

Edmonds Center for the Arts

ATTRACTIONS:
Best performing arts center

For more than three decades, arts, civic and business leaders in Edmonds dreamed of building a first-class, regional performing arts center in their city. In 2006, the dream become reality as the city opened the doors to the beautiful new Edmonds Center for the Arts. The center is on the campus of the old Edmonds High School, which later served as the Puget Sound Christian College. The original school building is on the State Register of Historic Places. Builders finished the renovations in September 2006. That fall, the Cascade Symphony Orchestra, the Olympic Ballet Theatre and the Sno-King Community Chorale put on preseason performances. In January 2007, Edmonds celebrated a gala grand opening. Initial renovations focused on the theater of the existing campus, which was first constructed in 1939. Art deco in style, its main façade is a convex wall flanked by two-story high pilasters. Bas relief decorative elements above the entry doors received new colors to accentuate the entrance. The reconstruction of the interior improved sight lines and acoustics, and also added to the elegance of the auditorium. During intermissions, audience members can step outside for a view of Puget Sound and the Olympic Mountains. A cultural resource for the entire region, Edmonds Center for the Arts provides first-class performing arts presentations, supports community partnerships and offers education outreach programs. The center is also available for rental.

410th Avenue N, Edmonds WA
(425) 275-4485
www.edmondscenterforthearts.org

Alan Turner Jewelers

FASHION: *Best jeweler in Edmonds*

For more than 50 years, Alan Turner Jewelers has been dazzling Edmonds shoppers with a selection of exquisite jewelry designs, from both its own designers and other leading firms. Alan Turner's lead designer, Greg Wilson, can design and create custom pieces to match your dreams and tastes. Alan Turner offers artisan jewelry from traditional English firms that long ago designed for Queen Victoria and currently for the Royal Family. As a full-service diamond merchant, the store carries rings and other pieces from such respected companies as A. Jaffe, Claude Thibaudeau and Camelot. The Lyric sterling silver collection contains artful combinations of silver, diamonds and pearls. At Alan Turner Jewelers, a gemologist assures your satisfaction by checking the quality and authenticity of every piece. Alan Turner is also the place to turn for elegant china and porcelain figurines from such world-famous sources as Hummel of Germany and Lladro of Spain. Owner Ann Turner and her staff are dedicated to quality, service and absolute integrity. They invite you to stop by their showroom and view the many precious adornments on display.

408 Main Street, Edmonds WA
(206) 546-1211 or (425) 744-7883
www.alanturnerjewelers.com

KinderBritches

FASHION: *Best children's clothing store in Edmonds*

You will find the trendiest, most unusual and classic designs in clothing, accessories, and gifts at KinderBritches. Tammy Miller opened KinderBritches in 1993 and made it her goal to stock must-have merchandise for babies and kids. The building where KinderBritches is located has housed a children's clothing store since 1962. Tammy remembers shopping there as a child, never dreaming that she would some day own her own shop in the same spot. Carrying on the tradition of her predecessors, the specialty store offers quality products for infants, toddlers, kids and "tweens," in sizes 0-7 for boys, and sizes 0-16 for girls. Tammy attends at least 10 trade shows every year to select from the best clothing lines, and her team researches products to ensure that customers will not have to look elsewhere to find the best of the best. From baby skincare products, jogging strollers and diaper bags for the younger set, to urban fashions and cool travel luggage for preteens, the knowledgeable staff can help you select gifts that will be appreciated for their uniqueness as well as their usefulness. Free gift-wrapping is first-class, and the KinderBritches 500 club grants a $25 gift certificate to customers who spend $500 in a year. Visit KinderBritches and carry on the tradition in downtown Edmonds.

422 Main Street, Edmonds WA
(425) 778-7600
www.kinderbritches.com

Mu·Shoe

FASHION: *Best women's designer shoes and handbags*

Edmond's first and only shoe store exclusively for women takes your feet to the cutting edge of fashion footwear. Susan Wilson, owner of Mu•Shoe, developed her eye and interest in shoes at an early age, thanks, in part, to her father, who owned a shoe store. After many years in the business world, Susan decided to unleash her love of shoes. A visit to a Venice shop filled with amazing shoes and a Florence shop filled with fine handbags forged her first partnerships and launched her business. Expect to see many designer labels in this posh shop, where artful displays include the latest styles by Coclico, Jocasi and Pazzo, alongside such fashion greats as Couture Donald

Pliner, Loriani Bags and DKNY. Susan carefully selects her shoes during seasonal visits to New York and Paris. She uses art gallery flair to exhibit shoes, handbags, hosiery and jewelry. The styles, textures and colors found here are appealing and fashion-forward, but never trendy. Mu•Shoe is perfect for businesswomen and busy women seeking professional, personalized services and an alternative to mall shopping. Susan named her shop after the popular Chinese dish, mu shu pork. Treat your feet to something sweet at Mu•Shoe Takeout, where Susan introduces new product lines and serves fortune cookies. Susan invites you to step out of your comfort zone with a visit to Mu•Shoe. You can try on the outfits that will accompany your shoes, receive encouragement and advice and walk out with a pair of sensational shoes.

403 Main Street, Edmonds WA
(425) 778-0125
www.mushoe.com

Running in Motion

FASHION: *Best sports store for runners and walkers*

If you're interested in maintaining a healthful lifestyle, walking and running are fabulous choices for attaining it. Running in Motion is an upscale sports store that's dedicated solely to running and walking enthusiasts. Owner Frank Yamamoto is a serious biped fanatic himself, so his store specializes in only three top brands of shoes—Mizuno, Saucony and New Balance. Frank's philosophy is that proper equipment and proper fit are crucial to achieving and maintaining fitness goals. He has a huge selection of those three brands, and Frank and his well trained staff make sure each customer is given the time to be properly fitted. If a shoe isn't right for your foot and your needs, Frank won't sell it to you. Running in Motion carries many top apparel lines, as well as all the accessories you'll want, like hydration bottles, gear bags and heart monitors. Frank hires the

high school's young track and cross-country runners to work at his shop and recruits the high school's coaches to advise at the running clinics he organizes every week. He also puts together charitable 5K runs, and when he'd been open only six months, he donated all the funds from one of these to Hurricane Katrina relief. Frank's dedication to the welfare of others extends not just to his customers and their health, but also to his community and beyond. If you want to stay in motion to stay in shape, Running In Motion is your next stop.

610 Main Street, Suite B, Edmonds WA
(425) 774-0637
www.runninginmotion.com

Nash Chiropractic & Massage

HEALTH & BEAUTY:
Best chiropractic clinic

Experience peace of mind while recovering from painful injuries and strains at Nash Chiropractic & Massage. Nash Chiropractic opened in 2000 and has since gained a strong reputation for excellence, due to its professionalism and one-on-one approach to patient care. Dr. Nash is a Palmer graduate and served as chiropractic consultant for famed soccer teams while residing in Scotland. He specializes in acute injuries, as well as chronic and long-term pain issues, including the treatment of old injuries. Patients appreciate the family-like atmosphere of the office and the friendly and personable attitude of Dr. Nash and his employees, who strive to make people feel as comfortable as possible, both mentally and physically. Nash Chiropractic staffs three licensed massage therapists, who work closely with the doctor to loosen up and elongate muscles prior to chiropractic adjustment, a step that improves results and eases stress for patients. Dr. Nash focuses on making individuals aware that they are in charge of their own health, and that the efforts they put into their own recovery will effect the amount of benefit they receive. A large percentage of Nash Chiropractic's clients come from referrals from patients who are delighted with the personalized treatment and kindness they receive. Trust your recovery to the professionals at Nash Chiropractic & Massage.

23303 Highway 99, Suite G, Edmonds WA
(425) 697-5188
www.nashchiropractic.com

Olympic Dance Sport

RECREATION: *Best dance classes in Edmonds*

If you ever wanted to learn how to dance in a comfortable, friendly environment, you will enjoy Olympic Dance Sport. The studio's staff members believe that dancing is a fun way to exercise and gain a positive outlook on life. The instructors at Olympic Dance Sport customize lessons to match your abilities and desires. After you learn basic dance moves in private lessons, you can practice your new skills in group sessions. Olympic Dance Sport offers instruction in traditional ballroom favorites, such as the waltz, tango and foxtrot. You can learn any of the popular social dances, including Latin and swing dances, and dance to music that ranges from classical to heavy metal. Olympic Dance Sport instructors teach competitive dancing and many of them, including owner Christina Singletary and her partner Marcus Rodriguez, have won or placed in regional and international dance competitions. Club members often spend their vacations together traveling to competitions. All instructors are members of the National Dance Council of America and are certified by the studio or by the NDCA. Dancers of all ages, from 12 to 80, are welcome to toss aside their rubber-soled shoes and take a turn on the dance floor. Whether you have two left feet or are an advanced dancer, Olympic Dance Sport can help you improve your moves.

9681 Firdale Avenue, Edmonds WA
(206) 546-8580
www.olympicdancesport.com

Girardi's Osteria

RESTAURANTS & CAFÉS: *Best Italian food in Edmonds*

Osteria is an Italian word that means "a place where people gather to eat, drink and trade stories." Owner Patrick Girardi, host and manager of Gerardi's Osteria, has created just that kind of place with this elegant, refined, yet cozy neighborhood restaurant. Girardi's Osteria serves a diversified menu that includes duck, chicken, lamb and filet mignon, but because Girardi's is a neighborhood osteria, Patrick also gets down to basics. He provides the same basic, daily menu, because it's composed of the selections his regulars love. But his weekly specials can run the creative spectrum from crab cakes and pesce to lamb *osso buco* to *risotto primavera con pollo*. The fish is fresh daily, and all the pastas are freshly made on site. There are also wonderful antipasti, such as *carpaccio* served with bread or *millefoglie* made from wild mushrooms, almonds, sun dried tomatoes and goat cheese. Patrick hopes that his clientele will gain an understanding and love for the complexities of northern and southern Italian cuisine when they see his menu. With its refined, personable service, combined with a rustic, cozy European atmosphere, Girardi's Osteria is the perfect place for a romantic evening or dinner after a long day at work. Local customers often say, "Let's go to Patrick's," because it really is their home away from home.

504 5th Avenue S, Edmonds WA
(425) 673-5278
www.girardis-osteria.com

Olives Café & Wine Bar

RESTAURANTS & CAFÉS: *Best Mediterranean food and tapas*

Olives Café & Wine Bar has been renovated by owner and executive chef Michael A. Young. Helped by friends and staff, he literally gutted and rebuilt this wonderful little restaurant with his own hands. Warm terracotta walls and a long, handmade bar provide a Mediterranean ambience the minute you walk in the door. Olives serves tapas, a small-plate dining tradition popular throughout Spain, Italy and Greece. Tapas are a selection of shareable dishes that create a varied dining experience, and Olives is the only place in town where you can get them. Chef Michael offers full-course meals, as well, and his gourmet soups, salads, panini and specialty sandwiches are all gustatory masterpieces. Olives features more than 50 wines by the glass from West Coast boutique wineries. Michael designs a new menu every week based on the season and the availability of fresh fruits, vegetables and quality meats in the local markets. Monday and Tuesday nights are half-price wine nights on select vintages, and Thursday is Crazy Wine Night. A complimentary wine tasting is held from 5 pm to 8 pm, with reasonably priced tapas and a fabulous time for one and all. The gregarious and attentive staff take their cue from Michael and his obvious passion for great food that is artfully prepared and absolutely delicious. Come in and let Olives give you a cheery, warm European-style welcome.

107 5th Avenue N, #103, Edmonds WA
(425) 771-5757
www.olivescafewinebar.com

LYNNWOOD

Lynnwood is the commercial center for south Snohomish County, just north of Seattle. Once a land of chicken farms, Lynnwood today is anchored by developments such as Alderwood Mall and the Lynnwood Convention Center. Lynnwood expects that the new City Center, under development, will become a vibrant commercial center. Projects currently underway will upgrade the city's transportation network, add new public spaces and parks and create a pedestrian-friendly environment. The city's historic Interurban Trail provides almost four paved miles for biking, walking and jogging, connecting to additional trails in Everett and Mountlake Terrace. Scriber Lake Park, a 20-acre bird sanctuary, is located in the heart of Lynnwood's commercial district.

PLACES TO GO

- Heritage Park
  19921 Poplar Way

- Lynndale Park
  18927 72nd Avenue W

- Wilcox Park
  5215 196th Street SW

THINGS TO DO

July
- Shakespeare in the Park
  Lynndale Park (425) 771-4030

Amante Pizza and Pasta

RESTAURANTS & CAFES:
Best pizza in Lynnwood

Amante Pizza and Pasta stands out among the competition in several ways. The pizza is exceptional. The non-pizza choices are unusually comprehensive, and they are very good, as well. After coming to the United States, owner Stan Dimitrov worked as a pizza delivery guy, saving his money and learning the business. He dreamed of opening his own restaurant and discovered that a chain franchise would not let him create the kind of restaurant he wanted to build. Today, Stan's pizza restaurant has a relaxed, friendly and family-oriented atmosphere. Dough and sauces are made fresh from scratch daily. Stan offers 24 specialty pizzas, from simple cheese to Thai House and Feta Fetish. There are 17 pasta dishes and 13 salads. Calzones, grinders and low-carb specialties are on hand. The Italian Buffalo wings are an unusual and tasty appetizer. Stan believes in giving back to the community, and his business received media coverage for the thousands of dollars it raised for tsunami victims. Amante Pizza delivers for free, and deliveries are actually the larger part of its business. As a result, it is normally easy to get a seat in the restaurant itself. The restaurant has banquet facilities and a sports bar. You will enjoy your visit to Amante Pizza and Pasta.

4730 196th Street SW, Lynnwood WA
(425) 640-6600
www.amantepizzaandpasta.com

MOUNTLAKE TERRACE

Mountlake Terrace and Lynnwood both lie on territory that was once known as Alderwood Manor. This area was first settled at the turn of the century when the logging industry flourished. Later, the land was platted into ranches for mink, chinchillas and poultry. Denser settlement began with returning WWII veterans and their young families. Civic-minded residents soon founded a municipal government. Today, Mountlake Terrace is a community of blue skies, mountain views, beautiful parks and quiet residential neighborhoods. Mountlake Terrace offers 262 acres of parks, playgrounds and recreational attractions, including nine- and 18-hole golf courses and an ice-skating rink.

PLACES TO GO

- Ballinger Park
  23000 Lakeview Drive

- Recreation Pavilion
  5303 228th Street SW

- Terrace Creek Park
  23200 48th Avenue

THINGS TO DO

July
- Tour de Terrace Parade
  City Hall (425) 776-7331

August
- Community BBQ & Market
  (425) 776-9173

Forest Crest Athletic Club

HEALTH & FITNESS: *Best tennis club*

If you are passionate about tennis, you will find a home at the Forest Crest Athletic Club. The club's three indoor and three outdoor tennis courts are open to members 24 hours a day, which allows early birds and night owls to get in their game. Forest Crest is friendly and family-oriented, with two modern remote ball machines and a pro shop with a stringing service. The club guarantees that with 48 hours notice it will set up matches for members based on their skill levels. The club's junior program is one of the largest and most successful in the Northwest, because as soon as students pass the beginner level, they are organized into ability levels, tested for placement and advanced accordingly. The club's coaches are certified by the U.S. Professional Tennis Association and the Professional Tennis Registry. Ted Sayrahder, head coach and club manager, has earned many honors and accreditations, and was voted 2003 Professional of the Year by the USPTA. Glenn Delany, Ted's deputy and head of the junior program for youngsters 10 and under, was voted USPTA Assistant Professional of the Year in 2001. Classes and many of the club's programs are open to nonmembers on a space-available basis. If you are passionate about tennis, the Forest Crest Athletic Club invites you to play.

4901 238th Street SW, Mountlake Terrace WA
(425) 774-0014
www.forestcrest.com

SEATAC

It is possible that more people have been to SeaTac than any other city on Puget Sound, Seattle included. Of course, many of them never made it out of the airport. Seattle-Tacoma International Airport, better known as SeaTac, gave its name to the surrounding town. In addition to the airport, SeaTac is a city of hotels, but also of more than 25,000 residents and an extensive park system.

PLACES TO GO

- Des Moines Creek Park
  2151 S 200th Street

- Grandview Park and Off-Leash Dog Area
  3600 S 228th Street

- Highline SeaTac Botanical Garden
  13735 24th Avenue S

- North SeaTac Park
  S 128th Street and 20th Avenue S

- Valley Ridge Park
  4644 S 188th Street

THINGS TO DO

June
- International Festival
  Angle Lake Park (206) 973-4680

July
- Shakespeare in the Park
  Angle Lake Park (206) 973-4680

October
- Juried Fine Art Exhibit
  City Hall (206) 973-4680

SeaTac Botanical Gardens
Photo by Gwen Osaki

Hillrose Pet Resort
ANIMALS & PETS: *Best pet resort*

Dogs need day care, too. If you are heading out of town on business or vacation without your much-loved pets, you needn't feel guilty about leaving them behind anymore. Your special companions can now have a vacation of their own at Hillrose Pet Resort. You and your pet will know you are at a resort the minute you walk in. There are luxury pet suites, pet taxi services and professional kennel technicians who will groom, walk and play with your animal while you are gone. The owners and staff live on site so there is care and security 24 hours a day. The staff of highly trained technicians works with and trains a second staff, composed of high school students with their requisite high energy. Your pet will have no end of entertainment and affection in your absence. The Pet Resort is always interested in your ideas for services and is constantly in the process of adding new ones. Look for massage therapy, aromatherapy and web cams in suites and play yards in the near future. Go in and take a tour of the Hillrose Pet Resort, formerly Atwood's Pet Resort. You may wish you could join your dog on vacation.

2040 S 142nd Street, SeaTac WA
(206) 241-0880
www.petresort.com

Photo by Scott McClain

Angle Lake Cyclery
RECREATION: *Best bike shop*

Celebrating more than 51 years as a full-service bike shop, Angle Lake Cyclery is the first and only bike shop on Pacific Highway in Seattle. Angle Lake Cyclery was created to provide a wide selection of standard and unusual bikes with an emphasis on high quality and solid design. Owner Dave Clark continued to maintain the family business after he inherited the shop from his father, Rex Clark. Dave is very low key and courteous. He values customer service and will patiently and politely answer any and all questions his customers might have. Since Dave wants Angle Lake Cyclery to be one of the best bike shops on the planet, he will not carry a product simply because it represents the latest technology on the market. At Angle Lake Cyclery, the products must meet Dave's standards for quality, have a valid concept and be bikes or accessories that he and his staff would use themselves. Dave prides himself on Angle Lake Cyclery's community involvement, which includes sponsoring bike rodeos to support the girl scouts and boy scouts. Bike rodeos enlighten the community about bicycle safety as well as the importance of bicycle helmets in preventing the tragic injuries faced by unprotected cyclists. The shop has also taken a prominent role in addressing the transportation needs of bike commuters. Stop in and visit Dave at Angle Lake Cyclery for all of your cycling needs.

20804 Pacific Highway S, SeaTac WA
(206) 878-7457
www.anglelake.com

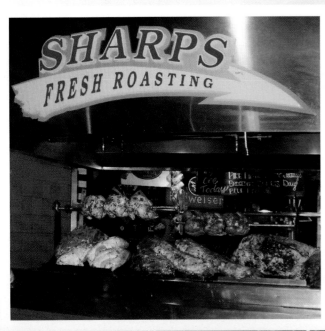

Sharp's Roaster & Ale House
RESTAURANTS & CAFÉS: *Best rotisserie roaster*

For more than 16 years, Sharp's Roaster & Ale House has been providing rotisserie meats, featuring a one-of-a-kind Radiant Roaster™. Located conveniently just outside of the SeaTac Airport, near all the major hotels in the area, Sharp's is known for having Seattle's best prime rib. This restaurant offers American barbeque, Northwest microbrews and a kid friendly atmosphere. Owner Timothy Firnstahl says he focuses on serving the highest quality food with the freshest ingredients at family prices. Sharp's Roaster also has a unique presentation of their dishes. The restaurant features a live smoker in the middle of the dining room and what is called a wagering wheel. This wheel spins every half hour and wherever it stops is the special for the next 30 minutes. When you are ready for a fun dining experience, head over to Sharp's Roaster & Ale House.

18427 Pacific Highway S, SeaTac WA
(206) 241-5744

Photo by Gwen Osaki

PLACES TO GO

- The Children's Museum
  305 Harrison Street (206) 441-1768

- Experience Music Project (EMP)
  325 5th Avenue N (206) 367-5483

- Frye Art Museum
  704 Terry Avenue (206) 622-9250

- Klondike Gold Rush National Park
  319 Second Avenue S (206) 553-7220

- Museum of History & Industry
  2700 24th Avenue E (206) 324-1126

- Nordic Heritage Museum
  3014 NW 67th Street (206) 789-5707

- Odyssey Maritime Discovery Center
  2205 Alaskan Way, Pier 66 (206) 374-4000

- Pacific Science Center
  200 2nd Avenue N (206) 443-2001

- Science Fiction Museum
  325 5th Avenue N (206) 724-3428

- Seattle Asian Art Museum
  1400 East Prospect Street (206) 344-5265

- Seattle Veterans Museum
  200 University Street (425) 821-0489

- The Seattle Aquarium
  1483 Alaskan Way, Pier 59 (206) 386-4300

- Woodland Park Zoo
  5500 Phinney Avenue N (206) 684-4800

- Alki Beach Park
  1702 Alki Avenue SW

- Discovery Park
  3801 W Government Way

- Golden Gardens Park
  8498 Seaview Place NW

- Green Lake Park
  7201 East Green Lake Drive N

- Japanese Garden
  1000 Lake Washington Boulevard

- Kubota Garden
  9817 55th Avenue S

- Lincoln Park
  8011 Fauntleroy Way SW

- Washington Park Arboretum
  2300 Arboretum Drive E

- Woodland Park
  Aurora Avenue N and N 59th Street

SEATTLE

Seattle was founded in the 1850s and named after Chief Seattle. It is the largest city in the Pacific Northwest, with 574,000 people within the city limits. Seattle is the hub of the greater Puget Sound region, a metropolitan area of about 3.8 million. Seattle is America's most educated large city. More than half its population 25 years and older holds at least a bachelor's degree. Seattle's reputation for heavy coffee consumption is well deserved. Its legendary rain, however, is exaggerated. Many East coast cities are wetter.

THINGS TO DO

May
- University District Street Fair
  (206) 547-4417

- Northwest Folklife Festival
  Seattle Center (206) 684-7200

May–September
- Butterflies and Blooms
  Woodland Park Zoo (206) 684-4800

June
- Fremont Fair
  (206) 649-6706

July
- Bite of Seattle
  Seattle Center (206) 684-7200

September
- What's Cooking in Wallingford
  (206) 632-3165

- Bumbershoot: Seattle's Music and Arts
  Festival
  Seattle Center (206) 684-7200

- Bungalow and Craftsman Fair
  Town Hall (206) 622-6952

- Fishermen's Fall Festival
  Fishermen's Terminal (206) 728-3395

October
- Feast at the Market
  Pike Place Market (206) 461-6935 ext. 160

- Seattle Home Show
  *Qwest Field and Exhibition Center
  (206) 381-8000*

November
- Fall Orchid Show and Sale
  Seattle Center (206) 684-7200

- Northwest Craft Alliance: Best of the
  Northwest Fall Show
  Magnuson Park (206) 684-4946

- Winterfest Worldfest
  Seattle Center (206) 684-7200

November-December
- Holiday Carousel and Wonderland
  Westlake Park (206) 623-0340

December
- KZOK Bob Rivers Show Twisted Christmas
  Party
  Paramount Theatre (206) 292-ARTS (2787)

Villa Heidelberg Bed and Breakfast

ACCOMMODATIONS:
Best bed and breakfast on Puget Sound

For old world charm on Puget Sound, spend a night or more at Judy Burbrink's Villa Heidelberg Bed and Breakfast. The location offers a great view of Puget Sound and the Olympic Mountains, yet is just 10 minutes from downtown Seattle. The Villa is a warm, comfortable and safe place for a single woman traveling alone.

In the common area, you'll find beamed ceilings, open staircases and leaded glass windows. You can dine each morning in the dining room or on the old-fashioned wraparound porch. Enjoy seasonal fruit, juice and gourmet coffee with the excellent breakfasts. At night you might rest in the Heidelberg room, with its king-sized brass bed, fireplace, crystal chandelier and view of the rose garden and South Puget Sound. Of the six *zimmers* (rooms) available, two have private baths. No matter which room you choose, you are sure to enjoy your stay at Villa Heidelberg.

4845 45th Avenue SW, Seattle WA
(206) 938-3658 or (800) 671-2942
www.villaheidelberg.com

Northwest Art & Frame

ARTS & CRAFTS:
Best frame shop

Northwest Art & Frame has a fabulous range of art supplies for everyone from the Sunday painter to the professional artist. The store is one of the best custom and ready-made frame shops in the Northwest, selling retail and also wholesale to some of the largest corporations in Washington. You can find an irresistible gift and extensive greeting card selection, with items to serve any gift-giving occasion. The staff at Northwest Art & Frame is unusually devoted and knowledgeable. Some staff members have been with the business for more than 20 years. These employees appreciate their working environment and are greatly respected by their colleagues, as well as by owner Dan Reiner. Many customers have shopped here for decades, with Northwest Art & Frame having been a west Seattle fixture for more than 37 years. It's a fun place to shop and a great place to work where the inquisitive owners are always looking for the latest exciting thing. For artist supplies, frames and gifts, head to Northwest Art & Frame.

**4733 California Avenue SW, Seattle WA
(206) 937-5507**

Bill Speidel's Underground Tour

ATTRACTIONS:
Best tour of Seattle

The Underground Tour is a leisurely, guided walking tour beneath Seattle's sidewalks and streets. While you roam the subterranean passages that once were the main roadways and first-floor storefronts of old downtown Seattle, tour guides regale you with humorous stories our pioneers didn't want you to hear, providing 50 years of history with a twist. The tour begins with a seated introduction inside Doc Maynard's, a restored 1890s saloon. Then you walk outside through historic Pioneer Square to three different sections of the underground, about three blocks in all. Be prepared for the underground landscape to be moderately rugged, where you'll encounter six flights of stairs, uneven terrain and spotty lighting. Dress for the weather and leave your spike-heeled shoes at home. The tour ends at the Rogues Gallery, where you'll find portraits of Seattle's colorful characters and other displays depicting Seattle's past. Whether you're shopping for shirts, shot glasses, *Sons of the Profits* (the book by Bill Speidel that launched the Underground Tour) or work by local artists, you will be sure to find the perfect memento of your Underground Tour adventure. Doc Maynard's offers a full menu, including snacks and espresso. It is a great place to unwind after your tour. Upstairs, Doc's game room features pool tables, pinball, darts, vintage video games and sports on TV. Doc Maynard's nightclub is one of Seattle's lively music venues, featuring a mix of the Northwest's favorite bands and national touring acts.

608 First Avenue, Seattle WA
(206) 682-4646
www.undergroundtour.com

ACT Theatre

ATTRACTIONS:
Best theater in Seattle

The best contemporary theater in Seattle is otherwise known as ACT. From its original base of 300 subscribers in its 400-seat facility in lower Queen Anne, ACT has grown to its present stature as a nationally-recognized theater serving nearly 10,000 subscribers, and along the way has received critical acclaim. Just a few of ACT's many awards have been sizable NEA challenge grants, the Washington State Governor's Arts Award and designation as Seattle's Best Theater by the *Seattle Weekly*. Forty years ago, ACT Theatre was created by Gregory and Jean Falls to provide a venue for innovative dramaturgy, a goal that still continues long after Gregory's 22 years as artistic director. In recent years ACT has added to its strengths. In 1994, ACT Theatre and the Housing Resource Group began a new initiative, a collaboration to restore the Eagles Auditorium, a neglected Seattle landmark. The new theater opened in 1996 to deserved acclaim, reinforcing ACT's national reputation as an outstanding regional theater. Each season ACT presents an exciting mix of American classics and new works by some of the leading contemporary playwrights. Consider a season ticket subscription to enjoy multiple membership benefits in addition to great theater.

700 Union Street, Seattle WA
(206) 292-7676
www.acttheatre.org

Nordic Heritage Museum

ATTRACTIONS: *Best place for Scandinavian history*

The Nordic Heritage Museum is a fascinating place where history comes alive. The people of Scandinavia have played a significant role in the history of the Pacific Northwest, so it is only fitting that Seattle should be home to a museum that honors them and their achievements. Enter the museum through the Dream of America exhibition and discover why so many Scandinavians left their homeland and how they made the arduous journey across America to the Northwest. Beautifully designed displays let you see what they saw on their travels. As you make your way through the museum, a remarkable selection of artifacts, such as Bibles, clothing, household china, folk art, tools and much more, provide an intimate look at the cherished treasures they brought with them and the lives they made for themselves in a new land. The second floor houses the Heritage Rooms, with special exhibits on fishing and logging, and galleries for exhibitions of historic and contemporary Scandinavian-American art, including seasonal displays of traditional Christmas villages. On the third floor, five galleries focus on immigrants from each of the five Scandinavian nations. The museum also houses a library of print material and the Gordon Ekvall Tracie Music Library, which includes rare field recordings of Nordic music and dances. For a wonderful look at this unique page of history, visit the Nordic Heritage Museum.

3014 NW 67th Street, Seattle WA
(206) 789-5707
www.nordicmuseum.org

Museum of Flight

ATTRACTIONS: *Best source of aviation history*

The Museum of Flight is known worldwide as a must-see destination in Seattle. Serving more than 400,000 visitors a year, its 12-acre campus consists of a 361,000-square-foot main building and a 35,000-square-foot Library & Archives annex. It is one of the largest air and space museums in the world. The Great Gallery is a three-million-cubic-foot, six-story glass and steel exhibit hall containing 39 full-size historic aircraft, 23 of which, including the nine-ton Douglas DC-3, hang from the space-frame ceiling in flight attitude. The Red Barn features displays on the birth of the aviation industry in the Northwest, as well as other aspects of pre-World War II aviation history. The Personal Courage Wing displays 28 World War I and II fighter aircraft. There is a 268-seat auditorium and extensive rental facilities for hosting private meetings, receptions, banquets and other special events. A full service, on the premises, catering kitchen is available. In addition to these facilities, the Airpark is the museum's outdoor, large-aircraft display area. The museum offers an extensive array of educational programs for youth and adults. The museum's new Aviation Learning Center experiential learning environment uses interactive workstations, including a full-size functional aircraft, to teach concepts such as aerodynamics, flight planning, navigation, aircraft design, aircraft identification, air traffic control, aviation weather and aviation careers.

9404 E Marginal Way S, Seattle WA
(206) 764-5720
www.museumofflight.org

Space Needle

ATTRACTIONS: *Seattle's number one tourist destination*

The symbol of Seattle, the Space Needle is one of the most recognizable structures in the world. In 1959, an unlikely artist was sketching his vision of a dominant central structure for the 1962 Seattle World's Fair on a placemat in a coffee house. The artist was Edward E. Carlson, then president of Western International Hotels. His space-age image was to be the focus of the futuristic World's Fair in Seattle; the Fair's theme would be Century 21.

Carlson and his supporters soon found moving the symbol from the placemat to the drawing board to the construction phase was not an easy process. The first obstacle was the structure's design. One drawing resembled a tethered balloon and another was a balloon-shaped top house on a central column anchored by cables. Architect John Graham, fresh from his success in designing the world's first shopping mall (Seattle's Northgate), turned the balloon design into a flying saucer.

Since the Space Needle was to be privately financed, it had to be situated on land which could be acquired for public use, but built within the fairgrounds. Early investigations indicated such a plot of land did not exist. Just before the search was abandoned, a suitable 120-foot-by-120-foot piece of land was found just 13 months before the World's Fair opened.

Construction, managed by the Howard S. Wright Construction Company, progressed quickly. An underground foundation was poured into a hole 30-feet deep and 120-feet across. It took 467 cement trucks an entire day to fill the hole, the largest continuous concrete pour ever attempted in the West. Once completed, the foundation weighed as much as the Space Needle itself, establishing the center of gravity just above ground. The five-level top house dome was completed with special attention paid to the revolving restaurant level and observation deck. The top house was balanced so perfectly that the restaurant rotated with just a one horsepower electric motor.

The 605-foot-tall Space Needle was completed in December 1961 and officially opened on the first day of the World's Fair, April 21, 1962. The Space Needle's elevators were the last pieces to arrive before the opening. New, computerized elevators were installed in 1993. The elevators travel 10 mph, 14 feet per second, 800 feet per minute, or as fast as a raindrop falls to earth. In fact, a snowflake falls at 3 mph, so in an elevator during a snowstorm it appears to be snowing up.

Storms occasionally force closure of the Space Needle, but it is built to withstand a wind velocity of 200 miles per hour. The Space Needle has withstood several tremors, too, including a 2001 earthquake measuring 6.8 on the Richter scale. The tallest building west of the Mississippi River when it was built, the Space Needle has double the 1962 building code requirements, enabling the structure to withstand even greater jolts.

During the World's Fair, nearly 20,000 people a day traveled to the top and the Space Needle hosted more than 2.3 million visitors. Nearly 40 years later, it is still Seattle's number one tourist destination. In 2000, a $20 million revitalization of the Space Needle was completed. The year-long project included construction of the Pavilion Level, SpaceBase retail store, SkyCity restaurant, O Deck overhaul, exterior lighting additions, Legacy Light installations, exterior painting and more. The Space Needle is located at Seattle Center.

Whatever your interests, theater, ballet, opera, sports, rock 'n' roll history, roller coasters, science, movies, shopping, exploring or just plain walking around, the city unfurls from the Space Needle.

400 Broad Street, Seattle WA
(206) 905-2100
www.spaceneedle.com

Olde Thyme Aviation, Inc.

ATTRACTIONS:
Best way to see Puget Sound

Olde Thyme Aviation offers scenic biplane rides in authentic restored antique biplanes at the famous Museum of Flight at Boeing Field in Seattle. The 10 planes used in these rides have a history ranging from 1927 to 1944. They are part of a private collection in Seattle, scrupulously maintained in airworthy condition. The planes available are two Travel Airs, two Waco UPF-7's, two Stearman Kaydets, and four Cabin Waco biplanes. Olde Thyme Aviation operates seven days a week on a first-come, first-served basis. They do take advance reservations and fly by appointment during the off season. At the end of each ride, passengers are given a certificate explaining the type of aircraft in which they have flown and its history. Gift certificates are available for rides, allowing you to extend the gift of flight and offer an exciting experience to remember.

1222 McGilvra Boulevard E, Seattle WA
(206) 730-1412
www.oldethymeaviation.com

Blake Island Adventure Cruise

ATTRACTIONS: *Best coastal experience*

Blake Island State Park is a magical island park just minutes from downtown Seattle by charter boat from Pier 55. With 475 acres of heavily wooded lowland forest, the island's 16 miles of hiking trails and five miles of saltwater beaches provide a natural wonderland on Seattle's doorstep. The cruise on Puget Sound from the Seattle waterfront past the Alki Point lighthouse and Bainbridge Island to Blake Island is a treat all by itself. Visitors to Blake Island can enjoy hiking, mountain biking or tent camping in one of the many campsites provided by Washington State Parks. Blacktail deer wander casually through campsites with spectacular views of the Seattle skyline, Mt. Rainier, passing ferries and surrounding islands. Watchable wildlife is a main attraction of the park, with otters, mink, chipmunks, raccoons and a wide variety of birds, including bald eagles, great blue herons, kingfishers and woodpeckers. With no permanent residents or traffic, the park offers a safe, family-friendly environment with old growth forests, pristine beaches, great picnic and recreational areas and restroom facilities with showers. On the north end of the island, the Tillicum Village Native American Indian Cultural Center offers a gift gallery and a snack bar and features a traditional Indian-style salmon bake, complete with a spectacular stage show of native dances and legends. Getting to the island via passenger tour boat is easy. The trip to Blake Island is a wonderful day tour or a great way to introduce young people to the world of camping.

2992 SW Avalon Way, Seattle WA (206) 933-8600 or (800) 426-1205
www.blakeislandadventures.com

Smith Tower Observation Deck

ATTRACTIONS: *Best panoramic views of Puget Sound*

Since 1914, the place to go for Seattle's most accessible view is the Smith Tower Observation Deck. It puts you in the middle of the downtown skyline and close to Seattle's historic waterfront. The Observation Deck on the 35th floor wraps around all four sides of the tower, providing panoramic views of Mt. Rainier and the Olympic and Cascade Mountains. It also provides the closest view in town of Safeco Field, Seahawk Stadium, the Colman Ferry Terminal and Pioneer Square. While at the tower, you must see its crown jewel, the Chinese Room, featuring a handcarved teak ceiling inset with 776 semiprecious porcelain disks. There are also 17th century works of art and a Wishing Chair, nearly 300 years old, that portends marriage within a year to single women who sit in it. Many couples rent the Chinese Room for their fairy tale weddings. The tower, envisioned by New York tycoon Lyman Cornelius Smith, was Seattle's first skyscraper. At 522 feet it was, in 1914, the fourth tallest building in the world. For 50 years, it remained the tallest building west of the Mississippi. The exterior is clad in Washington granite and white terra cotta. Interior finishes include Alaskan marble, floors of hand-laid mosaic tiles and a grand lobby paneled in Mexican onyx and watched over by 22 larger-than-life Indian heads. After a $27 million restoration in 1995, the tower is one of the most thoroughly wired buildings in Seattle and is home to many corporate offices and Internet companies. The building's 2,314 windows are encased in bronze frames. Most contain their original 1914 safety glass. Unlike modern skyscrapers, Smith Tower windows can be opened and closed. If the facts and numbers don't impress you, come to the Observation Deck. We guarantee the view will.

506 Second Avenue, Seattle WA
(206) 622-4004
www.smithtower.com

Rascals Restaurant & Casino

ATTRACTIONS: *Best Seattle casino*

Rascals started out in 1986 as a restaurant that featured mouth-watering baby back ribs and championship New England clam chowder. Since then, Rascals Restaurant & Casino has earned a three-star rating and expanded its menu to include barbeque, Asian and seafood. Also offered are good, inexpensive drinks. The casino features more than 14,000 square feet of gaming fun. There's a variety of live table games to choose from, including Blackjack, Pai Gow and Four Card Poker. Test your poker face with some of Seattle's finest poker players in their daily no limit Texas Hold 'Em tournaments. Or if Pull Tabs are your game, check out their new sports bar that has 42 bowls of the newest games. While you're playing, enjoy one of their fine microbrews on tap. Relax and enjoy all the games on their giant 12-foot, high-definition television. Enjoy the sounds of some really terrific bands while you dance the night away. You'll be pleasantly surprised to fine that Rascals is a tastefully decorated, clean, upscale neighborhood bar. The original facade from The Palace Saloon in Idaho is featured in the downstairs bar and dates to 1890. Stop by Rascals Restaurant & Casino, where you're sure to have a memorable dining and gaming experience.

9635 Des Moines Memorial Drive, Seattle WA
(206) 763-7428
www.rascalscasino.com

Ride the Ducks of Seattle

ATTRACTIONS: *Must-do water tour*

Ride the Ducks of Seattle has been voted a Must-Do in Seattle. Tour Seattle by sea in a WWII amphibious landing craft that has been redesigned to carry 36 passengers and one crazy Captain. The Coast Guard-certified Captain will take you on a wacky and informative land and water tour of Seattle. You'll see Pike Place Market, Pioneer Square, the Seattle waterfront, Safeco and Qwest Fields, and then splash into Lake Union to see a spectacular view of downtown Seattle and the famous houseboats. This is not your usual tour; the Captains are all entertainers and passengers are encouraged to participate in the action. There are sound effects, music and comedy for the entire tour. It's a floating adventure in an historic craft. The Ride the Ducks fleet have all seen real wartime service in Sicily and Normandy, as well as South Africa, but now the U.S. Coast Guard ensures that each Duck has been tested and certified to be safe. Visitors often say the 90-minute attraction, (60 minutes on land, 30 minutes in the water), is the most memorable thing they did in Seattle. It's guaranteed fun for all ages. Reservations are recommended, but walk-ups are welcome. Private parties and group tours are available.

516 Broad Street, Seattle WA
(206) 441-DUCK (3825) or (800) 817-1116
www.ridetheducksofseattle.com

TOUR STARTS AT SPACE NEEDLE   206-441-DUCK

LAND & WATER   LAND & WATER   TOUR

St. James Cathedral

ATTRACTIONS: *Most impressive Renaissance architecture*

In Seattle, St. James Cathedral is noted for its beautiful services, impressive Italian Renaissance-style architecture and extensive outreach to the poor. It serves as a gathering place, a crossroads for learning and a center for the arts. It is a place where ideas are explored in the light of the Gospel. Built in 1907, the Cathedral is the other church for the Catholic Archdiocese of Seattle and the parish church for a large and vital community. St. Frances Xavier Cabrini, the first American citizen to be canonized, worshipped in the Cathedral during its early years. In 1994, a restoration and renovation project renewed the beauty of this Seattle landmark, transforming it into a dynamic space for the celebration of the Church's liturgy and for ecumenical, cultural and civic events. The Cathedral's Mary Shrine, designed by Susan Jones, has received national and international architectural awards, and is definitely something to behold.

804 Ninth Avenue, Seattle WA
(206) 622-3559
www.stjames-cathedral.org

Tillicum Village

ATTRACTIONS: *Center honors Chief Seattle and Northwest Coast first nations*

Few cities have the natural advantages of Seattle. The surrounding mountains, inspiring waterways and islands create not only spectacular views, but also wonderful opportunities for close-to-home outings and adventures. One of the most exceptional offerings is the cruise from Seattle's downtown waterfront to Blake Island State Park and the Tillicum Village Northwest Coast Native American Cultural Center. Tiny Blake Island, just off the shore from the site of Seattle's founding settlement Alki Point, is home to Tillicum Village, believed to be the birthplace of the city's namesake, Chief Seattle. Tillicum Village opened in 1962 as a center for the preservation of the Northwest Coast First Nations culture, and especially the traditional method of preparing fresh Pacific salmon on cedar stakes around alder wood fires. Tillicum Village encompasses the best of the Northwest. The cruise across Puget Sound to Tillicum Village is followed by the tasty treat of steamed clams in a nectar broth. Guests watch as their salmon are removed from the fires and released from the five-foot cedar cooking stakes. Following a potlatch style feast, a spectacular array of Northwest Coast Native dances and legends are displayed on the elaborately decorated stage. Produced by world famous Greg Thompson Productions, Dance on the Wind will take you on an emotionally charged journey through the history and traditions of the First Nations that peopled the coastal areas from Washington to southeast Alaska.

2992 SW Avalon Way, Seattle WA
(206) 933-8600 or (800) 426-1205
www.tillicumvillage.com

SW Seattle Historical Society- Log House Museum

ATTRACTIONS: *Best museum of local history*

Historical artifacts and edifices fade or disappear all too quickly. The Southwest Seattle Historical Society does its best to slow that digression by working as advocates for the collection, protection and preservation of historic artifacts and sites. The Log House Museum is just one treasure they have preserved. The Museum resides in a renovated, 1904 log structure, which once served as a carriage house to the Fir Lodge. The Fir Lodge was one of the first year round homes built on Alki Beach, and was owned by prominent Seattleites, William and Gladys Bernard. Mr. Bernard had established the city's first soap company, Seattle Soap Co., and his wife Gladys was known for her devotion to orphaned children. Around 1908, the carriage house was moved from its original location on the estate to roughly where it is today. The carriage house, built of Douglas fir logs, was purchased by the Southwest Seattle Historical Society in 1995, restored, and converted into the Log House Museum. The Museum opened in 1997, the 146th anniversary of the landing of the Alki party on Alki's beach. Exhibits in the museum span prehistory to current times. Events sponsored by the Society include Homes With History tours, Garden Tea at the Villa Heidelberg, and Christmas Tea at the Homestead Restaurant. Visit The Log House Museum and wet your whistle with a draught from the deep well of local history.

3003 61st SW, Seattle WA
(206) 938-5293
www.loghousemuseum.org

Clipper Navigation

ATTRACTIONS:
Best water transportation

Since 1986, this wonderful company has been known as the travel expert for the Pacific Northwest and Western Canada. Victoria Clipper's three-catamaran fleet plies the coastal waters with travel from Seattle to Victoria and the San Juan Islands. You can book special destinations, day trips, sightseeing tours and packages that will take you anywhere from picturesque Vancouver to quaint Victoria to the breathtaking calm of the San Juan Islands. Enjoy a romantic getaway, Orca whale watching in the San Juans, the spectacular Skagit Valley Tulip Festival or sample fine wines from Eastern Washington. Clipper Vacations will handle the details for you. Clipper Navigation has been run by the same close-knit management team, headed by Meredith Tall, Darrell Bryan, Janis Smith, Joan Rasmussen and Steve Giorgio, for most of its 20-year history. Together they've forged a top-notch staff that is knowledgeable, courteous and professional, plus dedicated to making sure you and yours have a fabulous time. Clipper Vacations provides terrific tours year round, and includes many wonderful seasonal events on its itinerary. From the moment you arrive at Pier 69 until you leave for home, Clipper Navigation wants to make sure your trip is one that you will remember forever.

2701 Alaskan Way, Pier 69, Seattle WA
(206) 448-5000 or (800) 888-2535
www.clippervacations.com

Alki Auto Repair
AUTO: *Best auto repair in West Seattle*

Automobile owners in Seattle have been able to turn to Alki Auto Repair for expert care, timely service and fair prices for more than 83 years. Alki Auto Repair has received the Best of West Seattle award, as well as King County's Green Globe award for being a leader in the use of recycled and nontoxic products. The company is committed to running an environmentally friendly shop. Alki has reasons to want to preserve the landscape, such as the captivating beach view across the street. Whether you own a foreign or domestic car, John's mechanics will fix it right the first time with parts specifically made for your automobile. An integral part of the community for decades, John regularly donates to local schools and other causes. To find Alki from Interstate 5, take the West Seattle Bridge to the Admiral Way exit, turn right on 56th and left on Alki Avenue. When you seek quality auto repair care, call Alki Auto Repair. You will quickly discover why West Seattle treasures this shop.

2540 Alki Avenue SW, Seattle WA
(206) 935-8059

Remo Borracchini's Bakery
BAKERIES, COFFEE & TEA: *Best bakery in Rainier Valley*

Whether you're planning a celebration or need to pick up something elegant for a last-minute occasion, Remo Borracchini's Bakery has just the thing you're looking for. Located in the heart of the Italian community within Seattle, Remo Borracchini's Bakery carries everything from their popular cakes to cookies, biscotti, éclairs and doughnuts. Borracchini's, voted best bakery in Seattle by *Citysearch* in 2005, also has a large deli that boasts an abundant selection of meats and cheeses, as well as homemade bread straight from their own brick ovens, and olive oil imported all the way from Italy. Founded in 1922 and passed down by parents Mario and Maria Borracchini of Italy, owners Remo and his wife Betty and their family run the bakery themselves to maintain the famous tradition that makes their selections so special. Borracchini's carries only the highest caliber of cakes for weddings, birthdays, anniversaries, and even bar mitzvahs. They never use preservatives or bake anything from store-bought mixes. They have several different sizes, flavors, combinations and styles of cakes to make your occasion memorable. For weddings or larger events, Borracchini's offers several catering options, including delivery services that cover several areas in Washington, as well as packages to make planning easier. They also carry a large selection of champagne and wine at unbeatable prices. Remo Borracchini's Bakery is the perfect place for your event.

2307 Rainier Avenue S, Seattle WA
(206) 325-1550

Morfey's Cake Shoppe

BAKERIES, COFFEE & TEA: *Best cakes in Queen Anne*

One of the mottoes of Morfey's Cake Shoppe is We Do Cake, and, indeed, cake is the only thing that Morfey's makes. This specialization allows the shop to provide superior and professional results. Tired of dry, frozen pre-made cake? Move up to Morfey's made-to-order cakes. All cakes are handmade using only the finest ingredients. Morfey's specializes in wedding cakes. If you are planning a wedding, the shop encourages you to make an appointment for a wedding cake sitting. This will ensure that you have exactly the cake you want. If a particular design presents problems, Morfey's will tell you immediately rather than making substitutions. Cakes for any occasion are available with custom decorations. Cakes come in 17 flavors with any of 15 fillings and a variety of icing styles. Since 1960, Morfey's has been a fixture in Seattle's Queen Anne neighborhood. It is located just two blocks west of the Pacific Science Center (the location of the Space Needle). Deliveries are available. Get your sweet teeth over to Morfey's Cake Shop, where it tastes as good as it looks.

110 Denny Way, Seattle WA
(206) 283-8557
www.morfeyscake.com

Upper Crust Bakery

BAKERIES, COFFEE & TEA:
Best Danish, strudel, kringle and smorkager

Located in the heart of Magnolia Village in Seattle, the Upper Crust Bakery, with its delicious pastries, is a Seattle Treasure that shouldn't be missed. The delightful aroma of freshly-baked goodies greets visitors before they even open the door. Your mouth will be watering in anticipation before you first lay eyes on the many varieties of treats in this bakery. The Upper Crust Bakery is known for its incredible pecan sticky buns, apple pockets and Danish. One bite of these delicious treats will have you running back for more. The bakery's delectable peach Danish is a favorite, as are the light and flaky croissants and spicy Jalapeno-Cheese Rolls. The bakery specializes in Scandinavian and northern European recipes such as *kringle, smorkager* and various strudels. The bakery is owned by Geoff, Karla and Ken Haigh. Karla creates beautiful cakes and *petit fours* for any occasion. She can decorate them to your design and they taste as good as they look. From June through October, the Upper Crust Bakery operates a stall at the Magnolia Farmer's Market on Saturdays. Catch them at the market or in Magnolia Village.

3204 W McGraw Street, Seattle WA
(206) 283-1003

Harbor view of Seattle

Main Street Home Loans

"Good, bad, or ugly credit," that's the slogan and the commitment of Sandy Hickson and Tami Macias. With their combined 38 years of experience in the corporate lending world, these women really know their stuff. They also know that corporate interests are seldom the same as customers' interests. That is why they opened their own business. They really care about people and they are energized by successfully meeting their needs. Sandy and Tami are accustomed to taking the toughest situations and making them work, however long it takes. And it pays. They boast an impressive success rate and have built lasting relationships with their customers. True personal service is a rare commodity in the lending business and that is what Tami and Sandy bring to this community. Whatever your situation, at the comfortable office of Main Street Home Loans you will be treated respectfully and fairly. These community treasures can help you make your dreams come true.

Serving Metro Seattle
1024 Main Street, Sumner WA
(253) 862-9490

Nelson & Langer, PLLC

BUSINESS: *Legal experts for victims of brain and spinal injuries*

A serious injury causes many unanticipated stresses. The ensuing disability can lead to mounting medical and rehabilitation bills. Nelson & Langer, PLLC can help. They are a reputable Washington law firm emphasizing brain and spinal injury representation and the wrongful denial of disability benefits (both private and ERISA claims). Michael Nelson, founder of Nelson & Langer, is a seasoned litigator who has practiced law in Washington for more than 30 years. Mike, a survivor of a serious brain injury himself, has the knowledge, training and expertise necessary to provide the best legal representation possible. Frederick Langer is both a practicing attorney and a registered nurse. With his clinical and legal expertise, he has the ability to assess his clients' long-term care needs and the legal wherewithal to help provide for them. Nelson & Langer, PLLC believes in teamwork. Their teams of attorneys, paralegals, nurses and administrative staff, are dedicated to seeing that your case runs smoothly. Nelson & Langer want to remind you to check your auto insurance policy and verify you have Personal Injury Protection (PIP) coverage. PIP insurance provides coverage to protect your well being in case of a serious injury. Nelson & Langer, PLLC can be reached at their main office in Seattle or, if it is more convenient, their satellite office in Renton.

705 Second Avenue, 17th Floor, Seattle WA
(206) 623-7520
3300 Maple Valley Highway, Renton WA
(425) 255-9698
www.nelsonlangerlaw.com

Alki Mail & Dispatch

BUSINESS: *Best copy and coffee stop*

For 17 years, the folks at Alki Mail & Dispatch have provided a place in West Seattle that is the epitome of Northwest culture. Alki Mail & Dispatch is a business support service where you can ship anything to anywhere (U.S. Mail, UPS, FedEx or DHL), get a killer cup of coffee, make copies, print your resume, have documents notarized and much more. Need a classy greeting card or cool gift? You'll find that, too. At Alki Mail & Dispatch, the staff is friendly and the environment is relaxed, but these professionals know their stuff. You can get business done while connecting with people from the neighborhood. Your cup of joe is courtesy of Batdorf and Bronsons, an all organic, fair trade coffee. They use a spectacular Mexican blend. If you need some carbohydrates with that jump juice, Alki Mail & Dispatch offers a selection of scrumptious goods from local bakeries. They also have Internet access, so come in and use their computers or just bring in your own laptop to cruise the web. Lots of parking makes it a quick-in and quick-out. In addition to being a neighborhood gem, Alki Mail & Dispatch supports the people and the needs of the community. Connect with the locals and get your business done—what more could you ask for?

4701 SW Admiral Way, Seattle WA
(206) 932-2556
www.alkimail.com

www.alkimail.com • 932-2556

Barnard Intellectual Property Law, Inc.
BUSINESS: *Specialists in technology and intellectual property law*

Barnard Intellectual Property Law, Inc. is a Seattle-based law firm specializing in all areas of patent, trademark, copyright and unfair competition law. Attorney Delbert J. Barnard represents clients ranging from inventors and artists to multinational corporations. His firm helps clients obtain patents and trademarks, represents clients in both federal and state courts, and provides strategic counseling in intellectual property law. Del Barnard and his team can help with domestic and international technology licensing, collaboration agreements, due diligence studies, cease and desist letters, invalidity/non-infringement opinions, and any other legal services a client may need. Del Barnard graduated from Oregon State University with a B.S. in civil engineering. He received his law degree from American University in Washington while working as a patent examiner in the U.S. Patent and Trademark Office. Del has practiced before the Ninth Circuit and Federal Circuit Court of Appeals and the United States Supreme Court. On several occasions he has served as an expert witness or a court-appointed special master. He has been president of the Washington State Intellectual Property Association, has written several articles on intellectual property law and is frequently asked to speak on the topic. Del Barnard and his staff are committed to representing the client's interests while maintaining the highest degree of ethical integrity and competence. Let Barnard Intellectual Property Law protect your competitive edge.

1044 Industry Drive, Seattle WA
(206) 246-0568
www.barnardintellectualpropertylaw.com

Sweetie
FASHION: *Best off-the-map boutique*

There is much more to Sweetie than the cute name. Sweetie is a contemporary women's boutique where eclectic style reigns. Whether you are looking for dress clothes or jeans, Sweetie has it. *Eat.Shop.Seattle.* named it the Best Off-the-Map Boutique in the city. You will find dresses, skirts and tops from Diane van Furstenberg, Rebecca Taylor and many other top designers. You will also find the latest trends in casual wear. Expect a full line of accessories, too, including handbags, earrings and belts. Proprietor Joeanna Purdie loves that every day at Sweetie is new and exciting. As for the unforgettable name, *Eat.Shop.Seattle.* sees it this way: "Sweetie is a moniker for all things good and useful. When women want their guys to do something for them, the sentence always starts with 'sweetie.' It's a perfect word to help you get what you want, and this is a perfect boutique filled with everything you could ever want to wear." Drop by and see why many Seattle women consider Sweetie a fashion shopper's dream.

4508 California Avenue SW, Seattle WA
(206) 923-3533
www.sweetieboutique.com

smallclothes
FASHION: *Best used clothing boutique for kids*

Artist Stephanie Hargrave and her mother, Ruth, have created a shop, called smallclothes, which will give parents a whole new set of options. Nestled just south of the Admiralty District, smallclothes is a unique boutique that combines the best features of a thrift store and a crafts gallery. The shop offers high quality, lightly used, but very fashionable clothing for kids at reasonable prices. The goods are in pristine condition, some with the tags still intact, at prices ranging from 50 to 75 percent less than retail. You might, for example, steal a Petit Bateau outfit from them for $3, or come across brands such as Little Me, Baby Lulu, Mimi Rose, Zutano or Janie and Jack. Each room in the shop, which is nestled inside a classic Seattle bungalow, focuses on a specific age range. The parlor caters to infants three to 24 months old; one back room is reserved for three to six-year-olds; another for seven to 12-year-olds. The shop is more than a thrift store, however. Stephanie and Ruth offer handmade baby blankets and hand-painted baby furniture, art for youngsters' bedrooms, gifts, toys and books. The shop is kid friendly, with plenty of toys and books to keep the little ones busy as moms and dads browse the racks. So if your child (or someone else's) has outgrown their wardrobe, drop by smallclothes. The children you love will look like a million without costing you a zillion.

3236 California Avenue SW, Seattle WA
(206) 923-2222

Rocky Mountain Chocolate Factory
FUN FOODS: *Best destination for chocolate lovers*

One visit to any of the Rocky Mountain Chocolate Factory branches and you will discover why this store is such an attraction for chocolate lovers. The shop carries 15 varieties of rich, creamy, handmade fudge, freshly dipped huge strawberries and 20 varieties of caramel apples. You can also find hand-dipped clusters and truffles, barks, hard ice cream and many other delights. Rocky Mountain has low-carb chocolates and a huge assortment of sugar-free items approved for diabetics. You can watch as the staff dips crisp apples in thick, bubbling caramel from a traditional copper kettle. The caramel apple is then rolled in a rainbow of tasty toppings to complete your old-fashioned treat. A signature item is the humongous Pecan Bear Apple, which is dipped in caramel, rolled in roasted pecans, coated with milk or dark chocolate and drizzled with a white confection. Linger awhile longer and learn how fudge is made. Staff members fashion a creamy fudge loaf on a traditional marble slab, the old-fashioned way, right before your eyes. Everyone gets a free sample. Do not leave without picking up a gift of fine chocolate to share your experience. Gifts are elegantly crafted and beautifully packaged in boxes, tins and baskets. Stop in at Rocky Mountain Chocolate Factory, where they keep the kettle cooking for you.

1419 1st Avenue, Seattle WA (206) 262-9581 or (877) 276-0482
401 NE Northgate Way, Suite 2020, Seattle WA (206) 363-1399
99 Yesler Way, Seattle WA *(206) 405-2872*
1321 Columbia Center Boulevard, Suite 393, Kennewick WA
(509) 735-7187 or (800) 454-RMCF (7623)
www.rmcf.com

Cookies
FUN FOODS: *Best cookie supplies*

When you hear the word *cookies*, does your mouth water? If you have visions about eating, savouring, baking and decorating these time-tested and highly regarded treats, Caryn Truitt and Betsey Toombs, owners of Cookies in the Ballard neighborhood of Seattle, will accommodate you. They sell all manner of cookie supplies including plates, jars, cutters, and anything and everything that goes into preparing and serving cookies, right down to the apron you'll want to wear when tending the oven. Cookies is a place where people of all ages can connect with childhood memories. It's a nostalgic business at a time when people want to revive home and family. This is truly a one-stop place for entry to the cookie world. So if you're thinking cookies, Caryn, Betsey and staff are waiting for you. If they don't have it, they will get it. And if they can get it, you can bake it.

2211 NW Market Street, Seattle WA
(206) 297-1015
www.cookiesinseattle.com

Avalon Glassworks
GALLERIES: *Best glass studio*

Avalon Glassworks is a neighborhood experience of brightly colored fantasy and fancy. Jon and Shannon Felix, owners and artisans, bring an intense passion for the craft and years of experience to every piece of glasswork they design. Lucky customers have the opportunity to experience that passion coming to life as they watch these glass pieces being made on-site. Since the Felixes took over the 12-year-old company in 2003, they have cultivated a reputation for their unique, modern designs. As you walk in the gallery/ studio, you'll be surrounded with fabulous color, whimsy and one-of-a-kind work, including their famous Blossom and Luna vases. Both artists studied glassblowing at Tulane University, but this powerful artistic team also benefits from Shannon's background in graphic design and Jon's years as a glass chemist and four years working with Dale Chihuly. They love taking advantage of the chemistry in colored glass to create new color and pattern combinations, diversifying the process with various surface treatments. Through Jon and Shannon's vision, Avalon Glassworks has become a must-see destination for glass artists, art lovers and gift givers. From vases to bowls to garden floats, Avalon Glassworks is guaranteed to have the special piece you're looking for at a competitive price.

2914 SW Avalon Way, Seattle WA
(206) 937-6369
www.avalonglassworks.com

Agate Designs
GALLERIES: *Best gem shop*

A family business started in 1965 by Jim and Martha Kullberg has bloomed into a second-generation business that is still family-owned and operated. Agate Designs believes man can duplicate almost anything on earth, but he cannot match the beauty that Mother Nature has bestowed upon us. At Agate Designs in Seattle, owners Mark Kullberg and Terry Derosier make it their job to find and display nature's beauties for your lasting enjoyment. They stock natural, high quality, collectible crystals, gems, minerals and fossils. All are hand picked for quality and comprise the largest store of its kind in the Seattle area. Many visitors describe the shop as a little museum as they marvel over 500-million-year-old fossils and 250-pound amethyst geodes. While there, you will see fascinating specimens of rainbow obsidian, petrified wood and agate. They also provide a large assortment of all types of jewelry and handmade stone boxes of lapis, malachite and rhodonite, plus crystal balls, carvings and stunning Baltic amber.

120 1st Ave S, Seattle WA
(206) 621-3063

Seattle Glassblowing Studio
GALLERIES: *Best glassblowing school*

Founded in 1991 by glassblowing artist Cliff Goodman, Seattle Glassblowing Studio is centrally located in downtown Seattle. Offering classes, private lessons and weekend workshops, Seattle Glassblowing has the largest enrollment of any glassblowing school in the United States. Their gallery showcases numerous local artists, featuring splendid works of art. In addition to sculptures, vases, bowls and ornaments, Seattle Glassblowing's design team creates custom lighting, installations and commissions. The impressive roster of artists who have worked in the studio includes Martin Blank, Fritz Dreisbach, Scott Darlington and Aaron Tate. Adjacent to Seattle Glassblowing is Hot Glass Color and Supply, a store carrying the largest supply of German-imported Kugler colors in the United States. There is also a restaurant and espresso bar attached, serving delicious homemade Italian food, sandwiches, soups and desserts. For a fascinating experience, visit Seattle Glassblowing Studio and watch the magical art of glassblowing.

2227 5th Avenue, Seattle WA
(206) 448-2181
www.seattleglassblowing.com

Flury & Company, Ltd.
GALLERIES: *Best gallery of the American West*

Lois Flury, owner of Flury & Company, Ltd., has been collecting and dealing in photography and specializing in Edward S. Curtis' vintage material since 1972. Curtis was an artist, natural ethnographer and man of his time. The North American Indian was his lifelong labor and obsession. Through talent and tenacity, pioneer Curtis chronicled

a culture that was rapidly receding into the past. In making a record of what was past, and passing, he hoped to preserve it. He succeeded in publishing his work in a magnificent limited edition of 20 volumes of illustrated text and 20 accompanying portfolios of engravings. Located in historic Pioneer Square, the gallery is a wealth of information for those wanting to learn more about the history of the gallery and its collection of choice photographs and antique Native American art. Their catalogue of new, rare and out-of-print books and a selection of books on Edward S. Curtis and American Indian art and culture are available through the gallery.

322 First Avenue S, Seattle WA
(206) 587-0260
www.fluryco.com

Youngstown Cultural Arts Center
GALLERIES: *Best community renovation*

If a building can be the heart of a community, that heart for the community of Delridge is the Youngstown Cultural Arts Center. This lovely, old, brick building, built in 1917 to serve mill workers' children as Youngstown School, closed in 1989. The playground became choked with weeds and the building was a target for vandals. Delridge residents spurred its reincarnation by including it in the 1999 Delridge Neighborhood Plan. The redesigned and renovated building, a program of the Delridge Neighborhoods Development Association (DNDA), has become a hub of community activity. The center offers such events as free arts education for young people,

evening classes for adults that include dancing and drawing, and a 150-seat theater featuring world-class performances on weekends. You'll also find a recording studio, dance studio and classrooms rented for community use. The top floor contains live/work studios reserved for low-income artists and performers in the community. The building is also home to an alternative school and a few arts organizations. If you are in Delridge, come in and hear the heartbeat of a community at the Youngstown Cultural Arts Center.

4408 Delridge Way SW, Seattle WA
(206) 935-2999
www.youngstownarts.org

Photo ©2006 Denny Sternstein

Village Green Perennial Nursery
GARDENS, PLANTS & FLOWERS: *Best nursery for hard-to-find perennials*

If you're looking for unusual perennials, root roses or drought-tolerant native plants, visit Village Green Perennial Nursery in Seattle. Their beautiful, relaxing grounds will make you feel like you're in a park, especially when you get a chance to bird watch while you peruse their plant stock. Owners Vera Johnson and Bill Curtin created this business out of their love for gardening and the outdoors. Customer service is all-important to them, and their right-hand anchor, Donna Thomas, helps meet this goal. The gifts they offer are as varied as the plants. You will find pre-planted Vietnamese pots and handmade crafts in the gift shop. Twice a year they host high tea with the Daughters of the British Empire. There's an annual halibut cookout, and for fall there's the lighted pumpkin walk. Their Artists Fair features food and music, as well as art. Classes are offered spring through fall. If you're just starting out in the garden or changing your landscape, let the staff at Village Green Perennial Nursery help you make your dream garden come true.

10223 26th Avenue SW, Seattle WA
(206) 767-7735
www.villagegreenperennialnursery.com

The Flower Lady
GARDENS, PLANTS & FLOWERS:
Best locally grown flowers

The Flower Lady has been a popular stop for eighborhood people on their way home from work for more than 30 years. The shop makes beautiful, reasonably priced, hand-tied and paper-wrapped bouquets on the spot. The Flower Lady is a full-service florist that can handle arrangements for any of life's events. The business began as a small street-corner stand, where Vivian Darst sold irises, daffodils and gladiolas from her father's bulb farm on Whidbey Island. Vivian displayed her wares while seated beneath an umbrella. The stand gradually added other flowers from wholesalers and local farms and within a few years offered a full selection. Over the years, the stand moved to a few different locations. In 1981, a seven-year zoning battle with the city began that gained much media attention; in the same year, The Flower Lady moved into an indoor shop. Flowers are still set up outside. Today, however, the Flower Lady also sells gifts, cards and music. At The Flower Lady, people have the option to make their own arrangements, a service unique to this shop. Vivian continues to provide the warm service that has gained her a devoted clientele. Stop by and try your hand at arranging a personal bouquet.

3230-C Eastlake Avenue, Seattle WA
(877) 325-5751
www.seattleflowerlady.com

Apple Physical Therapy

HEALTH: *Voted top place to work in South Puget Sound*

Washington native Randy Johnson, partner and CEO of Apple Physical Therapy, opened his company in 1984 as a way to support his family. Since then his business has evolved into an organization that supports many families and serves individuals throughout the Puget Sound region with clinics in 23 locations. Company President and CEO Claude Ciancio came to work for Apple Physical Therapy in 1990 and achieved partnership in 1998. Ciancio comes from New York City, but his commitment to patients and the community aligns him firmly with Johnson's original goals for service to patients and the communities where patients reside. Randy and Claude believe in the Golden Rule, as well as five core elements, which they feel have made Apple Physical Therapy the success it is today. These five elements are, in order, Integrity, Knowledge, Compassion, Profit and Fun. For patients at any of the Apple facilities, these core tenets create a welcoming and comforting environment that is ideal for both working and healing. Employees, via a *Business Examiner* magazine poll, named Apple Physical Therapy as the number one place to work in the Puget Sound area. Whether you are searching for rehabilitation services or a new career, the staff at Apple Physical Therapy invites your family to become part of their family.

600 University Street, Suite 818, Seattle WA
(206) 957-3336
www.applept.com

Arbor Vitae Natural Medicine

HEALTH: *Best natural health clinic in west Seattle*

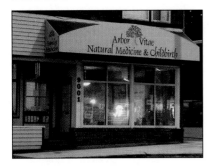

Arbor Vitae Natural Medicine in Seattle takes old-fashioned care seriously. It provides a comfortable setting, has deep roots in the community and balances the best of modern and traditional health practices for comprehensive primary care and midwifery services. "I believe in taking the time to really understand my patients and their health concerns," says owner Dr. Pushpa Larsen. "I try to use the best of modern, scientific medicine and traditional time-tested systems to support my patients in returning to health and balance." Dr. Larsen holds certificates in naturopathic midwifery, spirituality, health and medicine from Bastyr University. She is one of the only naturopathic physicians in the state who uses advanced cardiovascular testing to detect heart disease at the earliest stages. Such detection allows Dr. Larsen to prescribe effective treatments without surgical or pharmaceutical interventions. Independent professionals at Arbor Vitae enhance alternative healing efforts with acupuncture, nutritional counseling and massage. "We help young bodies and minds grow strong. We help older bodies and minds stay young," says Dr. Larsen. Whether you are looking for a primary care physician or face a specific health concern, Dr. Larsen and the gifted professionals at Arbor Vitae Natural Medicine are deeply committed to your health and harmony. Set up an appointment with Dr. Larsen and discover the difference natural medicine can make in your life.

9001 35th Avenue SW, Seattle WA
(206) 933-6087
www.arbor-vitae.com

Alki View Massage & Wellness Center

HEALTH: *Best massage center*

The Alki View Massage & Wellness Center puts a comprehensive team of wellness practitioners at your service, including experts in massage therapy, acupuncture and mental health counseling. The center is located in a converted beach house with a view of Puget Sound. Massage specialists here are Jessica and Michelle DeShayes, identical twins and graduates of the Brenneke School of Massage. Jessica and Michelle, in practice since 1997, believe that massage reconnects the mind and spirit with the body. They employ a variety of massage techniques, including Swedish and deep tissue massage. A signature treatment is the Twin Tandem massage, synchronized by the twins. All guests receive a complimentary foot soak. Molly Connelly provides the acupuncture services at the center. She holds a master's degree in acupuncture from the New England School of Acupuncture, the oldest acupuncture school in the country, and is licensed by Washington State and certified by the National Certification Commission for Acupuncture and Oriental Medicine. Molly has a special interest in illnesses that are particularly hard to treat. Come to the Alki View Massage & Wellness Center, where the staff will seek to leave you feeling like you're in heaven.

5963 SW Carroll Street, Seattle WA
(206) 387-3944
www.alkiviewmassage.com
www.alkiviewacupuncture.com

Super Supplements

HEALTH: *Voted best independent retail chain in the nation*

Science learns something new every day about the ways vitamins, herbs and nutritional supplements enhance health. Keeping up with all that cutting-edge information would be overwhelming without the help of experts. Super Supplements is a privately owned chain of 13 discount vitamin stores in western Washington. It was started in 1994 by John Wurts and bills itself as having some of the most knowledgeable staff members in the industry. John brings more than 18 years of experience in the vitamin industry to his operation, which was voted 2004 Best Retail Chain in the Nation by *Vitamin Retailer* magazine. The stores feature wide, inviting aisles, a vast array of supplements, sports nutrition, herbs, body care and homeopathic products, plus a well educated staff prepared to provide the most up-to-date and accurate product information available. Bring your questions to university students, naturopathic doctors or herbalists, or take advantage of Healthnotes, a touchscreen information system that retrieves research on natural remedies, illnesses and potential drug interactions from vitamin, herb and food combinations. You'll get 10 to 70-percent discounts on products at Super Supplements locations from Bellingham to Lakewood. The same great service and more than 30,000 products are available on the website. Visit Super Supplements to begin your journey to a healthier life.

4700 California Avenue SW, Seattle WA
(206) 838-5981
14355 Aurora Avenue N, Seattle WA
(206) 365-5240
4336 Roosevelt Way NE, Seattle WA
(206) 633-4428
Mail Order: (800) 249-9394
www.supersup.com

Uli's Famous Sausage

MARKETS: *Best sausages in town*

In the heart of Seattle's famous Pike Place Market, master butcher Uli Lengenberg's shop offers a tantalizing array of handmade German and international sausages. Using no coloring agents and restricting his use of preservatives to those needed for safety, Uli creates sausage masterpieces. With all-natural cuts of pork, lamb, chicken, beef and turkey, Uli honors his German background with specialties like Nurnberger rostbratwurst, but he knows his way around a Polish kielbassa and a Cajun andouille as well. Try the English bangers, Spanish chorizo, a French merguez or perhaps the pork apple bratwurst, made with locally-grown apples. There's more to choose from, including chicken dishes and fresh turkey sage sausage for the calorie-conscious. Born and raised in Siegerland, Germany, Uli learned the art of butchery in Germany. He then moved to Taiwan, where he practiced his craft for 12 years. Uli met his wife Jean there, where she was teaching at the Taipei-American School. Jean convinced him to bring his sausage-making skills back to her hometown of Seattle. In addition to serving his customers, Uli supplies sausage to many area restaurants. Come to Uli's Famous Sausage for delectable dishes of all varieties and you will have to come back for more.

1511 Pike Place, Seattle WA
(206) 839-1000
www.ulisfamoussausage.com

MarketSpice

MARKETS: *Best place for teas and spices*

Sweet, spicy aromas waft your way as you approach the MarketSpice store. Pause for awhile and enjoy the exotic and delightful experience of pure olfactory pleasure. MarketSpice can be traced back to 1911 when a tiny tea and spice shop in Seattle's Pike Street Market was established. The wonderfully fragrant, signature MarketSpice Tea is a blend of tea, spices and essential oils providing enjoyment to customers around the globe. In order to ensure optimum freshness, the tea is still crafted by hand in small batches at the company's Redmond facility. In addition to this gourmet tea, MarketSpice carries many high quality spices and tea blends that are unique to them. Over the years they have expanded their product line to include creamed honeys with spices and flavorings, tea cookies, candles, barbeque sauces and breath mints. The cinnamon-orange flavor of their famous tea is so popular that the taste has been incorporated into other products. For the very out of the ordinary, try their exclusive Dragon Phoenix Pearl or their popular anti-oxidant tea, African Red Bush. If you're in the area, drop into the store for a complimentary cup of tea. Once you have sampled the naturally sweet MarketSpice, you will want more. If you don't live near Seattle, don't despair. You can order MarketSpice and African Red Bush tea, as well as many other products, from the website. You may also call the store directly, as MarketSpice ships worldwide.

Seattle's Pike Street Market (to the left of the "Rachel the Pig" statue)
(206) 622-6340 or (425) 883-1220
www.amazon.com (under gourmet foods)

Olsen's Scandinavian Foods

MARKETS: *Best Scandinavian market*

Olsen's Scandinavian Foods is located in the Ballard neighborhood, in the heart of Seattle's Scandinavian community. Olsen's has been providing the Scandinavian populace with a taste of home for 46 years. Many of the authentic foods sold at Olsen's are prepared in house from

traditional Norwegian recipes passed down through several generations. Most of Olsen's other products are imported directly from Scandinavia. Olsen's Foods was founded in 1960. In 1997, it was bought by the Endresen sisters, Anita and Reidun, from Sandeid, Norway. Olsen's offers an extensive variety of Scandinavian food and gift products, including many types of fish, cheese, breads, condiments, kitchenware, cookbooks and other useful items. Everything in the store is carefully selected to create a place that looks, feels, and smells like a typical *forretning* in Norway. Along with operating an authentic foods store, the Endresen sisters have created a cornerstone of culture within the thriving Ballard neighborhood. For a big slice of Scandinavia, head over to Olsen's Scandinavian Foods.

2248 NW Market Street, Seattle WA
(206) 783-8288
www.scandinavianfoods.net

Fidalgo's Home Flair

HOME: *Best home accents*

Do you love decorating your home? Do you have a passion for finding that last perfect item that finally pulls all of your planning and hard work together? Fidalgo's Home Flair is just the place to find accents for your home, garden and patio. Manager Nancy Johnson delights in carrying inventory that puts the finishing touch on your interior. The knowledgeable and talented staff can explore decorating possibilities with you. The spaciousness of the store allows customers to view a variety of choices in an uncrowded, relaxed setting. With choices of French, Asian, contemporary and traditional styling, imaginative decorating solutions encourage you to break out of old patterns and try something different. Fidalgo's offers plentiful silk trees and plants along with custom installations. Choose from a delightful assortment of dinnerware, lamps, small media storage, vases and bistro sets. Wine bars, plant stands and baker's racks group collections together and form important focal points. Fidalgo's can change your relationship to your interior with soothing water fountains. Good design, style and function don't have to stop inside. Create personal living spaces outside with Fidalgo's complete selection of garden and outdoor living accessories. Holiday décor is a Fidalgo's specialty that begins in earnest the first week in November. Bring accent into your environment with a visit to Fidalgo's.

4100 4th Avenue S, Seattle WA
(206) 768-1000
www.fidalgoshome.com

Alki Bike & Board
RECREATION: *Best bike & board shop*

At Alki Bike & Board Shop, their goal and mission statement is fun, fun, fun and service, service, service. You might think those two ideas would be difficult to combine, but Stu Hennesy and his sons, Patrick and Julian, are experts at both. Stu and his sons wanted Alki Bike and Board to be different, and with differing generational viewpoints on what constituted fun and exercise, Alki Bikes and Boards was born. They specialize in two things: bicycles and boards, including skateboards, snowboards, mountain boards and long boards. This is a friendly, fun and very experienced team of men who believe in sports as a lifestyle, and are dedicated to helping people find and maintain a high standard of health through exercise. They service and maintain all the equipment they sell and carry a full line of parts and accessories. They also carry major brands of top-of-the-line active wear, so you'll definitely look the part, too. True sports enthusiasts of the highest order, this father and son trio are into extreme sports and have a deep and abiding belief that anywhere you can go on a moving piece of equipment, you should try to go as high and fast and far as you can. As Stu says, "Why should we ever have a customer come in and not have fun?" When was the last time you had an offer that good?

2606 California Avenue SW, Seattle WA
(206) 938-3322
www.alkibikeandboard.com

Alki Homestead Restaurant
RESTAURANTS & CAFÉS: *Best home-cooked meals*

Built in 1905, the Alki Homestead Restaurant is one of the last surviving original log buildings on Alki Point. A private home first, it became a boarding house for returning soldiers during World War II and finally a restaurant in 1950, when owner Doris Nelson started her 50-year career here. At Alki Homestead Restaurant, a small price gets you a piece of yesteryear and a delectable three-course meal with all the trimmings, served just as it would be in grandma's house, if grandma had impeccable taste and was a cook like Doris. You can savor the warmth of the fireplace and the glow of candlelight reflecting off her fine old crystal, silver, and lace tablecloths, while you enjoy a home-cooked meal served family style, with her special pan-fried chicken going round on platters and bowls of mashed potatoes with boats of giblet gravy passed hand to hand. As long-time employees say, "The dining room was her home and the customers were her family." Doris passed away in 2004, but her family and entire staff are committed to carrying on both her gracious legacy and her tradition of great service and great food, the kind you can rarely find anymore. Come to Alki Homestead Restaurant and join the legions of people who come back to Doris's special place again and again.

2717 61st Avenue SW, Seattle WA
(206) 935-5678

Elliott Bay Brewery Pub
RESTAURANTS & CAFÉS: *Best gourmet burgers*

Rumor has it that the best gourmet burgers in Seattle come oout of the kitchen at the Elliott Bay Brewery Pub. Perhaps it's because their popular beef burgers are made with all-natural Black Angus beef raised locally on Vashon Island and served on buns baked with spent grain, a high fiber by-product of their brewing process. Or maybe it's because the beer you wash the burger down with makes you smack your lips. In any case, owners Todd Carden and Brent Norton and head brewer Doug Hindman invite you to discover for yourself some of the region's highest quality pub food, including weekly soup and chili specials. You will probably want to order one of their hand-crafted beers first. You might choose Alembic Pale, a gold medal winning amber ale; Elliott Bay IPA, a bold and hoppy golden brew; Luna Weizen, light and refreshing with a hint of citrus; or No Doubt Stout, dark, robust and smooth. They use only certified organic pale malt as the base malt in the regular house beer. Elliott Bay Brewery Pub is a 100-percent smoke-free establishment. Since the pub's founding in 1997, staying involved in the local community has been a high priority at Elliott Bay. Staffers have served on numerous advisory boards and volunteered time and expertise during many charitable events. They also donate services, such as tours of the brewery with private tastings, for auction items at fundraisers. Visit Elliott Bay Brewery Pub, a business with a conscience and great burgers to boot.

4720 California Avenue SW, Seattle WA
(206) 932-8695 *www.ElliottBayBrewing.com*

Easy Street Records Café
RESTAURANTS & CAFÉS: *Best music café*

Easy Street Records Café has been nourishing West Seattle with music, great coffee and food for 18 years. This winning combination makes Easy Street a strong cornerstone of the community. The shop has the only Ticketmaster in the neighborhood; it's also the place to sit back and listen to music before you buy it while sipping a coffee drink or sampling the cafe's lively menu. For breakfast, consider the Johnny Cash special with steak and three eggs or the Frances Farmer

French toast. Your tunes will sound better than ever accompaniment from a Soundgarden burger or Dixie Chick chicken hoagie. Easy Street Records hosts live local and international music acts in the evenings. Easy Street is strategically located in the middle of a lively shopping district. President Matt Vaughan feels affection for this West Seattle community and seeks to support it while it, in turn, supports Easy Street. "Music is the sound track of your life. At Easy Street there's a passion and vulnerability you can't find in just any old chain of record stores. Add food to that, and there are good times to be had." When you must have music, stop, look, listen and eat at Easy Street Records Café.

4559 California Avenue SW, Seattle WA
(206) 938-EASY (3279)
www.easystreetonline.com

Photo: Nick Lobeck

Athenian Inn
RESTAURANTS & CAFÉS:
Pike Place tradition since 1909

Nestled into the historic Pike Place Market on Seattle's waterfront is the popular Athenian Inn Restaurant and Lounge, an eatery made famous by its incredible seafood, majestic views and cameo role in Tom Hanks' feature film, *Sleepless in Seattle*. The Athenian first opened in 1909 and has long been a popular favorite of locals and visitors alike, due to the restaurant's terrific seafood selection and friendly service. In commemoration of its film debut and famous visitor, the inn now features a stool at the fish bar, which boasts a plaque denoting that Mr. Hanks sat at that spot. Owner Louise Cromwell and long-time chef Lou Fox, who has been manning the kitchen for 40 years, are dedicated to using the freshest, highest quality ingredients in their entrées. Favored menu items include scrumptious fish and chips, along with hearty sandwiches and burgers. Customers also enjoy an old-fashioned ice cream soda fountain, and breakfast lovers can order generous portions all day long. The Athenian Inn offers a terrific selection of beer, including hundreds of bottled beers, 16 beers on tap and an array of microbrews. With a charming atmosphere reminiscent of a neighborhood café, the Athenian Inn is the ideal place to enjoy relaxing meals with friends or family. Experience a Pike Place tradition while savoring the comforting cuisine and exceptional views at the Athenian Inn.

1517 Pike Place Market, Seattle WA
(206) 624-7166

Herban Feast Catering
RESTAURANTS & CAFÉS: *Best catering for Northwest cuisine*

According to BJ Duft, owner of Seattle's Herban Feast, each catering opportunity is similar to a performance, where timing, presentation and quality make for a memorable affair. At Herban Feast, BJ and the staff are passionate about great food. They enjoy orchestrating all the details, including equipment rental and staffing, and work one-on-one with their customers to assure a smooth event that lives up to your expectations. Herban Feast delivers the bounty of the Pacific Northwest to its customers through creative, seasonal menus. The company supports local growers while providing exciting interpretations of Northwest regional cuisine. You'll find menus specially designed to take advantage of local delicacies, whether you seek a wedding menu, a special breakfast, lunch or dinner event. Herban Feast also creates wonderful appetizers and desserts. The Herban Feast catering service is an extension of the Sweet and Savory Pantry, a popular take-out deli. The deli sees a steady stream of busy folks stopping by for everything from quick to-go breakfasts to full dinner entrées. Take out options include homemade soups, salads, sandwiches, appetizers and desserts. Herban Feast and Sweet and Savory Pantry belong to Puget Sound Fresh, a coalition of local foodservice providers dedicated to the purchase of locally grown products. This commitment assures customers that ingredients will not only be the freshest possible, but the tastiest. Call Herban Feast or visit the storefront to enjoy fine foods for catered occasions and every day meals.

2332 California Avenue SW, Seattle WA
(206) 932-4717
www.herbanfeast.com

Huckleberry Square Restaurant
RESTAURANTS & CAFÉS: *Best huckleberry recipes anywhere*

With huge portions at modest prices, Huckleberry Square Restaurant will fill your tummy without emptying your wallet. This restaurant offers specialized dishes that feature the huckleberry, a wild berry found in abundance in the Northwest's mountains. Owner Dan Spadoni offers healthful, wholesome foods utilizing Northwest tastes and ingredients... and he glorifies the huckleberry. The huckleberry is considered special because, as the Native people say, it embodies the spirit of the Northwest. It is versatile, wild, and untamed. Huckleberry Square has a family oriented clientele with three and four-generation families that come regularly. Huckleberry Square has been around for 27 years and evolved from a hamburger drive-up. Today it is a beautifully decorated modern establishment that resembles a gallery filled with Native American art, sculptures, and artifacts. As part of Dan's tribute to Northwest Native cultures, all of the creations are made from original recipes. In addition to the distinctive and matchless huckleberry dishes, including the "to-die-for" huckleberry ice cream, delicious salmon dinners are extremely popular. Dan gives a lot of the credit for the success of the restaurant to Hostess Karen Rodriquez and the restaurant's first hostess, Beverly Anderson. He also could not have gotten this far without his siblings, Jim, Mary Ann, Irene, Betty, and Dick. When you want a taste of the Northwest, try Huckleberry Square Restaurant.

14423 Ambaum Boulevard SW, Seattle WA
(206) 246-7006

Matador West
RESTAURANTS & CAFÉS: *Best Tex-Mex*

West Seattle is taking its happy hours south of the border, thanks to Matador West in the bustling Junction neighborhood. With a serious selection of tequila, spicy Mexican and Tex-Mex fare, Matador West has quickly become a favorite night spot. Owners Zak Melang and Nathan Opper styled Matador West after their original Matador restaurant and tequila bar in Ballard. As longtime residents, Zak and Nate are deeply in touch with what makes their neighbors happy, thus happy hours at Matador West are among the happiest happy hours anywhere. The tequila connoisseur will have 50 varieties to peruse, from a respectable Sauza Gold to a smooth and sophisticated Don Julio Reál. Look for Tex-Mex specialties like ancho-chipolte baby back ribs or all natural beef carne asada. Mexican fajitas and an assortment of unusual enchiladas, like those made with habanero peppers or tomatillos, are popular. Rib eye steaks and burgers also have a wide following. The Arts & Crafts décor includes stylized wrought iron, wood inlays and a flaming stained-glass back bar, sure to melt tensions and induce relaxation. For fabulous food and an enjoyable departure from the ordinary, drop by Matador West and see why Seattle is so fond of this southern treasure in its midst.

4546 California Avenue SW, Seattle WA   (206) 932-9988
2221 NW Market Street, Seattle WA   (206) 297-2855
www.matadorseattle.com

Northlake Tavern & Pizza
RESTAURANTS & CAFÉS: *Best pizza tavern*

Northlake Tavern & Pizza House is a Seattle tradition that celebrated its 50th anniversary in 2004. In 1954, Herb Friedman started with an old Italian recipe and experimented with various crusts and toppings, until the Northlake Tavern pizza was born. Cheryl Berkovich and her husband took over in 1987 and have kept Herb's pizza standards. Northlake pizza is mouthwateringly fabulous, because it's really more of a cake than a pie, and while there are many succulent adjectives to describe this gustatory delight, one of the best is heavy. The crust is very thick, and the toppings run into the pounds, which is why they have to be cooked in the old-fashioned stone ovens for so long. "It's a long wait, but it's worth it," laughs Cheryl. Northlake has its own specially formulated recipe for dough, sauce and pepperoni, and every pizza is made with as much mozzarella as the pizza can hold—enough cheese to keep 35 dairy cows employed year round. Northlake Tavern & Pizza House takes pride in having the biggest and tastiest pizzas around, and though it's often compared to others, it's never been equaled. So pizza lovers, take note. Come hungry, but be prepared to take some home.

660 NE Northlake Way, Seattle WA
(206) 633-5317
www.northlaketavern.com

Luna Park Café
RESTAURANTS & CAFÉS:
Best milkshakes in town

To simulate a 1950s diner requires a few important elements, including a real ice cream milkshake, generous portions of home-cooked food and a tabletop jukebox. Luna Park Café manages this and more in an historic post-World War II building. The café is named in honor of an amusement park that crowded the pier from 1907 to 1913. This retro café, owned by John Bennett, came alive in 1989 following a careful renovation. The 1958 Seeburg jukebox near the counter plays 200 selections, which customers select for a quarter apiece from remote boxes located at individual booths and along the main counter. You can choose hot biscuits to go with huge three-egg breakfasts or enjoy dinner standouts, like their celebrated hamburgers. Their real milkshake can meet just about any taste requirement with a choice of 17 flavors. Families appreciate the special menu for children under 10. The café makes a few concessions to modern times, like vegetarian burgers and espresso. This throw-back to another era recalls the days when trolley cars used to run down the middle of the street in this city. In the tradition of the original Luna Park, the café features one amusement ride, the Batmobile, and a few other entertainments, such as a clown vending machine. For generous servings of food and nostalgia, bring your family to Luna Park Café.

2918 SW Avalon Way, Seattle WA
(206) 935-7250

Pacific Rim Brewery

RESTAURANTS & CAFÉS: *Best seasonal microbrews*

Take one sip of the beer offered at Pacific Rim Brewery in Seattle and you will want to come back for more. The flavorful selections are guaranteed to please. Pacific Rim Brewery is owned by Scott Swansen and Erik Barber. After purchasing the brewery in 2002, they have dramatically increased production and sales of their delicious ales. Head brewer Scott Lord worked with the former owner for 13 years and is now clearly a master brewer. The Brewery Tasting Room is open seven days a week and is the perfect spot to meet friends and relax. This popular hangout offers a wide assortment of seasonal ales, as well as beers available year round. During the autumn season, be sure to try the Pumpkin Patch Ale. This unique ale contains pumpkin pie seasoning and fresh pumpkin and is sure to please on a cold day. One of the popular summer ales is the delicious Ring of Fire. Every ale offered by the brewery is well balanced and smooth, with amazing flavor. While some ales are full-bodied and stronger, others offer delicate malt flavors. There is clearly something for everyone. Pacific Rim Brewery is known in Seattle as one of the finest microbreweries in town. Because of its popularity, the owners are expanding and will soon be offering a menu featuring local cuisine, with an upstairs level for pool, music and food.

9832 14th Avenue SW, Seattle WA
(206) 764-3844
www.pacificrimbrewing.com

Ovio Bistro Eclectica

RESTAURANTS & CAFÉS: *Best new restaurant*

Ellie Chin is one of those people who just loves to entertain. It is obvious from the moment you walk through the doors of Ovio Bistro Eclectica in Seattle that this restaurant is truly an extension of her home, and the employees are like her family. Ellie credits her excellent staff with much of Ovio's success, saying it was their hard work, sometimes in their spare time, which launched this fantasy bistro in 2002. Ellie and Shing Chin sold their partnership in the Market Street Grill to start Ovio, and named their new restaurant after an egg in honor of new beginnings. With an eclectic menu that spans the world and a great wine list with reasonably priced options, Ovio Bistro is a compelling dining option, often found bursting at the seams. Ovio has been well received by Seattle and by the press. *Seattle* magazine named Ovio Best New Restaurant in 2003 and named Ovio staffer Michael Tinsley Server of the Year. *Seattle Weekly* recommends the daily soups and the pan-fried oysters with red pepper aioli, along with the pan-seared pork tenderloin, flat-iron steaks and pumpkin ravioli. *Bon Appétit* likes the five-spice duck and the vibrant citrus-crusted lamb, accompanied by baby artichokes and kumquat compote. For food choices inspired by southern Europe, Asia and the American Southwest, along with stellar Emerald City hospitality, make a reservation at the engaging Ovio Bistro Eclectica.

4752 California Avenue SW, Seattle WA
(206) 935-1774
www.oviobistro.com

Pagliacci Pizza

RESTAURANTS & CAFÉS: *One of the best pizzerias in America*

America's passion for pizza is legion, so when 18 magazines, newspapers and websites name the pizza from one pizzeria "The Best Pizza in Seattle," you know it's good. Pagliacci Pizza has been the people's pick since 1979, when it opened in the University District without a cash register or even a sign for more than a year. Dorene Centioli-McTigue started the amazing community tradition of Pagliacci, and partners Matt Gavin, Pat McDonald and Pat McCarthy have carried it on. Pagliacci Pizza may have grown, but it hasn't changed. It still uses the same hand-tossed dough, whole milk mozzarella cheese and Italian-style hot brick ovens that are the reason why *Bon Appetit* crowned it as one of the eight best pizzerias in America. Not only is the pizza prized, but the exclusive training that Pagliacci store managers and staff receive has established a reputation for outstanding customer service, as well. Each restaurant is equipped with special high-tech ordering systems that ensure prompt delivery of the best, hottest and freshest pizza possible, whether you're in one of the restaurants or are having pizza delivered. To top it all off, there are now 20 Pagliacci pizzerias in the greater Seattle area, and just as the business has grown, so too has its commitment to community service. Pagliacci now funds two housing projects that provide lodging and assistance for those in need. Pagliacci Pizza is dedicated to great pizza, great service and the gift of giving, so come in and enjoy a combination that can't be beat.

Corporate: 423 E Pike Street, Seattle WA
To order: (206) 726-1717 or (425) 453-1717
www.pagliacci.com

Von's Grand City Café

RESTAURANTS & CAFÉS: *Best martinis and Manhattans*

Von's Grand City Café has been a downtown Seattle landmark since 1910. One of the reasons for its long-term appeal is its reputation for pouring the best martinis and house Manhattans in town. In fact, Von's serves 99 kinds of martinis. Area manager Gregg Galuska says that he and owner Timothy Firnstahl make sure that Von's provides the highest quality service and the finest ingredients for their patrons. Von's menu includes radiant roaster prime rib, horizontal spit-roasted chicken, 13-hour flavor-cycle fresh loin of pork, and a variety of other reasonably priced entrees. In addition to the traditional dining room, Von's offers outdoor seating, a television for catching favorite sporting events, and banquet facilities that can accommodate up to 100 people. If you prefer, you can order ahead and take your meal home with you.

Family friendly, they have booster seats and highchairs, a children's menu, and wheelchair access. Serving breakfast, lunch, dinner and, of course, happy hour, Von's Grand City Café, which is attached to the Roosevelt Hotel, is ready to take your order.

619 Pine Street, Seattle WA
(206) 621-8667

The Other Coast Café
RESTAURANTS & CAFÉS: *Best sandwich shop*

If you are passionate about great sandwiches, head to one of the Other Coast Café's two Seattle locations, where owner and sandwich aficionado Brent Bridenback serves East Coast sandwiches with a Northwest attitude. The original shop, housed in a former 1920s automotive shop, has been a community gathering spot for 50 years. The café prepares its made-to-order sandwiches with the freshest breads, baked locally each day, along with Boar's Head meats and Pacific Northwest cheeses. The results are so tender and delicious you'll want to try a different combination every time you visit. Brent and his friendly staff thoroughly enjoy creating custom sandwiches, and they work hard to make every customer feel like a friend. One of the café's most popular designer sandwiches is the Rajun Cajun, with thinly sliced Cajun turkey and generous layers of pepper jack cheese along with fresh tomatoes, onions and Brent's own spicy mayonnaise. The café relies on word-of-mouth advertising, an effective strategy, because just one of these savory sandwiches will have you singing in the streets and shouting praise from the rooftops. The Other Coast is rightly proud to have been featured in such publications as *Sunset* and *Seattle* magazine, and to have been named Best Sandwich Shop in Seattle by *Seattle Weekly*. To quote the *Weekly*, "the Other Coast Cafe blew Seattle's other sandwich shops out of the water." Experience the Other Coast Café, where a sandwich is never just a sandwich, it's a gourmet meal.

5315 Ballard Avenue NW, Seattle WA   (206) 789-0936
601 Union Square, Seattle WA   (206) 624-3383
www.othercoastcafe.com

Salty's on Alki Seafood Grill
RESTAURANTS & CAFÉS: *Best Northwest cuisine*

With sweeping views of Elliott Bay and the city skyline, Salty's on Alki Beach offers a perfect window through which visitors can experience the beauty of Seattle. But don't be fooled by the majesty of your surroundings. The focus at Salty's is, most definitely, on the food. Salty's is famous for its fresh Northwest seafood and produce. Owners Gerry and Kathy Kingen win awards annually, and critics praise their efforts. *Citysearch* calls Salty's Sunday brunch the nation's best. *The Seattle Post-Intelligencer* says, "their salmon preparation is the best we've encountered." Much of the credit must go to the culinary expertise of executive chef Jeremy McLachlan and catering chef Noah Maikisch. Whether you're dining in or are planning a catered event, this team will provide distinctive menus showcasing Northwest cuisine. The primary goal at Salty's is to make each guest feel like they're part of the family. Menu selections include salmon, Dungeness crab, oysters and prime, perfectly prepared, char-broiled steaks. The bar-café features live music on select evenings and a happy hour adored by locals. Although Salty's is a first-choice restaurant at any time of the year, when spring and summer arrive it is a particular treasure. Long summer days and evenings with refreshing saltwater breezes encourage Salty's guests to enjoy dining outside on the seaside patio or the wraparound deck. For a deliciously rich dining experience, either al fresco or accompanied by live entertainment, take a seat at Salty's on Alki.

1936 Harbor Avenue SW, Seattle WA
(206) 937-1600
www.saltys.com

Sport Restaurant and Bar

RESTAURANTS & CAFÉS:
Best restaurant for sports fans

When visiting Seattle, it is considered a must to spend at least a little time downtown exploring the area around the Space Needle. This is the heart of the Emerald City, and when you are here, you will quickly find that the locals have an intense interest in all things sports-related, especially if it has anything to do with their beloved Seahawks, Sonics or Mariners. Sport Restaurant and Bar is one of the most unique sports-themed restaurants on the planet, conveniently located just across the street from the distinctive architectural monument that is the Space Needle. A high-definition television set welcomes you in each booth, allowing you to catch all the action while you dine on chef/owner John Howie's remarkable culinary creations with friends or family. Displays of historic Major League Baseball artifacts and other sports memorabilia, worth thousands of dollars, make it seem like a sports museum, but there is nothing stuffy about a visit here. With a friendly menu highlighted by grilled king salmon and thin-crust pizzas, along with their delicious Haagan-Daz milkshakes, this is a place to visit with anyone who loves sports. The full children's menu creates a welcoming environment for the whole family. For a slam-dunk time for your whole party, and to add a final touchdown to your downtown Seattle itinerary, drop by Sport Restaurant and Bar.

140 4th Avenue N, Suite 130, Seattle WA
(206) 404-7767
www.sportrestaurant.com

Pacific Galleries Antique Mall

SHOPPING: *Best antique mall and auction in the region*

For more than three decades, Pacific Galleries in Seattle has conducted sales of superb antiques and fine art, earning a reputation for professionalism and integrity. Pacific Galleries is proud of its standing in the community. Their research team is experienced in the intricacies of the antique industry and it shows. Pacific Galleries works hard to bring together the region's most prestigious designers and antique dealers, in an auction setting, offering many unique items ranging from furniture and jewelry to fine arts and handcrafted artifacts. A stroll through the antique mall lets you see a sampling of the professional displays of individual boutiques. Pacific Galleries offers lots of cases, lots of spaces, says Pacific Galleries' chief operations officer Lynn Kenyon, resulting in a wide selection of high-end art, antiques and estate goods. With auctions usually beginning at 5:30 pm, you'll have an entertaining evening as you marvel at the amazing selection of antiques available in a single setting. Assorted furniture pieces of American oak, mid-century modern and European styles are augmented by artwork pieces, including china, crystal, silver, pottery and bronze. Pacific Galleries assists sellers by helping auction anything from an entire estate to a single item. See for yourself what is available, seven days a week, at Pacific Galleries Antique Mall, which offers locations in Seattle and Centralia.

241 S Lander Street, Seattle WA
(206) 292-3999 or (800) 560-9924
310 N Tower Avenue, Centralia WA
(360) 736-1282
www.pacgal.com

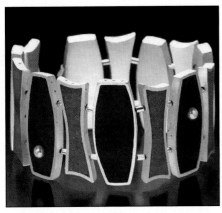

Click! Design That Fits

SHOPPING:
Best home accents in West Seattle

Click! Design That Fits features a hand-picked selection of gifts, home accents and furnishings, as well as unique jewelry by owner Frances Smersh. She and partner John Smersh created this West Seattle boutique to feature works with a modern flair by local artists and international designers. Home decor items include ceramics by local artist Timothy Foss, as well as collaborative vases by Brooklyn, NY-based Klein Reid and cultural icon Eva Zeisel. Click! is also home to an amazing selection of handbags, including all-vegan bags and wallets by Canadian company Matt & Nat; rich, luxurious bags made of Italian upholstery leather by Kisim; and upbeat handbag designs by Angela Adams, whose hand-tufted cotton rugs are also here. Frances Smersh's simple, sleek and modern jewelry is the centerpiece at Click!, and it is made in her studio right behind the store. Smersh has a penchant for unexpected materials in jewelry and most of her pieces are made with surprisingly lightweight colored concrete. Her award-winning "Kate" bracelet is made of nesting silver shapes filled with concrete and set with freshwater pearls. This handmade jewelry is the perfect complement to the contemporary design pieces throughout the store, making it truly design that fits.

2210 California Avenue SW, Seattle WA
(206) 328-9252
www.ClickDesignThatFits.com

Birth and Beyond

SHOPPING: *Best store for new moms*

Ten years ago, John and Lyndsey Starkey opened this wonderful store that caters to all your new family needs. Birth and Beyond brings together all those must-have items for families with a new baby on the way. Whether you are breastfeeding or bottle feeding, Birth and Beyond can provide you and your baby with all you need. They are the most complete breastfeeding center in the Northwest. The large selection of nursing bras is amazing and their sizes will fit almost all new moms. The Birth and Beyond staff are all experienced moms who are ready and able to assist you in finding products and information that have passed the real-life test of quality and practicality. Birth and Beyond designs and makes its own brand of slings and manufactures a full line of cotton diapers, swaddling blankets and burp cloths. They carry a variety of lotions, oils, herbs and soaps to spoil and pamper mom and baby. If you're pregnant, have a new baby or are just interested in learning more about childbirth, this store is a definite stop.

2610 E Madison Street, Seattle WA
(206) 324-4831
www.birthandbeyond.com

Dragon's Toy Box

SHOPPING: *Best toys that last*

Open your child's eyes to a world of wonder with the exciting and educational toys and games that line the walls of one of Seattle's hottest shops, Dragon's Toy Box. Mother-and-daughter team Gail Small and Brekke Hewitt opened the shop in 2005 to bring creative learning tools to the children of the community. Dragon's Toy Box specializes in quality educational toys that encourage children to think and explore. Gail and Brekke believe that toys that break quickly just emphasize the impermanence of today's disposable society, so they search local and international companies for well made toys that will last a lifetime and inspire curiosity. Dragon's Toy Box offers a wide selection of collectible toys, including Breyer Horses and the Schleich Collection. The shop also features modern learning toys, such as Learning Resource Reading Rods. Board games are always great choices, and Dragon's Toy Box stocks such creative choices as the exciting Catan series from Mayfair Games. Brekke and Gail, along with their staff of three, are committed to area schools. Dragon's Toy Box accepts school purchase orders and also offers discounts to educators. Give your children the toys they need to grow and explore now, while creating precious memories for the future, with the toys, books and games at the Dragon's Toy Box.

1525 1st Avenue, Seattle WA
(206) 652-2333
www.dragonstoybox.net

J.F. Henry

SHOPPING: *Best place for tableware and flatware*

Tom and Patty Henry take pride in their spectacular collection of tableware, flatware and kitchenware, beautifully gathered together at J.F. Henry in West Seattle. This 21-year-old business carries brand names customers have trusted for generations, such as Lenox, Waterford, Wedgwood and Spode. J.F. Henry is one of the select dealers for Pickard fine China, used by presidents on Air Force One and known for its incomparable table settings in 24-carat gold, pure platinum, and brilliant cobalt. J.F. Henry can special order thousands of patterns, offer a crystal wedding gift certain to become an heirloom, and meet your criteria for the perfect pastry brush or high performance bakeware. The J.F. Henry building is itself a tourist attraction, lovingly restored by the Henrys about 10 years ago and containing a remarkable chandelier and wrought iron railings from Seattle's Frederick & Nelson building, where Patty and Tom worked, met and married 25 years ago. J.F. Henry offers the largest selection of china, crystal and stainless in the Northwest at everyday sale prices, all under one roof. The Henrys decided years ago not to branch out into multiple stores, but instead to focus on offering fine merchandise and customer service. The store's manager, Carol Middleton, described by the Henrys as their "anchor," shares their commitment with more than 15 years of service. For a large selection of finery, turn to the experts at J.F. Henry.

4445 California Avenue SW, Seattle WA
(206) 935-5150 or (800) 281-4333
www.jfhenry.com

Laguna Vintage Pottery

SHOPPING: *One of the 20 must-see shops in the nation*

You have some fine pottery dinnerware from the 1920s through 1950s, and you're trying to find a replacement for the salad plate your child used as a frisbee, right? Then you're looking for Laguna Vintage Pottery in Seattle, one of the largest vintage pottery shops in America. Concentrating on exceptional quality, perfect condition, rare colors and unusual shapes, Laguna specializes in discontinued and collectible American dinnerware and art pottery. Collectors and owners Michael Lindsey and Bif Brigman scour the country for the finest examples of American pottery. They have been curators for local exhibitions and have lectured for the Seattle Art Museum, Historic Seattle and the National Antique Appraisers Association. Laguna has an inventory that includes all major American design styles of the 20th century: Mission/Arts and Crafts, Art Deco, Art Nouveau, California Modern, Mid-Century Modern and others. The store has thousands of patterns of discontinued American-made dinnerware in stock to replace your lost or broken pieces. Recently, *Elle Decor* featured Laguna as one of the nation's most comprehensive sources for 20th Century tableware and art pottery. *Country Home* called Laguna, "one of the 20 must-see shops in the nation." Harry L. Rinker, a national antiques and collectibles expert says, "Laguna is a Seattle landmark, equal to the Space Needle. Thank God I live on the East Coast; otherwise I would be in debtor's prison."

116 S Washington Street, Seattle WA
(206) 682–6162
www.lagunapottery.com

Magic Mouse Toys
SHOPPING: A *"Best of America"* store

Magic Mouse Toys has been serving the wholesome fantasy needs of Puget Sound since 1977, the same year founder Gilbert H. Gorilla earned his Ph.D. from Stanford, having majored in Fantasy, and graduated *summa cum cuddly*. A toy store which does not discriminate against adults, they offer a varied collection of elegant chess sets, backgammon, go and mahjongg sets, juggling equipment and European playing cards, including an extensive selection of tarot cards. Magic Mouse Toys occupies two floors of the gloriously ornamented Mutual Life Building, built in 1897, which is on the National Register of Historic Places. The German toy maker Steiff has designated Magic Mouse Toys as a "Best of America" store, as they carry a large selection of Steiff collectible teddy bears and animals. The two floors of quality and hand-chosen toys include an extensive game room downstairs featuring the best of children's American games, as well as the German brand Ravensburger. You can explore an excellent collection of children's books that covers the classics and the latest award winners. Whether you're looking for jazzy birthday party favors, that special French baby doll or a well engineered German tricycle, you will find it at Magic Mouse Toys.

603 1st Avenue, Seattle WA
(206) 682-8097
www.MagicMouseToys.com

Ye Olde Curiosity Shop
SHOPPING: *Most curious shop in Seattle*

"Everything in the world sardined into one fantastic shop," claims Ye Olde Curiosity Shop, located on Seattle's waterfront. When you walk in, you may not find *everything*, but you will find an amazing collection from the sublime to the sort of silly. Where else will you find Sylvester, one of the most well preserved mummies in North America? (It seems that Sylvester was coated in arsenic, thus his preservation.) You will also find the world's smallest shrunken head, a pig with three tails, Native American artifacts, and a ship made from Alaskan ivory. Since the store opened in 1899, Ye Olde Curiosity Shop has been an Indian trading post, where Northwest Coast and Alaskan Native Americans bring their crafts to sell. Says fourth-generation owner Andy James, "My great grandfather bought from the great grandfathers of some of the artists we buy from today." The result is an extraordinary collection of Native American art, including C. Alan Johnson figurines. Each figurine has its own name and personality. Not forgetting the *sort of silly* items, Ye Olde Curiosity Shop sports rubber chickens, celebrity dollar bills, lucky three-legged clay pigs and gator backscratchers, side by side with fine imports and jewelry. So come on in. The smallest ivory elephants in the world await, as does a 67-pound snail, a six-foot crab and countless other curiosities from every corner of the world.

1001 Alaskan Way, Pier 54, Seattle WA
(206) 682-5844 *www.yeoldecuriosityshop.com*

TUKWILA

Tukwila is a center of commerce—a crossroads of rivers, freeways and railroads. Tukwila contains Westfield Southcenter, Puget Sound's largest shopping complex, plus several Boeing facilities. The first macadam paved road in Washington State was in Tukwila.

PLACES TO GO

- Museum of Flight
  9404 E Marginal Way South
  (206) 764-5720

- Fort Dent Park
  6800 Fort Dent Way

- Joseph Foster Park
  13919 53rd Avenue S

- Tukwila Community Center
  12424 42nd Avenue S

- Tukwila Park
  15460 65th Avenue S

THINGS TO DO

July
- Tukwila Days
  Tukwila Community Center
  (206) 768-2822

P51 in Flight above the Cascades

Gordy's Steak & BBQ

RESTAURANTS & CAFÉS:
Classiest BBQ restaurant

Although Tukwila is a city known mostly for its small bars and taverns, Gordon and Kathy Harris have added something new and special over the past few years with the establishment of Gordy's Steak & BBQ. This community-oriented upscale dining establishment focuses on quality cuisine. Highlighted by business lunches and special occasion events, Gordy's is a perfect complement to the nearby Foster-Links Golf Course. General manager Jeffrey Stone has enjoyed watching the rapid growth of Gordy's Steak & BBQ, especially considering the skeptics who doubted how successful this endeavor would be. It has not taken long for people to see why this restaurant has become an accomplishment, and it continues to grow in popularity. Entering the foyer, the presence of the small but welcoming fireplace creates a comfortable setting and lets you know this will be a pleasant time for everyone in your party. Visit one of the newest sensations in the Tukwila area as you enjoy tasty BBQ cuisine in a relaxed and enjoyable setting, while sampling some of chef Tom Patterson's dynamic culinary creations.

13500 Interurban Avenue S, Tukwila WA
(206) 267-7427
www.gordysbbq.com

The East Side

The East Side

Biker riding through park

THE EAST SIDE is directly east of Seattle across Lake Washington. The region has enjoyed explosive economic growth, in part due to high-tech firms such as Microsoft. Renton, the most southerly of the Eastside communities, is a major retail center. It is home both to the Boeing 737 and to Greenwood Memorial Park, final resting place of Jimi Hendrix. North of Renton is Cougar Mountain Regional Wildland Park. With 36 miles for hiking and 12 miles for horses, the park is the largest urban wilderness in the United States.

Bellevue is the fifth largest city in the state, and its downtown is undergoing rapid change. The boom includes the Lincoln Square shopping complex, which opened in 2005. The city is a cultural center with several museums and festivals. Redmond, located northwest of Bellevue, is the home of Microsoft. By far the largest employer in the city, Microsoft has more than 30,000 full-time workers and more than eight million square feet of offices. The company intends to expand its Redmond campus by another 1.1 million square feet. With an annual bike race on city streets and the state's only velodrome, Redmond is known as a bicycle capital.

Kirkland, on Lake Washington west of Redmond, features an attractive downtown right on the lake. The main street is lined with bronze sculptures and hosts a lively nightlife. Further north is the town of Woodinville, famed for the Columbia and Chateau St. Michelle wineries. To the east and away from the general Eastside bustle is Issaquah, headquarters of Costco. The Issaquah Alps that surround the town feature hiking trails and other outdoor activities.

PLACES TO GO

- Bellefields Trailhead at Mercer Slough Nature Park
  1905 118th Avenue SE

- Bellevue Aquatic Center
  601 143rd Avenue NE

- Bellevue Botanical Gardens at Wilburton Hill Park
  12001 Main Street

- Bellevue Golf Course
  5500 140th Avenue NE

- Bellevue Skate Park
  14224 NE Bel-Red Road

- Chism Beach Park
  1175 96th Avenue SE

- Hidden Valley Sports Park
  1905-112th Avenue NE

- Lewis Creek Park and Visitor Center
  5808 Lakemont Boulevard SE

- Winters House
  2102 Bellevue Way SE

THINGS TO DO

June
- Bellevue Strawberry Festival
  Downtown Park
  (425) 453-1655

July
- Pacific Northwest Arts Fair
  (206) 363-2048

November
- Bellevue Magic Season
  Holiday festival, various locations
  (425) 453-1223

- Garden D'Lights
  Bellevue Botanical Garden
  (425) 452-2750

BELLEVUE

Founded in 1869 by William Meydenbauer and incorporated as a city in 1953, Bellevue covers 31 miles of rolling landscape between Lakes Washington and Sammamish, with the Cascade Mountain range to the east and the Olympic Mountains to the west. Bellevue has population of 117,000 people. The City boasts the 36,000-square-foot Meydenbauer Exhibition Hall. Residents support the Bellevue Philharmonic Orchestra and nearly 20 other visual and performing arts groups. Performing arts facilities include the Lee Theater at Forest Ridge School, Music Works Northwest and the Carlson Theatre at Bellevue Community College.

Photo by Marcela Suarez

Bellevue Arts Museum

ATTRACTIONS:
Best functional art museum

Bellevue Arts Museum reopened in 2005 following a sweeping makeover that put new life into this repository of fine art, craft and design. Thousands of new members joined the museum and 56,000 people visited in the first nine months after the opening. The museum specializes in design and craft art, the items of daily living that are often both utilitarian and artful. You'll find works in glass, wood and fiber, along with handmade furniture, textile design, fashion design and examples of industrial and interior design. At any given time, the museum displays from 300 to 500 pieces of craft and design art. Exhibitions rotate, with more than a dozen new shows each year. In recent time, Bellevue Arts Museum has showcased works from the Pilchuck Glass School and an installation of found objects from hurricane Katrina. Among the 2006 exhibits was a Japanese show featuring folding screens, kimonos and other items created with rozome, or Japanese batik. The museum grew out of the annual Bellevue Arts and Crafts Fair, held for 60 years on the last weekend of July. Fair volunteers wanted a permanent museum devoted to craft and design. They opened the predecessor to Bellevue Arts Museum in 1975. Today, the fair is held in and around the museum, and displays the juried work of more than 300 artists. The fair is a major regional event, and yearly attendance reaches 325,000. For an exciting exploration of functional art, visit the Bellevue Arts Museum.

510 Bellevue Way NE, Bellevue WA
(425) 519-0770
www.bellevuearts.org

Margrethe Agger
Day and Night Butterflies
Spelsauwool
2.14 x 1.75 m
Photo by John Olsen

Hilary Britton, Windermere Real Estate
BUSINESS: *Best in client satisfaction*

Anyone who has packed up their house and moved knows how stressful that process can be. Wouldn't it be wonderful to have help facilitating and expediting the whole thing? Hilary Britton, with Windermere Real Estate, can make it happen . Hilary has sold real estate since 1998 and knows the many challenges that face a family on the move. She is a full-time and accessible realtor, as well as an Associate Broker, who has been trained to do the footwork that makes the transition smooth and practically painless. She's tireless in her research and makes sure you know what the schools will be like, where the best retirement communities are and who to go to for everything from interior design or remodeling to shopping. Hilary is a great listener and troubleshooter. She knows what should be happening and when, and will orchestrate every detail of your move, which makes her more than your ordinary realtor. Hilary can set up house hunting trips and supply you with photos and information on new homes and homes under construction. She is an award-winning top producer who was awarded the Best in Client Satisfaction by her clients for *Seattle Magazine* in 2005. If you are relocating to the Greater Seattle area—or are moving from one Seattle location to another—let Hilary save you money, time and aggravation.

1200 112th Avenue NE, Suite B100, Bellevue WA (206) 817-1344
www.hilarybritton.com hilaryb@windermere.com

Windermere Real Estate/Bellevue Commons

Grand Event Rentals
BUSINESS: *Best way to stage a grand event*

Since opening in 2002, Eddie Redman, owner of Grand Event Rentals, has been Bellevue's choice for designing and supplying fabulous grand event décor for everything from thematic events to product launches to weddings. Grand Event Rentals offers everything you need for your next extravaganza, including high quality, durable tents that will keep Seattle's rain on the plain where it belongs instead of dripping merrily onto your guests. Eddie's organizational skills and attention to detail transforms utilitarian tents into warm, elegant spaces where your group, large or small, will feel comfortable and welcome. Each tent can be turned into a dazzling ballroom or enchanting dining room complete with coordinated draperies, table linens and chandeliers, while up-lights and votives will create a soft romantic setting. Sub-floor carpeting and safe heaters will allow your guests to comfortably mingle even when the mercury drops. Eddie and wife Kathy, who helps with stage design and planning, work closely with you, spending quality time getting a feel and understanding for your ultimate vision. Grand Event Rentals provides technical, structural and legal advice to ensure that your event is safe, hazard free and gloriously fun. Make sure your next event is memorable and marvelous with Grand Event Rentals.

1606 130th Avenue NE, Bellevue WA
(425) 462-7368
www.grandevents.com

Bellevue Square at night
Photo by Marcela Suarez

Main Street Home Loans
BUSINESS: *Best home lender*

"Good, bad, or ugly credit," that's the slogan and the commitment of Sandy Hickson and Tami Macias. With their combined 38 years of experience in the corporate lending world, these women really know their stuff. They also know that corporate interests are seldom the same as customers' interests. That is why they opened their own business. They really care about people and they are energized by successfully meeting their needs. Sandy and Tami are accustomed to taking the toughest situations and making them work, however long it takes. And it pays. They boast an impressive success rate and have built lasting relationships with their customers. True personal service is a rare commodity in the lending business and that is what Tami and Sandy bring to this community. Whatever your situation, at the comfortable office of Main Street Home Loans you will be treated respectfully and fairly. These community treasures can help you make your dreams come true.

Serving Bellevue
1024 Main Street, Sumner WA
(253) 862-9490

A Masquerade Costume

FASHION: *Best selection of costumes and masks*

Most adults think their dress-up days are over, but at A Masquerade Costume dressing up is all part of the business. Offering authentic replications of international and historical period costumes, A Masquerade Costume is the place to go for all your costume needs. At A Masquerade Costume they create seasonal, famous and fictional-character costumes, as well as classic masquerade and show girl costumes. Co-owner Kyra Stewart flies to France, Italy and many other places to shop for costumes. A Masquerade Costume has a large collection of masks that are shipped from Italy. Their collection includes the Commedia Bell Arte collection. All of their authentic Italian masks are works of art and make great accessories for 18th century costumes. Like the masks, all of the costumes are expertly designed to look authentic. They also carry modern costume wear, wigs, shoes and all costume accessories. If you can't find what you want in the shop, Kyra and Co-owner Angie Glasser will find it or construct it for you. They provide costumes for period weddings and parties, and will go on location to do fantasy photos for you. They also offer actors and event planning for murder mystery dinners and other occasions. A Masquerade Costume shop is a worker-owned cooperative. Visit the shop and let them dress you up.

12736 NE 15th Place, Bellevue WA
(425) 373-5990
www.amasquerade.com

Bellevue Square at night
Photo by Marcela Suarez

Rocky Mountain Chocolate Factory

FUN FOODS: *Best Chocolate*

One visit to any of the Rocky Mountain Chocolate Factory branches and you will discover why this store is such an attraction for chocolate lovers. The shop carries 15 varieties of rich, creamy, handmade fudge, freshly dipped huge strawberries and 20 varieties of caramel apples. You can also find hand-dipped clusters and truffles, barks, hard ice cream and many other delights. Rocky Mountain has low-carb chocolates and a huge assortment of sugar-free items approved for diabetics. You can watch as the staff dips crisp apples in thick, bubbling caramel from a traditional copper kettle. The caramel apple is then rolled in a rainbow of tasty toppings to complete your old-fashioned treat. A signature item is the humongous Pecan Bear Apple, which is dipped in caramel, rolled in roasted pecans, coated with milk or dark chocolate and drizzled with a white confection. Linger awhile longer and learn how fudge is made. Staff members fashion a creamy fudge loaf on a traditional marble slab, the old-fashioned way, right before your eyes. Everyone gets a free sample. Do not leave without picking up a gift of fine chocolate to share your experience. Gifts are elegantly crafted and beautifully packaged in boxes, tins and baskets. Stop in at Rocky Mountain Chocolate Factory, where they keep the kettle cooking for you.

1419 1st Avenue, Seattle WA (206) 262-9581 or (877) 276-0482
401 NE Northgate Way, Suite 2020, Seattle WA (206) 363-1399
99 Yesler Way, Seattle WA *(206) 405-2872*
1321 Columbia Center Boulevard, Suite 393, Kennewick WA
(509) 735-7187 or (800) 454-RMCF (7623)
www.rmcf.com

One of many beautiful parks in Bellevue
Photo by Marcela Suarez

1st Choice Acupuncture & Herbal Medicine

HEALTH: *Best choice for traditional Chinese medicine in Bellevue*

The moment you step into 1st Choice Acupuncture & Herbal Medicine clinic, you understand its name. Someone hands you a steaming cup of sweet herbal tea, and as you relax in the waiting room, the elegant décor and soothing fountain will envelope you in tranquility. At 1st Choice Acupuncture, you are what they care about. Howie Sun, nationally board certified and licensed acupuncturist and Traditional Chinese Medicine (TCM) practitioner, is dedicated to helping you achieve and maintain holistic personal wellness. TCM has been in use for more than 5,000 years. At 1st Choice, every treatment plan is tailored specifically for the individual. Part of the clinic's unique approach is to provide lifestyle counseling and support for each patient's treatment plan. TCM encompasses systemic medicines and techniques that include acupressure, Oriental massage and herbal remedies. Howie is a part of the third generation of healers in his family. He has earned a degree in holistic science, a second in biochemistry, a third in molecular cellular developmental biology and a MS degree in oriental medicine. With this unique background, Howie is able to fuse the best of both Eastern and Western traditions with his own passion for healing. Begin your journey to radiant health in the compassionate and caring world of 1st Choice Acupuncture & Herbal Medicine.

13401 Bel-Red Road, Suite A-12, Bellevue WA
(425) 392-8881
www.1stchoiceacupuncture.com

Apple Physical Therapy

HEALTH: *Voted top place to work in South Puget Sound*

Washington native Randy Johnson, partner and CEO of Apple Physical Therapy, opened his company in 1984 as a way to support his family. Since then his business has evolved into an organization that supports many families and serves individuals throughout the Puget Sound region with clinics in 23 locations. Company President and CEO Claude Ciancio came to work for Apple Physical Therapy in 1990 and achieved partnership in 1998. Ciancio comes from New York City, but his commitment to patients and the community aligns him firmly with Johnson's original goals for service to patients and the communities where patients reside. Randy and Claude believe in the Golden Rule, as well as five core elements, which they feel have made Apple Physical Therapy the success it is today. These five elements are, in order, Integrity, Knowledge, Compassion, Profit and Fun. For patients at any of the Apple facilities, these core tenets create a welcoming and comforting environment that is ideal for both working and healing. Employees, via a *Business Examiner* magazine poll, named Apple Physical Therapy as the number one place to work in the Puget Sound area. Whether you are searching for rehabilitation services or a new career, the staff at Apple Physical Therapy invites your family to become part of their family.

1750 112th Avenue NE, Suite E-175, Bellevue WA
(425) 289-0381
www.applept.com

Mt. Stewart's jagged peak

Sports Reaction Center
HEALTH: *Best sports medicine choice in Bellevue*

The professionals at Sports Reaction Center are dedicated to providing a unique rehabilitation approach for any active person. Owner and physical therapist Neil Chasan has 24 years of experience. He is long-time soccer coach and a function-oriented manual therapist. Neil and his staff incorporate what they've learned from athletics into their work and impart that knowledge to their patients. Sports Reaction Center treats everyone like an athlete. The therapy they offer is very progressive and more than standard physical therapy. Combining medical science with sports science, their patients are actively involved in their own well being. Creator of the Swing Reaction System golf-specific exercise program, Neil specializes in golf conditioning. This is a practical program of exercise and training for golfers who plan to take their game to the next level, with longer shots, more accuracy and lower handicaps. Neil wrote a book on golf conditioning titled *Total Conditioning for Golfers*. Sports Reaction Center also focuses on obesity, weight loss and preventative exercises. They treat clients from all over the world, including Australia, Germany and England. The Sports Reaction Center will help you work through any injuries or ongoing problems.

13434 NE 16th Street, Suite 210, Bellevue WA
(425) 643-9778 *www.srcpt.com*

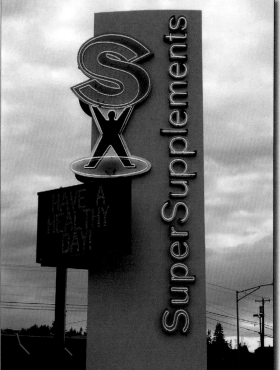

Super Supplements
HEALTH: *Voted best independent retail chain in the nation*

Science learns something new every day about the ways vitamins, herbs and nutritional supplements enhance health. Keeping up with all that cutting-edge information would be overwhelming without the help of experts. Super Supplements is a privately owned chain of 13 discount vitamin stores in western Washington. It was started in 1994 by John Wurts and bills itself as having some of the most knowledgeable staff members in the industry. John brings more than 18 years of experience in the vitamin industry to his operation, which was voted 2004 Best Retail Chain in the Nation by *Vitamin Retailer* magazine. The stores feature wide, inviting aisles, a vast array of supplements, sports nutrition, herbs, body care and homeopathic products, plus a well educated staff prepared to provide the most up-to-date and accurate product information available. Bring your questions to university students, naturopathic doctors or herbalists, or take advantage of Healthnotes, a touchscreen kiosk with encyclopedic information on natural remedies, illnesses and potential drug interactions from vitamin, herb and food combinations. You'll get 10 to 70-percent discounts on name brand products at convenient Super Supplements locations from Bellingham to Lakewood. The same great service and more than 30,000 products are available on the website. Visit Super Supplements to begin your journey to a healthier life.

14733 NE 8th Street, Bellevue WA
(425) 957-0787
707 Rainier Avenue S, Renton WA
(425) 226-2112
Mail Order: (800) 249-9394
www.supersup.com

Go To Your Room

HOME: *Best children's furniture store in Bellevue*

Janet Wixom and Noelia Baldazo have changed the implications of the parental command, "go to your room." The co-owners of Bellevue's favorite children's furniture and accessory store provide a treasure trove of fantastic possibilities to make anyone happy to go to their room. Janet and Noelia met in a prenatal class and became friends as they shopped together. They both recognized a lack of exciting, high-quality children's furniture available in the Seattle area and decided to fill the need. The 4,500-square-foot store's selection tends toward classically styled furniture that can be used for a long time. Rather than buy a crib and changing table that will outgrow its usefulness, you are encouraged to think about how the furniture can be transformed for use when your child grows. Janet and Noelia offer children's furniture that will change to a full-sized bed, and a majority of their cribs can be converted into daybeds. Loft beds have desk, dresser, and bookcase components that store underneath, taking the same floor space as a bed. Color schemes, bedding, and accessories can easily be changed to carry a child's room from infancy through the teenage years. Artists have created murals and stenciled art on the walls of several display-room vignettes to showcase the inventory and spark your creative abilities. As part of their outstanding customer service, the talented staff will be happy to help you design your child's dream room. Go To Your Room. You will be glad you did.

13000 Bel-Red Road, Bellevue WA
(425) 453-2990
www.gotoyourroom.com

From Russia With Love Deli

MARKETS: *Best Eastern European foods in Bellevue*

If you're looking for authentic Russian and Eastern European foods, then From Russia With Love Deli is the place for you. Owner Sergey Dunayev, a native of Vladivostok, guarantees good quality foods and excellent service. He places an emphasis on education in respect to all the different foods carried in the store. The clientele is just as varied as the foods. His customers come from all over Eastern Europe. The deli case is stocked full of smoked meats, dried fish, salads and blintzes. Since taking over the store in 1999 he's increased the number of items in stock tenfold. He's established a great bond of trust with his customers, too. If he recommends something and they find it unsatisfactory, his customers know they can always get a credit. "They don't even have to return it. I trust my customers and they trust me," he says. Their lunch menu consists of delicious homemade soups, salads and hot entrees all made from scratch in the deli and all at affordable prices. There's even an excellent catering menu. In the kitchen is his trusted employee, Tanya Dzhafarova, who likes to engage the customers with her lively personality as she turns out excellent dishes. Stop in at the deli and get a taste of Eastern Europe.

Store: 15600 NE 8th Street, K-16,
Bellevue WA
(425) 401-2093
Cafeteria: 1424 156th Avenue NE, Bellevue WA
(425) 603-0701
www.frwldeli.com

Firenze Ristorante Italiano

RESTAURANTS & CAFÉS: *Best Italian food in Bellevue*

Firenze Ristorante Italiano has been serving tantalizing traditional style Italian meals since 1992. The atmosphere is warm and inviting, with Mediterranean themed décor that includes stucco walls, terracotta floors, starched linens and candlelight. Soothing opera music, quiet conversations and the aromatic smell of Italian food all contribute to the ambience of this wonderful restaurant. Owner Salvatore Lembo will greet you in the traditional Italian fashion, and you can often find him visiting at tables, chatting with customers about his extensive and outstanding wine list, menu or just about anything at all. He's proud of the restaurant's reputation for quality, as well as the fact that Firenze has become a destination restaurant. It's the perfect place to have an intimate dinner, toast a business deal or have a celebration with family and friends. The menu features all your favorite traditional Italian dishes at reasonable prices. There's also a private banquet room that's available for parties, receptions or business meetings. Firenze also carries a large selection of fine cigars. The banquet room is available during the week and makes a great place to relax and enjoy one after dinner. So whether you're looking for that perfect spot for a large celebration or a dinner for two, stop in and enjoy an authentic taste of Italy at Firenze Ristorante Italiano.

15600 NE 8th Street, Bellevue WA
(425) 957-1077
www.firenzerestaurant.com

Crab Pot Restaurant & Bar

RESTAURANTS & CAFÉS: *Best seafood in Bellevue*

With locations in Seattle and Bellevue, the Crab Pot Restaurant & Bar is the best place to go for fresh seafood when you're visiting King County. The menu features nautical delights from fish and chips to *cioppino*, but the Crab Pot's specialty, the Seafeast, is a unique treat. They take a variety of crabs, clams, mussels, shrimp in the shell, salmon, halibut, oysters, potatoes, corn on the cob and andouille sausage steamed with mouth-watering spices and pour it right on the table. Then, no need for silverware, all you need is the bib and mallet they give you. Try any of the five varieties available and you won't be able to wait to try the others. The Crab Pot Restaurant & Bar is one of the most enjoyable places to eat in the Pacific Northwest. The Seattle restaurant is located on the waterfront. Either location is perfect for family and friends to enjoy a classic seafood meal. Groups of all sizes can be accommodated for lunch or dinner, and customers are welcome to walk right in. Both locations offer a homey atmosphere and friendly service.

Two Lake Bellevue Drive, Bellevue WA
(425) 455-2244
The Bay Pavilion, 1301 Alaska Way, Pier 57, Seattle WA
(206) 624-1890

Seastar Restaurant and Raw Bar

RESTAURANTS & CAFÉS: *Best raw bar in Bellevue*

When you consider that chef/owner John Howie of Seastar Restaurant and Raw Bar began his culinary career at age 15, it's no wonder that his signature style has earned his establishments such acclaim in the Pacific Northwest. Assembling a stellar team to see his vision come to life, John opened Seastar Restaurant and Raw Bar in March of 2002. With a menu featuring fresh regional food with varied influences drawn from around the world, Seastar has become known for it's unique raw bar offering shucked oysters, sashimi and sushi. Seastar has been honored for its wine list, receiving recognition and numerous distinctions within this area of the hospitality industry. In the 2005 Zagat Survey, Seastar received high ratings in the Top Cuisine-Seafood category, where the people polled described the fare as "delicious seafood creatively prepared," words that capture the character of this place. John believes in giving back to the community, serving on the board of the Gary Payton Foundation, which organizes efforts to assist at-risk youth in Seattle and Oakland. His appearances on national television programs such as *Good Morning America* and the Food Network have gone a long way towards raising the profile of his unique style of wonderfully eclectic dining fare. Spend an afternoon or evening in downtown Bellevue's financial district and enjoy the award-winning seafood selections of this amazing place.

205 108th Avenue NE, Suite 100, Bellevue WA
(425) 456-0010
www.seastarrestaurant.com

PLACES TO GO

- Blyth Park
  16950 W Riverside Drive

- Brickyard Rd. Park
  16800 Brickyard Road NE

- Park at Bothell Landing
  9919 NE 180th Street

- Sammamish River Park & Trail
  17995 102nd Avenue NE

- Thrashers's Corner Regional Park
  12th Ave SE & 208th Street SE

THINGS TO DO

June
- Father's Day Car Show
  Country Village Shops
  (425) 483-2250

July
- City of Bothell Freedom Festival
  (425) 486-7430

- Fourth of July Parade
  (425) 486-7430

- Music in the Park Concert Series
  Park at Bothell Landing Amphitheatre
  (425) 486-7430

August
- *Greater Bothell Arts & Crafts Fair*
  (425) 821-1127

- City of Bothell RiverFest
  (425) 486-7430

September
- La Fiesta Viva
  Country Village Shops
  (425) 483-2250 or (425) 821-1127

- Annual Fall Car Show
  Country Village Shops
  (425) 483-2250

October
- Harvest Festival
  & Pumpkin Painting Contest
  Country Village Shops
  (425) 483-2250

November
- Tree Lighting & Santa Arrival
  Park at Bothell Landing
  (425) 486-7430

BOTHELL

Bothell started as an isolated logging village housing a handful of hardy pioneers. George Bothell, who arrived in 1888 with his parents, was among four men who built the Bothell Shingle Mill Company. He became Bothell's first mayor after it was incorporated in 1909. Today Bothell is a multi-faceted city with a population of approximately 30,000. Over the years Bothell has taken on many roles: as a way station, mill town, local farm supply and services center, suburban bedroom community, and, within the last decade, regional employment center.

Downtown Bothell
Photo Courtesy of the Bothell Chamber of Commerce

Ada's Pottery Cottage

ARTS & CRAFTS:
Best in Polish Stoneware

Ada's Pottery Cottage offers the finest in Polish stoneware. Their pottery is supplied by the award-winning factory Ceramika Artystyczna in Boleswiec, Poland. This traditional art was started long ago by village craftsmen and peasants of Lower Silesia. They were first inspired by the wonder and beauty of the peacock's tail coloring and design, thus the eye of peacock feather motif was born. They used rudimentary tools such as carved potatoes to hand stamp patterns onto the clay. Today, the use of modern tools such as sea sponges have replaced the older techniques. Although most pieces are no longer handthrown, each individual piece is handstamped or handpainted by an artist, and ultimately touched by more than 14 careful hands helping it through the production process before it is fired. Once complete, the pottery continues to hold true to its incredible beauty and strength. The painters are trained for many years and a few become known as Unikat artists. Only those achieving the highest level of skill are awarded this designation, and may begin to design their own works of art. These patterns are signed and numbered, and the decorations are highly sought after. Ada's Pottery Cottage stocks a wonderful selection of the Signature series line. Their showroom is over 1,500 square feet of Polish stoneware and 60 percent of it is composed of the Traditional series collection. All stoneware is safe for use in dishwashers, microwaves and ovens. It is free of toxins such as lead or cadmium. They carry only the finest, first quality stoneware with a 100-percent customer satisfaction rate. Visit the website, or come into the Ada's Pottery Cottage showroom and experience the rich, visual poetry of Polish stoneware.

821 238th Street SE (Country Village Shop), Bothell WA
(425) 482-9104
www.adaspolishpottery.com

Chapters Photography

ARTS & CRAFTS: *Best portrait photography in Bothell*

Rob Resing began his photographic career at the age of 13 with an instamatic camera and a trip to the World's Fair. He returned home with 178 pictures of metal, dirt, people's shoes and one image of his family, who accidentally wandered in front of the lens. Now the owner of Chapters Photography, with his wife Karin, Rob has discovered Expressive Realism. This little known art form incorporates the elements of photography with the timeless presence of the painters Monet, Renoir and Manet. "We don't take pictures here," he says, "We create heirlooms. A portrait is an historical record of your life at this exact moment." Rob seeks the authentic self in each of his subjects. It takes patience, but he has an abundance of that. A generous amount of time is scheduled for each session. Rob says, "We never want our clients to feel rushed. We know that babies need time to adjust to new surroundings. Young children usually want to play with our fire engine before we get started. Our families and high school seniors love the beautiful spring flowers outside of the studio and the trees just up the walk. We have an entire outdoor studio within just a few feet of our door." Whether you would prefer portraits with your horses or in the studio, let Chapters Photography capture the next chapter in your life.

23716 8th Street SE, Suite E, Bothell WA
(425) 415-1267

Alexa's Café & Catering
The Monte Villa Farmhouse

RESTAURANTS & CAFÉS: *Best catering and event center*

Leigh Brink owns three interlocking businesses in Bothell. Together they form Alexa's Café & Catering and The Monte Villa Farmhouse. Locals have been coming to Alexa's Café for more than 15 years for breakfast and lunch. The food is fresh, uncomplicated and tasty. The breakfast menu contains almost anything you might imagine eating first thing in the day, including an outstanding hollandaise sauce on the eggs Benedict. Sandwiches, soups and salads dominate the extensive lunch menu. The basil tomato soup is another perfect dish. Like all the soups, it is homemade. The noise level in the café is low, encouraging conversation. The restaurant grew out of Leigh's catering business, which continues with a vast catering menu that offers dinner and reception fare not available at the café. Recently, Leigh bought the Monte Villa Farmhouse, which can be rented out for weddings, business meetings and other functions with catering by Leigh. Built in 1927, Monte Villa is a white clapboard structure tucked away among gardens and towering pines. It has a ballroom with hardwood floors and a bright, airy living room with French doors opening onto a veranda. Either room can be used for functions. The grounds are ideal for an outdoor wedding. For a great meal or a great event, try Alexa's Café & Catering and The Monte Villa Farmhouse.

Alexa's Café: 10115 Main Street, Bothell WA
(425) 483-6275 *www.alexascafe.com*
The Monte Villa Farmhouse: 3300 Monte Villa Parkway, Bothell WA
(425) 485-6115 *www.montevilla.com*

Papa's Place Restaurant & Catering

RESTAURANTS & CAFÉS: *Best French cuisine in Bothell*

The Food Network turns chefs into celebrities, but patrons of Bothell's Country Village Shops are keeping their local celebrity all to themselves. Chef Les Goetz, owner of Papa's Place Restaurant & Catering, is an accredited chef with 32 years of professional experience. He began at the age of 16 under the guidance of French chefs who taught him the art of cooking using traditional French ingredients and techniques. In designing the recipes for Papa's Place he kept the French techniques, but eliminated the fats, like butters and creams. The results are heart healthy European-American dishes. Les has perfected his culinary craft in top restaurants such as Cliff House, Mirabeau, Le Tastevin, and downtown Seattle's Columbia Tower restaurant. Since he puts his name on

every product, Les often pays more for the best ingredients. "It doesn't help to put pretty frills like flowers and branches on bad tasting or mediocre food," he says. Chef Les is trusted to prepare high quality foods with high level mastery. He prefers to focus on foods that are savory, but also bakes the best brownies and cookies you'll ever taste. Chef Les is living his dream and those who have discovered him hope he never leaves the area. When you need catering or a delicious dinner, come to Papa's Place Restaurant & Catering.

23716 8th Avenue SE, Suite C, Bothell WA
(425) 402-9362
papascatering.com

Stampin' in the Rain

ARTS & CRAFTS: *Best scrapbook supplies in Bothell*

The renewed popularity of stamp crafts and scrapbooking is making this cute little shop in the Pacific Northwest a huge success. Stampin' in the Rain offers you quality time spent with your creative side. Owner, artist and interior designer Kim L. Merboth believes that everyone who has imagination has creative potential, and a visit to her shop just might help you find it. Kim fell in love with this craft because it reminded her of how designing was done before the computer age. Stamping is hands-on creating, without restraints. She uses her design background to assist you in selecting the right tools to access your inner creativity. Whether you are designing wedding or party invitations, birthday or greeting cards, or any card for life's celebrations, stress and tension melt away when stamping. Stampin' in the Rain looks small from the outside, but is big on materials of inspiration. Offering numerous stamps, punches, embellishments and supplies, there are no rules or limitations at Stampin' in the Rain. Kim accommodates any shopping partners with a place to relax, read and enjoy complimentary candies while the stampers shop. Engaging activities include the Stamper's Afternoon Out on Sundays, where Kim or a guest art-instructor teaches popular ideas, tips and techniques. Kim will help you design anything you can visualize.

831 237th Street SE, Bothell WA
(425) 408-9050
www.stampin-in-the-rain.com

Country Village
SHOPPING: *Best un-mall in the region*

Bothell's Country Village Shops offer a full menu of seasonal fun for local shoppers and out-of-town visitors alike. The pleasant cluster of farm-style buildings is a perfect place to spend the day enjoying the specialty shops, day spa and restaurants that share the 13-acre grounds with the resident ducks, chickens and rabbits. Country Village is open seven days a week. You can stop in any time or you might want to schedule your visit to enjoy a special event. The Country Village Farmers Market is open every Friday from mid-May through September. More than 30 vendors gather here to sell their freshly picked produce and handcrafted items. With live music midday, it's the fun place to be on summer Fridays. Or maybe you'd enjoy a car show? Bring your own vintage car or come and enjoy everyone else's. The PT Cruiser Show and the Father's Day Car Show are in June. The Fall Car Show takes place in early September. Gardeners might prefer to visit the Fuchsia Show in August, or the Dahlia Show and the Koi Show in September. A Latino festival, La Fiesta Viva! is also in September and features lively music, craft booths and delicious food. Country Village is a wonderful place to gather with your friends and family, either in a casual setting at the company picnic field with its horseshoes, badminton, bocce court and putting course, or in the more elegant Courtyard Hall, a perfect spot for weddings, meetings and parties.

23718 7th Avenue SE, Bothell WA
(425) 483-2250
www.countryvillagebothell.com

Ante Nani's Lil Grass Shack
SHOPPING: *Best Makawa'o shopping experience*

Experience the spirit of Aloha by visiting Ante Nani's Lil Grass Shack in the Bothell Country Village. Why a Hawaiian kiosk in Bothell? "Because we missed Hawaii and wanted to bring it here," say Linda and William Aven, who are originally from Hawaii. Ante Nani's offers high quality Hawaiian *ono grinds* (good food). The *shoyu* (soy sauce) is not too salty, the coconut milk is well balanced, and both the mango and guava jelly taste like morning in Maui. Ante Nani's offers CDs of Hawaiian music, scented or unscented *ikaika* helmets and sterling silver Hawaiian heirloom jewelry. Body lotions and sprays with scents like plumeria, stephanotis and white ginger are sure to put a touch of Hawaii into your day on the mainland. You can find Hawaiian clothing, including men's Aloha shirts and mu'u mu'us for all ages. If you are planning a wedding or a graduation ceremony, William can create the perfect lei for you. If you drop by Ante Nani's Lil Grass Shack, William and Linda will talk story to you and then you will be *ohana* (family).

735 238th Street SE, Bothell WA
(425) 483-2017 *www.antenani.com*

Cranberry Cottage
SHOPPING: *Best home décor store in Bothell*

Take a step off the beaten path and discover a whole new way to shop for home décor and accessories with a visit to Cranberry Cottage. Owners Kelly Priebe and Theresa Ankney redesigned a 103-year-old barn to house this charming shop's many special finds. Kelly and Theresa, along with several guest designers, group the shop's exciting pieces in inspirational vignettes. The vignettes change frequently and show customers how pieces can benefit their homes. During the summer you can relax on the front porch with a cool beverage before heading inside to tour the beautifully designed rooms that display a wide variety of vintage and modern treasures. This is the ideal place to find pampering bath products, including soaps, lotions and spa products, along with sumptuous linens and pillows. Cranberry Cottage carries a wide range of home furnishings, as well as clocks, artwork, baby clothing and silk floral arrangements. Further treasures include ironwork and statuary for the garden, lamps, wicker pieces, and modern and vintage chandeliers. If you've been searching for something special and are unable to find it at Cranberry Cottage, Kelly and Theresa will order it for you, if it's available. Enjoy sensational service while searching for that must-have gift or décor piece with a visit to the welcoming and always changing Cranberry Cottage.

23929 Bothell Everett Highway, Bothell WA
(425) 481-7951

Ottoman Trading Company
SHOPPING: *Best variety of Turkish goods*

Halfway around the world and thousands of miles from Turkey is Bothell's own Ottoman Trading Company, offering a tremendous variety of ancient and modern Turkish décor, jewelry and clothing merchandise. Founded by Dena Sukaya, who is married to a Turkish-American engineer, this enterprise promotes and preserves traditional Turkish handicrafts from many of Istanbul's top textile, ceramic and fashion designers. To that end, Ottoman Trading Company travels to the region frequently and selects a variety of products from Istanbul's famed Grand Bazaar and other historically important marketplaces found in Turkey and the surrounding region. Every piece offered is authentic. You will not find the more common American-Bohemian replicas. In addition, the upscale feel here makes it a natural setting for what Dena calls Girl Celebrations, such as bridal showers, birthday parties and girl's nights out. To keep her connections active, she still manages a shopping service in Istanbul's historic bazaar district. Ottoman Trading Company is a window onto a part of the world you may not know, and a chance to bring these fascinating traditions and treasures home.

23634 Bothell Everett Highway, Bothell WA
(425) 368-0369
www.ottomantradingco.com

DUVALL

Duvall, with a population of 5,735, is one of the fastest growing communities in the state. The City was named after James Duvall, a logger, who homesteaded here in 1871. Duvall is located approximately 25 miles northeast of Seattle, halfway between Monroe and Carnation, and is fast becoming a favorite residential community for both commuters and for people who favor life in a small town setting.

PARKS

- Central Park
  27500 NE 150th Street

- Depot Park
  NE Stephens Street and Railroad Avenue

- McCormick Park
  East bank of Snoqualmie River adjacent to Snoqualmie Valley Trail

- Lake Rasmussen Park
  4th Avenue NE & NE Cherry Street

- Snoqualmie Valley Trail
  33-mile trail from Duvall to Vantage in Central Washington

EVENTS

June
- Duvall Days
  Parade, Fair, Fun Runs, and Art Show

July
- Sandblast Arts Festival
  McCormick Park
  (425)-788-3928

- Summer Stage Concerts
  *Wednesday nights 6:30 pm July to August
  McCormick Park*

September
- Outdoor Quilt Show
  Beautiful handmade quilts displayed along Main Street

Jazz concert in Duvall Park
Photo by Paul Schultz

BEARZABOUT

SHOPPING: *Largest collection of unique dolls & bears*

Carol and John Graham have gathered some of the most incredible dolls and bears imaginable. Bearzabout isn't a toy store for children. It is a collector's paradise. Serious collectors from around the world gravitate to Bearzabout. John and Carol travel to trade shows all over the country to find the newest and most unique dolls and stuffed animals. They preview the latest lines of all the top artists and manufacturers. Their intent is to carry the best and they have a keen awareness that overproduction kills the value and joy of collecting. It's all about treasures. Near the end of WWII, quantities of fabrics were too scarce to make fashions for live models. Designers saved on the cost of fabric by making doll clothes to represent the real fashions. They presented the dolls to wholesalers and retailers instead of staging expensive runway shows. Dolls representing this collection are available at Bearzabout. They carry the full line of Robert Toner, the designer of *Theatre de la mode*. These dolls, their hair styles, make-up and fashion trends are replicas of movie stars of many eras. Bearzabout carries John Wright's design of artist Thomas Nast's original Santa Claus and J.K. Rawling's approved Harry Potter dolls. Dolls by Ginny, Gene, Adora, Maggie Iacono, Zwergnase and Kathe Kruse are just a few of the lines that you'll be able to enjoy. Coveted Steiff bears are featured, and for promotions and special décor Carol and John can order extraordinarily life-like enormous stuffed animals. It may be the only way you can own an elephant or a giraffe. Bearzabout does it all with style.

15702 Main Street NE, Duvall WA
(425) 844-9100
www.bearzabout.com

ISSAQUAH

Issaquah sits on the edge of Lake Sammamish, surrounded by the Issaquah Alps, 17 miles east of Seattle. Issaquah shares a verdant valley with bald eagles, great blue herons, and thousands of spawning salmon. The city features a thriving arts scene, fine dining, historic treasures, extreme sports and unique shops. Parks and trails provide abundant connections to the natural world. Surrounded by stunning mountains and outdoor recreation, yet still close to urban centers, Issaquah is known as a Northwest destination for living, working, playing, and doing business in the 21st century.

PLACES TO GO

- Cougar Mountain Zoo
  19525 SE 54th

- Depot Park
  Across the Rainier Multiple Use Trail from Veteran's Memorial Field

- Francis J. Gaudette Theatre
  303 Front Street N

- Historic Train Depot and Gilman Town Hall
  Issaquah Historical Society

- Issaquah Community Center
  301 Rainier Boulevard S.

- Lake Sammamish State Park
  512-acre day-use park with 6,858 feet of waterfront on Lake Sammamish

- Pickering Farm
  1730 10th Avenue NW

- Talus Native Growth Protection Area
  SR 900 and Talus Development

THINGS TO DO

July
- Heritage Day Festival
  (425) 392-3500

September
- Hometown Issaquah Reunion
  (425) 392-3500

October
- Issaquah Salmon Days Festival
  (425) 392-0661

Cougar Mountain Zoo

Boehms Candies

FUN FOODS: *Most historic candy-making company*

In 1940, an Austrian mountain climber who once ran in the Olympics came to the United States. Julius Boehm was attracted to the Pacific Northwest by the allure of the Cascades. In 1943 he and a friend opened a candy-making shop called the Candy Kitchen in the Ravenna area of Seattle. In 1956, Julius and the business moved to the Issaquah foothills, where he built the Edelweiss Chalet above the candy factory. Julius left his mark on the landscape by building the Luis Trenker Kirch'l, a replica of a 12th century chapel near St. Moritz in Switzerland. Visitors to Boehms Candies can now tour Julius' house, as well as the candy-making facilities and chapel. Julius collected art, music boxes and toys, and filled his house with delightful reminders of his Alpine heritage. In the candy rooms downstairs, you can watch a variety of sweets, from Victorian creams to peanut brittle, being prepared and see the elaborate traditional hand-dipping process for making filled chocolates. The tour ends in the chapel that Julius dedicated to mountain climbers who have lost their lives while climbing. (Julius himself scaled Mt. Rainier when he was 81.) After the tour, you are invited to visit the gift shop and enjoy specialties such as Mozart-Kugeln and the chocolate-caramel Mount Rainier candy.

255 NE Gilman Boulevard, Issaquah WA
(425) 392-6652
www.boehmscandies.com

White Horse Toys

SHOPPING: *Best toy store in Issaquah*

Issaquah's Gilman Village is a one-of-a-kind open-air shopping center where all 25 shops are located in historic buildings that have been saved from demolition. One such building is the 1922 Schomber House/Garage building, now home to White Horse Toys. The business was created in 1995 by Molly and Bill Handley and their daughter, Debra Lewis. They started it in smaller quarters seven years before moving into the 3,000-square-foot barn in 2002. The shop offers a dazzling array of toys. Appropriately for a business that appeals so much to families, White Horse Toys is a multi-generational enterprise. In fact, opening a toy store was something Debra and Molly had wanted to do for many years before it finally became a reality. For Molly and Bill's 10 grandchildren, having a toy store in the family must seem like a dream come true. In addition to carrying European toys, White Horse Toys stocks high-quality manufactured toys, such as Steiff animals and William Britain soldiers (the same classic figures that were once made with lead, now made with safe materials). White Horse Toys offers free consultations for customers with special shopping needs and free gift wrapping.

317 NW Gilman Boulevard, #13, Issaquah WA
(425) 391-1498
www.whitehorsetoys.com

PLACES TO GO

- Houghton Beach Park
  5811 Lake Washington Boulevard

- Marina Park
  25 Lakeshore Drive

- Mark Twain Park
  10625 132nd Avenue NE

- Marsh Park
  6605 Lake Washington Boulevard

- Settler's Landing
  1001 Lake Street S

- Waverly Beach Park
  633 Waverly Park Way

THINGS TO DO

Monthly
- Downtown Art Walk
  Second Thursday of each month
  (425) 889-8212

March
- Little League Baseball Parade
  www.kall.org

May
- Kirkland Half Marathon and 5K
  (206) 729-9972

August
- Annual Garden Party
  (425) 893-8766

September
- Kirkland Triathlon at Carillon Point
  (503) 644-6822

November
- Kirkland Tree Lighting Ceremony
  (425) 893-8766

December
- Parade of Christmas Ships
  www.argosycruises.com

KIRKLAND

Kirkland lies on the northeastern shores of Lake Washington, a stone's throw from Seattle. No other city has as many waterfront parks on the lake as Kirkland. Tree-lined boulevards, a low-rise downtown, lanes of boutique shops and restaurants, intriguing outdoor sculptures, and a thriving arts scene make this city of 45,000 people a great place to live, visit and play.

Aussie Pet Mobile Eastside
ANIMALS & PETS: *Best mobile pet groomers*

When Aussie Pet Mobile Eastside comes to your door, your animals are treated to a full-service grooming in a highly sanitary, stress-free salon. Stress free means the environment is climate controlled for all weather conditions. Their experience is private, because multiple pets are not allowed in the area at the same time. Aussie Pet Mobile takes care of older pets by grooming on flat surfaces. There is even a geriatric support system to hold dogs up comfortably during treatments. There are no cages in the Aussie Mobile. Owner Geoff Andrist does not believe that there are ungroomable dogs or cats. He makes sure cats don't notice they are in water by the use of specially designed cones. In fact, they seem to like the heated hydrobath. Dogs love the new FURminator, which separates their coat, extracts loose hair and undercoat to stimulate hair follicles, increase circulation and leave their topcoat shiny and healthy. When pets are treated monthly or bi-weekly, shedding is reduced 60 to 80 percent. Geoff will schedule your pet's appointments at a time and location most convenient for you. You and your pets will love Geoff's award-winning Aussie Mobile because he provides one-on-one service in an atmosphere where pet owners are not just customers, but friends. Geoff volunteers his Aussie Mobile for events like Howel-O-Ween and local pet charities like HomewardPets.com. Call Geoff today and he will bring the Aussie Pet Mobile Eastside right to your door.

(800) PET-MOBILE (738-6624)
www.aussiepetmobile.com

Woodmark Hotel on Lake Washington

ACCOMMODATIONS: *Best luxury hotel in Kirkland*

For elegance and comfort on the shores of Lake Washington, The Woodmark Hotel is incomparable. At this luxury hotel you can enjoy spectacular views of the lake, the Olympic Mountains and the Seattle skyline from your beautifully appointed room or suite. There's a lakeside bistro, Waters, and the Spa at the Woodmark. They offer special touches like an invitation to Raid the Pantry for complimentary late-night snacks, a full schedule of seasonal special packages, and a restored vintage Chris-Craft for touring the lake. The Waters bistro has a warm and inviting atmosphere, and features Northwest cuisine with a Mediterranean accent. The menu includes delicious dishes like Rosemary Grilled Portobello Mushrooms, and Northwest Paella with shrimp, mussels, clams, halibut and chorizo with saffron rice. The Library Bar lounge offers afternoon tea, espresso, cocktails and *hors d'oeuvres*. For unwinding, the Spa offers an enormous selection of Aveda services. The packages include names like Panache, Pure Focus, Radiant Skin Facial, Fusion Stone Massage, Candlelight Soak, and Rosemary Mint Awakening Body Wrap. The Spa experience includes hydrotherapy, manicures, pedicures, massages, skin care, and body treatments—everything for rejuvenation and enjoyment. The Woodmark has a full set of amenities for the business guest as well as the vacationer. The hotel provides high-speed Internet, voice mail and data jacks, desks, in-room safes, a fitness room and concierge services. Just seven miles east of Seattle, this is the perfect place for a business conference.

1200 Carillon Point, Kirkland WA
(425) 822-3700 or (800) 822-3700
www.thewoodmark.com

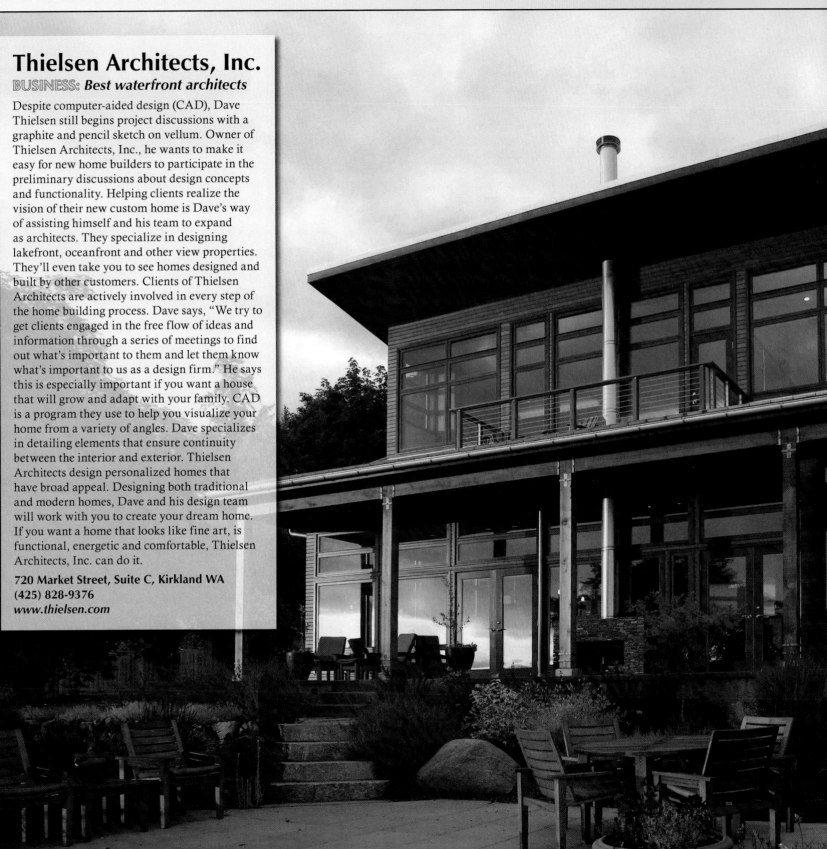

Thielsen Architects, Inc.

BUSINESS: *Best waterfront architects*

Despite computer-aided design (CAD), Dave Thielsen still begins project discussions with a graphite and pencil sketch on vellum. Owner of Thielsen Architects, Inc., he wants to make it easy for new home builders to participate in the preliminary discussions about design concepts and functionality. Helping clients realize the vision of their new custom home is Dave's way of assisting himself and his team to expand as architects. They specialize in designing lakefront, oceanfront and other view properties. They'll even take you to see homes designed and built by other customers. Clients of Thielsen Architects are actively involved in every step of the home building process. Dave says, "We try to get clients engaged in the free flow of ideas and information through a series of meetings to find out what's important to them and let them know what's important to us as a design firm." He says this is especially important if you want a house that will grow and adapt with your family. CAD is a program they use to help you visualize your home from a variety of angles. Dave specializes in detailing elements that ensure continuity between the interior and exterior. Thielsen Architects design personalized homes that have broad appeal. Designing both traditional and modern homes, Dave and his design team will work with you to create your dream home. If you want a home that looks like fine art, is functional, energetic and comfortable, Thielsen Architects, Inc. can do it.

720 Market Street, Suite C, Kirkland WA
(425) 828-9376
www.thielsen.com

Lakeshore Gallery
GALLERIES: *Best American-created crafts*

Wherever your final destination may be in Washington, as a visitor or a resident, Lakeshore Gallery should be on your itinerary. Allow plenty of time to visit their location in Kirkland, as you will be wonderfully lost in their abundant collection of hand-blown glass art, exquisite handcrafted jewelry, metal works, pottery and woodworks, as well as watercolors and other beautiful paintings. Lakeshore Gallery opened in 1983, and is owned by Georgie Kilrain, whose motto is Love the art you buy. Extremely authentic and carrying one-of-a-kind pieces, Lakeshore's focus is on American-created art and crafts. Customer service is paramount at Lakeshore, because the majority of their business comes from regular customers. Lakeshore Gallery has strong ties to the community. They were one of the galleries that began the local Art Walk years ago, and Lakeshore continues to be a dedicated participant today. Whether you're looking for a unique wedding gift or just want to expand or start your art collection, Lakeshore Gallery is a place you should look.

107 Park Lane, Kirkland WA
(425) 827-0606

Kirkland Dahn Yoga
HEALTH: *Best yoga classes in Kirkland*

Dahn Yoga is a holistic health program that combines deep stretching, breath work, meditation and movement to release and channel the flow of energy in your body. Dahn Yoga in Kirkland is one of 450 Dahn Yoga centers worldwide. In Korea in the 1970s, Ilchi Lee developed Dahn Yoga based on traditional Korean practices. Lee's method became tremendously popular, and major corporations, as well as the Korean military, soon adopted its practices. It was introduced into the United States in 1991. Open to anyone regardless of age, experience or current physical condition, Dahn Yoga can be a part of a physical fitness program or the beginning of a thoroughgoing lifestyle change. Highly skilled master trainers lead the Dahn Yoga classes. Different classes accommodate a range of fitness levels and goals. Regular yoga classes include stretching, deep breathing and meditation and are easy for beginners to follow, but challenging enough for advanced practitioners. A system of exercises and meditation called Brain Respiration uses the power of imagination and the mind-body-brain connection to awaken your potential. Tai Chi classes teach participants how to feel and use their vital energy. The graceful martial arts moves help release stress and recharge the body. Classes are available for children aged six and up. He Jung Jang, regional manager and master trainer, invites you to Kirkland Dahn Yoga.

10702 NE 68th Street, Kirkland WA
(425) 893-9642
www.dahnyoga.com

Apple Physical Therapy

HEALTH: *Voted top place to work in South Puget Sound*

Washington native Randy Johnson, partner and CEO of Apple Physical Therapy, opened his company in 1984 as a way to support his family. Since then his business has evolved into an organization that supports many families and serves individuals throughout the Puget Sound region with clinics in 23 locations. Company President and CEO Claude Ciancio came to work for Apple Physical Therapy in 1990 and achieved partnership in 1998. Ciancio comes from New York City, but his commitment to patients and the community aligns him firmly with Johnson's original goals for service to patients and the communities where patients reside. Randy and Claude believe in the Golden Rule, as well as five core elements, which they feel have made Apple Physical Therapy the success it is today. These five elements are, in order, Integrity, Knowledge, Compassion, Profit and Fun. For patients at any of the Apple facilities, these core tenets create a welcoming and comforting environment that is ideal for both working and healing. Employees, via a *Business Examiner* magazine poll, named Apple Physical Therapy as the number one place to work in the Puget Sound area. Whether you are searching for rehabilitation services or a new career, the staff at Apple Physical Therapy invites your family to become part of their family.

11821 NE 128th, Suite 203, Kirkland WA
(425) 285-1250
www.applept.com

Navy Memorial Sculpture, Kirkland

Madison House

LIFESTYLE DESTINATIONS: *Best upscale retirement community*

Nestled in Kirkland, near the eastern shores of Lake Washington with its picturesque parks, specialty shops and art galleries, you will find the best upscale retirement community in the area. For more than 26 years, Madison House has provided the best of retirement lifestyles with the ambience of a residential hotel. An elegant dining room provides a full menu of choices and three meals a day. The fitness center, heated indoor pool and spa, and other amenities assure that the residents feel like pampered guests. At Madison House, residents enjoy an active retirement with a wide variety of outings and scenic drives scheduled weekly. There is plenty of onsite fun, including art classes, theater, live music, movies and more. Residents are encouraged to meet their neighbors and participate in social activities, including Sherry Hour, High Tea and Happy Hour. Madison House offers luxurious one-bedroom and studio apartments, all featuring a full bath and separate kitchen. Residents who require assistance benefit from trained and attentive staff, including a registered nurse and therapeutic fitness coordinator. Madison House requires no upfront buy in or endowment fee, and offers monthly rentals that include all services and utilities except telephone. Small pets are welcome. Transportation to shopping, banking, hospital and healthcare services is provided daily.

12215 NE 128th Street, Kirkland WA
(425) 821-8210
www.madisonhouseretirement.com

Larry's Markets

MARKETS: *Best supermarket in Kirkland*

Larry, founder and owner of Larry's Markets, bagged groceries and ran errands at his parents' corner grocery store in Seattle. The entire family lived directly above the store. After graduating from the University of Washington in 1960, Larry worked at his father's newly purchased store at 144th and Pacific Highway South. In 1964 Larry opened his own store in the Central Seattle area. In 1974 Larry bought his father's store, and two years later replaced it with a 25,000-square-foot Larry's Market. Larry's now has six area locations and is the best supermarket chain in the region. In the summer of 1989 Larry's Markets expanded to the Eastside with the opening of the Kirkland Store. The 61,000-square-foot store has beautiful architecture and interior design, with departments like the Market Café, Produce Row, Market Deli and B.I.O. (natural, organic and environmentally friendly products). Located outside the store is the Apple Orchard, where 26 varieties of apple trees were planted in dedication to Larry's father, Marshal. Visit Larry's Markets in Kirkland or at any of their locations. They really are the best place to shop.

12321 NE 120th Place, Kirkland WA
(425) 820-2300
www.larrysmarkets.com

Tandoori Kitchen

RESTAURANTS & CAFÉS: *Best Indian and Pakistani cuisine*

The state of Washington is home to dozens of Indian restaurants, but none are better or more authentic than Tandoori Kitchen in Kirkland. Tandoori Kitchen prepares Indian and Pakistani cuisine just like you'd get it at a famous food market half a world away. Tandoori Kitchen is the creation of four brothers, Mansoor, Mughees, Maqsood and Shami Bhatti (their middle names, as all of them share the first name Mohammed), who drew on the heritage of mother Nusret's recipes, as interpreted by their chef father, Arshad. The food at Tandoori is mouth-watering, and the fact that it is low in fat and cholesterol is an added draw for the health-conscious. Word-of-mouth advertising has quadrupled the number of customers coming through the doors in recent years. Tandoori offers an extensive list of selections, including various kabobs of chicken, beef and lamb, Beef Nihari, Karahi Lamb, and Lamb boti Kabab that receive rave reviews, and a masterful naan bread that seems to go with everything. The curry dishes are so authentic that local British transplants say a meal here transports them back to their homeland, where world-class Indian and Pakistani chefs and restaurants are widely known. Once you stop by for a meal, or take advantage of their Taj Catering service, you will understand our enthusiasm for Tandoori Kitchen's authentic cuisine.

13108 NE 70th Place, Kirkland WA
(425) 827-0800

Rikki Rikki

RESTAURANTS & CAFÉS: *Best Japanese restaurant*

A visit to Rikki Rikki Authentic Japanese Restaurant & Sushi Bar during lunch or dinner offers the chance to enjoy some of the finest Japanese cuisine Washington has to offer. Owner Masahiro Tarada, known affectionately as Masa to everyone around here, opened Rikki 15 years ago. As the years have passed, his sales have continued to increase and the 120 seats Rikki Rikki has available are often filled, as visitors come by to enjoy the stylish décor and elegant jazz playing in the background not to mention the tremendous food. The reasonably priced menu is extensive and creative. In addition to the restaurant, Mr. Tarada has created a factory known as Rikki USA, where his popular sauces and salad dressings are created and shipped all over the world. As a neighborhood get-together spot, this is a perfect place for hanging out with friends or family, with an on-site formal room available by reservation. Though Mr. Terada does not talk about the famous customers who come through the door from time to time, including local pro athletes and some of the well known computer industry personalities, he is passionate about ensuring that each visitor will receive the best service and experience while there. Find out for yourself why Rikki Rikki is the best choice for Japanese food in Kirkland.

442 Parkplace Center, Kirkland WA
(425) 828-0707
www.rikkirikki.com

REDMOND

Surrounded by towering evergreen forests between the Cascade Mountains and Puget Sound, Redmond is known for natural beauty. In a city with 34 parks and more than 25 miles of trails, and just a short ride from great skiing, it's easy to forget you're within 20 minutes of downtown Seattle. Redmond is known for its arts and entertainment, with live theater, music, film and literary arts for every taste. Redmond sits in a fertile basin created by ancient glaciers that once covered much of King County. Thousands of years before the first fur trappers entered the area's dense forests, the rich bottomland of the Sammamish Valley provided shelter and food for Native Americans. Today Redmond is the seventh most populous city in King County and the sixteenth most populous city in the state of Washington, with a population of 49,900.

PLACES TO GO

- Idylwood Beach Park
  3650 W Lake Sammamish Parkway NE

- Luke McRedmond Landing
  15811 Redmond Way

- Sixty Acre Park
  NE 116th Street

- Watershed Preserve
  21760 Novelty Hill Road

THINGS TO DO

April
- Eggstravaganza
  (425) 556-2300

July
- Derby Days
  (425) 556-2299

August
- Seattle Chamber Music Society Summer Festival
  (206) 283-8808

- SweetFest Dessert Festival
  (206) 909-6175

September
- Canine Classic
  (425) 653-1020

Bridge over Sammamish River

MarketSpice
MARKETS: *Best tea and spices available*

The promise of sweet spices and exotic fragrances have been drawing customers to the MarketSpice store in Seattle's Pike Street Market since 1911. You are sure to enjoy the pure olfactory pleasure of spices, essential oils and teas found at this Seattle landmark. The teas here have won the hearts of tea lovers all over the world. To ensure optimum freshness, all of the teas and spice mixes are still handcrafted in small batches at the company's Redmond facility. Market Spice carries many high quality spices and tea blends that are available only under their label. The cinnamon-orange taste of their most famous tea is so popular that its flavor has been incorporated into other products. Over the years, MarketSpice has expanded its product line to include creamed honeys with spices, tea cookies, candles, barbecue sauces and breath mints. They have also created several new salt-free seasoning mixes, sold by mail and in their five stores. The Healthy Heart mix contains garlic, onion, coriander, paprika and other spices. The Seventh Wonder blend features sesame seeds, poppy seeds, paprika and more. For out-of-the-ordinary tea selections, try the company's exclusive Dragon Phoenix Pearl Tea or the popular Red Bush, with natural antioxidants. Drop into one of the MarketSpice stores for a complimentary cup of tea. It's certain you will want to try more.

85A Pike Place Market, Seattle WA
(206) 622-6340
Mail order and main office:
PO Box 2935, Redmond WA
(425) 883-1220

Tree Top Toys
SHOPPING: *Best toy store*

Whether you are looking for personalized service and competitive prices on top brand toys or specialty toys from small, independent companies, Tree Top Toys in Redmond can help. Owner Blanche Snipes tests every toy in the shop to ensure it is fun, educational and stimulating. Each toy also gets a safety and quality check before it goes on the shelves. Blanche's research reveals that some of the most popular toys are quite simple and often overlooked. Children love the butterfly gardens, puppets and costumes at Tree Top Toys. Also popular are the activity books, perfect for passing the time on long trips. School-age children will find subject-related toys and experiments, as well as games and puzzles. Tree Top also meets the demand for extracurricular fun, with arts-and-crafts projects, dolls and equipment for outdoor activities. Blanche stocks many well known brand names, including horses by Breyer Collectibles, Playmobil's endearing figures and Brio train sets. Tree Top Toys is the proud recipient of the Best of Seattle award, along with the Golden Booty award from Eastside Parent. Blanche and her staff can help you find age-appropriate merchandise for any child on your gift list. Visit Tree Top Toys next time you want to delight your child and inspire creative play.

15752 Redmond Way, Redmond WA
(425) 869-9713
www.treetoptoys.com

RENTON

Nestled on the south shore of Lake Washington, Renton sits in the heart of the Puget Sound area, 10 minutes from Seattle. Renton covers 17.2 miles and has a population of 57,000 people. A century ago, Renton was just a big open space on the trail from Seattle. Framed by densely wooded hills, and bisected by the Black and Cedar River, the land had long been home to the Duwamish Indians. Erasmus Smithers platted the town of Renton on land he and his wife owned under the Donation Land Claim Act of 1850, which allowed settlers coming into the Oregon Territory to claim 160 acres. In 1873, Smithers, with the financial backing of Captain William Renton, organized the Renton Coal Company. The Town was incorporated in September of 1901, having been declared a part of the Washington Territory after the Oregon Territory was divided in 1853.

PARKS

- Carco Theater
  1717 SE Maple Valley Highway

- Cedar River Park
  1717 SE Maple Valley Highway

- Gene Coulon Beach Park
  1201 Lake Washington Boulevard N

- Maplewood Golf Course
  4050 Maple Valley Highway

- Renton Historical Museum
  235 Mill Avenue S

- Talbot Hill Reservoir
  710 S 19th Street

- Veterans Memorial Park
  232 S Main

EVENTS

June
- Kidd Valley Family Concert Series
  Gene Coulon Memorial Beach Park

July
- IKEA Renton River Days
  (425) 430-6528

October
- Harvest Festival on the Piazza
  www.piazzarenton.com

Larkspur Landing
ACCOMMODATIONS: *Best hotel for business*

Larkspur Landing offers first-rate amenities and personalized service in a warm and inviting atmosphere. From custom-designed furniture and signature "FeatherBorne Beds" to exercise and spa facilities, you will find everything you need to rest, relax and stay in shape while you're on the road. Whether you're traveling for business or pleasure, you'll be kept up-to-the-minute and in touch with in-room high-speed Internet access and wireless Internet access in all public areas of the hotel. Business travelers will appreciate the full-size work desks and remote printing that allows you to send a print job from your guest room to a printer in the 24-hour business center. The Larkspur's library loans classic books, movies, CDs and games for quiet recreation. A complimentary Healthy Start breakfast is served seven days a week and complimentary Starbuck's coffee and herbal teas are available in the living room, as are fresh-baked cookies in the evening and fruit in the morning. With truly modern conveniences in a setting with Craftsman-style attention to detail and beauty, Larkspur Landing is sure to please even the most discriminating traveler.

1701 E Valley Road, Renton WA
(425) 235-1212 *www.larkspurlanding.com*

Cugini Florists

FLOWERS: *Voted top florist in Renton*

Whether you are expressing your sympathies, your love or your congratulations, do it in the language of flowers with help from the experts at Cugini Florists in Renton. Cugini has been serving King County residents since 1923 and has been in the capable hands of Owners Bill Gaw and Sharon Landes since 1984. Patrons appreciate Cugini's unusual designs and extensive gift selection. With fresh flowers arriving daily and deliveries made continuously throughout each day, you can count on quality and promptness from Cugini Florists. Whether your gift is destined for across the street, across town or across the globe, Cugini is your first and best choice for gifts, flowers and plants. They can put together everything from an elegant vase of red roses to a basket loaded with fruits and a live plant. Cugini also handles floral needs for weddings and other special occasions. Since 1995, every reader poll conducted by the *Renton Reporter* and the *South County Journal* has named Cugini as the top florist in the area. In 2002, the Renton Chamber of Commerce awarded it the Customer Focus Award. Cugini Florists is affiliated with the Society of American Florists, Teleflora and FTD. It also takes an active interest in the community through membership in the Renton Rotary Club and the Renton Chamber of Commerce. Stop in or call Cugini Florists next time you want to send flowers, and meet the folks who are making Renton a more beautiful place.

413 S 3rd Street, Renton WA
(425) 255-3900 or (877) 284-4640

Uptown Glassworks

GALLERIES: *Best glass art gallery in Renton*

Have you ever wanted to try blowing glass yourself? Uptown Glassworks can give you a chance to try this challenging art form, which will doubtless add to your admiration for the lovely work it displays. Uptown Glassworks is a 6,500-square-foot gallery that displays the works of almost 30 glass artists. It's also a place glass artists come to work and visitors come to watch glassblowing in progress. Glassblowing classes take place here, including Bead Me, an introductory class that meets monthly, and Hot Shots, a twice monthly class. Uptown Glassworks also hosts public events, such as holiday parties. Uptown is always glad to arrange for your private event, which could be a party for families or kids, a reunion or some other reason to spend a night out. Events always include the opportunity to try glassblowing. Uptown Glassworks can manage the catering for your event, or you can use your own caterer. The business is owned by Charles Divelbiss and managed by Ron Iverson and Kathleen Orndorff. The gallery also sells antique furniture from Charles's St. Charles Place store. The team at Uptown Glassworks invites you to enjoy its special glass creations, as well as the unparalleled experience of blowing glass.

230 Main Avenue S, Renton WA
(425) 228-1849
www.uptownglassworks.com

Impressions Dentistry

HEALTH: *Best family dentistry in Renton*

Impressions Dentistry will provide you with the most fun, relaxing visit to the dentist's office possible. Dr. Jack Chen and his well trained assistants provide a comfortable environment with the latest and most patient-friendly techniques and equipment. Impressions is a family dental practice. All ages are welcome. The brand new, state-of-the-art facility uses the most up-to-date equipment for maximum patient comfort. Digital x-rays are used because they reduce radiation exposure by more than 80 percent. To show patients exactly what to expect there are computers, digital cameras and large monitors that make it easy for you to understand your individual dental plan. Impressions is also an accomplished aesthetic dentistry provider. They offer whitening, veneers and restorations, as well as Invisalign, which replaces braces with a nearly invisible teeth-moving system. New patients who get their teeth cleaned and have x-rays taken also receive a complimentary teeth whitening. Dr. Chen knows that your time is valuable, so scheduling is planned with you in mind. He believes that a waiting room should not be for people waiting for an appointment, but for people who are waiting for the patient who has the appointment. For conscientious, friendly and professional dentistry in a state-of-the-art facility, Impressions Dentistry is the perfect choice.

1717 NE 44th Street, Suite A, Renton WA
(425) 226-2684
www.impressionsdentistry.com

Dr. Jack Chen

Apple Physical Therapy

HEALTH: *Voted top place to work in South Puget Sound*

Washington native Randy Johnson, partner and CEO of Apple Physical Therapy, opened his company in 1984 as a way to support his family. Since then his business has evolved into an organization that supports many families and serves individuals throughout the Puget Sound region with clinics in 23 locations. Company President and CEO Claude Ciancio came to work for Apple Physical Therapy in 1990 and achieved partnership in 1998. Ciancio comes from New York City, but his commitment to patients and the community aligns him firmly with Johnson's original goals for service to patients and the communities where patients reside. Randy and Claude believe in the Golden Rule, as well as five core elements, which they feel have made Apple Physical Therapy the success it is today. These five elements are, in order, Integrity, Knowledge, Compassion, Profit and Fun. For patients at any of the Apple facilities, these core tenets create a welcoming and comforting environment that is ideal for both working and healing. Employees, via a *Business Examiner* magazine poll, named Apple Physical Therapy as the number one place to work in the Puget Sound area. Whether you are searching for rehabilitation services or a new career, the staff at Apple Physical Therapy invites your family to become part of their family.

17650 140th Avenue SE, Suite B-07, Renton WA
(425) 430-0700
www.applept.com

King and Bunny's Appliances

HOME: *Best appliance dealer in Renton*

King and Bunny's Appliances is a little red store with a big warehouse that proudly claims to be the home of Whammer Deals. King and Bunny's carries the complete KitchenAid, Roper, Estate and Whirlpool lines of appliances. The store's salespeople are honest and well informed, and they will make sure you receive your new appliance quickly. Delivery, along with pick up and disposal of your old appliance, is available anywhere in the greater Renton/Seattle area. As a member of Nationwide, a group with buying power of more than $11 billion a year, King and Bunny's negotiates better prices from suppliers and passes the savings on to its customers. Owner King Parker comes to this business with 20 years of experience at Sears. He ended his Sears career as a division manager for major home appliances. King's wife, Bunny, oversees the finances, and their son Jason has worked in the store since it opened in 1982. King and Bunny's Appliances has been recognized by the Renton Chamber of Commerce for its customer service. King served on the Renton city council for eight years. The store sponsors FC Wild, a competitive girl's soccer team. If you need appliances, visit the experts at King and Bunny's. They want to make you a customer forever.

4608 NE Sunset Boulevard, Renton WA
(425) 277-0600
www.kingandbunnys.com

Shawn & Ted's Quality Meat Market

MARKETS: *Best sausages, smoked meats and jerky in Renton*

Shawn Beresford and Ted Coffman know a lot about meat. They have devoted their retail careers to its preparation. In 2004, they opened Shawn & Ted's Quality Meat Market, complete with a smokehouse. The residents of Renton and neighboring communities appreciate the market's freshly made sausages and smoked meats; the pepperoni and jerky are regionally renowned. On a Saturday, you will find customers lined up for the smoked baby back ribs. The market specializes in meat and poultry that are free of antibiotics or hormones. Misty Isle Black Angus beef and organic Smart Chicken are popular choices, along with meats that are ground on-site and frozen for your convenience. The market also carries quality fish, including wild salmon, halibut, sea bass and shellfish. Requests for custom cuts of beef, chicken and pork are always welcome. Shawn and Ted are great friends who worked together in Seattle's famed Pike Place Market for 15 years. They believe in having fun and making their meat market part of their life, not just a job. People who love to cook are sure to appreciate the quality of the products in this neighborhood butcher shop. For the kind of old-fashioned service and quality roasts and steaks that your grandparents took for granted, visit Shawn & Ted's Quality Meat Market.

5325 NE 4th Street, Renton WA
(425) 226-2422
www.shawnandtedsqualitymeatmarket.com

Top of the Hill Quality Produce

MARKETS: *Best produce market*

Selling produce at Top of the Hill Quality Produce in Renton is definitely a family affair. The Genzale family has been at it since 1927, when the family emigrated from Italy and started a produce business at Seattle's famous Pike Place Market. They were one of the original vendors at the market. Operations have expanded greatly since then to include Top of the Hill in Renton, plus locations in Newcastle and Burien. The family still runs a business at its original Pike Place Market location. The focus is always on outstanding, old-fashioned customer service. The staff at Top of the Hill are energetic and motivated. They are knowledgeable and clearly proud of their work. Because tradition is so important at Top of the Hill, the company strives to support area growers and vendors with whom it has done business for years. This means that the emphasis is on finding the finest, freshest fruits and vegetables from local farms. Top of the Hill carries organic produce, as well as gourmet cheeses, specialty foods, plants and beautiful bouquets. Top of the Hill is open all year, making it convenient for you to stop by at any time.

5325 NE 4th Street, Renton WA
(425) 226-4316

Photo provided by Bruce Hudson Photography

The Wine Alley

MARKETS: *Best wine market in Renton*

The Wine Alley specializes in fine wines from the Pacific Northwest and around the world. Inside this warm and inviting store you will find rack after rack of new or hard-to-find wines. Washington and Oregon are two of the fastest growing wine regions in the country, and Scott and Allison Helfen, owners of The Wine Alley, are excited to be able to bring these wines to their customers. The Wine Alley sponsors more wine-tasting events than most stores; many of them are informal and complimentary. The more formal tastings have a modest fee and include samples of their specialty foods. The store has three tastings a week. In addition to wine, The Wine Alley offers specialty beers. The Wine Alley carries beers from around the world, focusing primarily on the exceptional brewing areas of Belgium, Germany and England. The busy host or hostess will find specialty foods that go well with wine and beer, such as cheeses, smoked salmon and chocolates. The Wine Alley also carries wine and cheese accessories that make great gifts. While traveling in Italy, Scott and Allison found wine shops on every corner that offered local wines and specialty foods. Once home, they sought to create a store with the same atmosphere as the shops they fell in love with in Italy. Visit The Wine Alley and see how they have succeeded. They are located in the Fairwood Shopping Center.

14276 SE 176th Street, Renton WA
(425) 271-4501
www.thewinealley.com

Rockin' Horse Dance Barn

RECREATION: *Best dance venue in Renton*

Wouldn't it be great to get out and enjoy an evening of terrific dancing without having to worry about cigarette smoke, alcohol and the claustrophobic club scene? Thanks to the Rockin' Horse Dance Barn, you can. This fabulous, family-owned and operated dance venue first made the scene in 1988 when Dave Serfling, a life-long lover of dance, started teaching dance classes in various locations around Seattle. In 1992, Dave began renting Hagen's Barn, a Square Dance hall built in 1958, to host his own dance socials and classes. The Rockin' Horse Dance Barn officially moved into the old Hagen's Barn in 1998 after Dave purchased the landmark and changed its name. Today, Dave and his personable staff offer a myriad of classes. Go from the barn to the ballroom with Country, Swing, Ballroom, Latin and Line dance. Contemporary dance styles are also popular. Dave and his highly trained staff of professionals perform at weddings and other special events. They can assist you with everything from planning the reception and event coordination to handling the duties of master of ceremonies. Classes are open to both individuals and couples age 18 and older, and can be arranged as private, semi-private or group sessions. Whether you're looking for a regular Friday or Saturday night dance where you can show off your smooth moves, or want a fun way to stay fit, you can find the dance classes and parties that appeal to you at the Rockin' Horse Dance Barn.

11820 150th Avenue SE, Renton WA
(425) 255-9211
www.learn2dance4fun.com

Northwest Seaplanes

RECREATION: *Best sightseeing flights in the region*

You can see the Northwest Seaplanes difference as soon as you enter their offices at the Renton Municipal Airport. There you will find beautiful antiques, provided for the enjoyment of customers waiting for service. The Adirondack furniture on display provides a much more appealing sight than the drab plastic seats usually found in airplane waiting areas. Northwest provides free shuttle service from Boeing Field and Seattle-Tacoma International Airport. Clyde Carlson, owner of Northwest Seaplanes, has been in the airline business since 1981. He knew there was a market for flights from Puget Sound to the San Juan Islands and British Columbia, and he proved it. His fleet of seaplanes draws a range of customers from all walks of life, including businessmen, adventurers, sportsmen and anyone else who wants to see the beauty of the Pacific Northwest with an unobstructed view. The seaplanes operated by Northwest are DeHavilland Beavers, tough planes originally designed in the 1940s to serve some of the most rugged coastal terrain in the world. Clyde takes great pride in the fact that his planes are among the best maintained aircraft in service, operated by pilots whose professionalism is unequaled. You'll find information about Northwest's regularly-scheduled flights and charters on their website.

860 W Perimeter Road, Renton WA
(800) 690-0086
www.nwseaplanes.com

Armondo's Café Italiano

RESTAURANTS & CAFÉS: *Best wood-fired pizza in Renton*

Italian cooking at its best is awaiting your arrival at Armondo's Café Italiano. Located in downtown Renton, this beautiful and festive restaurant has long been a favorite of local residents and out-of-towners alike. Its wood-fired pizza, calzones and different types of fettuccine and sautés have been tempting and satisfying appetites in the same location since 1985. Armondo's was one of the first restaurants in Renton to have a wood-burning pizza oven. Each of their hand-spun pizzas and calzone are specially made to order. The colorful décor, blown-glass fixtures and upscale ambience combine to make this family-oriented restaurant a popular destination for any occasion. Owner and Renton local Armondo Pavone is committed to providing you with a memorable dining experience. So whether it's a great Italian lunch or dinner you're looking for, be sure to stop in and see why Armondo's Café Italiano has long been one of Renton's most successful restaurants.

310 Wells Avenue S, Renton WA
(425) 228-0759
www.armondos.com

Amante Pizza and Pasta

RESTAURANTS & CAFÉS:

Best pizza in Renton

Ivan and Dobremira Demirey opened Amante Pizza and Pasta to realize Ivan's dream. Ten years in the restaurant trade brought out Ivan's love of cooking and desire to run a pizza restaurant. Amante now has seven locations in the Puget Sound area. People turn to Amante's to feel at home and get good quality food with excellent service. Ivan and Dobremira have created a family atmosphere that includes a warm, personal connection between them and their patrons. The sauces at Amante are made from scratch; ingredients are fresh; and cheeses are Italian only. Pizza toppings are both traditional and inventive. The Bella Luna pizza features a Mediterranean combination of olive oil, fresh goat cheese and pine nuts, topped with fresh basil and roasted garlic. The pasta dishes feature flavor variety in the form of spaghetti, fettuccine, tortellini and baked manicotti. Order a veggie calzone or build your own from an assortment of meats, cheeses and vegetables. Customers counting their carbohydrates will appreciate Amante's low-carb meals, such as a no-dough pizza and chicken or eggplant Parmesan. Enjoy pizza or pasta at the restaurant or request a delivery. You will appreciate the flavorful food and the welcome at Amante.

4201 Sunset Boulevard NE, Renton WA
(425) 271-8985
www.amantepizzaandpasta.com

Photography by Robert Badgley

Melrose Grill
RESTAURANTS & CAFÉS: *Best steaks in Renton*

You'll find excellent steaks featuring high quality, corn-fed Nebraska beef at the Melrose Grill. This neighborhood steakhouse is located in a building originally constructed in 1901 as a three-story hotel, café and saloon by an Englishman named Ben Atkinson, who made his money in the gold fields of the Yukon. The saloon was a favorite haunt of coal miners and brick factory workers. During Prohibition, it flourished as a pool hall, card room and soda parlor. In 1928, fire destroyed the top two floors. Luckily, the saloon remained intact and the same mirrored back bar is still being used to this day. The building was purchased in 1997 by Armondo and Angela Pavone, Tim and Kimberly Searing, and Charles and Beverly Keeslar. The Melrose Grill opened to rave reviews in 2002. They restored and refurbished the building while still preserving its 100-year-old rustic charm. In addition to great steaks, other house specialties include salmon, pork and roasted chicken. The atmosphere is a blend of casual and upscale. Reasonable pricing, subdued lighting and historical photos of the building and former occupants all add to its flavorful ambience. Stop in and experience great food and service in this delightful and historic setting.

819 Houser Way S, Renton WA
(425) 254-0759
www.sansueb.com/melrose

The Met Coffee & Wine Bar
RESTAURANTS & CAFÉS: *Best coffee and wine bar*

Coffee and wine, two of life's great pleasures, come together at the Met Coffee & Wine Bar in Renton. Whether you are looking for that wake-up cup in the early morning or a light meal or wine tasting later in the day, The Met has what you need. Owner Mike Servis and his outgoing staff serve more than 50 Washington wines by the glass or bottle, along with fine coffee and foods. The bar grew out of Mike's wine collecting avocation. He and his staff are always pleased to share their extensive knowledge with customers. The comfortable atmosphere at The Met is a pleasant environment for wine tasting. The menu includes appetizers that complement the wines, such as a hummus plate, goat cheese with honey and walnuts, or antipasti. The Met also features a full lunch menu, with an assortment of sandwiches, soups and salads. Each Thursday night The Met features a specific winery and often hosts representatives from the winery. A wine club offers members a choice of two bottles of premium Northwest wine each month and discounts on additional wine purchases. The Met is available for private parties and provides catering. The staff is also glad to create a gift basket. Celebrate the Northwest's coffee and wine traditions from early morning until evening at The Met Coffee & Wine Bar.

232-C Burnett Avenue S, Renton WA
(425) 687-7989
www.themetwinebar.com

Plum Delicious
RESTAURANTS & CAFÉS: *Best breakfast in Renton*

"Be happy!" is the first training instruction that Plum Delicious owners Gary and Anita Johnson give their staff. Believing that extraordinary customer service is the key to business success, the Johnsons do their utmost to ensure staff job satisfaction. Gary's restaurant experience began in franchises, but his dream was to have his own establishment where everyone would feel welcome, which is why he refers to Plum Delicious as "your neighborhood kitchen." Kid friendly and sporting a menu for seniors, this restaurant has broad appeal. Gary encourages customer input and provides monthly specials. Monday night is family night, when kids eat free, and a movie plays on the big screen from 4 to 7 pm. Breakfast, which voters have called the best in Renton for several years running, is served all day. The salmon, eggs and hash browns are a Plum Delicious standout. The restaurant is famous for its prime rib dips, raspberry salmon, 10-ounce, hand-pressed burgers and summer salads. The homemade desserts, including carrot cake, earn much deserved praise. Accompany your food choices with a selection from the full-service bar, and be sure to try the restaurant's private label Merlot. Gary loves the restaurant business, where no two days are the same. His love for interacting with staff and customers and his joy in inventing culinary surprises will make your visit here Plum Delicious.

3212 NE Sunset Boulevard, Renton WA
(425) 255-8510

Fin N Bone

RESTAURANTS & CAFÉS: *Best Northwest cuisine in Renton*

One look at the menu explains where the Fin N Bone in Renton got its name: Salmon with pineapple mango salsa, Australian rock lobster, Dungeness crab cakes, New Zealand lamb chops, bacon-wrapped filet mignon. Then again, the name may underplay the prominence of such delicacies as stuffed chicken Milan and roasted raspberry duckling, which are associated more closely with feathers than either fins or bones. But we digress from the most important point, which is this: Fin N Bone is a great restaurant. Jerry and Yelina Jackson run this family-owned eatery with the help of their long-time friend, Paul Schmitt. Jerry's two decades of experience as a chef have meshed with Paul's long experience in fine dining to forge a perfect blend. Fin N Bone is known for its warm, spacious surroundings, its big-city restaurant atmosphere, and, of course, quality food. Located in the heart of Renton, Fin N Bone features a catch of the day, fresh salads and a comprehensive beverage list covering fine wines, beers and liquors. Jerry, who ensures that there's a wide range of fresh seafood on the menu, purchases seasonal vegetables from local growers. Open for lunch and dinner, with late hours, Fin N Bone features two happy hours a night. If you're planning a special occasion, Fin N Bone's banquet room will seat 50 people. The next time you are in Renton, visit the Fin N Bone and you'll understand why we put them in this book.

317 Main Avenue S, Renton WA
(425) 271-6644
www.finnbone.com

Jimmy Mac's Roadhouse

RESTAURANTS & CAFÉS: *Best Southern cookin'*

Wonderful inns and restaurants that sit at major intersections have always been called roadhouses, known for their down-home feel and great homemade country cooking. Especially in the West and South, fabulous steaks, chops and ribs are mouthwatering staples. Since 1998, Jimmy Mac's Roadhouse in Renton has borrowed a little bit of that Southern cooking tradition and brought it to the Northwest, along with menu additions like crab cakes, salmon and tuna. This Northwest roadhouse is also overflowing with famous Southern hospitality. Owner Scot Weisser focuses on serving terrific food with happy and attentive service, so you and your family are guaranteed a good old time. When you step in the door, you're greeted by country music and a big barrel of peanuts to enjoy while you wait, along with directions to relax, enjoy yourself, and throw your shells on the floor. You'll peruse their glass showcase of steaks, where you can pick out your own slab of beef. They'll cook it just like you want it and serve it up with their endless supply of famous homemade rolls with honey butter. Or you can enjoy their signature Hubcap Burger, a finger-licking burger served on, what else—a hubcap. The unique décor is old Western memorabilia, the atmosphere is casual and friendly, and the food is as fun as it is good. Enjoy a great country meal, but remember, at Jimmy Mac's Roadhouse, you gotta throw your shells on the floor.

225 SW 7th Street, Renton WA
(425) 227-6881
www.jimmymacsroadhouse.com

Jubilanté Restaurant & Jazz Club

RESTAURANTS & CAFÉS: *Best Jazz supper club in Renton*

The word jubilant means celebration, praise, a joyful noise, and that's exactly what Jubilanté Restaurant & Jazz Club inspires. As talented musicians and entertainers, owners Tess Guerzon-Cabrera and Caesar Cabrera know music is a way to bring people together. Their dream was to create a place where local entertainers could showcase their talents and the community could enjoy great music, great food and good times. When the chance came to buy the restaurant they performed in, they jumped at the opportunity, transforming the restaurant's atmosphere entirely. Now a fabulous jazz supper club with incredible international cuisine, Jubilanté is bright, warm and awash in Christmas lights, with different sections to give you a choice of atmosphere. The menu takes a trip through many different world cuisines, with an emphasis on Cajun. Each dish is made to order by Jubilanté's fantastic chef, using only the freshest, seasonal ingredients. The waitstaff is friendly, even during the busiest hours, and can help you make the difficult decision between dishes like Hawaiian teriyaki meatloaf or Vietnamese barbecued pork skewers. What's most exciting is that Jubilanté showcases live performances by local musicians five nights a week. Jubilanté's festive and spirited atmosphere is perfect for any celebratory occasion, from birthdays to business events. Jubilanté isn't just a restaurant or just a jazz bar, it's an experience.

305 Burnett Avenue S, Renton WA
(425) 226-1544
www.jubilante-restaurant.com

Whistle Stop Ale House

RESTAURANTS & CAFÉS: *Best regional microbrews*

Grab a Northwest regional microbrew and a specialty sandwich at a place where the staff will soon know you and your eating and drinking preferences. At the Whistle Stop Ale House, owners Melinda and Jeff Lawrence, together with bartenders Fran, Darren and Casey, create a family pub and community gathering place in the European tradition. You may hear singing from the kitchen, because many of the line cooks and their assistants are musicians. Those with an interest in wine will enjoy the Whistle Stop's monthly wine dinner, where patrons try wines from Washington and beyond. You can count on quality ingredients here with meats from Misty Isle Farms of Vashon Island and dairy products from Smith Brothers Farms. Melinda, Jeff and their staff believe that connecting people with each other through a neighborhood eatery draws a community together. Each year, they sponsor a fundraiser to benefit Renton area youth and family services. This family pub, in business since 1995, is a nonsmoking establishment. For good times, good beer and good food, visit the Whistle Stop Ale House.

809 S 4th Street, Renton WA
(425) 277-3039
www.whistlestopalehouse.com

St. Charles Place Antiques & Restorations

SHOPPING: *Best antique restorations in Renton*

Do you love the patina and warmth of antique furniture? If so, you will have a lot in common with Charles Divelbiss, owner of St. Charles Place Antiques & Restorations. Charles' affection for old things began with his father's gift of a collection of antique surplus. This gift inspired an interest in antiques that led him to open his own shop in the early 1970s. When Charles opened his shop 35 years ago, he was the only antique dealer in town. Today his store is an anchor in a thriving district that features a healthy cluster of antique dealers. Charles obtains much of his merchandise in Europe. Local purchases and consignments also find their way into his ever-changing inventory. It is exciting to browse beautiful selections that include American, English, French, Austrian, European and Asian styles. The experienced staff at St. Charles Place will graciously help you with your selections and can advise you when their skilled restoration would be worthwhile. Bring your questions about wood, glass, furniture, wiring and stripping to them. If they cannot accomplish the task, they will guide you to other resources. Fine representative pieces from the store are on display at the Glassworks Gallery. Charles also invites you to check out his bargain basement for special pricing on high-end antiques. Even if you don't find just what you want the first time, Charles promises you will enjoy the hunt. For antique quality you can trust, visit St. Charles Place Antiques & Restorations.

230 Wells Avenue S, Renton WA
(425) 226-8427

Cedar River Antique Mall

SHOPPING: *Best fine furniture, glass and memorabilia*

Antiques tell stories about the past and provide an opportunity for us to learn about the people who made and used them. Dieu Tien and Victoria Mai are passionate about learning the old stories and long dreamed of having their own antiques store. The Cedar River Antique Mall is the fulfillment of that dream. Formerly from Denmark, Dieu and Victoria provide special items for history lovers and antique collectors. The shop specializes in quality antiques and collectibles, including fine furniture, glass and memorabilia. Dieu is a collector who loves beautiful things and takes pleasure in searching the world for items to display in the shop's multicultural collection. Pieces come from America, Asia and many parts of Europe, particularly Scandinavia. Dieu and Victoria say that in the past, furniture came from the heart and soul of the maker. Discover some of that heart and soul at Cedar River Antique Mall.

916 S 3rd Street, Renton WA
(425) 255-4900

WOODINVILLE

At one time, Woodinville was heavily forested with trees so big their stumps could be used as houses, which, of course, drew loggers in droves. The saw and shingle mills are gone today, replaced by boutique wineries and specialty retailers. Woodinville is located in the north central section of King County, at the north end of the Sammamish River Valley. Woodinville, with an area of 5.6 miles and a population of 10,000, became the 32nd city in King County (out of 39 cities) in 1993.

PLACES TO GO

- Carol Edwards Center
  175th Street and 133rd Avenue NE

- Wilmot Gateway Park
  17301-131st Avenue NE

- Woodin Creek Park
  13301 NE 171st Street

- Woodinville Valley Trail
  1.5 miles south of downtown Woodinville

THINGS TO DO

April
- All Fools Day Parade
  (425) 481-8300

- All Fools Arts & Crafts Show
  (425) 546-7960

- Bassett Bash & Brigade
  (425) 483-0606

- Celebration of Arts
  (425) 398-9327

July
- COSI Summer Concert Series
  (425) 984-2346

August
- Shakespeare in the Park
  425-984-2346

October
- Harvest Happening
  (425) 984-2346

December
- Woodinville Light Festival
  (425) 398-9327

A pond on the Chateau St. Michelle winery grounds

Willows Lodge

ACCOMMODATIONS: *Best place to stay in Woodinville*

For a Northwest celebration of the senses, try the Willows Lodge in Woodinville. Located on five acres bordering the Sammamish River in the heart of Wine Country, the Lodge was recently named one of the best places to stay in the world by *Condé Nast Traveler,* one of only six Washington hotels and resorts to be listed. Willow Lodge offers 86 guest rooms and suites. The Barking Frog, a casual bistro, features Northwest cuisine with a European flair and an extensive Northwest wine collection. The world-renowned Herbfarm Restaurant is also nearby. A complimentary continental breakfast is served each morning at the Barking Frog and nightly wine tastings are offered in the Fireside Cellars. A different winery is featured each evening. Standard room amenities include a soaking tub designed for two, 300-count Italian linens, stone fireplaces, in-room safes with space for laptop computers, and a selection of robes. Outside the room, there is a 2,000-square-foot spa and fitness center, sauna and outdoor Jacuzzi. The Spa offers hydrotherapy, massage, body treatments and facials. If you or your company are looking for a challenge course to deliver team-building skills, the Lodge offers a 45-foot-high ropes course. Looking for romance? *Travel & Leisure* magazine, which named the Willows Lodge one of the Top 50 Most Romantic Getaways in the World, described a weekend at Willows Lodge as "the height of hedonism." At Willow Lodge you will experience a slower pace, a culinary awakening and a sensory delight.

14580 NE 145th Street, Woodinville WA
(425) 424-3900 or (877) 424-3930
www.willowslodge.com

Aussie Pet Mobile Eastside

ANIMALS & PETS: *Best stress-free pet salon*

When Aussie Pet Mobile Eastside comes to your door, your animals are treated to a full-service grooming in a highly sanitary, stress-free salon. Stress free means the environment is climate controlled for all weather conditions. Their experience is private, because multiple pets are not allowed in the area at the same time. Aussie Pet Mobile takes care of older pets by grooming on flat surfaces. There is even a geriatric support system to hold dogs up comfortably during treatments. There are no cages in the Aussie Mobile. Owner Geoff Andrist does not believe there are ungroomable dogs or cats. He makes sure cats don't notice they are in water by the use of specially designed cones. In fact, they seem to like the heated hydrobath. Dogs love the new FURminator, which separates their coat, extracts loose hair and undercoat to stimulate hair follicles, increases circulation and leaves their topcoat shiny and healthy. When pets are treated monthly or bi-weekly, shedding is reduced 60 to 80 percent. Geoff will schedule your pet's appointments at a time and location most convenient for you. You and your pets will love Geoff's award-winning Aussie Mobile, because he provides one-on-one service in an atmosphere where pet owners are not just customers, but friends. Geoff volunteers his Aussie Mobile for events like Howel-O-Ween and local pet charities like HomewardPets.com. Call Geoff today and he will bring the Aussie Pet Mobile Eastside right to your door.

(800) PET-MOBILE (738-6624) *www.aussiepetmobile.com*

Hypatia Aesthetics and Laser Treatment Clinic

HEALTH & BEAUTY: *Best state-of-the-art aesthetic treatments*

Hypatia Aesthetics and Laser Treatment Clinic specializes in restoring and maintaining the youthful appearance of your skin. Doing something about problem areas on your face and body is simpler than ever, thanks to Hypatia's state-of-the-art medical aesthetic treatments with an artistic touch. Located in downtown Woodinville, people come from all over the country to experience Hypatia's individualized medical cosmetic treatments, performed in a spa-like setting. The friendly staff is dedicated to their clients' aesthetic needs in ways that offer prompt results and little down time. Virginia T. Stevens, M.D. performs all consultations and therapies with patient comfort and safety in mind. Dr. Stevens pioneered Body Thermage, a non-invasive procedure that tightens skin, renews contours and boosts production of healthy collagen. She has performed more than 4,000 Body Thermage treatments, more than any doctor in the United States. Dr. Stevens was the first to introduce Contour Suture Threadlift Face and Necklifting to western Washington, a minimally invasive facelift procedure that changes lives. Dr. Stevens has done more of these procedures than any doctor on the West Coast. She is locally known as the aesthetic consultant for KOMO Channel 4. A University of Texas graduate, Dr. Stevens is board certified in internal medicine with a specialty in intensive care. Director of operations Michelle Reiger takes time to get to know each client's reasons for visiting the clinic. Whether you want to lift your face or brows without a surgical procedure, tighten loose skin or try an alternative to liposuction, Hypatia can deliver results in an environment that promises comfort and privacy. To look as youthful as you feel, consult the professionals at Hypatia Aesthetics and Laser Treatment Clinic.

14024 NE 181st Street, Suite 201, Woodinville WA
(425) 424-3416 or (866) 424-3416
www.hypatiaclinic.com

Bubbles Below Dive Center

RECREATION: *Best place to learn scuba diving*

If you can survive a wrestling match with an octopus, you can easily wrestle with running a scuba business, right? That is how Bud Gray feels about it. He now puts his efforts into caring for the customers who come through his door at Bubbles Below Dive Center in Woodinville. The incident with the octopus happened in 1970, when Bud was first learning to dive. He and his instructor brought an octopus to the surface and made the mistake of turning their backs on it. The octopus promptly taught Bud a lesson by wrapping up Bud's head, legs and arms. Bud recovered from that mugging and is now one of the Pacific Northwest's most recognized scuba instructors and diving center owners.

He became a PADI open water instructor in 1976 and eventually became a master instructor, qualified to teach more than 26 specialty courses ranging from Underwater Video to Marine Biologist. He has certified more than 3,000 students. Puget Sound is an excellent area to learn to dive. It is rated number three in the world for cold-water diving. If you want diving equipment or training, dive into Bubbles Below Dive Center.

17315 140th Avenue NE, Woodinville WA
(425) 424-3483
www.bubblesbelow.com

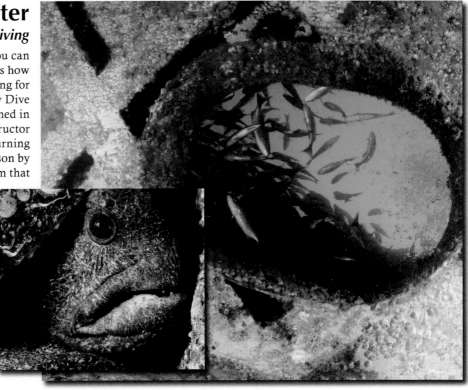

The Herbfarm Restaurant

RESTAURANTS & CAFÉS: *Best overall restaurant in the region*

Imagine a world where life is as perfect as you always hoped it would be. That's the goal of The Herbfarm Restaurant, where each night the lights go down, the candles come on and you are swept away to a nine-course dinner extravaganza that *Seattle Best Places* calls the fastest five hours you'll ever experience. The Herbfarm, located 20 minutes outside of Seattle in rural Woodinville, is dedicated to showcasing the foods and wines of the Pacific Northwest. *Frommer's Seattle* calls The Herbfarm the Northwest's most celebrated restaurant, "the ultimate expression of the Northwest's bounty." Each evening's dinner begins with a wine cellar open house and, weather permitting, a hosted herb garden tour. The *prix fixe* menu is set in the afternoon, featuring foods harvested, gathered, and rushed from farm, field and sea. Six wines are included with each night's dinner. The wines are chosen by The Herbfarm's wine staff to carefully enhance the menu flavors. The cellar houses more than 19,000 bottles and offers a staggering 3,275 different wines. Between courses you can explore the wine cellar, take snacks to The Herbfarm's pet recycling pig in the garden, or play a game of bocce on the restaurant's grass court. Dressy casual attire is suggested for this, the only AAA Five Diamond restaurant north of San Francisco and west of Chicago. Reservations required.

14590 NE 145th Street, Woodinville WA
(425) 485-5300
www.theherbfarm.com

Purple Café & Wine Bar

RESTAURANTS & CAFÉS: *Best café & wine bar in the area*

Purple Café and Wine Bar is a multifaceted food and wine concept specializing in an eclectic Northwest inspired menu coupled with an extensive global wine selection. This includes 75 wines by the glass, wine flights and hundreds more by the bottle. The atmosphere is often described as an urban retreat with rustic elements. The decor includes wrought iron furniture, used brick walls, concrete tabletops and a curved wine bar. Patio dining is available. The Purple Café specializes in sophisticated *hors d'oeuvres*, appetizers, homemade spreads, crackers and flat breads. Desserts are made from scratch. Purple Café & Wine Bar offers catering in three ways: Purple Direct, Purple Select and Purple House. Purple Direct is a quick and easy way to have fresh high quality food delivered to your home or office. You may have your selections served buffet style or boxed in individual meals. Purple Select features menus custom designed to your specific tastes and event style. Purple House is adjacent to the Woodinville location and is literally your *house* for your next business luncheon, rehearsal dinner or high tea. Visit one of the Purple Café's three locations, in Woodinville, Kirkland or Seattle, for the best in Northwest quality.

14459 Woodinville-Redmond Road, Woodinville WA
(425) 483-7129
323 Park Place, Kirkland WA
(425) 828-3772
1225 4th Avenue, Seattle WA
(206) 829-2280
www.thepurplecafe.com

Facelli Winery

WINERIES: *Best winery in the area*

Nestled away in the heart of Woodinville's Wine Country, you will find Facelli Winery. Upon entering the tasting room, you are likely to be greeted by at least one member of the Facelli family. Winemaker Lou Facelli, his wife Sandy and their three daughters, Lisa, Lori, and Kristi, take turns welcoming visitors each weekend. Celebrating over 24 years of winemaking using grapes from some of Washington's premier vineyards, the wines here should not be missed. Lou Facelli focuses on *reds* and small lots of various varietals, including a Late Harvest Syrah, believed to be the first in the state. At Facelli Winery there is very little blending.

With increasing interest in Italian varietals, new wines look promising in the future. Paying close attention to detail is a Facelli tradition. Taking tremendous pride in the bottles that bear the family name, they work hard to bring you a great bottle of wine at a reasonable price. The winery produces approximately 3000 cases annually from grapes grown in the Yakima and Columbia Valleys.

It is evident that this family loves what they do and they convey their enthusiasm from the moment you walk in. Whether receiving further education about their wine or a recipe to go with a glass of Sangiovese, you are likely to leave with a bottle in hand and a smile on your face. Autographed bottles are also a big hit.

16120 Woodinville-Redmond Road NE, #1, Woodinville WA
(425) 488-1020
www.facelliwinery.com

The Valley

The Valley

Water running through the woods

THE VALLEY, and the Green River, begin in the Cascades east of Tacoma, passing through lush farmland and through a series of cities between Tacoma and Seattle. The Green River gives its name to the valley, though some municipalities considered part of The Valley are outside of the actual Green River watershed. To the east, Mount Rainier looms over dense forest, alpine lakes and plunging waterfalls. Moving south from Seattle, you'll find Kent, which is built on some of the most fertile farmland in the world.

West of Kent, Des Moines enjoys easy access to Puget Sound and hosts a major marina. South along the Sound is Federal Way, which contains Dash Point State Park, with 3,301 feet of Puget Sound shoreline for marine life enthusiasts. West Hylebos Wetlands is one of southern King County's last remaining bogs, easily viewed from a boardwalk. Another Federal Way attraction is Wild Waves Enchanted Village, a major amusement/water park.

Inland from Federal Way, the city of Auburn is still the home of the Muckleshoot tribe, descendents of the Coastal Salish people who inhabited the eastern shores of Puget Sound for thousands of years. Across the Pierce County line to the south is Puyallup, which draws one million people a year to the largest annual fair in the state. Inland and east of Kent, Lake Wilderness and Lake Lucerne are within the city limits of Maple Valley. To the southeast, the little green city of Enumclaw is nestled in the foothills of magnificent Mt. Rainier. The many attractions, the pastoral landscape of protected farm land, and the peaceful ambience of the area make the Green River Valley an appealing haven for visitors to the Seattle area.

Flaming Geyser State Park, east of Auburn
Photo by Jenni Jones

AUBURN

Home of the Muckleshoot Indians, Auburn was originally incorporated as Slaughter, after pioneer William Slaughter. The main hotel in town was called the Slaughter House. In 1893, a large group of settlers from Auburn, New York moved to Slaughter, and renamed the town Auburn.

PLACES TO GO

- Auburn City Hall Gallery
  25 W Main Street

- Neely Mansion
  12303 SE Auburn Black Diamond Road
  (253) 833-9404

- White River Amphitheatre
  40601 Auburn Enumclaw Road

- White River Valley Museum
  918 H Street SE (253) 939-2783

- Brannan Park
  611 28 Street NE

- Flaming Geyser State Park
  23700 SE Flaming Geyser Road

- Game Farm Park
  3030 R Street SE

- Les Gove Park and Community Campus
  11 and Auburn Way S

- Roegner Park
  601 Oravetz Road

Washington National Golf Club

ATTRACTIONS: *Best public golf course in The Valley*

Playing golf at the Washington National Golf Club in Auburn might be as close as you're going to get to the PGA. Not only is the course designed to challenge all players, including professionals, it is also equipped with alabaster sand bunkers imported from Idaho and unique bent grass fairways. Home of the University of Washington's golf teams, Washington National Golf Club features themed golf carts to honor legendary UW sports alumni. They even have a cart in the colors and logo of each PAC-10 school. Owned by Heritage Golf Group, the golf club is extremely dedicated to making your experience a memorable one. A few years after opening, the golf club hosted the NCAA Women's National Championship in 2002, as well as several NCAA Regional Championships. Nominated as Best New Public Course for 2001, the club accommodates more corporate and charity golf events than any other course in Washington. Bring your clubs and reserve your favorite golf cart today.

14330 SE Husky Way, Auburn WA
(253) 333-5000
www.washingtonnationalgolfclub.com

Donel's Espresso

BAKERIES, COFFEE & TEA: *Best espresso stop*

You aren't likely to learn the secret recipe of the Zipperdoodle, but you can savor the super smooth richness of this Auburn favorite. The drink was created for people who want the experience of coffee, but can't stand the taste. Owner Donel Brinkman and manager Shelby Locke invite you to come and taste this locally famous drink, and while you're there, try any one of their more traditional-style espresso specialties. Customer service is the key at Donel's Espresso. The awesome staff will remember you, your name and your favorite drink after your second visit. Donel gives credit to her committed, outgoing and fun staff for the success of being the busiest coffee cart in South King County. Donel's Espresso is grateful for their popularity and shows it by giving back to the community. They enjoy being a facility that is a depository for donations to such programs as Toys for Tots, food banks, school camps, backpack and school supplies, and gifts for needy families at Christmas. In their first year in business they collected enough money to provide care for 30 needy families. Bring your donations to Donel's Espresso, and while you're at it, try that Zipperdoodle. You'll be back.

1404 A Street SE, Auburn WA
(253) 332-1900

Select Photography
BUSINESS: *Best portraiture in Auburn*

Located in the heart of downtown Auburn, Select Photography is a family-owned business with flair that specializes in weddings, high school senior packages and outdoor portraiture. Bill Higdon has more than 20 years of photography experience. Known as a problem solver, his special talent is combining technical ability with artistic skill to create beautiful and original photographs. His easy-going style and ability to create order out of wedding chaos has earned him a reputation as a dedicated, hard-working photographer who gets spectacular results. His wife, Laura, works as his valuable and indispensable assistant who attends to the bride, holds the reflectors and in general helps make it all go smoothly. You can choose traditional poses or a more photojournalistic approach or a combination of both. You are in control. Their non-time-based sessions allow you the freedom to enjoy being photographed without feeling rushed or pressured in any way. Exceptional images don't happen by accident. Bill is a photographic artist who understands composition, light and how to bring out your individual style. High School Senior packages offer a comprehensive assortment of looks, moods and attitudes in an outdoor setting. Far different than the usual stiff yearbook photo, your Select Photography Senior album will bring back memories to cherish for a lifetime. Make an appointment to see their work and discuss your needs. Bill and Laura would love the opportunity to sit down and discuss a custom package created just for you.

119 E Main, Auburn WA
(253) 333-7708 or (253) 381-6661
www.selectphotography.com

Photos by William E. Higdon

Apple Physical Therapy
HEALTH:
Voted top place to work in South Puget Sound

Washington native Randy Johnson, partner and CEO of Apple Physical Therapy, opened his company in 1984 as a way to support his family. Since then his business has evolved into an organization that supports many families and serves individuals throughout the Puget Sound region with clinics in 23 locations. Company President and CEO Claude Ciancio came to work for Apple Physical Therapy in 1990 and achieved partnership in 1998. Ciancio comes from New York City, but his commitment to patients and the community aligns him firmly with Johnson's original goals for service to patients and the communities where patients reside. Randy and Claude believe in the Golden Rule, as well as five core elements, which they feel have made Apple Physical Therapy the success it is today. These five elements are, in order, Integrity, Knowledge, Compassion, Profit and Fun. For patients at any of the Apple facilities, these core tenets create a welcoming and comforting environment that is ideal for both working and healing. Employees, via a *Business Examiner* magazine poll, named Apple Physical Therapy as the number one place to work in the Puget Sound area. Whether you are searching for rehabilitation services or a new career, the staff at Apple Physical Therapy invites your family to become part of their family.

720 12th Street SE, Auburn WA
(253) 735-3606
www.applept.com

Select Photography C (06)

Molen Orthodontics
HEALTH: *Best place for orthodontics*

When you see someone walking around the south end area with a spectacular smile, chances are they had their braces done by Dr. Molen. Known for the Molen Magic Smile that he creates, Dr. Bruce Molen opened his first orthodontic practice in Auburn in 1972. Through the years, he has had the opportunity to treat thousands of patients, including several generations of families. His son, Dr. Rick Molen, joined the practice in 2001 and made Molen Orthodontics a family practice that will continue creating beautiful smiles for many generations to come. By taking continuing education courses and staying on the cutting-edge of technology, the doctors are able to treat their patients in shorter amounts of time while creating exquisitely beautiful smiles. Their diagnostic approach involves evaluating the facial profile and the lip support provided by the teeth and developing individual treatment plans to have a positive impact on these critical aesthetic factors. The doctors utilize early interceptive treatment to correct problems associated with skeletal jaw growth. Early treatment, which is usually initiated around age eight, is a key factor in creating the Molen Magic Smile. Both doctors and their team display a deep respect for people and enjoy building positive, long-term relationships with their patients. When Dr. Rick was asked why he chose orthodontics as a profession, he replied, "Having the opportunity to change people's lives through giving them a beautiful smile is a feeling that I can't describe. It's a wonderful gift to be able to give." Changing lives by creating beautiful smiles is what Molen Orthodontics is all about.

1110 Harvey Road, Auburn WA
(253) 939-2552
16202 64th Street E, Suite 103, Sumner WA
(253) 863-0978
1771 Farrelly Street, Enumclaw WA
(360) 825-6578
www.molenorthodontics.com

Automatic:
The Underground Sprinkler Co.
HOME: *Best irrigation systems*

The McGowan family business is focused on expertly installed irrigation systems to perfectly meet the needs of their customers. With more than 30 years experience in both commercial and residential projects, they have been serving the Auburn area since 1986. Working within time and budget constraints, the professional staff designs the most efficient sprinkler systems in the industry. When installing in existing landscapes, they hand-cut turf and carefully preserve existing plantings. Restoration is assured. Automatic works closely with homebuilders and contractors in providing irrigation for new construction sites. Excellent service is the hallmark of this company. They renovate, repair, upgrade and winterize existing systems, and are also backflow certified. All of their design-build residential work is backed by a five-year parts and labor warranty. Automatic is also a friend to the do-it-yourselfer. The retail showroom provides irrigation and landscape lighting supplies. You can also take advantage of their design and technical assistance. For all your irrigation needs, Automatic: The Underground Sprinkler Co. is a name you can trust.

501 C Street SW, Auburn WA
(253) 804-1080 or (800) 474-3223
www.automaticsprink.com

White Knight Safe & Lock, Inc.
HOME: *Best locksmith in Auburn*

White Knight Safe & Lock is ready to come to your rescue. Armed with the latest techniques and equipment, they provide residential, automotive and commercial locksmith services. They also sell and install high-end traditional locks and safes for the home or office. In the last several years, the security field has undergone remarkable changes in order to meet the needs of an increasingly complex society. Computer and electronic applications are opening new avenues and keyless entry is gaining on conventional lock-and-key entry. White Knight is well versed in the new technologies and can take care of all of your locksmith needs. They are also ready to take care of your lock-outs, broken keys, master-key, and deadbolt installations. They carry every kind of key made and can make you a custom or designer key if necessary. Serving the Auburn area since 1974, White Knight Safe & Lock is as near as a phone call.

107 S Division Street, Auburn WA
(253) 833-1010

Frugals

RESTAURANTS & CAFÉS: *Best homegrown burger franchise*

Don't worry, you won't have to save your pennies for a hamburger here. At Frugals you'll get a delicious meal and still have change to spare. Peter and Sheila Stewart started their Frugals phenomenon in Port Angeles in 1988 with the goal of providing the highest quality food for the lowest possible prices. Their idea of a double drive-through with no indoor seating has proved to be wildly successful. Frugal's now has three locations, in Port Angeles, Tacoma and Auburn. The cool, retro-style stainless-steel building draws endless lines of satisfied customers. Despite its popularity, there is never a long wait at Frugals due to the staff's extreme efficiency. Arriving with the expectation of speedy service and low prices, diners are treated to the best tasting burgers in the area. With no need for fancy trappings, all expenses go to the quality of the food. Gardenburgers and hamburgers can be customized with a choice of cheeses, vegetables and thick-sliced bacon. Grilled chicken and great BLT sandwiches are on the menu, as are shakes, fries and soft drinks. Frugals consistently appears in the Best of the Olympic Peninsula for their burgers, shakes and fries. Time after time Frugals has taken best burger honors in newspaper polls. It's not just the food that's great, the staff is also efficient and fun-loving, evident in the lively camaraderie in the kitchen. The Stewarts have come up with a win-win recipe of simplicity, quality and value. They welcome you to drive through and enjoy their retro bistro.

1815 Howard Road, Auburn WA
(253) 333-0990 *www.frugalburger.com*

Auguri Ristorante

RESTAURANTS & CAFÉS:
Best place to experience classic Italy

If you crave classic Italian cuisine, and wonder whether you'll ever get to Italy for real Italian food, fret no more. Auguri's family-owned Ristorante will bring classic Italy to your table. John Latesta wanted to create a place where people in his community could come and have high quality authentic Italian food in a family atmosphere. With his daughter, Lindsey, he opened Auguri, a New York-style restaurant in the heart of Western Washington. Delight in a little taste of Rome with a piano bar on Wednesdays and live jazz on Friday evenings. There are three specials daily and always a meat special, a seafood special and a pasta special. Week-ends offer two intriguing specials and there is always something exquisite with a savory sauce. Create your own pizza by beginning with a plain cheese pizza and adding creative choices from their long list of possibilities, or choose from their regular list of tried and true and absolutely delicious entrées. Once each quarter Auguri features a special wine dinner with a 5-course meal. Once a month, they also sponsor cooking classes and wine tasting. This is a high-end restaurant that charges reasonable prices and serves fantastic Italian food. It's common sense to stop in and order.

18 Auburn Way S, Auburn WA
(253) 887-1559
www.auguriristorante.com

The Spunky Monkey Bar and Grill

RESTAURANTS & CAFÉS: *Best family restaurant in Auburn*

A visit to The Spunky Monkey Bar & Grill is an adventure for the whole family. Walk in the door and the first thing you see is a smiling spunky monkey hanging from the 3-D banana tree. Follow the smell of roasted garlic, you'll find yourself downstairs in the family dining room where you'll be seated in your own jungle hut. Each table boasts a bamboo basket filled with toys that even the adults can't resist playing with. Order your favorite Spunky Monkey special, including gorilla burgers, jungle salads and roaring pasta. Other popular favorites include pizza, panini and smoothies. Homemade soups and deli sandwiches are available for the soup and sandwich crowd. Looking for lighter fare? Spunky Monkey was the first Auburn restaurant to provide the Atkin's menu. No matter what your favorite food, you'll find something to treat your palate at Spunky Monkey. Menu specialties have catchy names, such as the Swinging Monkey and Gator Tail pasta. For meat lovers, there's a New York steak, and for seafood lovers, offerings of salmon and halibut. Special requests go to the indispensable Spunky Monkey manager, Elene Krofft, who is the mother of owner Donel Brinkman. The Spunky Monkey sports the largest karaoke in South King County. If you find yourself upstairs, you will enter the Monkey Bar. Whatever your choice, you'll be glad you visited the Spunky Monkey.

124 2nd Street SE, Auburn WA
(253) 804-9567

DES MOINES

The topography of Des Moines makes it easy to access Puget Sound, and there is a city-operated 840-slip recreational marina with moorage, boat launching and pier fishing. Six miles of shoreline includes public beaches, natural areas and waterfront parks. Saltwater State Park, on the shore, is the most popular state park on the Sound. Redondo Beach, a community within Des Moines, has a popular boardwalk.

PLACES TO GO

- Des Moines Marina
  22307 Dock Avenue S
  (206) 824-5700

- Des Moines Beach Park
  22030 Cliff Avenue S

- Field House Park
  1000 S 220 Street

- Mount Rainier Pool
  22722 19 Avenue S

- Redondo Pier, Boat Launch and Boardwalk
  Redondo Beach Drive and Redondo Way

- Saltwater State Park
  25205 8 Place S

THINGS TO DO

July
- Des Moines Waterland Festival
  Marina
  (206) 878-7000

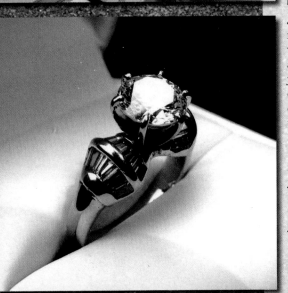

Kimberley's Exquisite Jewelry

FASHION: *Best re-designed jewelry*

Jewelry that once belonged to a beloved family member or ancestor isn't always suitable for wearing as-is, due to styling, disrepair or antiquated settings. Rather than resigning the jewelry and the memories it evokes to a bottom drawer, consider an update. Kimberley Simmons can turn that jewelry into a modern creation that suits your lifestyle and taste. Kimberley and her in-house technicians at Kimberley's Exquisite Jewelry in Des Moines can find a new setting for old stones or custom-design new jewelry to express your individual style. This full-service jewelry store can help you with all your jewelry needs, including jewelry repair, jewelry appraisal or the selection of jewelry from the store's stock of rings, earrings, necklaces and bracelets. Kimberley opened her shop five years ago and brings 28 years of experience in the jewelry business to her customers. Beyond her expertise as a jeweler, her customers find her very personable and discerning about their desires. Expect personal attention and exacting standards from Kimberley and her staff. Everyone, including the store's mascot, Kimberley's dog Max, is there to make your shopping experience pleasant and productive. Kimberly aims to help people celebrate the good things in life. Make jewelry a meaningful part of your life with a visit to Kimberley's Exquisite Jewelry.

22221 7th Street S, #C, Des Moines WA
(206) 824-4946
www.kimberleysexquisitejewelry.com

Athens Pizza & Pasta
RESTAURANTS & CAFÉS: *Best family pizza place*

Athens Pizza & Pasta serves first-class, but very affordable, meals the whole family can enjoy. This restaurant is operated by conscientious owners, who help support the local school system and are sponsors of the local school sport teams. The community-oriented Athens Pizza & Pasta is host to the popular Senior Spaghetti Bash, supplying food once each year. The restaurant features wonderful Greek and Italian entrées, specializing in grinders. These delicious oven-roasted submarine-style sandwiches made on a French roll are stuffed with tender meat. They have perfected many truly amazing recipes for a variety of pizza and pasta entrées. Owners Amar Bhamra and his wife Ramanpreef have owned Athens for five years, but the name has been established for a much longer time. The restaurant was founded by Tommy Tsantilas in 1973. As a result of Amar and Ramanpreef's golden talents, Athens Pizza has been given five stars for the past five years by the health department. The staff at Athens Pizza is extremely proficient and friendly. Athens Pizza & Pasta is the kind of fantastic restaurant that is comfortable for everyone, so come alone or bring the group. Athens Pizza & Pasta provides what you're looking for.

22340 Marine View Drive S, Des Moines WA
(206) 824-4454

Furney's Nursery

GARDENS, PLANTS & FLOWERS:
Best place to buy roses

Furney's Nursery traveled an unlikely path from fruit stand to full-service nursery. Edith and Everett Furney began selling peaches from their orchard at a small stand in 1929. Customers often asked the Furneys to find plants for them, and soon they were selling more plants than fruit. Demand for plants and trees grew to the point that they finally decided to open a retail nursery, which has continued to thrive. Furney's stocks a wide selection of trees, shrubs and smaller plants, along with more than 100 different varieties of roses. Seeds and seedlings are available for the home gardener. The nursery offers lectures throughout the year by some of the most knowledgeable people in the gardening and landscaping business. Curious gardeners can attend weekend classes on attracting birds, container gardening and sculpting with stones and flowers. The Furneys' son Robert acquired the business in 1967, and it has continued to flourish under his leadership. The staff has grown to 100 loyal employees, and Furney's has become a grower, as well as a retail outlet. Farms in Des Moines and Gresham, Oregon supply plant stock not only for Furney's retail business, but also for many other nurseries from Oregon to British Columbia. Visit Furney's Nursery. They're closer than you think, yet a world apart.

21215 Pacific Highway S, Des Moines WA
(206) 878-8761
www.furneysnursery.com

ENUMCLAW

Inland en route to Mount Rainier, Enumclaw is home to the King County Fairgrounds, which hosts a variety of events in addition to the King County Fair. The surrounding plateau is one of the largest thoroughbred horse breeding and boarding areas in the United States.

PLACES TO GO

- The Anderson Garden
  24921 SE 448 Street
  (360) 825-3201

- Federation Forest State Park
  49201 SE Enumclaw Chinook Pass Road

- Hanging Gardens State Park
  Enumclaw-Franklin Road SE

- Mud Mountain Dam and Recreation Area
  30525 SE Mud Mountain Road

- Nolte State Park
  36921 Veazie Cumberland Road SE

THINGS TO DO

July
- King County Fair
  Fairgrounds
  (206) 296-8888

- Scottish Highland Games
  Fairgrounds www.sshga.org

Molen Orthodontics

HEALTH: *Best place for orthodontics*

When you see someone walking around the south end area with a spectacular smile, chances are they had their braces done by Dr. Molen. Known for the Molen Magic Smile that he creates, Dr. Bruce Molen opened his first orthodontic practice in Auburn in 1972. Through the years, he has had the opportunity to treat thousands of patients, including several generations of families. His son, Dr. Rick Molen, joined the practice in 2001 and made Molen Orthodontics a family practice that will continue creating beautiful smiles for many generations to come. By taking continuing education courses and staying on the cutting-edge of technology, the doctors are able to treat their patients in shorter amounts of time while creating exquisitely beautiful smiles. Their diagnostic approach involves evaluating the facial profile and the lip support provided by the teeth and developing individual treatment plans to have a positive impact on these critical aesthetic factors. The doctors utilize early interceptive treatment to correct problems associated with skeletal jaw growth. Early treatment, which is usually initiated around age eight, is a key factor in creating the Molen Magic Smile. Both doctors and their team display a deep respect for people and enjoy building positive, long-term relationships with their patients. When Dr. Rick was asked why he chose orthodontics as a profession, he replied, "Having the opportunity to change people's lives through giving them a beautiful smile is a feeling that I can't describe. It's a wonderful gift to be able to give." Changing lives by creating beautiful smiles is what Molen Orthodontics is all about.

1771 Farrelly Street, Enumclaw WA
(360) 825-6578
1110 Harvey Road, Auburn WA
(253) 939-2552
16202 64th Street E, Suite 103, Sumner WA
(253) 863-0978
www.molenorthodontics.com

FEDERAL WAY

The name Federal Way came from U.S. Highway 99 (now Washington State 99), completed in the 1920s, which ran through the area on its way from Everett to Olympia. Federal Way is home to Weyerhaeuser, the largest private owner of softwood timberland in the world. Weyerhaeuser sponsors botanical gardens featuring rhododendrons and Bonsai trees. The Commons at Federal Way is a major shopping mall.

PLACES TO GO

- Rhododendron Species Foundation and Botanical Garden
  2525 S 336 Street
  (253) 838-4646

- Pacific Rim Bonsai Collection
  Weyerhaeuser Way S
  (253) 924-5206

- Weyerhaeuser King County Aquatic Center
  650 SW Campus Drive

- Wild Waves and Enchanted Village
  36201 Enchanted Parkway S

- Celebration Park
  1095 S 324 Street

- Dash Point State Park
  SW Dash Point Road

- Five Mile Lake
  Military Road S and S 364 Street

- Steel Lake Park
  2410 S 312 Street

- West Hylebos Wetlands Park
  S 348 Street and 4 Avenue S

THINGS TO DO

July
- Red, White and Blues Festival (July 4)
  Celebration Park
  (253) 835-6900

August
- Kid's Day at Steel Lake Park
  (253) 835-6926

Rhododendrons: the Washington State Flower

Apple Physical Therapy

HEALTH: *Voted top place to work in South Puget Sound*

Washington native Randy Johnson, partner and CEO of Apple Physical Therapy, opened his company in 1984 as a way to support his family. Since then his business has evolved into an organization that supports many families and serves individuals throughout the Puget Sound region with clinics in 23 locations. Company President and CEO Claude Ciancio came to work for Apple Physical Therapy in 1990 and achieved partnership in 1998. Ciancio comes from New York City, but his commitment to patients and the community aligns him firmly with Johnson's original goals for service to patients and the communities where patients reside. Randy and Claude believe in the Golden Rule, as well as five core elements, which they feel have made Apple Physical Therapy the success it is today. These five elements are, in order, Integrity, Knowledge, Compassion, Profit and Fun. For patients at any of the Apple facilities, these core tenets create a welcoming and comforting environment that is ideal for both working and healing. Employees, via a *Business Examiner* magazine poll, named Apple Physical Therapy as the number one place to work in the Puget Sound area. Whether you are searching for rehabilitation services or a new career, the staff at Apple Physical Therapy invites your family to become part of their family.

32030 23rd Ave S, Federal Way WA
(253) 946-4852
www.applept.com

Super Supplements

HEALTH: *Voted best independent retail chain in the nation*

Science learns something new every day about the ways vitamins, herbs and nutritional supplements enhance health.

Keeping up with all that cutting-edge information would be overwhelming without the help of experts. Super Supplements is a privately owned chain of 13 discount vitamin stores in western Washington. It was started in 1994 by John Wurts and bills itself as having some of the most knowledgeable staff members in the industry. John brings more than 18 years of experience in the vitamin industry to his operation, which was voted 2004 Best Retail Chain in the Nation by *Vitamin Retailer* magazine. The stores feature wide, inviting aisles, a vast array of supplements, sports nutrition, herbs, body care and homeopathic products, plus a well educated staff prepared to provide the most up-to-date and accurate product information available. Bring your questions to university students, naturopathic doctors or herbalists, or take advantage of Healthnotes, a touchscreen information system that retrieves research on natural remedies, illnesses and potential drug interactions from vitamin, herb and food combinations. You'll get 10 to 70-percent discounts on products at Super Supplements locations from Bellingham to Lakewood. The same great service and more than 30,000 products are available on the website. Visit Super Supplements to begin your journey to a healthier life.

1401 S 348th Street, Federal Way WA
(253) 529-0636
Mail Order: (800) 249-9394
www.supersup.com

Pat's Plumbing

HOME: *Best plumber in The Valley*

"When you prefer perfection" call on Pat's Plumbing. Pat's has been serving The Valley for nearly 20 years and has earned a reputation for excellent service. Pat's plumbers are real pros:

knowledgeable, courteous, and efficient. Their trucks are fully stocked so that nearly any job can be handled on the spot, saving time and keeping costs down. Clogged drains, leaking faucets, broken pipes, disposal installation; whatever the job, Pat's can do it. For both gas and electric service, Pat's sells Bradford White water heaters. These products exceed industry standards, providing greater efficiency and helping preserve our natural resources, as well as saving you money. Your time is valuable, so Pat's offers several time frames per week to fit your busy schedule. They are even open on Saturdays. And the bottom line: you will know the bottom line before the job begins. There are no hidden charges, absolutely no surprises on your bill. In the words of one long-term customer, "Pat's is always prompt, provides excellent work and good products." For all your plumbing needs, the name to trust is Pat's Plumbing.

30459 Military Road S, Federal Way WA
(425) 235-7038 or (800) 491-4081
www.patsplumbing.com

Spice Islands Trading Company

SHOPPING: *Best place for Balinese merchandise*

Spice Islands Trading Company is a family-owned and operated business originating in the waterfront community of Des Moines. After four years in Des Moines, a recent move expanded their offerings to a new, 4,000-square-foot location at The Commons Mall in Federal Way. The doors to the new venue opened on August 12, 2006. Spice Islands Trading Company offers a colorful and exotic mix of furniture, home accessories, jewelry and an abundance of gift items. The wide selection of handcrafted products from the island of Bali are offered at affordable prices with many one-of-a-kind pieces. Join Claudia Alderman, her daughter Christine, her son Noel and his wife Evie on a cultural journey through the Spice Islands and beyond. Whether you are looking for a distinctive home accessory or the perfect gift, browse and enjoy a shopping experience only to be found at Spice Islands Trading Company.

1916 S Commons, Federal Way WA
(253) 945-6191
www.SpiceIslandsTradingCo.com

Brickyard Pub

RESTAURANTS & CAFÉS: *Best pub food*

One of the best reasons to head on out Military Road South is to partake in the fun at the Brickyard Pub. Owners Gene Stewart and Karen Merkt aren't interested in just selling beer. The invigorating atmosphere makes everyone feel at home. Customer service is number one. You're invited to socialize with old friends or make new friends in this convivial tavern. The Brickyard is more than a pub. They serve some of the best food in town. Known for their generous portions and great low prices, they serve some meals that are no more than three dollars. Don't be in a rush if you go on Friday or Saturday night, prime rib is the big draw and waiting for your food is just part of the allure. The man who created all of this wishes to remain anonymous, but his vision was to be able to invite everyone into his living room to eat, drink and have good fun. Customers become family and create supportive relationships at this pub. You can scream at the game on the television like you do at home. Get involved in rooting for your favorite NASCAR driver; the NASCAR theme is evident throughout. Bingo is free on Sundays and a variety of other games will hold your attention as you compete for giveaways as elaborate as a vacation trip. Their catering service in the indoor/outdoor beer garden is just one more reason to get acquainted with all that is offered at the Brickyard Pub.

28845 Military Road S, Federal Way WA
(253) 941-8173

KENT

Until the 1960s, Kent was an agricultural center, once known as the Lettuce Capital of the World. Today, Kent is a major industrial and distribution center and is also home to about 85,000 people. In 2005, *Sports Illustrated* named Kent as Sportstown Washington. In 2006, Kent Station, a major new entertainment center, opened downtown. The Great Wall Mall is the largest full-service Asian mall in greater Seattle. Aromas of herbs, incense and cooking waft through the air to entice shoppers.

PLACES TO GO

- Kent Historical Museum
  855 E Smith Street
  (253) 854 4330

- The Kent Valley Ice Centre
  6015 S 240 Street
  (253) 850-2400

- Pacific Raceways
  31001 144 Avenue SE
  (253) 639-5927

- The Hydroplane and Raceboat Museum
  5917 S 196 Street
  (206) 764-9453

- Clark Lake Park
  12700 SE 240 Street

- Green River Natural Resources Area
  22000 Russell Road

- Lake Fenwick Park
  25828 Lake Fenwick Road

- Mill Creek Canyon Earthworks Park
  742 E Titus Street

THINGS TO DO

July
- Cornucopia Days
  (253) 852-LION (5466)

Strawberry picking in Kent
Photos by Laurel Fan

Apple Physical Therapy
HEALTH: *Voted top place to work in South Puget Sound*

Washington native Randy Johnson, partner and CEO of Apple Physical Therapy, opened his company in 1984 as a way to support his family. Since then his business has evolved into an organization that supports many families and serves individuals throughout the Puget Sound region with clinics in 23 locations. Company President and CEO Claude Ciancio came to work for Apple Physical Therapy in 1990 and achieved partnership in 1998. Ciancio comes from New York City, but his commitment to patients and the community aligns him firmly with Johnson's original goals for service to patients and the communities where patients reside. Randy and Claude believe in the Golden Rule, as well as five core elements, which they feel have made Apple Physical Therapy the success it is today. These five elements are, in order, Integrity, Knowledge, Compassion, Profit and Fun. For patients at any of the Apple facilities, these core tenets create a welcoming and comforting environment that is ideal for both working and healing. Employees, via a *Business Examiner* magazine poll, named Apple Physical Therapy as the number one place to work in the Puget Sound area. Whether you are searching for rehabilitation services or a new career, the staff at Apple Physical Therapy invites your family to become part of their family.

25012 104th Avenue SE, Suite C, Kent WA
(253) 856-3477
www.applept.com

Marina on the Puget Sound

Eagle Fitness

HEALTH: *Best fitness training and gym*

Eagle Fitness owner Steve Yanak has found that running a gymnasium is a wonderful business. "There is nothing more rewarding than seeing people join the gym and become happier and healthier," he says. Eagle Fitness is a community fitness club where everyone knows your name. The staff members are highly educated and athletic. Most are young people from the local area who are committed to the community. Eagle Fitness has new cardio equipment with heart rate monitors and Cardio Theater, an award-winning audio and video system that entertains and informs exercisers. The gym has multiple lines of strength equipment and offers tanning in large 32-bulb tanning beds. Machines are available that allow members to build strength even if they cannot lift weights. You can add to your workout by hiring a personal trainer. To put parents' minds at ease, Eagle Fitness provides a fully staffed Kid's Club with video monitoring. The gym is sparkling clean and the atmosphere is friendly. All memberships are on a month-to-month basis, which keeps staff members on their toes. An orientation is included with your membership. Join Eagle Fitness and rediscover how great it feels to be in shape.

23424 Pacific Highway S, Kent WA
(206) 878-3788
www.eaglefitnesskent.com

Fireside Hearth & Home

HOME: *Best showroom for fireplaces, stoves and hearth accessories*

When Tom Karwin and Bill Nirk started Fireside Distributors in 1982, their goal was to form long-term customer relationships based on superior products, service and workmanship. They drove the forklift, answered the phones and put in long hours to develop Fireside into the largest supplier and installer of fireplaces and related products in the Pacific Northwest. Fireside Hearth & Home is now the retail outlet for Fireside of Washington, now owned by John Waterstraat and William Nirk. Fireside revolutionized the industry with the 1993 Start Up program. Under the program, Fireside installed fireplaces in new homes during the rough-in process and then came back right before owner occupancy to test and adjust all products. The entire industry now practices similar programs to ensure that fireplace installations meet high standards. The main retail showroom in Kent is a fantastic resource for homeowners, builders and remodelers with its displays of more than 40 brightly burning models of the latest fireplaces and stoves and many hearth accessories. The knowledgeable sales staff can help you with gas, wood, pellet and state-of-the-art ambient electric fireplaces, along with a full array of mantels to complement your new fireplace. Fireside also sells and installs Armstrong heating and cooling systems. Factory-trained technicians provide repairs, maintenance and upgrades to all of the products Fireside sells. For years of lasting enjoyment, you can depend on Fireside Hearth & Home. Their mission is to provide a customer-focused buying experience that offers the most innovative hearth products and services, while building customer loyalty through quality and integrity.

7818 S 212th Street, Suite 109, Kent WA
(425) 251-9447
www.firesidehearthandhome.com

Farrington Court Retirement Community

LIFESTYLE DESTINATIONS:
Best retirement community in Kent

Fun, active aging is what Farrington Court Retirement Community is all about. Situated in downtown Kent, luxurious apartment homes are situated in a fun active environment. The location is right next to the Kent Station, the local shopping center, theater, local banks, library and commuter rail. They are managed by Leisure Care, who for nearly 30 years has led the industry in the development and management of elegant retirement communities that are all about five-star living. Dan B. Madsen bought the company in 2003 and continues holding true to the founding principles. You'll be able to meet new friends and entertain family in the beautiful restaurant inside the community, called Merlots. Sign up for an art class or start a new fitness program offered by Prime Fit. Book that travel excursion you've always wanted to go on. Whether you want to spend an afternoon in the library with a good book, enjoy a night out on the town with your sweetie, or want to socialize with friends, Farrington Court has it all. It's your life, on your terms. General manager Lorilyn Evers has been recognized for meeting or exceeding company standards of operations. She has developed a world-class community with the best staff, entertainment, and atmosphere, as well as excellent customer satisfaction. Spend a night in their guest unit, and they'll wine and dine you. They love to make new friends.

516 Kenosia Avenue, Kent WA
(253) 852-2737
www.leisurecare.com

Nature's Market

MARKETS:
Best natural and organic market

Since 1992, the folks in and near Kent have had a partner in the community dedicated to their well-being. That partner is Nature's Market, the largest, most complete natural products store in the area. Organic produce is offered exclusively. Organic wines, microbrews and organic meats are staples at the market. For those who need wheat-free, gluten-free products, the market caters to their needs by stocking more than 500 special products. Specializing in organic and natural foods, Nature's Market boasts a huge selection of the finest natural supplements and herbs. Included in the more than 30,000 products they carry, you will want to indulge yourself in the vast selection of natural health and beauty products. Maintaining the highest quality products at affordable prices is an important aim for owner Sally Honeysett, whose energetic and pleasant personality permeates all aspects of her business. The store emphasizes extraordinary customer care and the staff is friendly and well informed, with extensive knowledge on the uses and properties of the natural products available at the market. If your health and well-being are a priority, stop by, have lunch, and shop for the finest foods and supplements available anywhere.

26011 104th Avenue SE, Kent WA
(253) 854-5395

Café Siena

RESTAURANTS & CAFÉS:
Best Tuscan hideaway

When Café Siena opened in Kent two years ago, it was an immediate sensation. It's housed in a big, unusual and very beautiful building, which offers busy patrons a respite that is distinctly Italian in nature. This building's unusual styling features Tuscan-influenced architecture, a cozy hideaway filled with round, mosaic-topped tables and wrought iron chairs, and a bottom level devoted to four drive-thru windows and a walk-up espresso window. Catch up with friends in front of an outdoor fire pit while sampling gourmet soups and other Italian-influenced menu items. A panini bar, classic baked goods prepared on the premises (including a superior crostini), and music help define the many ways Café Siena revitalizes its patrons. Because Café Siena caters to busy people, this gourmet-quality fare is designed to be served quickly and conveniently by a friendly staff. Next time you need a break from the hubbub, but don't have time for a multi-course meal much less a trip to Italy, visit Café Siena for coffee, Italian baked goods and gourmet deli fare that will put everyday concerns on hold just long enough for you to amass new energy and get a second wind.

Café Siena: 24530 Russell Road, Kent WA
(253) 852-1806
Northwest Java Group: 1003 Main Street,
Sumner WA
(253) 891-3234

MAPLE VALLEY

Incorporated only in 1997, Maple Valley has its roots in a rural lifestyle with the many wonders of nature close at hand. Mount Rainier beckons in the near distance. Lake Wilderness Park provides canoeing, fishing, swimming and many other activities. Trails are rich with vine maples. You can hike, bike or ride horseback through town to the Cedar River or walk down the arboretum trails.

PLACES TO GO

- Lake Wilderness Arboretum
  22520 SE 248 Street

- Lake Wilderness Park
  23601 SE 248 street

THINGS TO DO

June
- Maple Valley Days
  Lake Wilderness Park
  www.maplevalleydays.com

August
- Wilderness Games
  Lake Wilderness Park
  (425) 413-8800 ext. 200

Wilderness Electric
HOME: *Best electricians*

For nearly 30 years, Wilderness Electric has been a trusted Maple Valley community favorite. They provide the highest quality electrical services and products to the community. Wilderness is well known for efficient, timely service and for treating customers and staff alike with courtesy and respect. Dedicated to fairness and equality in all dealings, they are experienced in working with homeowners, builders, and contractors. Safety is number one at Wilderness, and all of their accredited, journey-level electricians ensure that every installation meets the National Electrical Code. Their well stocked vans carry everything needed for almost any job: from installing hot tubs, ceiling fans and landscape lighting to wiring large, complex buildings. Visit the website for electrical safety tips, current code updates, and company specials delivered right to your in-box. Serving residential, commercial and industrial concerns, Wilderness Electric is your resource for electrical systems installed professionally and with pride.

**23220 Maple Valley Highway SE, Suite 205, Maple Valley WA
(425) 432-1747**
www.wildernesselectric.com

SUMNER AND BONNEY LAKE

Sumner and Bonney Lake are two small cities across the county line in Pierce County. Sumner was named for Charles Sumner, an anti-slavery senator and member of Lincoln's cabinet. Bonney Lake is one of the fastest growing communities in Washington. These towns provide country living with easy access to city amenities.

PLACES TO GO

- Sumner Ryan House Museum
  1228 Main Street
  (253) 863-8936

- Allan Yorke Park
  Bonney Lake Boulevard and W Tapps Highway

- Daffodil Valley Sports Complex
  Washington Street E, Sumner

- Lake Taps North Park
  2022 198 Avenue E, Sumner

- Loyalty Park
  1300 Park Street, Sumner

THINGS TO DO

August
- Sumner Summer Arts Festival
  (253) 863-6366 ext. 3024

- Bonney Lake Days
  Allan Yorke Park
  (253) 261-0023

Main Street Home Loans

BUSINESS: *Best home lender*

"Good, bad, or ugly credit," that's the slogan and the commitment of Sandy Hickson and Tami Macias. With their combined 38 years of experience in the corporate lending world, these women really know their stuff. They also know that corporate interests are seldom the same as customers' interests. That is why they opened their own business. They really care about people and they are energized by successfully meeting their needs. Sandy and Tami are accustomed to taking the toughest situations and making them work, however long it takes. And it pays. They boast an impressive success rate and have built lasting relationships with their customers. True personal service is a rare commodity in the lending business and that is what Tami and Sandy bring to this community. Whatever your situation, at the comfortable office of Main Street Home Loans you will be treated respectfully and fairly. These community treasures can help you make your dreams come true.

1024 Main Street, Sumner WA
(253) 862-9490

VanLierop Garden Market

GARDENS, PLANTS & FLOWERS: *Best all-around garden market*

At the VanLierop Garden Market you will find more than you expect, from an extensive collection of unusual annuals and perennials, to cut flowers, garden art and food. Since starting the year round market for garden-style living in 1998, Anne VanLierop-Johnson and April and Bonnie VanLierop have successfully created a service-oriented business. Using both local floral deliveries and Teleflora, VanLierop Garden Market is able to cater to individual needs for the freshest flowers available. They carry beautifully artistic holiday décor for every season, as well as the exclusive candle line by Illume and the pottery line Aw. In addition to the market, there is a large outdoor garden featuring numerous Northwest artists and plantings of the newest annuals. The garden houses a unique collection of water features and Rocknoggins rock carvings, taking yard art to the next level. In January of 2005, Sorci's Delicatessen di Roma opened in the same location, with chef and owner Patrick Amato offering a full-service Italian deli specializing in imported and domestic meats, cheeses, breads and pasta. Whether or not you wish to take the time to work on your own yard, check out the VanLierop Garden Market and marvel at what they've done with theirs.

1020 Ryan Avenue, Sumner WA
(253) 862-8510
www.vanlieropgardenmarket.com

Molen Oral & Facial Surgery

HEALTH: *Best comprehensive care for dental surgery*

Established in 2005, Molen Oral & Facial Surgery maintains a distinctive level of quality service for patient care and integrity. Owners David Molen, DDS MD, and practice manager Crystal Molen facilitate the needs of their patients first. When David was in dental school, he saw how much the oral surgeons helped the children. He was moved to become an oral surgeon. After going to college in Utah and University of Washington School of Dentistry, Dr. Molen trained at the highly acclaimed Mayo Clinic in Minnesota. Dr. Molen practices a full spectrum of treatments such as facial rejuvenation, TMJ disorders, jaw surgery, wisdom teeth removal and dental implants. Although most patients are fearful of seeing an oral surgeon, Dr. Molen feels it's important to consult personally with every patient before surgery. Dr. Molen calls all of his patients on the night of their surgery, and provides his personal number for after-hours needs. Molen Oral & Facial Surgery employs a highly trained, energetic, friendly and caring staff. We hope you never do, but if you face dental surgery, visit Molen Oral & Facial Surgery, where the needs of patients come first.

16202 64th Street E, Suite 105, Sumner WA
1026 Harvey Road, Auburn WA
(253) 470-5020 (both locations)
www.molensurgery.com

Molen Orthodontics

HEALTH: *Best place for orthodontics*

When you see someone walking around the south end area with a spectacular smile, chances are they had their braces done by Dr. Molen. Known for the Molen Magic Smile that he creates, Dr. Bruce Molen opened his first orthodontic practice in Auburn in 1972. Through the years, he has had the opportunity to treat thousands of patients, including several generations of families. His son, Dr. Rick Molen, joined the practice in 2001 and made Molen Orthodontics a family practice that will continue creating beautiful smiles for many generations to come. By taking continuing education courses and staying on the cutting-edge of technology, the doctors are able to treat their patients in shorter amounts of time while creating exquisitely beautiful smiles. Their diagnostic approach involves evaluating the facial profile and the lip support provided by the teeth and developing individual treatment plans to have a positive impact on these critical aesthetic factors. The doctors utilize early interceptive treatment to correct problems associated with skeletal jaw growth. Early treatment, which is usually initiated around age eight, is a key factor in creating the Molen Magic Smile. Both doctors and their team display a deep respect for people and enjoy building positive, long-term relationships with their patients. When Dr. Rick was asked why he chose orthodontics as a profession, he replied, "Having the opportunity to change people's lives through giving them a beautiful smile is a feeling that I can't describe. It's a wonderful gift to be able to give." Changing lives by creating beautiful smiles is what Molen Orthodontics is all about.

Sumner office:
16202 64th Street East, Ste. #103
(253) 863-0978
Auburn office:
1110 Harvey Road
(253) 939-2552
Enumclaw office:
1771 Farrelly Street
(360) 825-6578
www.molenorthodontics.com

Apple Physical Therapy

HEALTH: *Voted top place to work in South Puget Sound*

Washington native Randy Johnson, partner and CEO of Apple Physical Therapy, first opened his company in 1984 as a way to support his family. Since opening he has helped his business evolve into an organization that supports many families and serves individuals throughout the Puget Sound region with clinics in 23 locations. Company President and CEO Claude Ciancio came to work for Apple Physical Therapy in 1990 and achieved partnership in 1998. Ciancio comes from New York City, but his commitment to patients and the community aligns him firmly with Johnson's original goals for service to patients and the communities where patients reside. Randy and Claude believe in the Golden Rule as well as five core elements, which they feel have made Apple Physical Therapy the success it is today. These five elements are, in order, Integrity, Knowledge, Compassion, Profit and Fun. For patients at any of the Apple facilities, these core tenets create a welcoming and comforting environment that is ideal for both working and healing. Employees, via a *Business Examiner* magazine poll, named Apple Physical Therapy as the number one place to work in the Puget Sound area. Whether you are searching for rehabilitation services or a new career, the staff at Apple Physical Therapy invites your family to become part of their family.

19820 State Route 410 E, Suite 201, Bonney Lake WA
(253) 863-7510
www.applept.com

Feather Your Nest

HOME: *Best home décor in Sumner*

Feather Your Nest is a home décor store that inspires people to look at their homes in a different light. This family-oriented business, owned by Kurstyn Schober and run with help from her mother, sister, husband and five children, features two different kinds of country décor, cottage and classic American, and specializes in items that will help homeowners create a welcoming space where friends and family can gather. Kurstyn started out as a home crafter and the shop came about almost accidentally to provide an outlet for her creativity. With an emphasis on home furnishings, she chose a name based on her mother's favorite saying, "I need a little something to feather my nest." The store features antiques and gifts, as well as decorating items, with the emphasis shifting according to the seasons. In winter, items such as the Winterland Friends Collection of snowman-themed decorations are highlighted, and gardening items are brought to the forefront during the spring and summer. You can find something delightful for any time or season, and with a wide range of prices, everyone can take something home regardless of budget.

1103 Main Street, Sumner WA
(253) 891-2149
www.featheryournestofsumner.com

Golden Rule Bears

SHOPPING: *Best teddy bear store*

Golden Rule Bears is well-known as a teddy bear lover's dream come true. Featuring thousands of bears and other stuffed animals, this shop has one of the largest inventories of Steiff, Cherished Teddies and Boyds Bears in the world and a vast array of Gund, Ty, R. John Wright, Deb Canham Artist Designs, Bearington, Ganz and Muffy VanderBear. They are honored to be a Boyds "Gold Paw" Dealer, as well as the only Cherished Teddies Cherished Retailer in the Pacific Northwest. They are an authorized club store for many of their lines. From miniatures and figurines, to puppets and toys, you'll find just what you are looking for snuggled in the heart of downtown Sumner. Tom and Lorraine Young founded the store in 1986 and pride themselves on exceptional customer service, as well as unmatched selection. Their sales associates are all collectors themselves and are knowledgeable about details of their diverse lines. Golden Rule Bears has built a 20-year international reputation of excellence. Visit them in Sumner and see why.

1115-B Main Street, Sumner WA
(253) 863-0280 or (800) 932-2327
www.goldenrulebears.com

Bistro Thyme

RESTAURANTS & CAFÉS: *Best international cuisine*

Bistro Thyme is a fine-dining establishment with an international flair, but it is more than that. Chef Rose Fahimi Ighani has a deeply spiritual connection to her many friends and the larger community. She has carried a life-long concern for the well-being of women and children. Ighani hosts a Circle of Healing twice a month where women of any faith can come to pray together in a spirit of unity. Rose traveled a long and perilous path to get where she is today. Of the persecuted Bahai faith, Rose and her children escaped from Iran by foot and on horseback through forbidding mountainous terrain into Turkey. Eventually, they were able to join family members in Canada. While working in a deli and taking English lessons, she met her future husband, Paul Webber. Rose has a gift for saving struggling restaurants and turning them into successful businesses. She has performed that miracle several times, and then gone on to other challenges. In 2004, she and Paul moved to Bonney Lake. They bought the last parcel of the Ochsner farm. Rose opened Bistro Thyme, and much of the farm-fresh produce and herbs she uses in her cooking come right from their own garden. The menu features foods of many cultures and once a month Rose has an ethnic buffet. She is an incredible chef. Homemade soups, salads, dressings, and sandwiches are served, as well a changing array of the entrées she enjoys developing. Rose, her family, and Bistro Thyme are real treasures in the Bonney Lake community.

20870 State Route 410 E, Bonney Lake WA
(253) 862-1171

Baron Manfred von Vierthaler Winery & Restaurant

RESTAURANTS & CAFÉS: *Best Bavarian-style restaurant*

Come visit a Bavarian-style winery restaurant and enjoy good food, great wine and a fantastic view of the Sumner Valley, especially at sunset. After lunch or before dinner on weekends you can also visit the Baron's Train Museum. Besides a display of just about every engine that ever ran on American rails, including at least 12 currently running trains, a huge 3,800-square-foot operating layout is also under construction. Baron Manfred and Baroness Ingeborg von Vierthaler's restaurant features authentic German cuisine. Among the home-cooked meals you will find venison, several kinds of schnitzels and a good assortment of traditional German dishes and desserts. Besides their own wines, you can also have a real German draft beer imported from Muenchen in Bavaria. On the American side of the menu, you will find a variety of juicy, tender prime cuts of steak, as well as seafood and pasta dishes. They also offer samples of their own private label wines made to the Baron's own formulas in the tasting area of the restaurant. Specialties include white and red late harvest (Auslese) slightly sweet wines.

17136 Highway 410, Sumner WA
(3 miles east of Sumner)
(253) 863-1633

New England Saltbox
SHOPPING: *Best interior decorating in Sumner*

The New England Saltbox in Sumner features a collection of country décor and antiques for your home, as well as a variety of giftware. Lodge furniture and décor has recently been added in the shop. Home decorating services are also offered. Marlene Grantham, shop owner, developed a love for the homey New England look after spending 17 years on the East Coast during her husband's naval career. Upon their return to the West Coast, she wanted to open a shop that encourages an appreciation for New England décor, and the New England Saltbox is the result. In 2002, the shop received the Judges Award for Best Interior Decorating for the Boardwalk Home at the Pierce Country Street of dreams in nearby DuPont. Some of the things you will find during your visit to the shop include upholstered furniture, lodge furniture, Shaker cupboards and furniture area rugs by Country Cat Loom and Weymouth. They also carry Old Heritage reproductions, Lt. Moses lighting, framed prints and faux wall finishes. Other favorites are quilts, American folk art, Olde Century paint, wrought iron, pottery, baskets, dolls, including Byers Choice dolls, tinware, samplers, vintage fabrics and candles. With this extensive selection, the New England Saltbox is sure to have something you will love.

1115 Main Street, Sumner WA
(253) 826-3506

Nifty's Toy and Novelty Company
SHOPPING: *Best toy store in Sumner*

Nifty's Toy and Novelty Company is an old-fashioned toy store in Sumner. Nifty's offers fun and unique, non-electronic games and toys for children ages 1 to 99. At Nifty's, the idea is to provide the opportunity for kids to have fun and use their imaginations by offering hands-on children's toys and novelties. The store is browser friendly, while original painted murals give it a warm and fun atmosphere. Kay Kiser has owned Nifty's (formerly The Button Patch) for a decade. She stocks a wide selection of wooden toys and puzzles, including train sets, ramp racers and pull toys. For infants, there are soft and safe cuddle and teething toys. Little girls enjoy the fairy dresses, ballerina jewelry boxes and dolls. There is also an extensive selection of art supplies and kits. For boys, there are die-cast cars, kites, sport balls and yo-yos. In addition, there are board games for every age. With a gift from Nifty's, the fun has only begun.

1117 Main Street, Sumner WA
(253) 826-2635

South Puget Sound

State Capitol Building in Olympia at dusk

South Puget Sound

THE SOUTH PUGET SOUND

focal points are Olympia and Tacoma. A visit to Olympia, the state capital, can include a trip to the Temple of Justice to watch a state Supreme Court hearing, a run around Capitol Lake, and a stop at one of many small boutiques, coffee shops and bakeries downtown. The popular farmer's market is known for its size, quality and the variety of vendors. Olympia has a flourishing music scene. The experimental, non-traditional Evergreen State College thrives, as well, and makes a major impact on the culture and economy of Olympia.

Olympia's nearest neighbor, Lacey, is the host of Lacey Museum and St. Martins College. Tumwater lies next to Deschutes River Falls south of Olympia. The famed Tumwater Thunderbirds won four state high school football titles under legendary coach Sid Otton.

East of Olympia, Fort Lewis, the Nisqually Indian Reservation and the Nisqually National Wildlife Refuge form a natural break between the Olympia area and Tacoma.

Tacoma, a major port, was nicknamed the City of Destiny because it was the western terminus of the Northern Pacific Railroad in the late 1800s. The city took the motto When Rails Meet Sails. Tacoma has had a campus of the University of Washington since 1990. It was the first city in the state to build a modern electric light rail line, and has restored the Thea Foss Waterway downtown to modern glory.

Tacoma at Sunset
Courtesy of Washington State Tourism
Photo by J. Poth

LACEY

Immediately east of Olympia, Lacey was a resort community in the early 1900s. Horse racing enthusiasts flocked to Lacey from all over the Northwest to watch horse races and relax at the lake resorts. Lacey is close to many lakes and forests and in particular to the beautiful Nisqually Valley, which separates the Olympia-Lacey area from Tacoma. Lacey has 33,000 people to Olympia's 44,000, so Lacey and Olympia are effectively twin cities.

PLACES TO GO

- Jacob Smith House
  4500 Intelco Loop SE (360) 491-0857

- Lacey Museum
  829½ Lacey Street SE

- Huntamer Park
  7th Avenue SE

- Rainier Vista Community Park
  5475 45th Avenue SE

- St. Martins Park
  College Street SE and Carpenter Road SE

- Wonderwood Park
  Brentwood Drive SE

- Woodland Creek Park
  Pacific Avenue SE

THINGS TO DO

March
- Nisqually River Basin Land Trust Auction
  Saint Martin's College (360) 458-1111

May
- International Migratory Bird Day
  (360) 753-9467

June
- Dixieland Jazz Festival
  St. Martins College (360) 943-9123

July–August
- Thurston County Fair
  Fairgrounds (360) 786-5453

October
- Children's Day
  Huntamer Park (360) 491-0857

View from Hurricane Ridge in the Olympic National Park

Meconi's Italian Subs
RESTAURANTS & CAFÉS: *Best sub shop*

Like many East Coast transplants, when Wayne and Nancy Meconi arrived in Olympia in the early 1980s, they were glad to be there, but they also missed some things from home. Their loss resulted in a big gain for Olympia when they opened the first Meconi's Italian Subs in 1986. The Meconis left Pennsylvania when Wayne was laid off from the steel mills. Life was good in Olympia, but Wayne couldn't find a good sub shop, at least nothing like the family-owned shops that seemed to be on every corner back in Williamsport. He remodeled a three-car garage in his spare time with the idea of starting his own shop and creating a little side job. After plenty of research and tracking down the right ingredients for authentic East Coast flavors, he opened the doors on what remains his Lacey Boulevard location. The sub shop was an immediate hit and Nancy quit her job to work full-time in the shop. In 1993, daughter Maria joined the business as manager for a second location near the Capitol Building in downtown Olympia. With homemade sub rolls made fresh and ingredients that agreed with Wayne's very particular taste buds, it's no wonder that the Daily Olympian has voted Meconi's the Best Sub Shop every year since the voting began. Visit Meconi's Italian Subs and find out for yourself just what Wayne was missing when he set about bringing an East Coast-style sub shop to the West Coast.

1051 Capitol Way S, Olympia WA (360) 534-0240
5225A Lacey Boulevard SE, Lacey WA (360) 459-0213
www.meconissubs.com

LAKEWOOD

Incorporated in 1996, Lakewood was once known as Prairie, the Nisqually Prairie, to be precise. Land disputes with the Nisqually Indians led to the establishment of Fort Steilacoom. Later, relations improved. Indians and settlers partied together on the prairie. The city's modern name reflects its many lakes. The largest are American Lake, Lake Steilacoom and Gravelly Lake.

PLACES TO GO

- Fort Lewis Museum
  4320 Main Street, Fort Lewis
  (253) 967-7206

- Lakewold Gardens
  12317 Gravelly Lake Drive SW
  (888) 858-4106

- American Lake Park
  Veterans Drive SW

- Fort Steilacoom Park
  Steilacoom Boulevard SW
  and Elwood Drive SW

- Harry Todd Park
  N Thorne Lane SW

- Seeley Lake Park
  Lakewood Drive SW

THINGS TO DO

May
- Lakewood International Festival
  Pierce College
  (253) 964-7327

June
- Summerfest
  Fort Steilacoom Park
  (253) 589-2489

September
- Oktoberfest
  Elks Club
  (253) 588-5466

December
- Christmas at Fort Steilacoom
  (253) 582-5838

Aquarium Paradise
ANIMALS & PETS: *Best aquarium store*

Aquarium Paradise was established in 1992 by Lonzo and Joan Fanony. Fish had always been a hobby for Lonzo and he dreamed of having his own store. This dream was realized when he opened Aquarium Paradise. Well educated in the fish world, Lonzo maintained a great interest in marine biology. Originally, Aquarium Paradise started from modest beginnings with 1,000 square feet. It has grown to more than 10,000 square feet, making it the largest pet fish store in the Pacific Northwest. They specialize in custom installations and maintenance, as well as customer service. Aquarium Paradise has always been family-owned. At first, Lonzo felt working in the store was a way for his four sons to earn their way through college. Currently, Domenic, Loren, Justin and Delano Fanony enjoy keeping their father's dream alive, and the opportunity to spend time with the family. From fish to corals and freshwater to saltwater, Aquarium Paradise will become your one-stop fish shop.

11724 Pacific Highway SW, Lakewood WA
(253) 584-FISH (3474)

PLACES TO GO

- Bigelow House Museum
  918 Glass Avenue NE (360) 753-1215

- Boston Harbor Marina
  312 73rd Avenue NE (360) 357-5670

- Olympic Flight Museum
  7637-A Old Highway 99 SE (360) 705-3925

- Salmon Run art exhibit
  The Olympia Center, 222 Columbia St. NW

- Washington State Capitol
  416 14th Avenue SW (360) 586-3460

- Heritage Park Fountain
  330 5th Avenue SW

- Percival Landing
  405 Columbia Street NW

- Priest Point Park
  2600 East Bay Drive NE

- Watershed Park
  2500 Henderson Boulevard SE

- Yashiro Japanese Garden
  900 Plum Street SE

THING TO DO

February
- Ethnic Celebration
  The Olympia Center (360) 753-8380

April
- Spring Arts Walk
  (360) 753-8380

June
- Olympia Artist Studio Tour
  (360) 753-8380

- Olympic Air Show
  Airport (360) 705-3925

July
- Capital Lakefair
  Heritage Park (360) 943-7344

August
- Sand in the City
  Port Plaza (360) 956-0818

September
- Olympia Harbor Days
  www.harbordays.com

- Percival Play Day
  Percival Landing (360) 753-8380

October
- Fall Arts Walk *(360) 753-8380*

OLYMPIA

The number of things to see and do is almost endless in Olympia, Washington's capital city. Olympia is a hub for artists and musicians. Music ranges from alternative to classical. Olympia is also a great town for boating and other outdoor recreation. You can visit a festival almost every month of the year.

Ramada Governor House
ACCOMMODATIONS:
Best hotel in Olympia

A stay at the Ramada Governor House in Olympia is more than a well-appointed room. It's the opportunity to stay in an exceedingly well run establishment where general manager Sandra Miller and her staff put people first. The employees here are approachable and energetic. They enjoy their work, adore their boss and will do everything possible to meet your needs. Sandra puts the focus squarely on people in all aspects of her life and work. She caters not only to her guests, many of whom are legislators, but also reaches out into her community. She housed victims of Hurricane Katrina who were trying to relocate in Washington, and has been honored for her efforts to improve the work environment for employees raising families. The Governor House has 119 spacious guestrooms, plus a fitness facility, heated outdoor pool, sauna and whirlpool. Guests enjoy complimentary high-speed Internet, safes in the rooms, laundry services and superior dining and room service from Southern Kitchen restaurant. Banquet and meeting rooms are also available. For pleasure, you couldn't be better placed, with convenient access to the Olympic peninsula and the Pacific Ocean beaches. The State Capitol , several museums, the Farmer's Market and the Percival Landing Waterfront Park are all nearby. Whether you come for business or pleasure, you can be sure you are in good hands with Sandra and her team at Ramada Governor House.

621 S Capitol Way, Olympia WA (360) 352-7700
http://cendant.netopia.com/olympia00198
www.ramada.com

Audio Northwest
AUTO: *Best car audio store*

For car audio, video or security systems that are customized to individual needs, fairly priced and backed by great warranties, the residents of Thurston County turn to Audio Northwest. This reliable company has built a stellar reputation over more than 20 years with great products and careful service. Owner Jesse Peterson believes in selling people what they need. After 10 years as a corporate manager for a retail audio company, Jesse jumped at the opportunity to work for a business that was grounded in the community and treated customers and employees with integrity. Today, he owns that business and continues to spoil Olympia with top-notch customer care. Jesse was born and raised in Olympia and believes in giving back to his community. Audio Northwest is the place to turn for invisible audio systems, Sirius satellite radio, sound damping, navigation systems and back-up cameras. Whether you need woofers and amplifiers or heated seats, you can count on Audio Northwest installers to find solutions. The company honors all product warranties and prides itself on honest prices. Next time you need to customize the sound or security on a vehicle, turn to the experts at Audio Northwest. They will treat you and your vehicle like they intend to know you for a long time.

107 Franklin Street NE, Olympia WA
(360) 786-9512
www.audionorthwest.com

Hands on Children's Museum
ATTRACTIONS: *Best family attraction*

The Hands On Children's Museum is the most visited family attraction in the South Puget Sound, offering award-winning programs and exciting exhibits. Located on the State Capitol's campus, the museum features more than 50 interactive exhibits in six main galleries. The Good for You! Gallery features a child-size farmer's market where young children can buy and sell fresh fruits, vegetables, bakery goods and cheeses. In the family kitchen, they can prepare a home-cooked meal and then visit the neighborhood climbing space. The museum also features a Build It! Gallery, where young children can build their own house, complete with windows, doors and roof, and also

operate a dump truck. In the Working Waterfront, they can board a three-story cargo ship to be the captain, cook meals in the galley and load logs into the cargo hold. The museum's Young at Art studio features more than 50 different bins of new and recycled materials where visitors can make their own creations. The TotSpot Early Learning Center is designed for very young children and offers sensory experiences, including a lentils table, Playdough table, dress-up nook and several activity stations. The Hands On Children's Museum is a non-profit organization dedicated to stimulating curiosity, creativity and learning. The Museum offers an experiential preschool, camps, field trips, and its signature event, Sand In The City, held the fourth weekend in August on Olympia's boat-lined waterfront.

106 11th Avenue SW, Olympia WA
(360) 956-0818 *www.hocm.org*

Photo by Barbara McConkey, InForm Design

Monarch Sculpture Park
ATTRACTIONS: *Most interesting park*

Whether you are an art connoisseur or just a curious traveler, make sure to stop by Monarch Sculpture Park in Olympia. With numerous statues and sculptures, the park features work from more than 80 local, national and international artists. Along with several styles and themes of artistic sculpture, the park has a beautiful Japanese Garden and an enormous, rare hedge maze in the shape of a butterfly, one of very few maze-design hedges left in the country. Inspired by European influences, including creative effects and layouts from Denmark and Sweden, founders and fellow artists Myrna Orsini and Doris Coonrod opened Monarch Sculpture Park in 1995. With no entrance fees and 80 acres of displays, Monarch Sculpture Park is a donation-run gathering

of professional and emerging artists who come together through Artist-in-Residence Programs or inspiration in celebration of fine art. While the park is available for viewing year round, special events include painting and recycled art exhibits, workshops and several other events worth viewing. While its purpose is to display, select pieces from the park are available for purchase. Come and enjoy the view, and the blending of culture and style at the Monarch Sculpture Park.

8431 Waldrick Road SE, Olympia WA
(360) 264-2408
www.scattercreek.com/~monarchpark

Richard Taylor

Lattin's Country Cider Mill and Farm
BAKERIES, COFFEE & TEA: *Best jam and cider*

The word *farm* is truly defined at Lattin's Country Cider Mill and Farm in Olympia. They boast more than 23 varieties of pies, including their popular white chocolate mousse with raspberry topping, large apple fritters and warm doughnuts. Lattin's also offers a full assortment of produce fresh from their farm. Owner Carolyn Lattin and her late husband, Victor, began producing their

award-winning cider with just a small apple press 30 years ago. Now with the aid of their two daughters, Carolyn continues to fulfill that just-out-of-the-oven craving for country-style food. Nationally recognized, Lattin's Country Cider Mill and Farm won two awards from the North American Farmers' Direct Marketing Association in 2004 for making the best cider and strawberry jam in the nation. They also have a petting farm, complete with everything from a pony to peacocks. A horse-drawn carriage provides transportation to their pumpkin patch during the fall. The farm is rich with history, continuing the tradition of good, healthful, homemade products and a comfortable atmosphere.

9402 Rich Road SE, Olympia WA
(360) 491-7328

Photos by Paul & Shirley Bragg

Wagner's Bakery & Café
BAKERIES, COFFEE & TEA: *Best wedding cakes*

Wagner's European Bakery & Café in Olympia is the oldest bakery and café in the Puget Sound area. Since 1939, four generations of the Wagner family have owned, operated or worked at the business, consistent in their commitment to bring their customers the very best. The friendly atmosphere provides an ideal spot for community gathering, and a gracious and attentive staff ensures the customers are well taken care of. Wagner's is also renowned for their distinctive and

beautiful wedding cakes. Located one block north of Hands On Children's Museum and two blocks north of the Capitol Building, Wagner's bakery is the perfect place to enjoy breakfast, lunch or dessert when out visiting the city's sites. In addition, the family also owns and operates the Marketplace Bakery, located in the Olympia Farmer's Market and the Lacey Farmer's Market. The Wagner family's dedication to quality food, good service and community involvement is the reason Wagner's is still thriving after 66 years.

1013 Capitol Way S, Olympia WA
(360) 357-7268

Vento Photography
BUSINESS: *Best commercial photos*

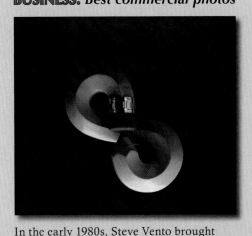

In the early 1980s, Steve Vento brought commercial photography to the community of Olympia. Today, his photography is intricately woven into the Olympia scene, appearing on billboards, in annual reports and on phonebook covers. Vento Photography has done a little bit of something for every type of business in town. Vento knows how to deliver an idea or capture audience imagination with his work. He also handles restoration photography work, and has a great reputation as a portrait photographer. Vento has put the very best light and angle on portraits of families, governors, state and corporate officials. He is a supporter of Olympia's Chamber of Commerce and takes an active part in community functions. The photography that goes into a credit card or a lottery ticket is very possibly Vento's work. His work also appears in numerous magazines. The Vento Photography website functions as a stunning portfolio of his talents. A few quick clicks take you through some of the variety Vento has encountered. The businesses of Olympia know him for his professional work, fair prices and community involvement. Next time you need a professional photographer capable of portraying the heart and soul of your business, turn to Vento Photography. He'll put his creativity to work for you.

120 State Avenue NE, Olympia WA
(360) 786-1206
www.ventophotography.com

Bartels Men's Store

FASHION: *Best high quality men's store in Olympia*

Bartels Men's Store is a refreshing change in the men's apparel market for a number of reasons. For instance, the staff of Bartels is friendly and knowledgeable about the unique concerns of men looking for traditional and updated apparel. They provide very high quality clothing choices, including custom-tailored clothes, shoes and accessories. In addition, the staff is well trained and friendly, and Bartels has created a comfortable shopping experience that allows customers to get appropriate clothing for their body type and personal fashion taste. They believe that whatever looks good on you is what fashion is all about, and they will extend their services to include whatever it takes for you to look good when you leave their store. They carry many lines of clothing, including Tommy Bahama, St. Croix, Pills Khais, Swiss Army Apparel, HS Trask, Tallia, Remy Leathers and Cutter and Buck. For a comfortable and welcoming excursion into men's clothing options, include a visit to Bartels Men's Store on your Olympia schedule.

501 Capitol Way S, Olympia WA
(360) 786-6634

Dorthea's by Design

FASHION: *Best store for plus sizes*

Dorthea's By Design has been providing beautiful clothing for plus-size women in downtown Olympia since 2002. Owner Dorthea Paulson, a professionally trained fashion designer and seamstress, had been working in alterations and tailoring for 15 years prior to opening her own store. She had always felt the need to design clothing for plus-size women, and still feels like the retail industry could be doing a better job in this area. When she saw the need for a plus-size boutique in the Olympia area, she took it as an opportunity to open her very own store. With behind-the-scenes support and encouragement from her husband, Dorthea is now able to offer items not found in regular department stores. She personally selects clothing that is unique, easy-care and good quality. She's known for her personal service, such as free fitting and hemming, and does the sewing herself, right in the store. Dorthea's design training comes in handy when selecting styles and doing alterations, because she knows fabrics as well as body types and what works best for the individual. Dorthea can custom design and make one-of-a-kind outfits by special request. Stop in at Dorthea's By Design in downtown Olympia and discover this wonderful boutique that specializes in beautiful clothing for women of size and great accessories for everyone.

418 Washington Street SE, Olympia WA
(360) 753-8706

Bonaventure

FASHION: *Best upscale women's shoe boutique*

Owner Jeanne Carras is fulfilling her dreams with an upscale boutique catering to women. Located in the New Caldonia building, her shop is called Bonaventure. Jeanne and her staff are dedicated to helping people buy shoes, as well as handbags and hosiery. They focus on educating customers in buying the correct shoes for their feet, personal style and needs. They serve customers by measuring and fitting them in the old-fashioned shoe store style. Jeanne's commitment to quality came from her parents, but her daughter was the inspiration behind opening the store. Jeanne initially considered opening a clothing shop. She quickly realized the one thing downtown Olympia lacked was a shoe store and Bonaventure was born. The name of her boutique is very important to her, as it came from her old family Bible. Bonaventure was a saint whose name means good fortune, and he was known to spread peace in the community. Jeanne is also a peace spreader; she believes in giving back and appreciates all of those who have helped her succeed. She has strong convictions about contributing to the community and is involved in the Olympia Downtown Association, Thurston County Chamber and the Olympia Symphony Orchestra. Jeanne believes that shoes aren't just an accessory, but the most important part of a woman's wardrobe. Visit her at Bonaventure on your next trip to Olympia.

116 5th Avenue SE, Olympia WA
(360) 943-4899 or (877) 943-4899
www.bonaventureshoes.com

Fair Portia
FASHION: *Best handcrafted jewelry*

Nestled beneath the glass atrium in the New Caledonia building, you will find Fair Portia, a tiny jewel box of a boutique, offering one-of-a-kind handcrafted jewelry by Gina Vitale Syrja. Timeless jewelry with a romantic edge, Gina's designs sparkle at a black tie event, yet are just as easily worn with a favorite pair of jeans. The ethereal effect of her jewelry stems from textile techniques such as crocheting and knitting bejeweled threads of fine silver and gold wire. The results are captivating, subtle, highly wearable works of art for any occasion. Gina is particularly known for her elegant, original jewelry for wedding parties. Gina chose Shakespeare's fair Portia as her muse to capture the romantic style of her jewelry. She goes to great lengths to find exquisite materials for her jewelry and from vintage Swarovski to sapphires, every gem tells a story. Fair Portia began when Gina's close childhood friend, Didi Jones, heard of Gina's desire to be home with her young daughter and sent her some jewelry tools. More than a decade later, Gina is still adding to her repertoire. Gina appreciates the gift of family, affectionately referring to her mother as "my hero" and gratefully acknowledging the support of her husband and daughter. Fair Portia presents an annual fashion show featuring women who have made positive contributions to the Olympia community. In addition, Gina donates her pieces to important causes in the Olympia area and serves on committees benefitting the arts. If you are looking for gorgeous hand-hewn jewelry, visit Fair Portia and let Gina assist you.

116 5th Avenue SE, Olympia WA
(360) 359-5307

Panowicz Jewelers
FASHION: *Best collection of jewelry designs*

From the minute you step into Panowicz Jewelers, you know you have found one of the real gems of the Northwest. You find yourself welcomed into the store like you would welcome a friend into your home, and that may be the perfect way to describe the Panowicz Jewelers experience. Elegant yet inviting, the warm tones of the decor showcase a remarkable collection of fine jewelry from around the world. Founded in 1948, and located across from Olympia's Farmers Market, Panowicz Jewelers is family-owned and operated. Rob and Linda Panowicz provide their clients with exquisitely beautiful, yet very wearable collections of jewelry. Whether it is from world-renowned designers like Hearts on Fire and Roberto Coin or a custom design, their commitment to excellence and client satisfaction will come shining through, giving you a lifetime of pleasure while becoming an heirloom to be treasured by future generations. Ready to welcome you is a team of jewelry professionals who share this passion for fine jewelry. Forget their years of jewelry experience. Forget the wall covered with their professional qualifications. What you will find is a wonderful group of people united in their desire to help you commemorate the celebrations of life, whether that be a wedding, the birth of a child, a promotion, or "just because." Rob and Linda genuinely and warmly invite you to get to know them and their special way of doing business.

111 Market Street NE, #104, Olympia WA
(360) 357-4943
www.panowicz.com

Doria's

FASHION: *Best women's boutique in downtown Olympia*

In the heart of downtown Olympia is Doria's, a women's boutique designed to meet all aspects of a lady's fashion needs from prom to motherhood. Tami Perman created her shop in 2000, naming it after her late grandmother who was a tremendous inspiration and a contributor to her flair for fashion. Like its namesake, Doria's is very involved in the community, and the staff of this fine enterprise believes it is the giving back that measures success. The staff of Doria's is well versed and experienced in assisting with a wide variety of fashion needs. While perhaps best known for their formals, this shop has everything else a woman might need, from cute tops to shoes and accessories. The energy present during the busy times of the year, such as a prom or fashion show, is only part of what makes this place special. It is the old-fashioned service and care that the staff shows to each and every customer that really stands out, and it is said that you won't leave Doria's without making a friend. For a chance to experience why people come all the way from Seattle, start a new friendship at this special place next time you're in Olympia.

418½ Washington Street SE, Olympia
(360) 753-1088

Precious Metalsmith
FASHION: *Best custom jewelry*

The art of custom jewelry design is alive and well at Precious Metalsmith, located in the New Caldonia Building in Olympia's historic district. Precious Metalsmith is a full-service jewelry store with a team of talented jewelers and designers who combine Old World quality with modern craftsmanship. Christopher and Joanna Thornton pride themselves on creating distinctive pieces for individuals, couples, families and groups. They specialize in uniquely crafted wedding rings and appreciate being part of those special moments. Chris and Joanna's talents are especially showcased in their use of an ancient Japanese technique called *Mokume Gane* that uses contrasting metals to achieve a wood-like pattern. Because this technique forges two metals into one, it is a fitting metaphor for marriage. Many cultures are represented in their stylish creations, including Celtic-inspired pieces that reflect their Scottish ancestry. Other custom metal products include candle sticks and teapots. Precious Metalsmith is known for taking on challenging repair work many other jewelers don't have the skills or tools to handle. Joanna's natural talents were evident from the time she was a child. She began her design career by making souvenir jewelry for tourists in her Michigan hometown. Chris uses his background in computers to design and manufacture jewelry with the aid of high-tech equipment. Joanna and Chris invite you to see the wonderful artistry on display at Precious Metalsmith.

120 State Avenue NE, #271, Olympia WA (360) 870-4391
www.preciousmetalsmith.com

Floral Ingenuity and Weiks Wild Bird Shop
GARDENS, PLANTS & FLOWERS: *Best Olympia florist*

The many loyal customers of Floral Ingenuity and Weiks Wild Bird Shop comment on the friendliness and courtesy of the staff. It is obvious the owners believe in building long-term relationships. Buck and Elly Weiks, and their son Leon, have been serving their community since 1981 with their creative, unique floral design abilities and their knowledge of backyard birding products. On the floral side of the business, the designs are easily recognizable due to the distinctiveness of their creations. Floral Ingenuity creates high style and unusual designs, but also handles the more traditional types of arrangements. Their flowers are professionally processed and pampered for long-lasting beauty. Every order receives personal attention to assure the best quality. Floral Ingenuity provides local delivery, using their own delivery staff, to ensure careful handling of their delicate creations. Orders can also be sent globally using their worldwide floral wire service. The community is so trusting of Buck's skill that customers often request a "Buck Do," which shows Buck's ingenious and distinctive expression. On the bird side of the business, customers can choose from a large selection of bird and squirrel food, feeders, houses and seed. Leon, who is also important to the operation, is the creator of the Weiks Mix Bird Seed, their top-selling product. Call Floral Ingenuity and see firsthand what makes this combination floral and bird shop such a special place, or check out their website.

2704 Pacific Avenue, Olympia WA (360) 786-0101 or (800) 864-3871
www.floralingenuity.com

Great Western Supply and The Barn Nursery
GARDENS, PLANTS & FLOWERS: *Best garden supplies*

Although owner Dan O'Neill didn't start Great Western Supply and The Barn Nursery until 1978, the legacy of the O'Neill family business reaches back to 1896. Dan began Great Western when he recognized that dairy farmers had excess manure and consumers had a need for well-mixed soil for their lawns and gardens. It was a win-win situation and Great Western Supply was created. As the bulk products expanded, many baseball fields and community gardens were built with donated material. Dan says, " The customers planted a seed, no pun intended, to start a nursery by exclaiming over and over, I drive all the way out here to buy my manure, it certainly would be

kind of you to sell a rhododendron or rose." In 1986 they turned the old red barn next to Great Western Supply into a nursery and called it The Barn Nursery. The O'Neill family has made it a priority to provide a variety of educational resources and job-related opportunities in cooperation with the Olympia Tumwater Foundation, South Puget Sound Community College Foundation and the Community Foundation. Their community involvement has won them the award for the Best Small Business in Thurston County. Whether you need topsoil, plants or a special tool, the O'Neill family will help you beautify your landscape and better the community.

9418 Old Highway 99 SE, Olympia WA (Great Western Supply) (360) 754-3722
9510 Old Highway 99 SE, Olympia WA (The Barn Nursery) (360) 943-2826
www.thebarnnurseryolympia.com

Apple Physical Therapy

HEALTH: *Voted top place to work in South Puget Sound*

Washington native Randy Johnson, partner and CEO of Apple Physical Therapy, first opened his company in 1984 as a way to support his family. Since opening he has helped his business evolve into an organization that supports many families and serves individuals throughout the Puget Sound region with clinics in 23 locations. Company President and CEO Claude Ciancio came to work for Apple Physical Therapy in 1990 and achieved partnership in 1998. Ciancio comes from New York City, but his commitment to patients and the community aligns him firmly with Johnson's original goals for service to patients and the communities where patients reside. Randy and Claude believe in the Golden Rule as well as five core elements, which they feel have made Apple Physical Therapy the success it is today. These five elements are, in order, Integrity, Knowledge, Compassion, Profit and Fun. For patients at any of the Apple facilities, these core tenets create a welcoming and comforting environment that is ideal for both working and healing. Employees, via a *Business Examiner* magazine poll, named Apple Physical Therapy as the number one place to work in the Puget Sound area. Whether you are searching for rehabilitation services or a new career, the staff at Apple Physical Therapy invites your family to become part of their family.

3015 Limited Lane NW, Suite B, Olympia WA
(360) 709-0700
www.applept.com

A rocky beach on the Puget Sound

Premiere Salon & Spa

HEALTH & BEAUTY: *Best salon spa*

Kelly Bakala believes in the power of touch to relax people and make life better in her hometown of Olympia. Her Premiere Salon & Spa is an urban retreat. Patrons can take advantage of 20 years of experience in body care while building the kind of relationships that allow them to slip into a calming state of mind and enjoy the many services she offers. Located just across from the Olympia Farmer's Market, Premiere is a full-service spa with a highly educated and knowledgeable staff. Respected for their use of top products, such as the Aveda line of body and skin care treatments, the staff feels it doesn't matter who you are or what you do, you will always be welcome here. Kelly and her employees strive to bring the latest trends and styles in hair, nail, skin and body care to customers. When you're in Olympia next, spend an afternoon in restful luxury surrounded by a fantastic team of specialists who are concerned only with your relaxation and satisfaction.

111 Market Street NE, Suite 101, Olympia WA
(360) 753-3299
www.premieresalonandspa.com

Accent Import Stone, Inc.

HOME: *Best natural stone and tile*

Rod Dresser's father taught him the importance of pursuing his passion, and instilled a drive to do things right the first time. Rod has taken his father's lessons to heart as owner of Accent Import Stone in downtown Olympia. Rod learned the craft of stone and tile design, fabrication and maintenance under his father's guidance. Even though Rod, Sr. passed away in 1993, Accent Import Stone remains a family-owned and operated business. Rod's mother Pauline is the showroom manager, with 50 years of experience to her credit; and all six of Rod's children are involved in the business in various capacities. The moment you walk in the door, it is clear that superior products and service are of utmost importance. The Dresser family is committed to working with you to make your vision a reality. Accent Import Stone specializes in exceptional products including durable, contemporary glass tile, elegant natural stone and beautiful Mexican handcrafted ceramic tiles. Also featured is the energy efficient NuHeat radiant heat floor system that keeps tile floors warm and toasty. Everything you need for proper installation and care of your stone and tile is available, along with expert advice and outstanding customer service. The Dresser family invites you to visit the showroom at Accent Import Stone. The selection, service and quality you find will surely exceed your expectations.

112 State Avenue, Olympia WA
(360) 956-0309
www.accentimportstoneinc.com

Canvas Works

HOME: *Best source of all things canvas*

When Nancy Graybeal started making kites and windsocks for her children, little did she know that her beachside hobby would turn into a business to showcase her expertise. Recognizing a need for good canvas work, especially canvas bags and custom boat coverings, Canvas Works was born. For more than 25 years, Canvas Works has been a family-owned and operated business. Nancy's husband, Gary, along with their children Amy, Brandon and Lia share a passion for the fiber arts and are all avid hobbyists. They love their jobs, especially when they have the opportunity to educate people and help them find what they need. Canvas Works specializes in top quality marine canvas products and hardware, awnings and patio furniture coverings. An excellent selection of apparel, outerwear, and decorator fabrics, patterns and accessories are also available. Canvas Works' also includes a knitting shop, with an incredible fabric assortment and a jaw-dropping array of colors and textures. Whether you're a beginner or looking to improve your knitting and purling skills, they have class for you. Canvas Works is closed on Sundays, but is open late on Mondays to allow customers to socialize, have a cup of tea and share their latest fabric creations and patterns. The Graybeals invite you to visit their new 8,000-square-foot downtown Olympia facility and experience the superiority and selection of all things fiber at Canvas Works.

525 Columbia Street SW, Olympia WA
(360) 352-4481
www.canvasworks.net

Olympia Fireplace & Spa

HOME: *Best fireplace and spa company*

Owner Dick Sowell and his staff at Olympia Fireplace & Spa know a lot about staying warm while enjoying the good life. They sell gas, wood and pellet fireplaces and stoves, plus barbecues, spas and awnings. The store displays more than 50 models of fireplaces and stoves. You can view freestanding and built-in barbecues in the patio display area, or step in and literally test the waters in the spa area. Olympia Fireplace & Spa carries only the highest quality products. Look for spas by Sundance and Nordic, barbecues by Weber, Ducane and Lynx, and fireplaces and stoves by such respected manufacturers as Vermont Castings, Heat N Glo Country Stoves and Quadrafire. Olympia Fireplace & Spa sells directly to consumers and works with about 75 area contractors. Staff members are heating experts with from six to 20 years of experience in their fields. You'll receive thoughtful advice from some of the best problem solvers in the field and the knowledge that you have chosen a quality product from a trusted local supplier with the expertise to install and service your purchase. Good old-fashioned customer service has earned Dick and his staff countless compliments and the gratitude of many homeowners. Dick takes his commitment to his employees seriously, and has a close working relationship with his veteran staff. Visit Olympia Fireplace & Spa to put fashionable and hardworking fireplaces, stoves and spas in your home. A second store is located in Chehalis.

506 E 4th Avenue, Olympia WA
(360) 352-4328
1331 NW Louisiana Avenue, Chehalis WA
(360) 740-6910
www.olympiafireplace.com

Selden's Home Furnishings

HOME: *Best home furnishings in Olympia*

George Koehler worked for the original owners of Selden's Home Furnishings for 31 years before purchasing the store from the Selden family in 1973, and you can still spy George from time to time as you visit the shop. The integrity and high quality merchandise that the store has offered at this location since 1947 draws many people to the heart of Olympia for their home furnishing needs. Selden's has a wide variety of home furnishings from such famous names as Ekornes, Thomasville, Lane, Broyhill, La-Z-boy, Karastan, Montana, Spring Air and Tempur-pedic. With two floors of showroom display and qualified designers, Selden's is a fun place to get ideas for your home. High-end quality at a good price and involvement in the community are important aspects of what Selden's offers, but friendly employees and the personalized assistance they represent are just as valuable. As a family-owned business that has been around for nearly 60 years, Selden's has a large community of loyal customers who appreciate the special touch of old-fashioned service. With the ability to make customized drapes and carpets, as well as provide personal decorating consultations, Selden's has stayed on the cutting edge of the home furnishings market. Take the time to visit this downtown Olympia icon.

220 Legion Way SE, Olympia WA
(360) 357-5531
www.seldensofolympia.com

Meconi's Italian Subs
RESTAURANTS & CAFÉS:
Best sub shop

Like many East Coast transplants, when Wayne and Nancy Meconi arrived in Olympia in the early 1980s, they were glad to be there, but they also missed some things from home. Their loss resulted in a big gain for Olympia when they opened the first Meconi's Italian Subs in 1986. The Meconis left Pennsylvania when Wayne was laid off from the steel mills. Life was good in Olympia, but Wayne couldn't find a good sub shop, at least nothing like the family-owned shops that seemed to be on every corner back in Williamsport. He remodeled a three-car garage in his spare time with the idea of starting his own shop and creating a little side job. After plenty of research and tracking down the right ingredients for authentic East Coast flavors, he opened the doors on what remains his Lacey Boulevard location. The sub shop was an immediate hit and Nancy quit her job to work full-time in the shop. In 1993, daughter Maria joined the business as manager for a second location near the Capitol Building in downtown Olympia. With homemade sub rolls made fresh and ingredients that agreed with Wayne's very particular taste buds, it's no wonder that the *Daily Olympian* has voted Meconi's the Best Sub Shop every year since the voting began. Visit Meconi's Italian Subs and find out for yourself just what Wayne was missing when he set about bringing an East Coast-style sub shop to the West Coast.

1051 Capitol Way S, Olympia WA
(360) 534-0240
5225A Lacey Boulevard SE, Lacey WA
(360) 459-0213
www.meconissubs.com

Nonna Rosa Café & Tea Room
RESTAURANTS & CAFÉS: *Best tea room in Olympia*

The Nonna Rosa Café & Tea Room serves a wonderful international variety of dishes. Located on New Caldonia Avenue in downtown Olympia, surrounded by specialty boutiques and art displays, proprietor Nancy Omana Caiafa offers her guests a taste of Europe and a touch of the Orient. Nancy was born in the Philippines and spent most of her adult life in Europe. She inherited fine dining from her mother, who was a caterer, and her expertise in Italian food from her mother-in-law, Rosa. Visitors have come from all over the world, and Nonna Rosa Café displays a guest book saturated with compliments. The atrium provides a relaxed atmosphere for a light lunch, midday coffee or tea break, or the chance to refuel during a marathon shopping spree. Try a hot or cold *panini* filled with assorted meats and cheeses, fresh garden salad, chicken buns and noodle soup. Nonna Rosa's traditionally British afternoon tea is served in charming tea dishes, along with petite

portions of sandwiches, and warm scones smothered with English clotted cream, lemon curd or jam. Freshly brewed Vesuvio coffee, English, Ceylon, China and Indian tea, and Italian sodas are available. Nancy is known for her delightful tea parties and other special events that involve music, good food and excellent service with door prizes and lots of surprises. Unique gift items are on sale for all occasions. When in Olympia, stop at Nonna Rosa and say hello to Nancy, sample the wonderful food, and be sure to sign the guestbook.

116 E 5th Avenue, Olympia WA
(360) 705-0850 or (360) 480-2197

Plenty Restaurant & Catering
RESTAURANTS & CAFÉS: *Best late night dining*

When it comes to late-night dining options in Olympia there is one option that really stands out. Plenty Restaurant & Catering is a family-owned and operated business with a staff composed of all different ages, styles and personalities. The interior of the restaurant possesses a unique character and atmosphere, painted with random colors in fun and whimsical patterns. Upon entering Plenty you know you're in an fun place. Owners Jim and Nichol Butigan, along with daughter Sophie, are all involved with the running both the restaurant and catering side of the operation. They all love the downtown atmosphere of Olympia and enjoy offering live music on Thursday

nights to enhance the experience of visiting their establishment. Jim was raised in Olympia. After living in Chicago for a time, he returned to open the restaurant. With the establishment of Plenty Restaurant, the Butigans can offer a place where the community can get something to eat when everything else is closed. They are considered one of the best catering companies in town, offering a wide variety of options for almost any occasion. Whether you need a late-night bite, a weekend brunch, or catering for a party, Plenty Restaurant & Catering will have plenty of good options.

200 4th Avenue W, Olympia WA
(360) 705-3716
www.plentyrestaurant.com

Ranch House BBQ

RESTAURANTS & CAFÉS: *Best BBQ of the South Sound*

The people at Ranch House BBQ know a thing or two about real barbeque. Pitmaster and Founder Amy Anderson and her team have traveled the national competition circuit for more than 13 years. They have won grand championships at the Washington, California, Arizona and Nevada state BBQ competitions. They took the Grand Championship at the Canadian International and the World Championship in Ireland in 2000. FoodNetwork filmed them for a show called BBQ Country Cook-Off as they participated in the Jack Daniel's World Championship Invitational in Lynchburg, Tennessee under the name Mad Momma & the Kids. Shortly thereafter, Amy and Co-founder Melanie Tapia, Olympia natives, stumbled across a building they knew would be perfect for a barbeque house. They opened the doors in 2004. At Ranch House BBQ, the staff prepares authentic, finger-licking barbeque just for you. The meats are seasoned with Amy's secret dry rub seasoning or glazed with her award-winning BBQ sauce. Then they are cooked low and slow. Chicken and pork ribs smoke for six hours over apple and cherry wood from the Anderson family farm. Pork shoulder and beef brisket smoke for up to 18 hours and are so flavorful that they require no sauce. Add some sides and you have a meal you will never forget. The restaurant also offers takeout and full-service catering. Since opening, Ranch House BBQ has continued to win awards. The FoodNetwork recently visited Olympia to film Amy, Melanie and the rest of the staff for a special called Grill Girls that premiered in June. The Ranch House BBQ is a must visit for all.

10841 Kennedy Creek Road SW, Olympia WA
(360) 866-8704
www.ranchhousebbq.net

Southern Kitchen

RESTAURANTS & CAFÉS: *Best Southern cooking*

Olympia is a long way from Alabama, but that distance closes considerably when you walk into Southern Kitchen, located in Olympia's Ramada Governor House. Owner Gloria Martin hails from Alabama, where her father taught her the art of cooking. She learned not only to prepare marvelous Southern dishes from scratch, but to sprinkle those dishes with generous helpings of love and hospitality. Her first Southern Kitchen opened in 1995 in Tacoma. Its popularity eventually led to the opening a second restaurant a decade later. Gloria and her staff bring fun and energy to the restaurants. She loves her staff like family, and she personally teaches her chefs how to create dynamite Southern dishes out of whole foods. Gloria believes Southern cooking is to be shared, so she created restaurants that pass on the traditions of Southern hospitality by encouraging people to get to know each other over a great meal. Come to Southern Kitchen hungry, because the portions are generous. Try the chicken fried steak made with Gloria's secret batter and a strawberry lemonade. You'll find all the Southern staples here, like black-eyed peas, collard greens, catfish, liver and onions and fried green tomatoes. Southern Kitchen has served many celebrities and looks forward to serving you. Enjoy great food and true charm at Southern Kitchen, where the best of the South meets the Pacific Northwest.

621 Capitol Way S, Olympia WA
(360) 943-8300
1716 6th Avenue, Tacoma WA
(253) 627-4282

Veritas Olympia
RESTAURANTS & CAFÉS:
Best arty café

Veritas Olympia is a Christian café devoted to the visual and performing arts. Dan and Randi Schaubert launched Veritas in the fall of 2005. The classy space features local art, uplifting music and wireless Internet access. Veritas works in conjunction with Track10.com to find the best talent in the Northwest Christian music scene. It also offers comedy acts, a family game night, an open mike and a Karaoke night. The food menu is simple but delicious. It aims toward Italian bistro with paninis, pasta and Caesar salads. Top beverage choices include Caffé D'arte espresso, Tempest teas and blended drinks. Dan and Randi believe in supporting the organizations they believe in and use profits from Veritas to fund Family Life Skills, a nonprofit service organization. Proceeds from the local art displayed at Veritas go into a kid's art program called Light of the World. Randi believes in helping children find creative skills at an early age, and still recalls the thrill of winning her first blue ribbon for artwork she created in kindergarten. Veritas rents its upstairs loft for meetings and business luncheons. For a peaceful environment with quality food and entertainment, the Schauberts invite you to visit Veritas Olympia, a downtown family hot spot that is making a difference.

109 N Capitol Way,
Olympia WA
(360) 352-4920
www.veritasolympia.com

Waterstreet Café & Bar
RESTAURANTS & CAFÉS:
Best progressive American cuisine

Waterstreet Café owner Jeff Taylor was raised in Olympia by a family committed to fresh food, and it shows in his diverse and eclectic menu. Long regarded as one of the region's most innovative and original chefs, Taylor's newest project builds on the traditions of fantastic food and stellar service that have long been a hallmark of his restaurant endeavors. With a mix of inventive dining options ranging from American to Italian classics, Waterstreet Café enhances the culinary experience with gorgeous views of the Capitol Campus and nearby Capitol Lake. It is a favorite hangout of locals, but has increasingly become a haunt of visitors from all over the world who are impressed that such a fine restaurant exists outside of a major metropolitan area. In the spring and summer, Waterstreet offers a five-course tasting menu using fresh ingredients purchased from local fisherman, ranchers and farmers. They offer an extensive and affordable wine list, as well as the only on-staff wine steward in the Olympia area. To see how Taylor has taken formerly common foods and updated them to become uncommon specialty cuisine, make Waterstreet Café & Bar a stop on your Olympia itinerary.

610 Water Street SW, Olympia WA
(360) 709-9090 *www.waterstreetcafeolympia.com*

Basilico Ristorante
RESTAURANTS & CAFÉS: *Best Italian cuisine in Olympia*

When two northern Italians, Samuele Lucchese of Genova and Arlindo Moraes of Bologna, met in Tacoma over a very good bottle of Barolo wine, their conversation turned to home and the lack of authentic northern Italian food in the South Puget Sound area. It wasn't spaghetti-and-meatball American Italian cuisine they craved, but regional Italian recipes and handmade, hand-cut pastas. In late 2005, the two men opened Basilico in downtown Olympia. Samuele and Arlindo believe in keeping food simple in the true Italian way, an art that allows the food to express its own flavor. They and their crew prepare every meal, every sauce and every pasta variety from scratch. Patrons can view the pasta chef preparing and cutting the pasta just moments before it is served. They really know Italian food, and guests will get a true taste of Italy. There's much to savor on

the Basilico menu, including *filetto al sale tartufato*, a filet mignon grilled with truffle salt and served with potatoes shaped as mushrooms, or *maltagliati all'antica con pesto*, freshly made pasta tossed with pesto and served with green beans and potato. The well rounded menu features a long list of tantalizing antipasti appetizers, plus top-notch soups and salads. To complement your meal, Arlindo and Samuele offer some of the best Italian wines available at surprisingly reasonable prices. For freshness you can see and taste, visit Basilico Ristorante.

507A Capitol Way S, Olympia WA
(360) 570-8777

Percival Landing
Photo by Jonathan Spangler

Brewery City Pizza

RESTAURANTS & CAFÉS:
Best pizza in Olympia

Our Pizza Tops 'Em All! That has been the slogan at Brewery City Pizza since the opening of their first restaurant in Tumwater in 1982, just one mile south of the old Olympia Brewing Company. Two more restaurants have since opened in nearby Olympia. Local ownership, long-standing management, and commitment to community have helped make these restaurants hometown favorites for almost a quarter of a century. Good food, attentive service, and spotless restaurants are the focal points of success for Brewery City Pizza. All sauces, original hand-tossed and new thin-crust dough, focaccia bread, and tomato basil soup are made fresh daily. Menu creations are assembled and served by an exceptionally loyal and friendly staff. What started as one restaurant offering pizza, sandwiches, and a salad bar has evolved into three restaurants with full service menus. Gone is the salad bar and in its place are entrée salads. Added to the menu are appetizers, pastas, calzones, bistro pizzas, and focaccia sandwiches. Stop in and sample a shrimp cocktail, garden fresh spinach salad or perhaps chicken parmigiana pasta. If your heart is set on pizza, Brewery City Pizza is the place to go. Choose from their many original favorites or bistro pizzas, or create your own masterpiece from their large list of toppings. Handcrafted and baked to order, Brewery City pizzas top 'em all.

4353 Martin Way East, Olympia WA
(360) 491-6630
2705 Limited Lane Northwest, Olympia
(360) 754-7800
5150 Capitol Boulevard, Tumwater WA
(360) 754-6767

BREWERY CITY
- EST. 1982 -

Finders Keepers Antique Mall

SHOPPING:
Best antiques in Olympia

The slogan at Finders Keepers Antique Mall is The most fun place to shop in Olympia. Finders Keepers is known for great prices and the highest percentage of quality merchandise in the area. This mall has something for everyone, from romantic, edgy, retro vintage clothing, to delicate teacups and stunning furniture. They have a ratio of 90-percent authentic to 10-percent reproduction. Finders Keepers, with extended hours for the after-work crowd, was voted the 2005 Best of Olympia in the antique store category. If you are looking for something specific and can't find it at Finders Keepers, you can add your name to the want list and the dealers will treasure shop for you. Owner Deena Collins has always loved treasure hunting at garage sales and antique stores. She decorated her house this way. When the opportunity arose for her to become an antique mall owner, she took it and ran. Deena is doing what she loves. Her dream was to be a part of the downtown and have an organized, clean, high-end store a reputation for being a destination for antique buyers. This shop a treasure trove. Visit Finders Keepers to find your own buried treasure.

501 4th Avenue E, Olympia WA
(360) 943-6454

Archibald Sisters

SHOPPING: *Best bath products*

Archibald Sisters is a great one-stop shopping destination for any young-at-heart shopper looking for fine bath products, lotions, fragrances, gifts or jewelry. Archibald Sisters makes packages and sells its signature lotions and fragrances right at the store. You'll receive top-flight service from owners Susie Archibald and Phil Rollins and their 15 creative and exceedingly helpful employees. The store opened in 1975 as the dream child of sisters Susie and Shelley Archibald, with Phil handling the fragrances and lotions. It was their dream to sell usable products that would satisfy varied needs. The store has seen continuous growth over the years, but basically sells a product line much like the one first offered. You will find concentrated perfume oil essences, a hand-and-body lotion that perfectly blends vegetable moisturizers with vitamins, massage oil made from natural sweet almond oil, plus special shampoos and soaps. Men will approve of the popular Uppercut fragrance in spray cologne, and the pH balanced Aftershave Balm. The jewelry, toys and cards are all worth your attention. A visit to Archibald Sisters will make clear the reason for this store's success. Come smell the scents and find personal care products you will not want to live without. Once you've visited Archibald Sisters, you'll understand why this special store has so many faithful customers and a thriving mail order business.

406 Capitol Way S, Olympia WA (360) 943-5914 or (800) 943-2707
www.archibaldsisters.com

Wind Up Here

SHOPPING: *Best specialty toy store*

Conveniently located in downtown Olympia is a truly old-fashioned specialty toy store. Wind Up Here was created by its four local owners with a handshake around a kitchen table back in 1993. They're committed to helping you have a positive experience while you're in the store by helping you find exactly what you're looking for. They steer away from toys generally carried at the larger chain stores, with a focus away from violent toys, gender stereotyping and commercial licenses. They specialize in entertaining games, puzzles, infant gifts, novelties and wind-up toys. This is the store to visit if you're looking for unusual, zany or hard-to-find toys. You'll find the store fully stocked with more than 5,000 items. No matter what your age, there's a tremendous selection of toys, arts and crafts, and science-related items that will fascinate and stimulate your mind. Also featured is a glow-in-the-dark room, a dress-up boutique, specialty layette and baby equipment, and active and outdoor toys. Wind Up Here was voted Best Toy Store in South Sound for six years and has earned the Small Business of the Year award from the Economic Development Council. All the owners believe that play and learning are good for the heart. They're also responsible for starting the now nationwide Good to Grow program to identify great toys for children with special needs. Bring the kids and stop in at Wind Up Here when you're in downtown Olympia, and re-discover toys in a casual and relaxed environment.

121 Fifth Avenue SE, Olympia WA (360) 943-9045 or (800) 531-2616
www.winduphere.com

Photo courtesy of Salty's on Alki

PUYALLUP

Puyallup is home to the Puyallup Fair, which is the largest annual fair in Washington, attracting more than one million people a year. The Puyallup Fair is also one of the largest fairs in the country. The city itself is built around the Puyallup Fairgrounds. You can get an excellent view of the fairgrounds from the neighboring town of South Hill. The fair serves as an anchor for a host of one-of-a-kind businesses. The Daffodil Festival, in April, winds through Tacoma, Puyallup, Sumner and Orting.

PLACES TO GO

- Karshner Museum
  309 4th Street NE (253) 841-8748
- Meeker Mansion
  312 Spring Street (253) 848-1770
- Bradley Lake Park
  531 31st Avenue SE
- Clark's Creek Park
  1700 12th Avenue SW
- Pioneer Park
  324 S Meridian
- Wildwood Park
  1101 23rd Avenue SE

THINGS TO DO

April
- The Daffodil Festival *(253) 863-9524*
- Puyallup Spring Fair *(253) 841-5045*

May
- Art & Wine Walk
  Downtown (253) 840-6015

June
- Meeker Days Festival *(253) 840-2631*

September
- Puyallup Fair *(253) 841-5045*
- Puyallup Pro Rodeo *(253) 841-5045*

October
- Art & Wine Walk
  Downtown (253) 840-6015

Photo by Tom Harpel

The Wild Side

ANIMALS & PETS: *Best pet store in Puyallup*

Pets are tantamount at The Wild Side. Open since 2004, The Wild Side is a unique pet store specializing in every type of pet and pet product you need, including household and exotic pets such as hedgehogs, coveys, ground squirrels and wallabies. Owners Cindy Taylor and Cari Aida have more than 60 years of experience in the pet industry. They opened The Wild Side to give

the community a resourceful place for good information, quality animals and the best products. The staff is extraordinary. Customer service is a top priority, so when you visit, you can expect to have a great experience. It is one of the few pet stores in the area that is USDA licensed. They are renowned for their quality animals. Every pet comes with a seven-day health guarantee and a free veterinary exam. At The Wild Side, they are focused on making the right match of animal to human rather than just making sales. They do their best to ensure all animals are placed into a good home and that new owners receive the most compatible pet. Visit The Wild Side and take home a new family member.

11012 Canyon Road E, Suite 3, Puyallup WA
(253) 538-WILD (9453)
www.thewildsidepetswa.com

The Quilt Barn

ARTS & CRAFTS: *Best quilt shop in Puyallup*

The Quilt Barn has everything you need for quilting from start to finish. Owner Pam Hewitt has more than 20 years experience in the quilting industry. Her staff of Sue, Robin, Denise, Carol, Lynda and Gretchen are all quilters, with close to 20 years experience between them. The Quilt Barnis known for its extensive fabric selections. Not only do they have a large variety and selection, they carry more than 4,000 bolts of fabric with specialties such as batiks, florals, and flannels. The Quilt Barn offers a range of classes from beginner to intermediate. Pam teaches most

of the classes herself and actually taught classes at the store before she bought it. In addition, they host quilt clubs that allow people from all skill levels to get together and quilt. Pam has a great visual gift with an eye for color and detail. She sews daily just for the fun of it. Visit The Quilt Barn to see her many creations all over the shop. The Quilt Barn will inspire you to let your creative juices flow.

1206 E Main, Puyallup WA
(253) 845-1532
or (800) 988-BARN (2276)
www.quiltbarn.com

Cascade Off Road

AUTO: *Best place for truck and SUV accessories in Puyallup*

Since 2003, Cascade Off Road has been Puyallup's favorite place to go for truck and SUV accessories. Owners Joe and Heidi Zaichkin specialize in gas and diesel performance, intakes and exhaust. But they are especially known for their customer service and the very knowledgeable and friendly staff they employ. They offer a full line of interior and exterior accessories, including nerf bars, running boards, winches and many other off-road products. Cascade Off Road carries parts for Chevy, Dodge, Ford, Toyota and Nissan, as well as other foreign and domestic trucks. Cascade Off Road is a full service shop featuring installation, information and service. Joe and Heidi opened Cascade Off Road because they were unable to find the quality of service they desired from an accessory shop. Cascade Off Road offers the best selection of accessories in the area for your vehicle. Go to Cascade Off Road for your truck or SUV accessories.

15012 Meridian Street E, Suite 1, Puyallup WA
(253) 840-1171
www.cascadeoffroad.com

Korum Automotive Group

AUTO: *Best family-owned dealership*

The intersection of Meridian and River Road is popularly known as Korum Korners, reflecting the growth of the Korum family of automobile dealerships. If you want to purchase a car in Puyallup, you will undoubtedly come in contact with a member of the Korum clan. Mel Korum came to Puyallup in 1956 and opened a Dodge dealership. Mel's son, Jerry, joined him in 1962. Together they were instrumental in opening several other dealerships in the community. These dealerships have generally been sold to other family members, so that almost every car dealership in town is owned by a Korum relative. Korum Automotive Group sells Ford, Hyundai and Mitsubishi vehicles. Jerry's formula for business success has been to put his employees first, his customers second and the community third. It's a formula that has had outstanding results. The whole family supports the community through their numerous philanthropic activities. The Korum for Kids Foundation was established to promote and improve the health, welfare and future of young people through donations to qualified organizations. If you happen to be in Puyallup on September 7, allow time to celebrate Korum Korners Day. Remember, too, Korum Automotive Group sells great cars and provides outstanding service. Time magazine nominated Jerry Korum and the Korum Automotive Group for the 2006 Quality Dealer Award. Welcome to Korum Korners; it's sure to be the beginning of a satisfying relationship between you and a great car family.

100 River Road, Puyallup WA
(253) 845-6600
www.korum.net

Martin Henry Coffee Roasters

BAKERIES, COFFEE & TEA:
Best coffee roasters

For a better cup of coffee, look no further than Martin Henry Coffee Roasters. Debbie and Dan Bennett acted on their desire to provide people with a distinctively better cup of coffee when they established Martin Henry Coffee Roasters. The name Martin Henry was selected in memory of Dan Bennett's grandfather. Based largely in part to Debbie's former employer and her infectious personality, the exemplary service at Martin Henry rivals that of service received from the larger retailers. Dan and Debbie's background in retail has helped them to maintain a high standard of excellence and provide the type of customer service they require at Martin Henry Coffee Roasters. The service is a fitting accompaniment to the extraordinary coffee served. Martin Henry does not pre-blend the green beans. Each one is roasted separately and then blended to create the most desirable characteristic and original flavor. At Martin Henry, they use a 100 percent chemical free Swiss water decaf process which uses only pure water. Upon completion of the very detailed process, the coffee beans are ready to be roasted into the best cup of coffee you will taste. Martin Henry Coffee Roasters strives to be the best, not the biggest, with a mission to provide the finest tasting coffee you can buy. Debbie and Dan invite you come into Martin Henry Coffee Roasters and find quality in every cup of coffee.

1114 River Road, Puyallup WA
(253) 848-3110
11401 Steele Street, Tacoma WA
(253) 848-6427

Pioneer Bakery

BAKERIES, COFFEE & TEA: *Best apple fritters*

Get in line early if you're headed to the Pioneer Bakery, because the locals have the showcases empty by 9 or 10 in the morning. One reason is the award-winning Pioneer Bakery apple fritter. The family-owned and operated Pioneer Bakery is a Puyallup hot spot. Jake and Patti Bostwick grew up in Puyallup. They bought the bakery, which has been in business since 1959, in 2005. Entering the bakery feels like stepping into the old West. Western décor and covered wagons help to create a warm environment. It is a place where locals and visitors can congregate and experience downtown Puyallup. If you are too late for the apple fritters, go for a donut. These baked goods are the best in town. Pioneer Bakery is also known for their homemade soups and huge chocolate chip cookies. Bread, sandwiches, pies, brownies and cheesecakes are also among the temptations you'll find hard to resist. Patti starts baking at four o'clock in the morning. Typically, she starts out making 200 donuts, after that she makes the breads and the cookies. There is always something rising or baking. The Pioneer has become a family affair, with all six of the Bostwick children working. A treasured employee makes the soups. Patti says, "We're that great little hole-in-the-wall bakery you look for when you travel to other places…" Visit the Pioneer, but try to get there early.

120 S Meridian Street, Puyallup WA
(253) 845-8336

Home Team Northwest

BUSINESS: *Best mortgage broker who's also a mortgage banker*

Doug Davey, owner of Home Team Northwest, opened his real estate business with a commitment to offer the community excellent service. The Home Team vision alters the traditional structure of the real estate business by utilizing a core support staff and Realtor® teams. The staff and agents, led by broker Terri Olson, are encouraged by the company to engage in intern and apprenticeship programs that offer education in hands-on field work and classroom theory. Giving such opportunities for personal growth and leadership development, while earning an income, is one of the many advantages Home Team Northwest offers their agents. The Home Team vision of serving clients at the highest level requires a team of specialized agents, such as buyer's specialists, listing specialists, land specialists, transaction specialists, and new construction specialists. Doug's philosophy, "The whole is much greater than the sum of the parts," led to his structure for the company. "Always being a trusted advisor to my clients, providing excellent service with integrity, putting others first, and building win-win relationships is paramount. I can meet and exceed that commitment with some of the best in the business, and I am excited about that." No matter what your real estate need, call Home Team Northwest.

2929 5th Avenue NE, #A, Puyallup WA
(253) 435-1515
www.hometeamnw.com

Mortgage By Design
BUSINESS: *Best loan specialists*

"You talk, we listen" is the motto of Mortgage By Design. Owners Michelle Cate and Kisha Weir, along with their dedicated and professional staff, represent more than 100 years of experience in the financial field. They are known for their caring attitudes and thrive on meeting the expectations of their clients. Financing a new home or investment property is a complicated process, with ever-changing conditions such as interest rates and financial markets. The staff at Mortgage By Design knows that every person and transaction is unique, and they will assist you in meeting all requirements in an efficient manner. Committed to effective communication, they keep you informed all the way through the loan process. Your peace of mind is important to them. Mortgage By Design will provide you with their written commitment to excellence of service. Michelle, Kisha and all the staff are very involved in their community and are a major benefactor of Helping Hand House. You can trust all your mortgage needs to a good neighbor; Mortgage By Design.

510 E Main, Suite D, Puyallup WA
(253) 864-6222
www.mortgagebydesign.com

The Liberty Theater
BUSINESS: *Best place for weddings, banquets and events*

The Liberty Theater is a reborn community treasure in Puyallup. Dominic Constanti built The Liberty Theater in 1924. Back then it was the most modern theater of its time, and was equipped with the latest-model projector equipment and a Wurlitzer organ. It featured seating for 900, a stage, dressing rooms, indirect stage flood lighting and an elaborate ventilation system. In 1999, Tom Neumann remodeled the theater and restored all of its finer points. Today, the Liberty is a full corporate event facility and grand event hall, complete with catering, bar, DJ services and complete video and audio production. The theater hosts such events as weddings, parties, dances, live concerts and expo shows. The Liberty is constantly being upgraded with the latest technology to keep this theater the most modern of its time. The Liberty Theatre has become the premier event facility in the Northwest. More than 1,650 weddings have taken place in the transformed building. For Tom, the restoration of old theaters is a way to recapture the days when life moved at a slower pace. As he says, "Strangers greeted one another on busy downtown streets, gentlemen

tipped their hats to address ladies, and warm hospitality was cherished by all." If you want to touch this more gracious time, visit The Liberty Theater.

116 W Main Avenue,
Puyallup WA
(253) 864-8116
www.thelibertytheater.com

Mac's Septic Service
BUSINESS: *Best septic service*

Virgil and Alice McKort established Mac's Septic Service in 1952. The McKorts retired in 1987, and their long-time employees Keith and Joyce Shotwell bought the business. Keith and Joyce knew the septic business well. Keith had the experience with septic systems, and Joyce had the office knowledge to continue the successful business started by the McKorts. They began ownership with only $2,000 in savings, but they knew they could make it work. With the grace of God, the business is flourishing. They give their customers great service, a fair price and a personal touch. They enjoy a large volume of business from realtors, as well as home and business owners. In 1995, Joyce bought Keith four portable toilets for a Christmas present. Keith said, "Well, I guess we're in the portable toilet business." He bought an old truck and converted it to service the portable toilets. Keith then purchased 10 more toilets. Today they have more than 200. They named the portable toilet business Mac's Affordable Portable, and Keith is now known as the "Colonel of the Urinal." Call the colonel if you need help with you septic system.

813 Shaw Road E, Puyallup WA
(253) 845-9517

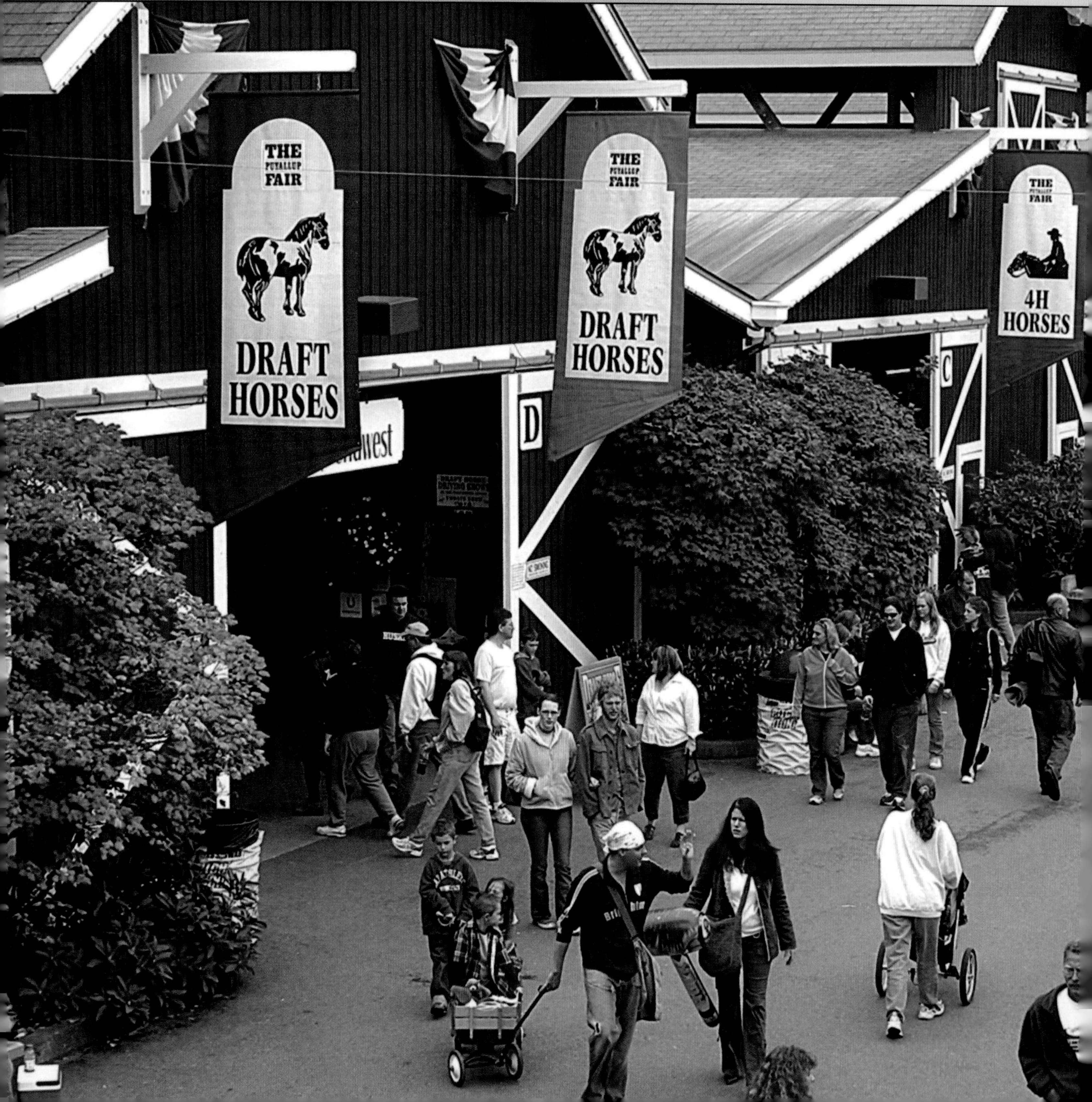

THE
PUYALLUP
FAIR

DRAFT
HORSES

THE
PUYALLUP
FAIR

DRAFT
HORSES

THE
PUYALLUP
FAIR

4H
HORSES

Puyallup Fair & Events Center
EVENTS:
Home of the best county fair

You know you're at the fair when the smell of popcorn, barbecue and hay merge with a kaleidoscopic array of color, and a chorus of midway hawkers and giggling children sing in your ear. The Puyallup Fair was conceived in June 1900 by a group of local businessmen, farmers and residents. Since then, it has become the sixth largest fair in the nation and eighth largest in the world. The Puyallup Fair & Events Center is a self-supporting, nonprofit organization that runs without government subsidies. The facility exists to support animals, agriculture, education and family values. It is a hub for community outreach programs, and hosts numerous events throughout the year, including the famous Puyallup Pro Rodeo and the Puyallup Spring Fair. Fairgoers are delighted with the abundant attractions, including the new ShowPlex Exhibition and Conference Center, which offers more than 122,000 square feet of high-tech, ground-level space and a professional staff dedicated to the highest levels of customer service. The Puyallup Fair & Events Center finds a myriad of ways to celebrate Puyallup, including Oktoberfest, art galas and home shows. Rodeos, expos and more than one annual fair keep this center buzzing with activity. For family entertainment and good times, visit the Puyallup Fair & Events Center.

110 9th Avenue SW, Puyallup WA
(253) 841-5045
www.thefair.com

Island Freeze Smoothie & Nutrition Center

FUN FOODS: *Best smoothies*

You may feel like you are on vacation when you walk into Island Freeze Smoothie & Nutrition Center. The décor is decidedly tropical. Palm trees and bamboo surround you as you are greeted with friendly smiles. The atmosphere is warm and relaxing, so take your time deciding on one of the more than 25 different smoothies they offer. Randall Pruitt is the brainchild behind Island Freeze. He and his wife, Shannon, have been in business since 2003. Randall had almost 20 years of experience as an executive chef, and it disturbed him that he couldn't find a really great smoothie with fresh ingredients instead of artificial flavoring and syrups. He set out to create a bold-tasting smoothie that didn't just taste wonderful, but was nutritional, too. Island Freeze Smoothie uses the finest and freshest fruits and real fruit juices. You won't hear a can opener opening a single can or find a drop of syrup in the place. There's an entire menu of nutritional supplements to add to your smoothie as well, for that extra healthful punch to your wildly-good-for-you drink. Another fun thing about Island Freeze is that they are crazy about their customers. They're happy to make you happy, and if you don't see the smoothie you want on the menu, think up your own and they'll be glad to make it for you. Come in and fuel up in a healthful way that'll keep you going all day.

**13609 162nd Street Court E,
Puyallup WA
(253) 841-7304**

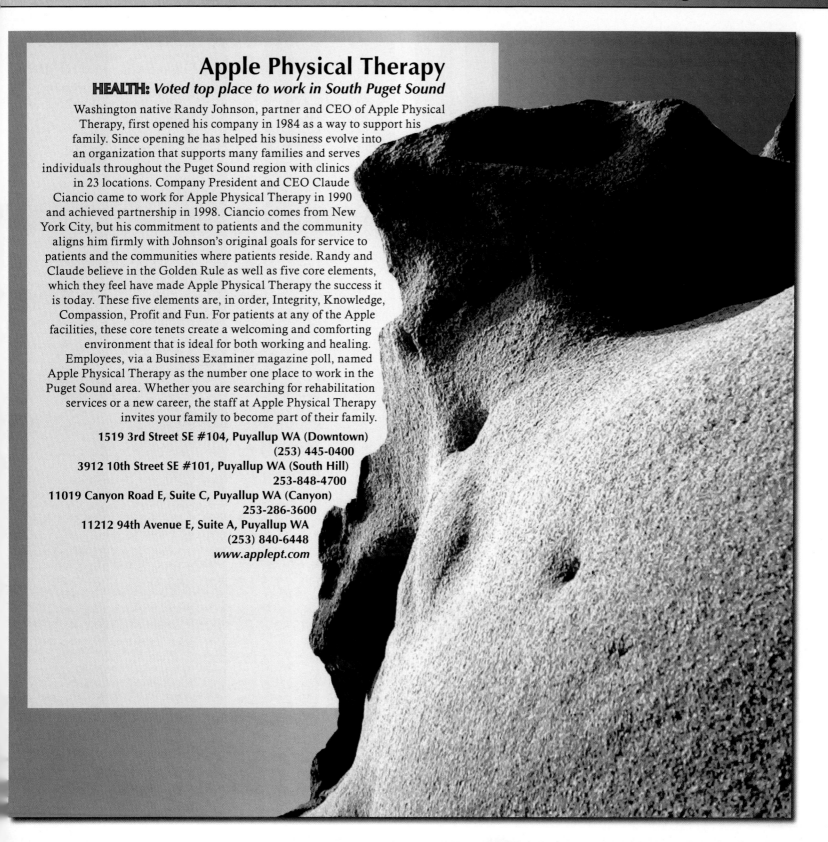

Apple Physical Therapy

HEALTH: *Voted top place to work in South Puget Sound*

Washington native Randy Johnson, partner and CEO of Apple Physical Therapy, first opened his company in 1984 as a way to support his family. Since opening he has helped his business evolve into an organization that supports many families and serves individuals throughout the Puget Sound region with clinics in 23 locations. Company President and CEO Claude Ciancio came to work for Apple Physical Therapy in 1990 and achieved partnership in 1998. Ciancio comes from New York City, but his commitment to patients and the community aligns him firmly with Johnson's original goals for service to patients and the communities where patients reside. Randy and Claude believe in the Golden Rule as well as five core elements, which they feel have made Apple Physical Therapy the success it is today. These five elements are, in order, Integrity, Knowledge, Compassion, Profit and Fun. For patients at any of the Apple facilities, these core tenets create a welcoming and comforting environment that is ideal for both working and healing.

Employees, via a Business Examiner magazine poll, named Apple Physical Therapy as the number one place to work in the Puget Sound area. Whether you are searching for rehabilitation services or a new career, the staff at Apple Physical Therapy invites your family to become part of their family.

1519 3rd Street SE #104, Puyallup WA (Downtown)
(253) 445-0400
3912 10th Street SE #101, Puyallup WA (South Hill)
253-848-4700
11019 Canyon Road E, Suite C, Puyallup WA (Canyon)
253-286-3600
11212 94th Avenue E, Suite A, Puyallup WA
(253) 840-6448
www.applept.com

Cherry Creek Hair Company

HEALTH & BEAUTY:
Best hair salon

Jennifer Roberts is the owner and stylist of Cherry Creek Hair Company. She opened the shop in 2000 and has since become one of the most popular and reputable salons in the Puyallup area. In September of last year, she christened a new salon between Pioneer and East Main. The new home, in a Belle Époque-style house full of character and charm, has been transformed into a chic, upscale salon with a soothing and relaxing feel. Cherry Creek is staffed by a talented team that offers the latest in coloring and cutting techniques. The staff attends hair shows and hands-on classes to stay up to the moment with the new trends. The stylists pride themselves on their return clientele. When Roberts opened Cherry Creek, she dreamed of a place where you could get a fabulous cut for a reasonable price. She wanted a place with friendly stylists who could offer the best advice for every hair type and complement each personal lifestyle. She achieved her dream of opening a hip and trendy place that is affordable, with an atmosphere that is fun and friendly, and where the stylists are highly skilled and educated. Call Cherry Creek Hair Company. They'll make you look fabulous.

202 5th Street SE, Puyallup WA
(253) 848-4775

Competitive Edge Performance Training

HEALTH & BEAUTY: *Best training facility for school-age young people*

Competitive Edge Performance Training is an amazing sports facility in Puyallup. It is a club designed specifically for school-aged children. Owners Joe Albers and Brian Petersen created Competitive Edge to include conditioning, agility and weight training, and it is geared toward the safety and health of growing young people. Competitive Edge is known specifically for their work with athletes, helping youngsters prepare for their particular sport. The staff is highly educated in this area. Many athletes from their program have earned scholarships and gone on to play college sports. Competition is not the entire focus at Competitive Edge. Joe and Brian wanted to create a place where they could work with children in a positive environment. At Competitive Edge, they not only help young people attain physical development, they also mentor them by building confidence, social skills, leadership skills and life skills so they will become healthy functioning adults in their communities. Parents bring their children from all over the South Puget Sound area to become part of the Competitive Edge program. High school youth can earn their physical education credits through the program, and volunteer opportunities are available. Visit Competitive Edge, where they build confidence by developing competence.

16719 110th Avenue E, Puyallup WA (253) 840-8581 *www.gottheedge.com*

Mocha Cabana Experience

HEALTH & BEAUTY: *Best tanning salon*

Exhausted? Overworked? Too tired to think? Are you caught in a reverie of faraway places? Dream no more and treat yourself to the Mocha Cabana Experience. Owner Lisa Boyer and her festive and friendly staff guarantee you the micro-mini vacation of your life. "Walk out of your daily life and pamper yourself in a vacation atmosphere," Lisa says. You may think you have just arrived in the Bahamas. The décor inside Mocha Cabana is tropical right down to the burning tiki lights. The Mocha Cabana Experience offers the best in tanning lotions, the most affordable tanning prices, and an incredible variety of delicious espresso drinks. Choose indoor or outdoor seating,

where you can relax and enjoy table games or the small bookshelf of pleasure reading materials. Bring a bit of the experience home with something from the gift shop. If you think you can't get away because of the kids, think again, because Mocha Cabana is kid friendly. Your children can have their own mini-vacation with the Nintendo and educational games stocked in The Kid Zone. They will have fun and be happy while you are pampering yourself. Want an espresso on the run? Call in your order and the baristas at Mocha Cabana will have it waiting for you.

711 E Main St, Puyallup WA
(253) 770-5540
www.mochacabana.net

Puyallup Athletic Club
HEALTH & BEAUTY: *Best athletic club*

If you long to see a slimmer, healthier and more fit you in your future, Puyallup Athletic Club is just the place to go. Established in 1985, the club is a full-service health club without high pressure sales or an intimidating atmosphere. Co-managers Pam Strickling and Heather Anchita are proud to offer simple membership options with no long-term contract obligations. The nationally certified staff is trained to meet expectations of friendly and superior customer service. Experts in giving helpful guidance that is geared toward meeting and maintaining realistic fitness goals, they are trained to provide service to a variety of fitness levels, diverse ages, and individual preferences. Available classes include fitness, yoga, F.A.S.T., A.C.E (Anyone Can Exercise) and SilverSneakers for Seniors. Facilities include a weight room, racquetball courts and cardiovascular equipment. PAC provides sports physical therapy to those recovering from orthopedic injuries, and prides itself on teaching people about proper alignment, body mechanics and improving core stability. A great way to meet new friends and have exercising fun is to join the Saturday and Sunday morning hikes organized from May through September. Another appealing option is the 12-week New Year Program that is a complete exercise, nutrition, hair and clothing make-over. This is a comfortable, informal club with a focus on fitness and activity for real people with real goals.

15406 Meridian E, Puyallup WA (253) 845-7620 *www.puyallupathleticclub.com*

Super Supplements
HEALTH & BEAUTY: *Best independent retail chain in the nation*

Science learns something new every day about the ways vitamins, herbs and nutritional supplements enhance health. Keeping up with all that cutting-edge information would be overwhelming without the help of experts. Super Supplements is a privately owned chain of 13 discount vitamin stores in western Washington. It was started in 1994 by John Wurts and bills itself as having some of the most knowledgeable staff members in the industry. John brings more than 18 years of experience in the vitamin industry to his operation, which was voted 2004 Best

Retail Chain in the Nation by *Vitamin Retailer* magazine. The stores feature wide, inviting aisles, a vast array of supplements, sports nutrition, herbs, body care and homeopathic products, plus a well educated staff prepared to provide the most up-to-date and accurate product information available. Bring your questions to university students, naturopathic doctors or herbalists, or take advantage of Healthnotes, a touchscreen information system that retrieves research on natural remedies, illnesses and potential drug interactions from vitamin, herb and food combinations. You'll get 10 to 70-percent discounts on products at Super Supplements locations from Bellingham to Lakewood. The same great service and more than 30,000 products are available on the website. Visit Super Supplements to begin your journey to a healthier life.

4307 S Meridian, Puyallup WA
(253) 604-0700
Mail Order: (800) 249-9394
www.supersup.com

CleanTech Housekeeping Referral Service, Inc.
HOME: *Best housekeeping service*

Pat Bayer loves the South Sound area. She grew up here and stays active and involved to give back to the community. Her business, CleanTech Housekeeping Referral Service, Inc., has been a licensed house cleaning employment agency with the State of Washington since 1995. When asked why she started a cleaning business, she says she is a born nurturer. When you see the abandoned animals she nurses back to health and the huge buffet she provides for her house cleaners every Friday, you will get an idea of how true that is. Pat's goal is to make a difference in people's lives every day. Her work involves the clients and the housekeepers, and she strives to match them in the best combination. She wants clients to have high quality housecleaning so their days are easier. In many cases, a personal relationship has grown between Pat and her clients. Clients often call from other states and countries to set up housecleaning for their loved ones in town. She also loves her housekeepers, and makes their lives easier by scheduling their hours and taking care of correspondence and financial matters. She recently moved her business because she inherited a home and commercial property from her brother. She has brought her enthusiasm into this new neighborhood in hopes of keeping her brother's place alive and benefiting the community. Call Pat at CleanTech. It's a great service.

108 W Meeker, Puyallup WA
(253) 770-2255 or (877) 708-8100

Newell Hunt Furniture

HOME: *Best furniture store*

Established in 1946, Newell Hunt Furniture features three floors of distinctive home furnishings, design consultants, and excellent delivery and set-up services. The furniture at Newell Hunt is high quality and of great value. The customer base is very loyal because of the personal consulting and service that comes with shopping at Newell Hunt. Owner Arla Cuddie worked for Warren and Dorothy Hunt, of the original family, for many years prior to purchasing the store with partner Rodger Gustafson in 2002. They have continued to run the store with the same integrity and style. Arla's own children are involved in helping out around the store with continual painting projects and events on the weekends, continuing the store's family tradition. Naturally, weekends are a busy time at Newell Hunt. Still, you are always greeted with a smile, a full jar of cookies and coffee, or Arla's special hot wassail during the holidays. The atmosphere at Newell Hunt Furniture is just like being in your own home; it's warm, welcoming and it even smells good. The staff is made up of well educated designers. Their goal is to provide affordable, quality furniture that suits each family's lifestyle. They are passionate about helping people with their home furnishing needs. Arla calls her staff Lifestyle Consultants; their intent is not to "sell you," but to create opportunities for you to buy furnishings that fit your lifestyle. Visit Newell Hunt Furniture to renew your style and make your home more livable.

113 W Stewart, Puyallup WA
(253) 845-1735
www.newellhuntfurniture.com

Calla Lily Designs

HOME: *Best interior design*

The staff at Calla Lily Designs want you to surround yourself with beauty and comfort. Their interior decoration, design and redesign services help customers turn their homes into stylish havens. Owners Patricia and Callie Drotz, and the other members of the Calla Lily design team, love to work on the big picture with their customers. They understand that all clients have their own timelines and budget constraints. Calla Lily can create a detailed plan just for you, taking into consideration your unique needs. Calla Lily specializes in re-design—using what you already have. Team members add fresh color, accessories and plants for a new look. The shop has a unique and ever-changing inventory of home decorating items that includes art, lamps, pillows, mirrors and candles. It also has an extensive array of high-quality permanent botanicals, ranging from peonies to palm trees, to spruce up your home or office. Staff members can help you choose the right accessories for your project. If you find yourself stumped trying to accessorize a bookshelf, mantle or any other area, Calla Lily can help you find the solution. Visit Calla Lily Designs and let the fresh thinking of its staff inspire you.

17530 Meridian E, Puyallup WA
(253) 841-4757
www.callalilydesigners.com

Dance Explosion & Dynamite Dancewear

RECREATION: *Best dance studio*

With razzle-dazzle energy and theatrical emphasis, the students at Dance Explosion are taught to give 110 percent to the audience with facial expressions, feelings and movements. Owners Jessica and Ana Reese make a remarkable team. These sisters originate from Austin, bringing with them their Texas hospitality and warmth. Jessica has an extensive dance background and has trained across the U.S., as well as internationally. Ana handles the business aspect of the studio and influences Jessica's curriculum with her theater background. Together they create an awesome twosome and a truly unique, family-oriented dance studio. These sisters offer a fresh, comprehensive and fun learning experience. "We believe that everyone should have the opportunity to dance, whether it is for fun and exercise or whether you would like to make a career of it," Jessica says. They encourage the love of dance no matter what age, level or style. Among their diverse selection of classes are ballet, tap, jazz, hip-hop, cheerleading, belly dancing, break dancing, cardio and yoga. Dance Explosion also holds auditions for more serious dancers for their award-winning competitive dance troupes to give students experience performing at local and national competitions. In addition, Jessica and Ana provide a very nice selection of dance clothing and shoes in their Dynamite Dancewear section of the studio. Dance Explosion is a studio with something for everyone.

10227 139th Street Court E, Building C1-4, Puyallup WA
(253) 445-8110
www.DanceExplosionStars.com

Alexander's Restaurant
RESTAURANTS & CAFÉS: *Best French onion soup*

As a customer at Alexander's Restaurant, you can be part of the real life dream of chef Robert Shultz and his wife, Jodi. Robert has always had a passion for food. He has been a professional chef since 1980. He discovered his love of cooking when he was nine years old and began working toward the dream of having his own restaurant. Robert puts a lot of love into his culinary creations. His colleagues have accused him of being a perfectionist, but he believes you use all of your senses when you eat. Well known in the area for their beef ribs, Alexander's also serves fantastic French onion soup, a rib-sticking Tommy burger and satisfying Southwest chicken salad sandwiches. You'll discover your favorite selections when you take advantage of the relaxing atmosphere and the invitation to settle in and make yourself comfortable. Personal service from Robert, Jodi and their loyal server Brandy Anderson are three reasons to feel at home at Alexander's. You're invited to come in on your lunch break, bring a business client or just break away from your usual routine. Non-alcoholic wines and beers are available to complement your food choice. The skilled staff will also cater any event to your tastes. When cooking is the chef's passion, who knows what he'll come up with next? Stop by Alexander's Restaurant and find out.

213 Meridian Street N, Puyallup WA
(253) 435-8833

Mrs. Turner's Hometown Café
RESTAURANTS & CAFÉS: *Best place for comfort food*

Comfort food. There are times when nothing else will do. Mrs. Turner's Hometown Café is the epitome for comfort, rib-sticking good food, plus friendly service and always a warm welcome. The Café's origins date back to 1966, when it was named the Plantation Chicken and Pancake House. The Plantation introduced Colonel Sander's Kentucky Fried Chicken to the Puyallup Valley. In 1993, Mr. and Mrs. Paul Patrick took over the café. They were dedicated to keeping the same atmosphere they remembered when they brought their sons in for pancakes. With the passing of Mr. Patrick in 2004, James and Starla Feldbush became the new owners. James grew up in the restaurant business, and Starla had been working at Mrs. Turner's since 1991. Starla and husband James intend to keep the hometown traditions and want the café to remain a warm, friendly place where people always feel welcome and the food is always delicious. Mrs. Turner's serves daily breakfast, lunch and dinner specials. Their mile-high strawberry shortcake and huge, delicious cinnamon rolls are some of the customer favorites. Come to Mrs. Turner's Hometown Café to meet old friends or make some new ones. It won't be long before you are a regular.

701 E Main, Puyallup WA
(253) 848-7761

Po-Boy & Bar-BQ
RESTAURANTS & CAFÉS: *Best BBQ in Puyallup*

Scott Percival, owner of Po-Boy & Bar-BQ, says, "People who are BBQ fanatics will drive until they find their flavor." It doesn't necessarily mean he is the best, but when people make a point of coming to Po-Boy, it means Scott has their flavor. His theory was proven by a San Francisco couple who were on their way to a wedding in Vancouver, BC. They had eaten at Po-Boy two years earlier and were hoping it was still there. They flew into SeaTac, rented a car and drove to Puyallup before driving to the wedding. For Scott and his crew, that was the ultimate compliment. Scott's crew consists of his daughters, Megan, Stephanie, Jennifer and Amber. The family togetherness is apparent in the comfortable, friendly atmosphere. The Percivals have owned and operated the restaurant since 1989. They serve the finest meats available on the market, and smoke them with seasoned Alder wood in their outdoor smoker. The smoker was brought from New Orleans for "true" barbeque flavor. All of the side dishes are prepared fresh daily, including baked beans, potato salad, macaroni salad and creamy or crunchy coleslaw. They serve their own special blend of homemade barbeque sauce, and "napkins are a must." If you can resist the tempting smells of barbeque, there are additional satisfying Po-Boy sandwiches. Eat in or take-out, but whichever you choose, top it off with a slice of their luscious chocolate cake.

15019 Meridian Street, Puyallup WA (253) 848-8548

Café Beso
RESTAURANTS & CAFES: *Best downtown café*

Café Beso, in historic downtown Puyallup, is a deliciously quaint spot to sit down and enjoy breakfast or lunch. Since 2004, owners Kenneth and Moani Brumet have offered patrons freshly roasted coffee from Batdorf and Bronson, and specialty sandwiches, soups, salads and desserts created by chef Troy Guilao. On Friday evenings, they host their wine tasting event, featuring a new region every Friday to visit vineyards around the world and savor their award-winning wines. In addition, they offer a nice selection of microbrews. When in downtown Puyallup, you'll find that Café Beso is the perfect place to relax and enjoy a bite to eat.

109 S Meridian, Puyallup WA
(253) 770-0150

Casa Mia of Puyallup
RESTAURANTS & CAFÉS: *Best New York-style pizza*

In 1952, the first Casa Mia restaurant opened in a storefront in Hoquiam. It was started by Phil Bellafato, an Italian-American who grew up above one of the original Italian restaurants and pizzerias in New York. After a stint in the Army, Bellafato settled in the Northwest. At that time, pizza was virtually unknown in the area. Casa Mia, one of the first Italian restaurants in Washington, helped to change that. To this day, the Casa Mia menu is centered on Phil's original recipes, with nearly everything made the old-fashioned way. Pizza is hand-tossed, with fresh dough made daily, then baked on a brick hearth. There are now nine Casa Mia Italian Restaurants throughout the state of Washington, but none are finer than Casa Mia of Puyallup. In 1994, Casa Mia was selected as one of four finalists by Hunt-Wesson foods in the Prima Pizza recipe contest. Since then they have won first prize in the Pizza Across America contest, and have twice been selected as winners in *Pizza Today* magazine's Pizza Festiva International Pizza Recipe Contest. Stop in Casa Mia and get a taste of what Phil brought to Northwest all those years ago.

505 N Meridian, Puyallup WA
(253) 770-0400
www.casamiarestaurants.com

Victoria Sells Antique Mall
SHOPPING: *Best antiques mall*

For 10,000 square feet of antiques and collectibles, visit Victoria Sells Antiques on South Meridian. If that's not big enough for you, then try the Fircrest location on Regents Boulevard, between Tacoma and University Place. It covers 14,400 square feet. In either shop, you will find numerous dealers selling an extensive selection of upscale antique furniture, home décor, estate jewelry, black Americana, reproduction Victorian lamp shades and period lighting. You can also expect to see, linens, primitives, sports memorabilia, glass and a whole lot more. The Fircrest location includes a frame shop and a bistro. In either location, you will find a very friendly atmosphere with music from the 1920s and 30s in the air. Now and then you'll see people dancing. Customer service is high because the employees are the owners of the products they sell. Mall owners Jack and Judy Doepke have been antique collectors for what seems like forever. Opening the malls was a natural extension of their lifelong passion for antiques. Visit Victoria Sells for all your antique needs.

125 S Meridian, Puyallup WA
(253) 445-8330
1115 Regents Boulevard, Fircrest WA
(253) 565-2500

J.C.'s Music

SHOPPING: *Best downtown music store*

Opened in 2001, J.C.'s Music has been the premier musician's store in Puyallup. J.C. and Lenora McCormick opened J.C.'s Music with talent and a dream. J.C. has been a guitarist and entertainer for more than 40 years, and had previously worked for Puyallup Music. When the opportunity to open his own music store arose, he did just that. J.C.'s passion for music and his desire to share is evident in the store that bears his name. As you walk down the streets of downtown Puyallup, melodies waft from the outside speakers at J.C.'s. In his heart, J.C. wanted to create a place where musicians and entertainers of any caliber or age, from beginner to advanced, could feel welcome to come in and play the instruments. J.C.'s Music is a place that inspires young musicians to realize a dream. At J.C.'s, you will see people of all ages come in and gaze around before they begin playing the instruments and enjoying themselves. Regulars often come in to buy equipment, such as strings, and end up hanging out to enjoy the ambience for a while. Visit J.C.'s Music for a place where musical dreams come true.

124 S Meridian, Puyallup WA
(253) 864-9911

PLACES TO GO

- Art On Center
  1604 Center Street (253) 230-1673

- Children's Museum of Tacoma
  936 Broadway (253) 627-6031

- Fort Nisqually Living History Museum
  5400 N Pearl Street #11 (253) 591-5339

- Job Carr's Cabin Museum
  2350 N 30th Street (253) 627-5405

- LeMay: America's Car Museum
  325 152nd Street E (253) 536-2885

- Museum of Glass
  1801 Dock Street (253) 284-4750

- Point Defiance Zoo and Aquarium
  5400 N Pearl Street (253) 591-5337

- Tacoma Art Museum
  1701 Pacific Avenue (253) 272-4258

- Washington State History Museum
  1911 Pacific Avenue (888) 238-4373

- Working Waterfront Maritime Museum
  705 Dock Street (253) 272-2750

- W.W. Seymour Botanical Conservatory
  316 South G Street (253) 591-5330

- Tacoma Nature Center/Snake Lake
  1919 S Tyler Street

THINGS TO DO

February
- Wintergrass Bluegrass Festival
  Tacoma Sheraton (253) 428-8056

April
- Tacoma Jazz and Blues Festival
  www.tacomajazzfestival.com

- Norwegian Heritage Festival
  Pacific Lutheran University (253) 535-7532

June
- Small Ships Tacoma
  Dock Street Marina (253) 476-2295

July
- 4th of July Freedom Fair and Air Show
  Ruston Way (253) 682-1446

- Tacoma Old Town Blues Festival
  www.tacomaoldtownbluesfest.com

August
- Maritime Fest Juried Art Show
  (253) 927-3627

TACOMA

Tacoma is the second-largest city in the Puget Sound area. It is named after Mount Rainier, which was originally known as Mount Tacoma. The view of Mount Rainier from Tacoma is impressive. The mountain really seems to be part of the town. Tacoma has many distinct neighborhoods, which add variety and encourage civic spirit. *America's Most Livable Cities* has named Tacoma-Pierce County one of the nation's most desirable regions in which to live.

Tacoma's Union Station
Photo by Jan Tik

Silver Cloud Inn

ACCOMMODATIONS:
Best place on the Tacoma waterfront

If you're looking for a service-oriented hotel in Tacoma, travel to the Silver Cloud Inn, where guests rave about the service and hospitality the staff delivers on a daily basis. Located in historic Old Town, the Silver Cloud Inn is the only hotel on the Tacoma waterfront with water views from every guestroom. The Inn, with 90 spacious guestrooms and suites, features complimentary Silver Cloud breakfast, in-room high-speed Internet access, in-room coffee, refrigerator, microwave, hair dryer, iron and ironing board, and free local calls and voice mail. They also offer free laundry facilities, complimentary parking, and a boardroom for small meetings. Adjacent to Old Town and its quaint shopping and wonderful restaurants, the Inn is also within a few miles of the Washington State Historical Museum, the Point Defiance-Tahlequah ferry, Museum of Glass, Point Defiance Park and Zoo, Tacoma Dome, and Tacoma Landmark Convention Center. Check the website for special packages.

2317 N Ruston Way, Tacoma WA
(253) 272-1300 or (866) 820-8448
www.silvercloud.com/13home.htm

Tacoma Art Museum

ATTRACTIONS: *Best place to view art*

Situated in Tacoma's dynamic cultural district, Tacoma Art Museum shimmers in its sleek architecture, designed by Antoine Predock. Tacoma Art Museum opened its present facility in May 2003, giving them twice the space of their previous home, and allowing the museum to expand on its vision and mission. The building features flexible exhibition space in a series of galleries that wrap around an open-air, interior stone garden. The galleries showcase Tacoma Art Museum's permanent collection, which includes American, European and Asian art, plus traveling national and international exhibitions. The interior reflects the museum's spirit, from the emphasis on educational spaces, which are designed to make art accessible, to the framed views of Mt. Rainier. Tacoma Art Museum showcases traveling national and international exhibitions, and is dedicated to collecting and presenting Northwest art. The Museum's rich collection contains more than 3,200 significant works and key holdings in modern and contemporary Northwest, 19th century European, 20th century American and Asian works. The Museum also features a stunning permanent installation of Dale Chihuly glass, dating 1977 to the present. In addition to several varieties of art, Tacoma Art Museum offers a studio for art-making and resource center for art study open to visitors of all ages. Visitors can also enjoy lunch or coffee in the indoor/outdoor café, and shop for distinctive items such as jewelry, books and regionally hand-crafted items in the Museum store.

1701 Pacific Avenue, Tacoma WA
(253) 272-4258
www.TacomaArtMuseum.org

Washington State History Museum

ATTRACTIONS: *Best place to learn local history*

The Washington State History Museum is where fascination and fun come together. People of all ages can explore and be entertained in an environment where characters from Washington's past speak about their lives. Through interactive exhibits, theatrical storytelling, high-tech displays and dramatic artifacts, learn about Washington's unique people and places, as well as their impact on the country and the world. Begin your journey through Washington with an architectural masterpiece designed by Charles Moore and Arthur Andersson. The 106,000-square-foot museum building stands proudly on Pacific Avenue in Tacoma. The museum boasts soaring spaces and dramatic archways that consciously echo the Beaux Arts architecture of the nearby Union Station and invite you into a history experience full of colors, textures, sights and sounds. The museum, which opened 10 years ago, helped to spark the City of Destiny's dramatic downtown renaissance.

1911 Pacific Avenue, Tacoma WA
(888) BE-THERE (238-4373)
www.wshs.org

Museum of Glass

ATTRACTIONS: *Best glass art displays*

The Museum of Glass is an international center for contemporary art with a sustained focus on glass. It's both a unique museum and the cultural cornerstone of Tacoma's $150 million redevelopment along the Thea Foss Waterway. The Museum's most distinctive architectural feature, a tilted 90-foot tall cone wrapped in stainless steel, houses the Hot Shop Amphitheater. In this dynamic glass blowing studio, visitors watch artists engaged in the creative experimentation and exploration that makes glass one of the most exhilarating mediums in the art world today. In addition to the Hot Shop Amphitheater, the museum features three galleries with intriguing exhibitions, a 180-seat theater, a hands-on art studio, a museum store and café. The museum's exhibition schedule introduces works by internationally known artists who illuminate trends in contemporary art, highlighting glass within a full range of media. Clear, expert commentary in the form of interpretive text panels, guided tours and other programs ensure a museum experience that is meaningful and engaging to visitors. The museum's outdoor plazas are also noteworthy. Three large reflecting pools hold a variety of large art installations. The Chihuly Bridge of Glass, a 500-foot pedestrian bridge with art by Tacoma native Dale Chihuly, leads from the museum's rooftop plaza to downtown Tacoma.

1801 Dock Street, Tacoma WA
(253) 284-4750
www.museumofglass.org

Photos by Craig Wyzik

Celebrity Cake Studio

BAKERIES, COFFEE & TEA:
Best special occasion cakes

Elegant wedding cakes, artistically finished special occasion cakes and delectable desserts are just some of the temptations at the Celebrity Cake Studio. This family-owned and operated business is managed by sisters Odette D'Aniello and Mary Ann Quitugua along with their cousin, Wallace Bolo. All three learned their craft during years of baking and cake decorating for family-owned bakeries. Odette and Mary Ann design and decorate all of Celebrity Cake Studio's wedding and special occasion cakes and are famous in the area for their attention to detail and fine workmanship. The shop uses only the finest ingredients, such as sweetened butter from local dairies and imported Belgian chocolate. Celebrity Cake Studio's growing popularity is shown by the number of repeat customers who trust Odette and Mary Ann to make a spectacular cake or dessert that tastes as good as it looks. Celebrity Cake Studio is particularly known for its custom wedding cakes, which have graced thousands of weddings in the area and are recommended by many caterers and venues. Several area publications, including *Seattle Bride* and *The Knot*, have featured the shop. Browse through Celebrity Cake Studio's online catalog and marvel at the possibilities in cake design. Schedule a free cake tasting and enjoy the chef's choice of cake flavors, such the popular pink champagne swirl with Belgian white chocolate mousse. Order your next special occasion or wedding cake and experience why Celebrity Cake Studio is the area's premier cake and dessert destination.

602 E 25th Street, Suite 2, Tacoma WA
(253) 627-4773
www.celebritycakestudio.com

Main Street Home Loans
BUSINESS: *Best home lender*

"Good, bad, or ugly credit," that's the slogan and the commitment of Sandy Hickson and Tami Macias. With their combined 38 years of experience in the corporate lending world, these women really know their stuff. They also know that corporate interests are seldom the same as customers' interests. That is why they opened their own business. They really care about people and they are energized by successfully meeting their needs. Sandy and Tami are accustomed to taking the toughest situations and making them work, however long it takes. And it pays. They boast an impressive success rate and have built lasting relationships with their customers. True personal service is a rare commodity in the lending business and that is what Tami and Sandy bring to this community. Whatever your situation, at the comfortable office of Main Street Home Loans you will be treated respectfully and fairly. These community treasures can help you make your dreams come true.

(Serving all of Metro Seattle)
1024 Main Street, Sumner WA
(253) 862-9490

Apple Physical Therapy

HEALTH: *Voted top place to work in South Puget Sound*

Washington native Randy Johnson, partner and CEO of Apple Physical Therapy, opened his company in 1984 as a way to support his family. Since then his business has evolved into an organization that supports many families and serves individuals throughout the Puget Sound region with clinics in 23 locations. Company President and CEO Claude Ciancio came to work for Apple Physical Therapy in 1990 and achieved partnership in 1998. Ciancio comes from New York City, but his commitment to patients and the community aligns him firmly with Johnson's original goals for service to patients and the communities where patients reside. Randy and Claude believe in the Golden Rule, as well as five core elements, which they feel have made Apple Physical Therapy the success it is today. These five elements are, in order, Integrity, Knowledge, Compassion, Profit and Fun. For patients at any of the Apple facilities, these core tenets create a welcoming and comforting environment that is ideal for both working and healing. Employees, via a Business Examiner magazine poll, named Apple Physical Therapy as the number one place to work in the Puget Sound area. Whether you are searching for rehabilitation services or a new career, the staff at Apple Physical Therapy invites your family to become part of their family.

3315 S 23rd Street, Suite 210, Tacoma WA (central) (253) 572-8684
1119 Pacific Avenue, Suite 105, Tacoma WA (downtown) (253) 284-4441
www.applept.com

Northern Tacoma as seen from the 11th Street Bridge

Super Supplements
HEALTH & BEAUTY: *Best independent retail chain in the nation*

Science learns something new every day about the ways vitamins, herbs and nutritional supplements enhance health. Keeping up with all that cutting-edge information would be overwhelming without the help of experts. Super Supplements is a privately owned chain of 13 discount vitamin stores in western Washington. It was started in 1994 by John Wurts and bills itself as having some of the most knowledgeable staff members in the industry. John brings more than 18 years of experience in the vitamin industry to his operation, which was voted 2004 Best Retail Chain in the Nation by *Vitamin Retailer* magazine. The stores feature wide, inviting aisles, a vast array of supplements, sports nutrition, herbs, body care and homeopathic products, plus a well educated staff prepared to provide the most up-to-date and accurate product information available. Bring your questions to university students, naturopathic doctors or herbalists, or take advantage of Healthnotes, a touchscreen information system that retrieves research on natural remedies, illnesses and potential drug interactions from vitamin, herb and food combinations. You'll get 10 to 70-percent discounts on products at Super Supplements locations from Bellingham to Lakewood. The same great service and more than 30,000 products are available on the website. Visit Super Supplements to begin your journey to a healthier life.

Highway 16 & Pearl Street, Tacoma WA
(253) 584-7300
Mail Order: (800) 249-9394
www.supersup.com

Body Evolution
HEALTH & BEAUTY:
Best fitness center

Body Evolution is the newest wave in health and fitness enhancement centers, using cutting-edge technology to help men and women achieve good looks and good health.
Body Evolution started in 2000, as Spa Beyond, under the direction of owner and founder Misha Anderson. The spa combines traditional therapies, such as detoxifying treatments, tightening body wraps and rejuvenating facials, with advanced technology designed to help you achieve a leaner, healthier physique. Body Evolution offers the latest in computerized muscle training programs, which allow you to lie back and lose inches while small electrical pulses help you develop firm, toned muscles and shed inches in a short period of time. Other popular treatments include Endermosonic Cellulite Therapy, which uses vibrations to massage and reduce both cellulite and stress. This procedure is both highly effective and noninvasive; it improves circulation while reducing the appearance of cellulite dimples. One of Body Evolution's most unique services is the Alpha Thermogenic and Infra-red Aromatherapy Weight Loss Sauna, another vibration therapy that, in this case, stimulates the lymphatic system, both increasing circulation and accelerating your metabolism. Exceptional service and individualized care make Body Evolution the ideal place to enhance your overall well-being, regardless of your current physical condition. Develop a healthy and revitalized physique at Body Evolution in Bellevue or in the new Tacoma location. Franchise opportunities available.

Bellevue: (425) 957-7280 Tacoma: (253) 627-2222 *www.body-evo.com*

Frugals

RESTAURANTS & CAFÉS: *Best homegrown burger franchise*

Don't worry, you won't have to save your pennies for a hamburger here. At Frugals you'll get a delicious meal and still have change to spare. Peter and Sheila Stewart started their Frugals phenomenon in Port Angeles in 1988 with the goal of providing the highest quality food for the lowest possible prices. Their idea of a double drive-through with no indoor seating has proved to be wildly successful. Frugal's now has three locations, in Port Angeles, Tacoma and Auburn. The cool, retro-style stainless-steel building draws endless lines of satisfied customers. Despite its popularity, there is never a long wait at Frugals due to the staff's extreme efficiency. Arriving with the expectation of speedy service and low prices, diners are treated to the best tasting burgers in the area. With no need for fancy trappings, all expenses go to the quality of the food. Gardenburgers and hamburgers can be customized with a choice of cheeses, vegetables and thick-sliced bacon. Grilled chicken and great BLT sandwiches are on the menu, as are shakes, fries and soft drinks. Frugals consistently appears in the Best of the Olympic Peninsula for their burgers, shakes and fries. Time after time Frugals has taken best burger honors in newspaper polls. It's not just the food that's great, the staff is also efficient and fun-loving, evident in the lively camaraderie in the kitchen. The Stewarts have come up with a win-win recipe of simplicity, quality and value. They welcome you to drive through and enjoy their retro bistro.

10727 Pacific Avenue S, Tacoma WA
(253) 535-9775
www.frugalburger.com

A Renaissance Café

RESTAURANTS & CAFÉS: *Most innovative cooking*

Keith Flowers has a whimsical outlook on life, and his restaurant, A Renaissance Café, reflects his view. Keith makes the food for his café fresh and from scratch, and he sometimes uses cooking tools in unexpected ways. For example, to create his steam-scrambled eggs, he cooks them using the wand from an espresso machine. This extremely quick cooking method allows Keith to cook the eggs using no oil and to make the fluffiest eggs possible. It also allows Keith to say, "We put the fast in breakfast." You can have nearly anything added to your eggs, including ham, vegetable combos or chicken. If you choose chicken, Keith will tell you that you have ordered the Chicken and the Egg. Breakfasts and espresso are available all day. For lunch, the café offers grilled sandwiches and a sweet and spicy barbecue sandwich. Soups are homemade seafood chowder or vegetarian chili, and fresh salads are available. Keith makes real fruit smoothies and milkshakes, including his signature espresso milkshake, which Keith claims may spoil your appreciation for any other espresso drink. While the restaurant can get crowded, it is also a place where you can sit for a bit and enjoy life. Make any day special with a visit to A Renaissance Café for breakfast or lunch.

1746 Pacific Avenue, Tacoma WA
(253) 572-1029

Hawthorn Tea Room

RESTAURANTS & CAFÉS:
Best tea room in Tacoma

Jan Coad's two lifelong passions are antiques and high tea. The natural outcome of these loves is the Hawthorn Tea Room, which she opened in an historic building in Old Town Tacoma. Her Victorian-style tearoom serves lunch from 11 am to 3 pm and tea anytime. Reservations are recommended for the elegant afternoon high tea, which includes all of the traditional elements, such as homemade scones with Devonshire cream or jam, tea sandwiches and specialty desserts. The Hawthorn Tea Room holds a monthly children's theme tea, complete with activities and games. Birthday celebrations for the 11 and younger set begin with playing dress-up in Jan's collection of vintage gowns and furs. After a special lunch, the children can play games or make jewelry. The shop offers a large variety of teas, including the house special Hawthorn Signature Peach, Raspberry and Vanilla flavored black tea. It also sells antiques and heirloom gifts. Jan's daughter, Allie, was one of the inspirations for the shop. Jan's good friend Nicolle Wray helps her with the business. Nicolle makes her salsa in the Hawthorn Tea Room kitchen. Her special Blue Tomato Salsa is available at the tearoom and at *www.bluetomatosalsa.com*. Visit the Hawthorn Tea Room Tuesday through Saturday and share Jan's passion for tea and antiques.

2208 N 30th Street, Suite 101, Tacoma WA
(253) 238-9021

Red-necked Phalarope
Photo courtesy U.S. Fish and Wildlife Service

East and West Café
RESTAURANTS & CAFÉS:
Best market-fresh food

The best advertising is word of mouth. Just ask the regulars of East and West Café in Tacoma where owner Vien Floyd and her family have created a soothing atmosphere where you can get good, fresh, healthful food at an affordable price. The cafe is busy all the time. Diners enjoy sitting inside surrounded by warm wood tones and a beautiful collection of art glass, or outside on the patio surrounded by the fragrant herb and flower garden. The garden is the source of many of the vegetables and herbs used at East and West, while the rest come from local Tacoma markets. No MSG is used in the restaurant. Fat is removed from the meats to ensure the leanest, healthiest portions, and vegetarian dishes are available. Among the savory Vietnamese and Thai offerings you are sure to find personal favorites for lunch or dinner. Menu items change often, but once an item is introduced you can always request it.

5319 Tacoma Mall Boulevard, Tacoma WA
(253) 475-7755
www.eastandwestcafe.com

Southern Kitchen

RESTAURANTS & CAFÉS: *Best Southern cooking*

Olympia is a long way from Alabama, but that distance closes considerably when you walk into Southern Kitchen, located in Olympia's Ramada Governor House. Owner Gloria Martin hails from Alabama, where her father taught her the art of cooking. She learned not only to prepare marvelous Southern dishes from scratch, but to sprinkle those dishes with generous helpings of love and hospitality. Her first Southern Kitchen opened in 1995 in Tacoma. Its popularity eventually led to the opening a second restaurant a decade later. Gloria and her staff bring fun and energy to the restaurants. She loves her staff like family, and she personally teaches her chefs how to create dynamite Southern dishes out of whole foods. Gloria believes Southern cooking is to be shared, so she created restaurants that pass on the traditions of Southern hospitality by encouraging people to get to know each other over a great meal. Come to Southern Kitchen hungry, because the portions are generous. Try the chicken fried steak made with Gloria's secret batter and a strawberry lemonade. You'll find all the Southern staples here, like black-eyed peas, collard greens, catfish, liver and onions and fried green tomatoes. Southern Kitchen has served many celebrities and looks forward to serving you. Enjoy great food and true charm at Southern Kitchen, where the best of the South meets the Pacific Northwest.

621 Capitol Way S, Olympia WA
(360) 943-8300
1716 6th Avenue, Tacoma WA
(253) 627-4282

Vin Grotto Café and Wine Bar

RESTAURANTS & CAFÉS: *Best cheese plate in town*

Vin Grotto Café and Wine Bar is known for having the best cheese plate in town. Owner Kris Blondin was born and raised in Tacoma. In 2003, she opened Vin Grotto Café and Wine Bar. The wine shop has more than 200 selections, and their wine bar offers more than 70 selections by the glass. The staff is professional, knowledgeable and approachable. Vin Grotto serves light fare such as salads, soups, appetizers and desserts. As the owner knows, "wine is romantic and intriguing." The focus behind Vin Grotto Café and Wine Bar is to provide the community with a gathering spot offering great food, wine and atmosphere at an affordable price. She keeps the prices reasonable in order to have the opportunity to see familiar faces every week, instead of every month. Rated with four out of five stars in *The Tacoma News Tribune*, and four out of five forks in the *Olympian* newspaper, Vin Grotto is as extraordinary as it is eclectic. From starters such as the tasty cheese plate to afterthoughts such as a rich crème brulee, Vin Grotto Café and Wine Bar is just the right place for a first date, or a regular meeting spot for friends.

813 Pacific Avenue, Tacoma WA
(253) 722-5079
www.vingrotto.com

Pacific Northwest Shop
SHOPPING: *Best Northwest-made gifts*

At the Pacific Northwest Shop you can find personal or corporate gifts which, as the shop's slogan says, are made in our corner of America. Since 1978, this family-owned business has carried gifts of specialty foods and Pacific Northwest wines. You can find regional books and stationery, and the Pacific Northwest theme is carried out in clothing, throws and pottery. North Coast Indian merchandise includes spirit boxes and ceramic tiles with native designs. You will find one of the largest selections of Mount St. Helens volcanic ash art glass in the region. The store stocks gift boxes, such as the exclusive Mt. Rainier Box filled with Taste of the Pacific Northwest specialty foods. Delicious alder-smoked salmon, Walla Walla sweet onion mustard, and regional wines are just a few of the hundreds of gourmet food choices available. A new item is the Rub with Love spice rubs. For sweets, consider chocolate truffles, huckleberry jam or cashew roca. Located in Proctor, one of Tacoma's 12 urban villages, the Pacific Northwest Shop is near the University of Puget Sound in the city's beautiful North End. It offers complimentary gift wrap and can arrange to ship your purchases anywhere in the country. Of course, you can order online from the shop's website. Come to the Pacific Northwest Shop, where you are sure to find the perfect gift for a business colleague or a loved one.

2702 N Proctor Street, Tacoma WA
(253) 752-2242 or (800) 942-3523
www.pacificnorthwestshop.com

TUMWATER

Founded in 1846, Tumwater was the first American settlement on Puget Sound. It is one of three cities that make up Greater Olympia, together with Lacey and Olympia itself. The city's early growth was promoted by the power-generating falls of the Deschutes River, nearby saltwater access for transportation and the local abundance of timber.

PLACES TO GO

- Crosby House Museum
  702 Deschutes Way N
  (360) 754-4217

- Henderson House Museum
  602 Deschutes Way N
  (360) 754-4217

- Pioneer Park
  Henderson Boulevard SE

- Tumwater Falls Park
  200 Deschutes Way SW

- Tumwater Historical Park
  777 Simmons Road SW

THINGS TO DO

June
- Duck Dash
  Tumwater Falls Park
  (360) 491-9195

September
- Bluegrass in Tumwater
  American Heritage Campground
  (360) 943-8778

September–November
- Salmon Running
  Tumwater Falls Park
  (360) 943-2550

October
- Harvest Festival
  Tumwater Falls Park
  (360) 754-4217

Southern end of Tumwater Falls
Photo by Jenni Jones

Hexen Glass Studio

ARTS & CRAFTS: *Best stained glass studio in Tumwater*

Hexen Glass Studio specializes in custom stained glass that can be used in windows, entryways and cabinet doors. In addition to designing stained glass for your home or business, Hexen Glass offers classes you can take to learn the craft yourself. Hexen Glass is run by the mother-and-daughter team of Renate (mom) and Gabriela Cowan (daughter). The women, who founded Hexen Glass Studio in 1994, pride themselves on maintaining the highest quality of workmanship. When producing your custom order, Hexen Glass works closely with you to create a beautiful and personal addition to your windows or entryway. Adding art glass in cabinet doors brings a sparkle to your kitchen and is a great way to dress up any other room in your home or office. The Hexen Glass shop carries a selection of beautiful, one-of-a-kind stained glass and fused glass items, many of which were created by Gabriela. The shop also has bevels, tools and supplies, as well as books and patterns. It carries selected fusing supplies. The Cowans maintain high standards in the classroom as well as the studio. They believe that if you have a thorough understanding of the basics, you will be more comfortable creating your own glass art. Renate teaches classes in lead and copper foil technique. She offers workshops every month on topics such as Stepping Stones, Mosaics, Lamp Making, Basic Fusing and several others. If stained glass interests you, Hexen Glass Studio is a must destination.

3006 29th Avenue SW, Tumwater WA
(360) 705-8758
www.hexenglass.com

The Valley Athletic Club

HEALTH & BEAUTY: *Best athletic club in Tumwater*

For more than 30 years, the Valley Athletic Club in Tumwater has been changing people's lives. It is one of the largest and most complete health clubs on the West Coast, with fitness solutions tailor-made to suit any age or interest. It also holds surprises you won't find at just any fitness facility, like a full-service day spa and a pro shop ready to outfit you for the activity of your choice. From successful weight loss programs to physical therapy services, your health and wellness are top priority. With so much to recommend it, it's no wonder so many physicians recommend it to their patients. A helpful staff including nationally certified personal trainers and instructors set the tone for this club. The Valley features four swimming pools, five weight rooms, two gyms, plus raquetball, indoor and outdoor tennis, yoga studios, more than 70 exercise classes weekly and dozens of youth athletic programs. The V spa is the new gem in this stellar line-up, with specialty massages and a full array of body treatments, facials, manicures and pedicures to keep every inch of you looking and feeling great. Creative spa packages for men and women relax the mind and rejuvenate the body.

If looking and feeling better are important to you, the Valley Athletic Club is the perfect place for you. With a preschool and day care, a café, travel agency and even a dry cleaner, there is a lot to love. Try out the Valley Athletic Club soon, where all guests are welcome.

4833 Tumwater Valley Drive, Tumwater WA
(360) 352-3400

Photo courtesy of USGS/Cascades Volcano Observatory

Vancouver to Mount St. Helens

Vancouver to Mount St. Helens

An elk laying next to a stream

VANCOUVER TO MOUNT ST. HELENS is linked by I-5, which is in many ways the Main Street of the West Coast. Most Far West residents live within 100 miles of the highway.

At Washington's southern border, Vancouver is often seen as a suburb of Portland, but this city is actually the oldest European settlement in Washington. It was founded in 1825 by Dr. John McLoughlin, chief factor of the Hudson's Bay Company, to serve as a center for the fur trade. Fort Vancouver residents included many Indians and even Hawaiians, but a majority of the inhabitants were from Quebec, and the language of the settlement was French.

After Vancouver became American territory, Hudson Bay's business declined and the fort was eventually handed over to the United States military. North along the Colombia River is Longview, a planned city built by a lumber company to provide homes for its workers. It is one of the largest planned communities in the country. In 1852, residents north of the Colombia River met at Monticello, now a Longview neighborhood, to petition Congress to create Washington Territory.

The visitor's center for Mount St. Helens is the next stop north on I-5. Tourists flock to see the site of the most deadly and costly volcanic eruption in US history. A little further on, historic U.S. Highway 12 leads to Mount Rainier National Park. Each year, two million people visit the park, home of the highest peak in the Cascades. Next comes Centralia, founded by a freed slave named George Washington, which grew as a stopover for stagecoaches operating between the Columbia River and Seattle.

Star trails above an erupting Mount St. Helens
Photo courtesy of USGS/Cascades Volcano Observatory

MOUNT ST. HELENS

On a Sunday morning in May 1980, Mount St. Helens erupted. The explosion tore off the top of the mountain. Nearly 230 square miles of forest were blown down or buried. A mushroom cloud of ash rose thousands of feet in the air and drifted east, turning day into night as ash fell over much of eastern Washington. In 1982, the Federal government created the 172-square-mile National Volcanic Monument, a wilderness area dedicated to research, recreation and education. In 2004, the volcano began to steam, and thousands of small earthquakes shook the area. Climbing was suspended until July 2006, when the mountain was deemed quiet enough to let the public back in. Visitors can make several stops on their tour of the volcano. Immediately off I-5, the Mount St. Helens Visitor Center at Silver Lake provides exhibits on the area before, during and after the eruption. The Center offers a walk-through volcano model. About 40 miles to the east, the Coldwater Ridge Visitor's Center paints an amazing picture of how plants and animals recovered after the blast. Stroll the quarter-mile Winds of Change interpretive trail and enjoy panoramic views of the mountain, newly formed lakes and the debris-filled Toutle River Valley. Nine miles further, at the end of the highway, the Johnston Ridge Observatory lies at the heart of the blast zone. The Observatory's state-of-the-art displays graphically portray the sequence of geologic events that led up to the eruption. Read amazing eyewitness accounts from eruption survivors. Take a one-half mile walk on the Eruption Trail and see the lava dome, the crater and landslide deposits. Mount St. Helens will give you an utterly unique look at the power of nature.

**42218 NE Yale Bridge Road, Amboy WA
(Monument Headquarters)
(360) 449-7800
3029 Spirit Lake Highway, Castle Rock WA
(Silver Lake Visitor's Center)
(360) 274-0962**
www.fs.fed.us/gpnf/mshnvm

Mount Saint Helens as seen from the Oregon side of the border

Mount Rainier up close and personal

MOUNT RAINIER

Mount Rainier, the very emblem of Washington State, exerts a powerful influence on everyone who sees it. A volcano, Mount Rainier is encased in more than 35 square miles of snow and ice. It was originally known as Tacoma, from a Puyallup Indian word meaning mother of waters. Mount Rainier National Park, established in 1899, contains outstanding examples of old growth forests and subalpine meadows. Nearly two million people come to enjoy the grandeur and beauty of Mount Rainier each year. They may camp along glacier-fed rivers, photograph wildflowers or simply admire the view. The Wonderland Trail winds more than 90 miles around the mountain. Nearby ski areas include Crystal Mountain and White Pass. While many visitors try to see the park in a day, others find they can easily spend a week or more in the area. You can explore historic Longmire in the southwest corner of the park. Try Bourbon Buffalo Meatloaf at the Paradise Inn. From Stevens Canyon, take a short hike to the Grove of the Patriarchs, a spectacular virgin forest. Sunrise, a high point, is popular from July to October, and provides outstanding views of the mountain and its glaciers. Guided snowshoe walks are offered in winter and may be suitable for older children. Mountain climbing can be arduous. Even expert climbers require two to three days to reach the summit. About 10,000 people attempt the climb each year. See Mount Rainier up close, and you will feel its draw.

**Tahoma Woods, Star Route, Ashford WA
(360) 569-2211**
www.nps.gov/mora

CENTRALIA

Centralia is famous throughout the Pacific Northwest as a premier destination for antique hunting. Hundreds of antique dealers offer an incredible range of antiques, from fine china and quality furniture to unusual collectibles.

PLACES TO GO

- Riverside Park and Twin City Skate Park
  Judson Road

- Fort Borst Park
  Johnson Road W

THINGS TO DO

July
- Air Fair
  Chehalis-Centralia Airport
  (360) 748-1230

- Antique and Art Fest
  Downtown Centralia
  (360) 807-1244

- Summerfest Celebration (4th of July)
  Fort Borst Park
  (360) 748-8885

August
- Southwest Washington Fair
  Fairgrounds
  (360) 736-6072

September
- Southwest Washington ARTrails
  The Depot
  www.artrailsofsww.org

- Chehalis River Watershed Festival
  Riverside Park
  (360) 330-7512

Blockhouse of Fort Borst on the Chehalis River near Centralia, Washington, ca. 1898

McMenamins
Olympic Club Hotel & Theater
ACCOMMODATIONS: *Best hotel, theater and pub in the region*

Opened in 1908, McMenamins Olympic Club Hotel and Theater boasts a colorful and thoroughly checkered past. From brawling outlaws and infamous poker games through the scandalous 1920s, this gentlemen's resort managed to stay on remarkably good terms with the local constabulary. A classic railroad hotel, the Olympic thrived throughout Prohibition, purportedly spiriting hidden Canadian liquor from the tracks through tunnels leading to the Club's basement. Over time, owners of the establishment have seen fit to respect the impressive 1913 remodel. The splendid mahogany bar, in what is now the Olympic Club Pub, is an extraordinary example of the era, as is the massive Round Oak woodstove. By the 1930s, the Olympic had earned a reputation for good and plentiful food, and people stood three deep waiting for a seat at the counter. The McMenamins contribute to the reputation with pristine produce, hormone-free Oregon country beef and the freshest seafood found anywhere. The Olympic Club Brewery serves McMenamins' vast array of artisan beers, including Hammerhead Ale and Terminator Stout. The hotel's 27 guestrooms are fully restored in period style, with in-room sinks and private bathrooms down the hall. Each room pays homage to a colorful, historic local character. The classic billiards parlor features some of its original Brunswick pool tables, while the vintage 1920s movie theater screens new releases. For good food and unique accommodations, revel in a century of local history at McMenamins Olympic Club Hotel & Theater.

112 N Tower Avenue, Centralia WA
(360) 736 - 5164
www.mcmenamins.com

Up the Creek Antiques
SHOPPING: *Best antique store in Centralia*

When Dan and Sue Horwath moved to Centralia from Maryland's Eastern Shore in 1975, they needed a way to furnish their first house. Those efforts blossomed into a wholesale business called Up The Creek Antiques, a fitting name for a business that began 15 miles from the nearest town, close to Lincoln Creek. They dealt in American antique furniture purchased their old hunting grounds on the East Coast. Over time their business gathered a retail following, so they opened the American Antique Furniture Market in 1990. When they discovered that the name Up The Creek Antiques was popular, they decided to bring it back into their business name, so they are now officially Up The Creek Antiques – American Antique Furnishings. In 2004, Up The Creek Antiques purchased their own building, restored its original tin ceilings and walls, wooden floors and period appointments. The 7,000-square-foot showroom displays antique furniture, and some custom pieces, in a variety of periods, styles and woods along with vintage appointments appropriate to the furnishings. Their restoration shop is staffed by experienced craftsmen committed to restoring pieces authentically. Whether you need a chair re-glued or wish to explore their expertly restored building and showroom, Up The Creek Antiques is the place to go.

209 North Tower, Centralia WA
(360) 330-0427 or (800) 246-0868
www.upthecreek-antiques.com

Pacific Galleries Antique Mall

SHOPPING: *Best antique mall and auction in the region*

For more than three decades, Pacific Galleries in Seattle has conducted sales of superb antiques and fine art, earning a reputation for professionalism and integrity. Pacific Galleries is proud of its standing in the community. Their research team is experienced in the intricacies of the antique industry and it shows. Pacific Galleries works hard to bring together the region's most prestigious designers and antique dealers, in an auction setting, offering many unique items ranging from furniture and jewelry to fine arts and handcrafted artifacts. A stroll through the antique mall lets you see a sampling of the professional displays of individual boutiques. Pacific Galleries offers lots of cases, lots of spaces, says Pacific Galleries' chief operations officer Lynn Kenyon, resulting in a wide selection of high-end art, antiques and estate goods. With auctions usually beginning at 5:30 pm, you'll have an entertaining evening as you marvel at the amazing selection of antiques available in a single setting. Assorted furniture pieces of American oak, mid-century modern and European styles are augmented by artwork pieces, including china, crystal, silver, pottery and bronze. Pacific Galleries assists sellers by helping auction anything from an entire estate to a single item. See for yourself what is available, seven days a week, at Pacific Galleries Antique Mall, which offers locations in Seattle and Centralia.

241 S Lander Street, Seattle WA
(206) 292-3999 or (800) 560-9924
310 N Tower Avenue, Centralia WA
(360) 736-1282 or
www.pacgal.com

Common Folk Company

SHOPPING: *Most inviting specialty store in Centralia*

Inviting, charming, approachable. These are terms customers use to describe the Common Folk Company, a store that is anything but common. Imagine walking into a shop that literally takes your breath away with its huge floral arrangements and beautiful selection. Now imagine the smell of fresh baked pie and steamy espresso drifting towards you from the adjoining Good Lunch Café. Kathryn and Eric Straub and their long-time employees offer beautiful gifts and home décor with highly personalized service. You will find unusual antiques, fabulous and funky purses, European soaps, statuary, decorations for your home and other useful items. Since its establishment in 1989, Common Folk continues to hold seasonal holiday events featuring festive décor and regional folk artists. Stop by and let the Common Folk Company provide you with a new item to brighten up your life.

125 E High Street, Centralia WA (360) 736-8066

CHEHALIS

When the Northern Pacific Railroad built northward to Tacoma, it ignored Claquato, then the Lewis County seat. Settlers decided that, if the railroad would not go to the county seat, the county seat must go to the railroad. By 1874, the county seat was moved to the new settlement of Chehalis, leaving Claquato little more than a historical landmark.

PLACES TO GO

- Stan Hedwall Park
  1501 Rice Road

- Recreation Park, including Penny Playground
  221 SW 13th Street

- Vintage Motorcycle Museum
  545 N Market Boulevard

- Veterans Memorial Museum
  100 SW Veterans Way

THINGS TO DO

July
- ChehalisFest
  (360) 748-3635

Chehalis-Centralia Railroad Association

ATTRACTIONS: *Steam railroading*

Enjoy the sights, sounds and nostalgia of steam railroading at the Chehalis-Centralia Railroad Association, which began when a group of volunteers wanted to restore a 1916 logging locomotive. The locomotive had been in the City of Chehalis Recreation Park for 30 years. After the restoration began, several other railroad cars were acquired. Operations began in the summer of 1989. Trains operate over a nine-and-a-half mile section of track that weaves through scenic rolling hills and farmland, over several wooden trestles and along the Chehalis River. It is one of the few steam-powered, standard-gauge tourist railroads in the state. Dinner trains are operated on a seasonal schedule and special charters are available. During late May and early June, special trains are scheduled for school classes. Murder Mystery Dinner Trains are also scheduled on specific dates. Browse their website, and pick your event.

1945 S Market Boulevard, Chehalis WA
(360) 748-9593
www.ccrra.com

Veterans Memorial Museum

ATTRACTIONS: *Sobering reminder of sacrifice*

Dedicated to the men and women who honorably served the United States in the Armed Forces during times of both peace and war, the Veterans Memorial Museum in Chehalis is an extraordinary place. Co-founders Lee and Barbara Grimes and Loren and Patti Estep opened the museum on Veterans Day 1997, releasing the floodgates of painful yet incredibly important memories of our nation's history. They wanted to provide a place for veterans to congregate, release emotions and revisit their heroic efforts. Museum director Lee Grimes is often overwhelmed with personal reflections and stories of combat, sacrifice and honor. Entering the museum, visitors are greeted by a USO canteen and World War II era music. The main gallery is host to 85 glass display cases housing a variety of military effects, arranged in chronological order from the Revolutionary War through Iraq. A government-issued baseball bat and glove representing fun contrast sharply with the sobering reality of war that accompanies a body bag and nurse's uniform. The Oral History Room, named after Stanton Price, a local veteran who survived more than three years in Japanese POW camps, provides video footage of battles, interviews and other military history. The Veterans Memorial Museum is an unforgettable experience. It is a place to pay homage to those who made this country what it is today and to ensure that they shall not be forgotten.

100 SW Veterans Way, Chehalis WA
(360) 740-8875
www.veteransmuseum.org

Sowerby's

RESTAURANTS: *Authentic British fare and High Tea*

British travelers heading up and down I-5 often do a double take around Exit 77 when they see the little house with the Union Jack prominently displayed on its roof. If they're curious enough to stop they'll find Sowerby's Restaurant, where Sue Smith, who was born and raised in the British Isles, will make them feel right at home. Sowerby's name is a tribute to Sue's mother, Vera Sowerby, and its bill of fare pays homage to Vera's native land with traditional United Kingdom dishes done right, such as shepherd's pie, fish and chips, and haggis. Sue does make a few concessions to traditional American tastes, most notably with her special chicken, which is made from a secret recipe that delights customers no matter where they're from. The traditional English food didn't catch on right away. Sue estimates that only about 10 percent of her customers ordered anything British when the restaurant first opened, but once the word spread, locals as well as visitors from across the Atlantic started tucking into treats like steak and Guinness pie. In August 2004 Sue began offering high tea, as well. It's a reservation only affair: a wonderful repast of real English tea, watercress sandwiches, Scotch eggs, shortbread biscuits, and much more, served in a properly cozy manner. You don't want to miss Sowerby's.

227 SW Riverside Drive, Chehalis WA (360) 748-8060

ROCHESTER

The town of Rochester was founded by Swedish immigrants, and two of the community's festivals reflect that heritage.

THINGS TO DO

May
• Prairie Appreciation Day
Glacial Heritage Preserve
(360) 570-0083

June
• Swede Day Midsommar Festival
Swede Hall
(360) 273-7974

August
• Sleep in the Park!
Community Camp Out and Barbecue
Rochester Community Center
(360) 273-0398

December
• Lucia Queen of Light Celebration
Swede Hall
(360) 273-7974

Rochester Motocross, January 2006

How 'bout A Basket?

SHOPPING: *Best place to buy creative enjoyment packages*

How 'bout A Basket? is a truly fun place. Owner Vikki Vice wanted a business that would let her stay home with the kids. A basket company was her solution. But this isn't just any basket company. Vikki creates creative enjoyment packages. Several of her most popular baskets illustrate what is possible. The Blue & Gold basket, for instance, is filled with crackers, cookies, sparkling cider, Ghiradelli coffee, chocolates and nuts. Night @ the Movies features fabulous ceramic popcorn bowls filled with everything needed for movie watching, including a movie rental card. NW Breakfast is filled with the ingredients for a terrific breakfast, Northwest-style, including pancake mix, Marionberry jam, Lowery's coffee and much more. Vikki has baskets aimed at gardeners and sports fans, coffee drinkers and tea lovers. How 'bout A Basket? prepares custom baskets that let realtors and other businesses present themselves in a classy and eye-catching manner. Vikki can work with company colors and incorporate your logo into the baskets. She offers free delivery to businesses from Lacey to Chehalis and nationwide shipping. Vikki consistently supports area communities by donating to fundraising efforts. For a perfect gift rapidly prepared with professionalism and high quality, call How 'bout A Basket?

18940 Marble Street, Rochester WA   (360) 352-1421 or (888) 773-GIFT (4438) *www.howboutabasket.com*

Spirit Lake
Photo courtesy of USGS/Cascades Volcano Observatory

VANCOUVER

When the Lewis and Clark expedition camped at Vancouver in 1806, Lewis wrote that it was "the only desired situation for settlement west of the Rocky Mountains." That observation may have been a bit hard on the rest of the Oregon Country, but it certainly is true that Vancouver was a great place to settle.

PLACES TO GO

- Clark County Historical Museum
  1511 Main Street
  (360) 993-5679

- Fort Vancouver National Historic Site
  612 E Reserve Street
  (360) 696-7655

- General Oliver Otis Howard House
  750 Anderson Street
  (360) 992-1820

- George C. Marshall House
  1301 Officers Row
  (360) 693-3103

- Pearson Air Museum
  1115 E 5th Street
  (360) 694-7026

- Ulysses S. Grant House
  1101 Officers Row
  (360) 694-5252

- Esther Short Park
  800 Columbia Street

- Marine Park
  SE Marine Park Way and Columbia Way

- Old Apple Tree Park
  112 Columbia Way

- Salmon Creek Park/Klineline Pond
  1112 NE 117th Street

- Vancouver Lake Park
  6801 NW Lower River Road

- Waterfront Park
  115 Columbia Way

- Water Works Park
  Fourth Plain and Ft. Vancouver Way

Salmon Run Bell Tower in Esther Shore Park
Photo Courtesy of SW Washington Convention and Visitors Bureau

Columbia River Renaissance Trail
Photo courtesy of SW Washington Convention and Visitors Bureau

THINGS TO DO

June
- The Family Fair
  Esther Short Park
  (360) 695-1325

July
- Fort Vancouver Rodeo
  Clark County Saddle Club
  (360) 896-6654

- Fourth of July fireworks
  Fort Vancouver
  (360) 816-6200

August
- The Taste of Vancouver
  *Esther Short Park www.
  thetasteofvancouver.com*

- Vancouver Wine & Jazz Festival
  Esther Short Park
  (503) 224-8499

September
- Vancouver Sausage Festival
  St. Joseph School
  (360) 696-4407

October
- Old Apple Tree Festival
  Old Apple Tree Park
  (360) 619-1108

December
- Skyview Jazz Festival
  Skyview High School
  (360) 695-3565

Pearson Air Museum

ATTRACTIONS: *Oldest airfield in the US*

Pearson Air Museum is at historic Pearson Field, the oldest continuously-operating airfield in the United States and part of Vancouver's National Historic Reserve. The museum sports a small collection of well-restored aircraft housed in the country's second-oldest wooden aircraft hangar. A 1913 Voisin III is one of the oldest aircraft on display. The museum offers a hands-on learning center where kids of all ages can learn about aerodynamics. A theater shows aviation films on demand. Visitors can tour the maintenance shop, where volunteer mechanics restore antique aircraft. In the summer, the museum hosts Cruz-in the Runway, a weekly fly-in event that features classic aircraft plus pre-1974 cars. The current museum is the first step in a project to recreate the Army Air Corps field that existed in the 1920s and 1930s. The field was originally the polo grounds of the Vancouver Barracks. In 1912, Silas Christofferson flew the first airplane to land here. He launched his Curtis-type pusher aircraft from the roof of the Multnomah Hotel in Portland. A replica of this plane is in the museum. Pearson Field really took off during World War I, when the Army used the site to mill wood for airplanes. The Army put up a building for the mill in 1918. In 1921, this became the field's airplane hangar. It housed Italian prisoners of war during World War II. Browse through the exhibits and displays at Pearson Air Museum and discover the pioneering days of aviation in the Pacific Northwest.

1115 E 5th Street, Vancouver WA
(360) 694-7026
www.pearsonairmuseum.org

Heathman Lodge

ACCOMMODATIONS: *Best lodge in Vancouver*

The Heathman Lodge is an Alpine-style lodge filled with the art and charm of the Pacific Northwest. General manager Brett Wilkerson describes it as an unexpected urban retreat that offers travelers and visitors from the Portland/Vancouver area a blend of "heart-felt service, business amenities, and rustic mountain lodge comfort." The Lodge itself is an impressive work of rustic architecture built by craftsmen out of wood from Northwest forests. As you walk into the lobby, you'll see shining stone floors, gleaming wood and wonderful handwoven blankets. The Heathman Lodge website has an intriguing feature that allows a virtual visitor to stand in the lobby or several other locations and slowly turn in a full circle, seeing the full scope of the furnishings. Hudson's Restaurant features Iron Chef winner Mark Hosack preparing handcrafted American food in the rustic setting. From the hand-carved newel posts in the lobby with their representations of the Raven and a powerful North Coast Indian figure to the custom-made furniture throughout, you will find many treasures of the region at the Heathman Lodge. What you will also find are 121 spacious guest rooms, 21 signature suites, a business level, indoor pool, whirlpool, sauna and fitness center, excellent communications amenities, including data ports, and private dining rooms that can seat up to 300, along with service that can't be matched.

7801 NE Greenwood Drive, Vancouver WA
(360) 254-3100 or (888) 475-3100
www.heathmanlodge.com

The Bedford

LIFESTYLE DESTINATIONS: *Best independent living in Vancouver*

Since 1998, the Bedford has been giving seniors seeking a retirement residence in the Vancouver area a superior choice. The Bedford offers several roomy floor plans with full kitchens, full-sized washers and dryers, walk-in closets and cozy fireplaces. The secure environment and beautiful grounds assure your comfort and safety, and several comfortable transportation options promise your continued independence. Residents can enjoy the company of friends and neighbors while dining on nutritious, chef-prepared meals. The Bedford provides a range of activities to assure an active retirement lifestyle. Take advantage of an exercise room, an indoor heated pool and spa, plus a library, hair salon, billiards room and lounge with a large-screen television. There's always a game, movie or class awaiting your participation. The Bedford is conveniently located near hospitals, shopping and a golf course. On a clear day, some of the apartments feature views of Mount Hood and east Portland. Managers live on-site and provide round-the-clock service. Holiday Retirement Corporation owns and manages this stunning property, along with gracious retirement living centers across Canada, the United States and Great Britain. With all that experience, you can be assured this corporation provides the kind of gracious retirement living today's seniors demand. Print out the coupon on the Bedford website for a free lunch and tour of this prestigious independent living community.

13303 SE McGillivray Boulevard, Vancouver WA
(360) 891-6898 or (800) 322-0999
www.the-bedford.com

Vancouver National Historic Reserve

PARKS: *Best historical monument*

Fort Vancouver and its associated sites form the most important historic monument in the Northwest. Fort Vancouver was the main regional supply depot for the western part of North America in the early 1900s and was known as the New York of the West. The Vancouver sites, known collectively as the Vancouver National Historic Reserve, include Fort Vancouver, the Vancouver Barracks and the Pearson Field aviation site. Millions of archaeological artifacts lie under the ground, left by American Indians, Hudson Bay Company employees and their families, U.S. Army soldiers and their families and others who once lived or passed through here. You can join more than a dozen different tours at the reserve. Park rangers offer guided tours of the reconstructed fort daily. Attend living history demonstrations in the kitchen, blacksmith shop, period garden and elsewhere. Several tours teach visitors about the science of archeology or let them view some of the 1.5 million artifacts found at the site. Rangers introduce children to the past through Kids Digs and the Counting House Exhibit. The Vancouver Barracks, on the ridge above the fort, were a major Army center for a century. Many officers who later gained fame were stationed at Vancouver early in their careers, including George McClelland, Ulysses Grant and George Marshall. Even today, units of the U.S. Army Reserve are based in parts of the barracks. Neighboring Pearson Field is one of the oldest airports on the West Coast. Here, you can visit the Pearson Air Museum at the Jack Murdock Aviation Center. Other attractions managed by the reserve include the Columbia River Waterfront Park, the Water Resources Education Center and even the McLoughlin House in Oregon City, Oregon. You can easily spend a day enjoying the past at Vancouver National Historic Reserve.

612 E Reserve Street, Vancouver WA
(360) 696-7655
www.nps.gov/fova

Photo courtesy of Southwest Washington Convention & Visitors Bureau

Pasta Cucina
RESTAURANTS: *Best Italian food*

The Academy, Vancouver
Photo courtesy of Southwest Washington Convention & Visitors Bureau

When you are looking for delicious and reasonably priced Italian food, look no further than Pasta Cucina. Pasta Cucina is the perfect place for authentic homemade dishes served in a home-like setting where children are always welcome. A customer favorite dish, Tortellini Rosé, is made from cheese-filled tortellini tossed with sun-dried tomatoes and served in a rosé sauce. Another favorite entrée is a boneless breast of chicken wrapped with Italian bacon and topped with mozzarella and Gorgonzola cheeses. Choose from a good selection of sumptuous salads in addition to a variety of appetizers and desserts. The house wine is Luna di Luna Merlot. Beer and wine are also available. Owners Jason Lawson and Dawn and Brandon Clark established Pasta Cucina in the same location more than five years ago. In addition to the restaurant, they offer catering services. For an authentic taste of Italy, be sure to stop in at Pasta Cucina.

212 NE 164th Avenue, Vancouver WA
(360) 882-5122

WOODLAND

Incorporated in 1906, Woodland, located 20 miles north of Vancouver, is the southern gateway to Mount St. Helens. Woodland is a growing city with a passion for tradition.

PLACES TO GO

- Hulda Klager Lilac Gardens
  115 South Pekin Road

THINGS TO DO

April–May
- The Lilac Festival
  Hulda Klager Lilac Gardens
  (360) 225-8996

June
- Planter's Days
  Downtown Woodland
  (360) 225-9888

October
- Annual Apple Pressing
  The Cedar Creek Grist Mill
  (360) 225-5832

Empress Palace

ACCOMMODATIONS: *Best place for special events in Woodland*

Approaching the Empress Palace in Woodland, you first see ornamental iron entry gates guarded by two mythical, winged lions on tall masonry gate posts. Upon entering the property you will be amazed by the garden court that features 35 spiraled columns, and enormous Corinthian-style columns supporting a massive Italian-style portico with arched and coffered ceilings. A stunning marble entryway with a 40-foot-high masonry rotunda (the largest privately owned masonry dome in Washington) awaits. Empress Palace, a 13,000-square-foot French-Italian Renaissance edifice, is an enchanting place. This has to be the perfect spot for a wedding. It's a secluded mountaintop retreat on a seven-acre estate overlooking the Columbia and Lewis Rivers. The Neuschwanders, who purchased the property in 2000, have pledged to give the best quality service, making every celebration in this idyllic setting unique and exceptional. Their mission is to "create a sense of place that stirs the imagination to the royal pageantry and splendor of the French-Italian Renaissance period." Their impressive services and facilities include everything you need to create an unforgettable occasion. The Empress Palace, sometimes called the Taj Mahal of the Northwest, came alive through the imagination of Dr. Ronald Gerne of Woodland nearly two decades ago. The Neuschwanders have finished the work of art that was more than 15 years in the making, and are delighted to offer this lovely location for your special events.

460 Empress Lane, Woodland WA
(360) 225-4468 or (800) 474-6994
www.empresspalace.com

Photo by Stefan Isaacs

The Olympic Peninsula

The Olympic Peninsula

Mountain stream

THE OLYMPIC PENINSULA is dominated by nature. In the center, Olympic National Park soars with glaciers and saw-toothed peaks. Home to animals found nowhere else, the park is an international Biosphere Reserve and a World Heritage Site.

On the northern shore of the peninsula, the forests of Canada's Vancouver Island loom in the distance. To the west, massive trees draped with moss form a temperate rain forest where Pacific Ocean breakers collide with the rugged coast.

If you explore the peninsula from east to west, you will first land at Port Townsend, the second-oldest city in the state and a cultural oasis. Once a bustling port, the economy collapsed in the 1890s when the railroads turned Seattle into the great northwestern terminus. As a result, Port Townsend kept its original buildings and now boasts one of the densest collections of Victorian architecture in the country.

Further west is Port Angeles, which is the commercial hub of the Olympic Peninsula. Above the town rises Hurricane Ridge, a stunning viewpoint and ski area, one mile up and only 19 miles inland.

From Port Angeles, you have a choice of scenic drives. You can parallel the Strait of Juan de Fuca, past wild beaches littered with driftwood, and end at Ozette, a hiker's paradise on the Pacific Coast. You can turn inland, past Lake Crescent, home of the Beardslee trout. You then enter the Olympic National Forest and the Sol Duc valley, a unique jungle-like ecosystem dominated by Sitka spruce and Western hemlock.

FORKS

The City of Forks is nestled between a million acres of national park and the Pacific Coast. Forks has traditionally been a timber town, but technology is taking a major role. A loop of fiber-optic cable around the Peninsula was recently laid. Local schools are among the most wired schools in the nation, and the Bill & Melinda Gates Foundation has chosen Forks High School as a model for High Tech High. Forks has an incubator for tech start-ups, a new industrial park, an airport, and a community aquatic center. Forks is located near the Olympic National Park's Pacific Ocean beaches and the Hoh River Rain Forest. With a population of nearly 5,000 people, Forks is the largest city between Port Angeles and Aberdeen.

PLACES TO GO

- Olympic Natural Resources Center- University of Washington
  1455 S Forks Avenue (360) 374-3220

THINGS TO DO

April
- Fabric of the Forest Quilt Show
  (360) 374-2531

- RainFest
  Various locations around Forks

June
- Surfing and Tradition
  A cultural board and kayak surf competition
  (360) 374-4090

July
- Forks Old Fashioned 4th of July
  (360) 374-5412

- Clallam Bay /Sekiu Fun Days
  www.clallambaysekiufundays.com

- Quileute Days Tribal festival
  www.forkswa.com

August
- Wild Blackberry Festival
  www.joycewa/joycedaze.htm

- Forks Family Festival
  (360) 374-5412

Rafting the Elwha River
Courtesy of Washington State Tourism
Photo by Jim Poth

Kalaloch Lodge

ACCOMMODATIONS: *Best resort*

Kalaloch Lodge, perched on a bluff overlooking the Pacific, is one of Olympic National Park's most memorable resorts. When Charles W. Becker, Sr. acquired roughly 40 acres of land just south of Kalaloch Creek, there were no roads to the property. Milled lumber that washed up on the beach was used to construct the first buildings, erected in the late 1920s. After the Olympic Loop Highway (now Highway 101) provided better access to the area, more cabins were built. The complex, known as "Becker's Ocean Resort," offered simple lodging to auto travelers. In 1942 the U.S. Coast Guard established a beach patrol station there, adapting the buildings to suit its needs. After World War II, the buildings reverted back to recreational use and the Beckers made a variety of improvements, including adding a new Main Lodge. In 1978, the National Park Service purchased the property. Soon after, the resort was renamed Kalaloch Lodge. Kalaloch offers the only year round lodging in Olympic National Park. Visitors can stay in comfortable accommodations in the Main Lodge, secluded Seacrest House, or cozy cabins with Franklin fireplaces. Fresh and artfully prepared coastal cuisine and spectacular views abound in the Kalaloch Lodge Restaurant. Enjoy the grandeur of this glorious coastal land where the wonders of the Pacific are right outside your door. Kalaloch became part of the Olympic Coast National Marine Sanctuary in July of 1994. This Sanctuary is our nation's 14th marine sanctuary and covers an area of approximately 3,300 square miles.

157151 Highway 101, Forks WA
(866) 525-2562
www.visitkalaloch.com

PORT ANGELES

Port Angeles covers 10.1 square miles, with a population of 19,000. It is the activity center of the North Olympic Peninsula and the seat of Clallam County. The downtown shopping district is full of shops, flowers and outdoor art. Rising above the city is snow-capped Hurricane Ridge in Olympic National Park. The community is served by the award-winning Port Angeles Symphony and the Port Angeles Fine Arts Center, a noteworthy museum of contemporary art.

PLACES TO GO

- City Pier
  Lincoln Street on the waterfront

- Francis Street Park
  Main access point for Water Front Trail

- Harbor View Park - Ediz Hook
  Located at the end of Ediz Hook

- Haynes Viewpoint
  Located on Front and Peabody

- Sail & Paddle Park
  Located on Ediz Hook

THINGS TO DO

April
- Olympic Bird Festival
  (360) 681-4076

- Jazz in the Olympics
  (888) 933-6143

May
- Juan De Fuca Festival
  (360) 457-5411

June
- North Olympic Discovery Marathon
  (360) 417-1301

July
- Art Ranger Tour
  (360) 457-3532

August
- Port Angeles Heritage Weekend
  (360) 460-1001

October
- Dungeness Crab & Seafood Festival
  (360) 457-6110

Sol Duc, west of Port Angeles
Courtesy of Washington State Tourism
Photo by Jim Poth

Domaine Madeleine

ACCOMMODATIONS: *Most romantic getaway*

An unmistakable feeling of serenity permeates the air at Domaine Madeleine bed and breakfast, a quiet paradise snuggled between the Olympic Mountains and the Straits of Juan de Fuca. The twinkling lights of Victoria and the starlit sky in the evening, as well as the call of the eagles and whales during the day, create an unequaled atmosphere. The gardens are superb, with a Monet garden replica, woodland garden, cottage garden, rose garden and bamboo garden all vying for attention. The food is exquisitely presented and delicious. A few of the delights may include fresh asparagus and mango salsa placed alongside fresh salmon with Crème Brule for dessert; a Dungeness crab omelet with European-style vegetables and bananas flambé for dessert; and apple crepes covered with fresh berries accompanied by smoked ham, with black rice pudding and coconut milk for dessert. Resident chef Victor makes sure everything is done to perfection and any dietary need is met. For a room, pick from the Ming Suite, Monet, Renoir Suite, Rendezvous or Cottage. All have outstanding views of either the mountains or water. Each has its own entrance for privacy. *Sunset* magazine named Domaine Madeleine one of the 20 Best Seaside Getaways along the Pacific Coast, and was named Best Romantic Bed and Breakfast in the Pacific Northwest by viewers of *Northwest Backroads*. With only five rooms available, summer bookings fill up fast.

146 Wildflower Lane, Port Angeles WA
(360) 457-4174 or (888) 811-8376
www.domainemadeleine.com

A Hidden Haven

ACCOMMODATIONS: *Best bed & breakfast inn*

A Hidden Haven Bed & Breakfast is nestled on 20 secluded acres in lush forest at the foothills of the Olympics. This piece of heaven, a luxury destination and a naturalist's paradise, provides the ultimate romantic experience. Here you will find an ambience full of enchantment and wonder with waterfalls, ponds, gardens, plants and wildlife. The fairy-tale setting makes this a perfect place to have a small wedding, honeymoon, business retreat, family reunion or just to take some time off to relax. There is an abundance of wildlife—some guests report seeing more birds at Hidden Haven than in Olympic National Park. Hidden Haven's three suites and two cottages offer luxury amenities that include private decks and entrances, whirlpool tubs, fireplaces, in-room massage, satellite television and more. In the morning, savor a hot breakfast basket delivered right to your door, or your cottage may be stocked with breakfast goodies. For a truly extraordinary experience, feed the private deer herd, walk the woodland nature trail or feed the koi and trout. End your day with a romantic evening stroll in the lighted gardens. A Hidden Haven is a great place to stay.

1428 Dan Kelly Road, Port Angeles WA
(877) 418-0938 or (360) 452-2719
www.ahiddenhaven.com

Karon's Frame Center
ARTS & CRAFTS: *Best frame store*

Where do you have your unframed artwork hiding? Many of us have family heirlooms and other keepsakes packed away under the bed, in the attic, basement closet or dresser drawers. It seems the only time we ever see these things is when we move or have a garage sale. Well, now is a great time to find it and have it professionally framed at the largest and best equipped full service framing center on the peninsula, Karon's Frame Center. In 1991, Karon Nichols began working at a gallery on the waterfront in Port Angeles. Six months later she became their framer. After eight-and-a-half years, with the encouragement and support of her late husband Al, she opened Karon's Frame Center. The center has grown and expanded in the last six years with a friendly, professional and gifted staff of four and state-of-the-art equipment such as the Wizard, a computerized mat cutter. The Wizard makes it possible to complete decorative mats and multiple opening mats more efficiently and economically. Stop in to see their large selection of ready-made frames, browse through their extensive catalogs or search for art on computer with a database of more than 110,000 images. As Karon's motto says, "If it's worth remembering, it's worth framing."

625 E Front St, Port Angeles WA
(360) 565-0308

Ruddell Auto Mall
AUTO: *Best auto mall on the peninsula*

Starting in 1940, The Ruddell name became synonymous with integrity, quality and automotive reliability in both sales and service. That tradition continues today in its third generation with Howard Ruddell and his team at the clean, modern, state-of-the-art location on Golf Course Road in Port Angeles. The staff are friendly, well trained and helpful. Recognizing that people prefer to do business with people they like and respect, Ruddell Auto Mall promises that the "only thing lower than the price is the pressure." They maintain an impressive inventory of new cars and many more can be available in 24 hours. If you are looking for a hard-to-find vehicle, Ruddell Auto Mall can help you locate it. When it comes to maintenance and repair, the ASC-certified shop represents more than 270 years of combined experience and is presently the highest trained GM service department in the Northwest. While you wait, check out the Parts Pro Shop, where you will find automotive collectibles, apparel and NASCAR items. Don't miss the waiting areas with comfortable couches, wireless Internet access and lots of old car memorabilia. Trust your vehicle purchase and service to Ruddell Auto Mall and you will understand why it has been a community treasure for more than 65 years.

110 Golf Course Road, Port Angeles WA
(360) 452-6822
www.ruddellautomall.com

Bella Rosa Coffeehouse
BAKERIES, COFFEE & TEA: *Best coffeehouse in Port Angeles*

Port Angeles natives Kevin and Linda Berglund have built their professional lives around coffee and work to bring the best coffee possible to visitors and residents in their hometown. Linda named the Bella Rosa Coffeehouse after her Italian mother. The welcome at Bella Rosa is warm and heartfelt, and the Berglunds think of their employees as family. With the lively mix of enthusiastic and caring baristas, there is never a dull moment. You can pop in for a quick espresso to go, but this is a coffeehouse that invites you to linger. Bella Rosa was voted Best Coffee in Port Angeles for five years in a row. Free wireless Internet access means you can do homework or check your email while relaxing with great coffee. Linda uses the freshest, highest quality beans and provides continual training for the baristas to maintain a superior level of drink preparation. Join discriminating coffee drinkers for the best coffee in town. Life is short; drink good coffee.

403 S Lincoln Street, #1, Port Angeles WA
(360) 417-5402

Premier Party Rentals
BUSINESS: *Best party rentals*

Mae Graves, owner of Premier Party, loves what she does, exercising her inborn talents for helping people create fun and memorable events. Premier Party is the perfect place to do this. It is large enough to have a good selection and great prices, but small enough that you can almost always work with the owner if you want to. Mae enjoys helping her customers come up with unique party themes and ideas. Not all of us have a vision for decorating, but in the party business, it is a must and Mac has it. At Premier Party you will find supplies for birthdays, weddings, luaus, over the hill, school dance and holiday décor. They also have you covered for balloon bouquets, inflatable bounces for children's parties and company picnics, costumes, and balloon arches. Stop by Premier Party even if you don't have an excuse for a party… they'll help you think of one.

315 E 1st Port Angeles WA
(360) 457-7368

Susan Parr Travel, Inc.
BUSINESS: *Best vacation planners*

Susan Parr Travel is the kind of good, old-fashioned storefront service that is increasingly hard to find. This is truly a family-style business. Susan's father is not only a great supporter of his daughter's enterprise, he is also the bookkeeper. When you enter the office you will feel as though you are in an exotic hotel in a tropical paradise. It is as bright and cheerful as the highly qualified staff. They will sit down with you and spend as much time as it takes to arrange the vacation of your dreams. In addition to planning all types of travel around the world, Susan specializes in international adoption arrangements. Fully versed in this process, the staff can help families through the often delicate steps in what can often be an emotional journey. Passports, visas, vaccinations, tickets, accommodations and even seat assignments are among the considerations the agency will assist you with. No matter what your travel plans, Susan Parr Travel understands that leaving home can mean leaving your comfort zone. The staff provides personal attention to ensure that you travel comfortably and secure in the knowledge that arrangements are confirmed and you are well prepared. When you plan your journey with Susan Par Travel, you are planning for the best trip you have ever taken.

1234 E Front Street, Port Angeles WA
(360) 452-2188
www.susanparrtravel.com

Angeles Beauty Supply & Salon
HEALTH & BEAUTY: *Best beauty supplies on the north peninsula*

From the time she was 12 years old, Marti Oldham wanted to be a hairdresser and she knew she would have her own salon one day. She realized that dream when she bought Angeles Beauty Supply in 1994. In her capable hands, the business continues to be the largest supplier of professional beauty products on the North Olympic Peninsula catering to local residents and salons. Marti has expanded her services in the process. She combines an expertise in hair design and the latest techniques with an eye toward bringing out the best in each client. She also carries lovely jewelry and hair accessories for that extra sparkle. Adding manicure, pedicure and tanning services makes this a one-stop shop for all your personal needs. Marti even brought in a HEX Upright Tanning System booth in which you stand to tan. This provides even coverage and cuts tanning time in half, helping you "keep your golden glow year round." In addition to carrying top-of-the-line professional product lines, Marti's salon is the Peninsula's exclusive carrier of Kera Vita products. Enjoy the pampering of caring hands, get a tan and pick up the hair and skincare products you need, all in one place at Angeles Beauty Supply.

205 E 8th Street, Suite A, Port Angeles WA
(360) 452-4060

Julie's Shear Elegance
HEALTH & BEAUTY: *Best salon in town*

In conversations about landmark places in Port Angeles that are a part of the community in a big way, you can't leave Julie's Shear Elegance out. They specialize in hair coloring, but they do it all, and you won't be disappointed. Excellence is achieved by maintaining a highly trained enthusiastic staff that is devoted to teamwork. There is no stuffiness at Julie's Shear Elegance. The salon's atmosphere is fun, easy-going and approachable. Helping others feel wonderful is the name of their game. They want more than just making you feel and look good on the outside–they want you to feel good on the inside too. The salon has been in business for over 30 years. When founder Julie Pruss passed away, Tracy Smith, who had been manager for 18 years, was encouraged by the staff to buy the business. With her management background and over 28 years of hairdressing experience, she was more than qualified. Tracy is proud that her employees are like a close knit family. All are homegrown Port Angeleans and all feel a loyalty to keeping alive the foundation and ambiance of the treasure Julie started for the community. It's fun, and you will feel like family. They like to say it's the "big city salon in the small town with the small town prices."

210 E 4th, Port Angeles WA
(360) 457-7993

Fairchild Floors
HOME: *Best flooring*

If you are familiar with the stress of remodeling, or have put off replacing your old floors and carpets because you don't want to deal with the hassle and mess, help is available. Fairchild Floors makes purchasing and installing new floors a stress-free experience. They want to get in and out of your house without you noticing they've been there. Owned by Dave and Linda Fairchild, Fairchild Floors has been a trusted name in flooring ever since Dave's father, Darrell, started laying floors in 1947. Darrell was committed to conducting his business the right way. "My Dad taught me everything about the business," Dave says, "and I stand firm in my commitment to quality products and service." Since taking over the business, Dave has expanded and added a showroom. Dave and Linda work well together and have an excellent reputation for extraordinary customer service. Services and products include carpet, ceramic and marble tile, vinyl and hardwood flooring, window coverings and counter tops. Fairchild Floors offers remodeling counseling and the services of a personal planner for interior design. Assistance in coordinating color and design is graciously provided. Procrastinate no longer. Fairchild Floors will make your remodeling and flooring experience a pleasure.

1404 E 1st Street, Port Angeles WA
(360) 457-1411

Spa Shop & Pellet Heat Company
HOME: *Best place to buy spas and stoves*

The Spa Shop & Pellet Heat Company showroom in the heart of Port Angeles is the place to find top-quality spas and stoves. The professional and courteous staff at the shop have focused on quality products and customer service for more than 22 years. The licensed spa technicians have an average of more than 16 years of experience. The shop carries spas from Hot Spring, Calders, Tiger River, Hot Spot and Solana. Stoves are from Jotul, Mendota and Harmon. You can find a complete line of spa chemicals and accessories, including premium grade pellet fuel, hearth pads, spa and stove vacuums and custom-made spa covers. The shop has an extensive in-house parts department and a computerized water analysis lab. Owner Mike DeRousie makes it a priority to see that his customers' expectations are met and exceeded. "I am very proud of all our employees. They take pride in their work and it shows," says Mike. The average length of employment for each crew member is more than 12 years, and the shop's people enjoy giving back to the area. Mike and two other staff members are volunteer firefighters/EMTs. Another is a baseball coach and one is a volunteer librarian. Visit Spa Shop & Pellet Heat Company for your spa and stove needs.

230-C E First Street, Port Angeles WA
(360) 457-4406
www.spashop.com

Elwha Fish Company
MARKETS: *Best place to buy seafood*

Elwha Fish Company promises they are the best place to get fresh seafood and their customers agree. Originally the Hegg & Hegg Smoked Salmon Company, the company was purchased by the Lower Elwha Klallam Tribe in 2002. For hundreds of years the Elwha Nation has harvested salmon from the sea. In the olden days food storage for cold winters was required for survival. The time-honored tradition of curing fish by smoke was used and continues on at the Elwha Fish Company. Their hand-packed, canned seafood has been enjoyed by millions of people for more than 50 years. The Elwha Fish Company is known worldwide for their smoked salmon. Their fresh Dungeness crab is another favorite. They put together special gift packs that include vacuum packed and freshly canned gifts from the sea. You will want to try their Hood Canal oysters, tuna, and fresh sockeye and coho salmon. They'll pack and ship your selection anywhere you wish. Stop by or call the Elwha Fish Company for their ocean fresh, smoked or frozen seafood. All of their products are guaranteed to be locally caught in the bountiful waters of the Pacific Ocean and the Straits of Juan de Fuca, and delivered fresh to your door.

801 Marine Drive, Port Angeles WA
(360) 457-3344 or (800) 435-FISH (3474)
www.elwhafish.com

Café Garden Restaurant
RESTAURANTS & CAFÉS: *One of the best in Washington*

Dave and Laura Reynolds offer a unique dining experience at the Café Garden Restaurant. The food is superb, they have an in-house bakery, and everything on the menu is fresh, even the salad dressings. From the Belgian waffles and specialty egg dishes at breakfast, to the stir fries and deli sandwiches at lunch, everything is made to meet the highest standards of quality and consistency. Short cuts are never taken here. At dinner, Café Garden Restaurant features an extensive wine list, including wines that have been maturing in their wine cellar since the early 1990s to complement their diverse menu of braised steaks, pastas and fresh seafood. Dave and Laura's mission is to provide the most professional service possible. They fulfill that promise with the help of an outstanding staff, many of whom have been with the restaurant for at least a decade. For them, the Café Garden Restaurant is as much a home as it is a business. The cooks are incredible and they will fix anything you specially request, even if it's not on the menu. With such great food and service, it's no wonder the Café Garden Restaurant is consistently ranked among the best places to eat in Washington.

1506 E First Street, Port Angeles WA
(360) 457-4611

Frugals

RESTAURANTS & CAFÉS: *Best homegrown burger franchise*

Don't worry, you won't have to save your pennies for a hamburger here. At Frugals you'll get a delicious meal and still have change to spare. Peter and Sheila Stewart started their Frugals phenomenon in Port Angeles in 1988 with the goal of providing the highest quality food for the lowest possible prices. Their idea of a double drive-through with no indoor seating has proved to be wildly successful. Frugal's now has three locations in Port Angeles, Tacoma and Auburn. The cool, retro-style stainless-steel building draws endless lines of satisfied customers. Despite its popularity, there is never a long wait at Frugals due to the staff's extreme efficiency. Arriving with the expectation of speedy service and low prices, diners are treated to the best tasting burgers in the area. With no need for fancy trappings, all expenses go to the quality of the food. Gardenburgers and hamburgers can be customized with a choice of cheeses, vegetables and thick-sliced bacon. Grilled chicken and great BLT sandwiches are on the menu, as are shakes, fries and soft drinks. Frugals consistently appears in the Best of the Olympic Peninsula for their burgers, shakes and fries. Time after time Frugals has taken best burger honors in newspaper polls. It's not just the food that's great, the staff is also efficient and fun-loving, evident in the lively camaraderie in the kitchen. The Stewarts have come up with a win-win recipe of simplicity, quality and value. They welcome you to drive through and enjoy their retro bistro.

1520 E Front Street, Port Angeles WA
(360) 452-4320
www.frugalburger.com

Gordy's Pizza & Pasta

RESTAURANTS & CAFÉS: *Best pizza on the North Olympic Peninsula*

For more than 40 years, three generations of the Sexton family have served great Italian food at Gordy's Pizza & Pasta in Port Angeles. This is an old-fashioned pizza place where everything is made from fresh ingredients to ensure that each dish tastes great. Gordy's Pizza & Pasta has often been voted the Best Place for pizza and Italian food by the citizens of the North Olympic Peninsula. It also has the distinction of being the first pizza restaurant on the Peninsula. Gordy and Pat Sexton opened Gordy's in 1961, and now their children Randy Sexton and Cynthia Dawson run the restaurant, with their grandchildren working there, as well. "We can't thank the community enough for their support throughout the years," Randy says, "We grew up in the restaurant and look forward to serving future generations great food." Gordy's offers a wide variety of pizzas, including the restaurant's signature pie, The Works. If it's pasta you're looking for, Gordy's offers a wide selection. They also serve calzones, specialty sandwiches, salads, soups and mouth-watering desserts. Customers can dine in or pick up, including take-and-bake pizzas. They also deliver. Gordy's Pizza & Pasta can accommodate a group of up to 50 in a private dining room. Reservations are not required, but are appreciated for large groups.

1123 E First Street, Port Angeles WA
(360) 457-5056
www.gordyspizza.com

Bushwhacker Seafood Restaurant

RESTAURANTS & CAFÉS:
Best seafood in Clallam County

In 1976, Robert Grattan came to Port Angeles from Montana to manage the Bushwhacker Restaurant. He didn't realize that he'd find love as well as a vocation. When he hired a vivacious woman named Julie as a waitress, he never guessed that they'd get married and run the business together. Now Julie's daughter, Sadie Rose, is in training to take over the family business. The Bushwhacker is known for its fresh local seafood and prime rib, served in a relaxed atmosphere. Their homemade bread and clam chowder, as well as a huge salad bar keep bringing satisfied customers back. The *Peninsula Daily News* named The Bushwhacker as having the Best Seafood, Best Steak, Best Clam Chowder, Best Salad Bar, Best Happy Hour and Best Dessert in Clallam County. Robert and Julie go out of their way to support the community that has judged them so generously by contributing to many local causes. Visit The Bushwhacker and see why they are known as the best at what they do.

1527 E 1st Street, Port Angeles WA
(360) 457-4113

Blue Flame BBQ

RESTAURANTS & CAFÉS: *Best fire pit BBQ on the Peninsula*

True barbecue lives in beautiful Port Angeles. Friends and family urged Blue Flame owner Brad Norman to "step up to the plate" (literally and figuratively). In October of 2004, he did so in a big way, opening the best BBQ joint on the Peninsula. At the Blue Flame, you'll find yourself choosing samples of baby-back pork red spuds, chicken, lamb chops, bleu cheese, spare red spuds, and some of the best steelhead you've ever tasted. Brad offers free samples to all newcomers and travelers. He can do it with confidence knowing they will be back for a meal. Many of their local fans visit Blue Flame multiple times a week. All meals are accompanied by pit-roasted baby red spuds, romaine finger salad and a fresh dinner roll. Blue Flame is a direct fire pit BBQ. It's the REAL deal. Want BBQ, but want to relax at home? Call ahead for pick up and they'll have it ready for you. Brad and his staff quip that "the Olympic Peninsula is completely void of strangers. There are only friends we haven't met yet." It's a truth that applies to Blue Flame BBQ, too. Join them. They want to see you and have you delight in their delicious food as much as they do.

2947 E Highway 101, Port Angeles WA
(360) 452-6355

Dupuis' Restaurant

RESTAURANTS & CAFÉS: *Oldest restaurant on the North Peninsula*

The North Olympic Peninsula's oldest restaurant, Dupuis' Restaurant in Port Angeles, has quite the pedigree. Opened as a bar in 1920, it became Dupuis' Sea Food Inn in 1935. Though it has expanded its offerings over the years, the neon crab sign still stands outside and you can still get the cold cracked Dungeness crab that has drawn flocks of customers for decades. Now managed by Clallam County native Maureen McDonald, Dupuis' Restaurant is proud of its history. The original bar is now the Tavern Dining Room where, among other treats, diners can enjoy whole crabs and garlic bread, cedar plank salmon and Steak Dupuis, which is a filet mignon robed in bacon, topped with fresh Dungeness crab, a burgundy wine sauce and shiitake mushrooms.

The Fireplace Dining Room offers cozy seating around a brick fireplace. All rooms are decorated with historical memorabilia and charming collectibles. A real treat at Dupuis' is the Sunday brunch, featuring such delights as Crabby Bill's Frittata, made with fresh crab, chanterelles and sun-dried tomatoes. Enjoy discovering Dupuis' award-winning menu for yourself.

256861 Highway 101, Port Angeles WA
(360) 457-8033
www.dupuisrestaurant.com

Thai Peppers Restaurant
RESTAURANTS & CAFÉS: *Best Thai cuisine*

Guests at the Thai Peppers Restaurant in Port Angeles will be enticed by the aromas wafting through the air even before setting foot in the door. With its water view dining, this is truly a Washington treasure. Owner Sonthaya Itti has always had a love of cooking. As a young boy,

he dreamed of opening his own authentic Thai restaurant to bring a taste of Thailand to the people of the Northwest. His dream came true when Thai Peppers opened 10 years ago. Thai Peppers offers an amazing array of mouth-watering dishes. High quality ingredients are used in every selection. While many of the dishes are prepared with the traditional spiciness, Thai Peppers aims to please all customers, so dishes can be prepared on the mild side if requested. Thai Peppers Restaurant was voted the Best Asian Restaurant in Clallam County in 2003, was a recipient of the AAA Diamond Rates Awards in 2003, and was included in *Best Places Northwest* in 2002 and 2003. The restaurant also had the honor of serving first lady Laura Bush and her closest friends in July of 2003. Visit Thai Peppers Restaurant for a delicious lunch or dinner.

222 N Lincoln Street, Port Angeles WA
(360) 452-4995

Toga's
RESTAURANTS & CAFÉS: *Best Northwest cuisine*

For the finest in Northwest and international cuisine, come to Toga's in Port Angeles. Toga's uses only the finest ingredients in superb dishes ranging from Dungeness crab cakes and sautéed prawns Provençal to *sauerbraten* with Bavarian potato dumplings. Specialties include Jagersteins, stones heated to 500 degrees on which guests can cook their own choice of meats, and Toga's fondues, including original Swiss cheese, Northwest seafood, and the meat lover's fondue. The fondues require a 24-hour advance reservation, and they're more than a delicious meal. They're a social event. Don't miss out on the desserts, either. Toga's signature dessert is a chocolate macadamia mousse torte Executive chef and co-owner Toga Hertzog apprenticed in Germany after he graduated from Port Angeles High School. He honed his considerable skills in resort hotels in Hawaii, as well as aboard the Royal Viking Sun cruise ship. Returning to his hometown with his wife, Lisa, he opened Toga's in 1995 and has received numerous local and national accolades. In addition to fine food, Toga's features a wine list with selections from the Northwest and around the world, German beer on tap, and local microbrews, as well. Toga's is located in a remodeled 1943 home which boasts Olympic Mountain views. Reservations are recommended. Make it a point to eat at Toga's when you visit Port Angeles.

122 W Lauridsen Boulevard, Port Angeles WA
(360) 452-1952

Camaraderie Cellars
RESTAURANTS & CAFÉS:
Best winery on the Peninsula

For more than a decade, Don and Vicki Corson have been crafting some of Washington State's finest wines at Camaraderie Cellars. Dozens of major international medals have come their way from significant competitions in San Francisco, Los Angeles, New York and Dallas. Additionally, wine ratings in the 90s by national publications validate the words of the *Seattle Times* wine advisor that Camaraderie Cellars "gets good fruit and does it proud." Don, as wine maker, sources grapes from well known vintners such as Artz Vineyards on Red Mountain, and Paul Champoux at Mercer Ranch. Camaraderie's Cabernet Sauvignon, Merlot and other Bordeaux-style red and white wines are found in some of the state's finest restaurants. Visiting Camaraderie Cellars is more than a tasting experience. They are known for warm hospitality, where all guests are invited to celebrate their philosophy that the best things in life are meant to be shared. Views of the Olympic Mountains and an intimate garden picnic location with a giant slab of granite as your table will make your visit to Camaraderie Cellars a memorable one.

334 Benson Road, Port Angeles WA
(360) 417-3564
www.camaraderiecellars.com

PORT HADLOCK

Port Hadlock, Chimacum, and Irondale are commonly referred to as the Tri-Area. It's the hub of eastern Jefferson County and the most populated area in the county. This commercial hub is the gateway to Marrowstone and Indian Islands, popular for camping and seafood harvesting. Port Hadlock is surrounded by natural beauty, from the jagged peaks of the Olympic Mountains to the lush valleys of Chimacum and the crystal waters of Puget Sound

PLACES TO GO

- Anderson Lake State Park
  (888) CAMPOUT

- Fort Flagler State Park
  Eight miles northeast of Port Hadlock on the northern tip of Marrowstone Island

- Old Fort Townsend State Park

- Mystery Bay Park

- Marrowstone Island

- Chimacum Park

- East Beach Park

- Marrowstone Island

- Gibbs Lake

- Lake Leland

- Lower Hadlock

- H.J. Carroll Park

THINGS TO DO

June
- Olympic Music Festival
  (206) 527-8839

July
- Hadlock Days
  www.porthadlock.org

September
- Bunker Hill Memorial Golf Tournament
  (360) 379-3236

December
- Chimacum Arts and Crafts Fair
  (360) 732-4015

- Tri Area Christmas for Children
  (360) 385-2442

The Inn at Port Hadlock
ACCOMMODATIONS: *Best inn*

The Inn at Port Hadlock is nestled on the southern shore of Port Townsend Bay, just a short trip from Seattle. This 1903 inn is rich in history, has unbelievable views and features an incredible dining experience. The landmark Inn offers 46 rooms, 13 of which are deluxe suites with private patios and beautiful bay views. The rooms include exquisite works of art, unique and colorful furniture, and all the amenities of home. Many come with fireplaces. Stop by the lounge in the Inn's award-winning restaurant, Nemo's, for a beverage and appetizer, while viewing the beautiful stained-glass windows that were designed by local artists. For fine dining, experience the Inn's extensive menu of fine food and its exceptional wine collection while enjoying the spectacular harbor views. The Inn offers many activities, from historical walking tours to art and music festivals, and several unbelievable hiking trails. The land around the Inn was once a Salish tribal village known as Tsetsibus, which means "where the sun rises." The land is established as one of the oldest continuously occupied areas in all of Washington, going back over 12,000 years. This is one place you will want to stay.

310 Hadlock Bay Road, Port Hadlock WA
(360) 385-7030 or (800) 785-7030
www.innatporthadlock.com

Ajax Café
RESTAURANTS & CAFÉS: *Most fun café*

The Ajax Café is a little out of the way, but way out of the ordinary. The Ajax Café is a fun, friendly, casual dining spot for dinner. The major emphasis is on fresh seafood, choice steaks, delicious pasta concoctions, soul satisfying soups, addicting ribs and a selection of fine wines. The food is spectacular and the dining occurs in an unpretentious environment. Ajax Café is located in the old Galster House, where the founder of Port Hadlock lived in the late 1800s. Present owners Eileen Steimle, Laura Ferguson and Kristan McCary were waitresses for the previous owner. When he was going to sell the restaurant, no one wanted the place to change. With community support and one incredible investor, they were able to buy the restaurant and preserve its quirky ways. The atmosphere and décor of Ajax Café is stimulating, warm, intimate, lively, friendly and colorful, yet somehow peaceful. It is painted in bright, cheerful colors and a crazy array of hats and ties hang everywhere for guests to wear during their meals. The party continues with live music every weekend. You can enjoy the beautiful saltwater view from the deck and in late September the Ajax Café hosts an annual Dinghy Festival for boats measuring less than 17 feet.

21 N Water Street, Port Hadlock WA
(360) 385-3450
www.ajaxcafe.com

PORT LUDLOW

Port Ludlow is a recreational and residential community of 1,450 people at the west end of the Hood Canal floating bridge. Port Ludlow was founded by Andrew J. Pope and Captain William C. Talbot in the mid 1800s. The town has a rich history as a mill town and center for boat building. The town is built up around the shores of Ludlow Bay with beautiful views across Hood Canal, Admiralty Inlet and Puget Sound. There is a marina and boat launches for sailing, power boating, fishing, windsurfing, and kayaking. Golfing is a year round activity at the Resort at Port Ludlow Bay's 27-hole course. The climate in Port Ludlow is warmer, and with more sun than many other areas of the Northwest. The daily temperature is about four degrees warmer than Seattle and receives less rain.

PLACES TO GO

- Port Ludlow Golf
  1 Heron Road, Port Ludlow

- Port Ludlow Marina
  west shore of Admiralty Inlet, at the mouth of Hood Canal

- Shine Tidelands - State Park, Day Park
  West of Hood Canal Bridge

- Timberton Loop Trail
  Paradise Bay Road and Timberton Drive

- Wolfe State Park, Day Park
  Off Paradise Bay Road / Seven Sister Road

THINGS TO DO

August
- Ice Cream Social
  Port Ludlow Marina

September
- Port Ludlow Fun Fest
  (360) 437-7677

October
- Fort Worden Wildlife Art Expo
  (360) 344-4401

December
- Holiday Home Tour
  (360) 437-5123

The Resort at Port Ludlow

ACCOMMODATIONS:
Best resort

The Resort at Port Ludlow is tucked into a quiet bay where you'll find the activities and lifestyle you've dreamed of. Enjoy Port Ludlow's resort facilities: 27-hole championship golf course, 300-slip marina with permanent and guest moorage, waterside Inn with luxurious accommodations (relax with an in-room spa treatment), restaurants, walking trails, gorgeous grounds for parties and get-togethers, and facilities for productive business meetings and retreats. In this lovely setting, you will enjoy a plentiful mix of leisure activities, take part in local festivals and events, explore the Olympic Mountains, or visit the historic towns of Port Townsend and Port Gamble. You can enjoy everything Port Ludlow has to offer in a drier climate with more sunshine than other Puget Sound areas, thanks to the rain shadow effect of the Olympic Mountain range. From the mountains to the Sound, from forests to the beaches, and with sun on the sea, at Port Ludlow is a true gem of the Pacific Northwest. And this resort makes it all even better.

1 Heron Road, Port Ludlow WA
(360) 437-7000 or (877) 805-0868
www.portludlowresort.com

PORT TOWNSEND

Originally named Port Townshend in 1792 after the Marquis of Townshend, Port Townsend was founded in April 1851. With a population of 8,400, Port Townsend is known for its historic charm, maritime heritage, and natural setting. From recreation in the Olympic Mountains to drama at the downtown theater, life here is connected to the land and the people. Discovery Bay, the Strait of Juan de Fuca and Port Townsend Bay surround the city where it sits at the northeast end of the Quimper Peninsula It is the seat of Jefferson County.

PLACES TO GO

- Fort Flagler
  North end of Marrowstone Island

- Old Fort Townsend
  South of Port Townsend on Sims Way/Hwy 20

- Pope Marine Park
  On the water across from City Hall

- Protection Island Wildlife Refuge
  Discovery Bay in the Strait of Juan de Fuca

- Rothschild House
  Franklin Street at Taylor Street

- Union Wharf
  Downtown

THINGS TO DO

April
- Maritime Swap Meet
  (360) 385-3628

June
- Summer Chamber Music Festival
  (360) 385-3102

August
- Jefferson County Fair
  (360) 385.1013

September
- Wooden Boat Festival
  (360) 385-3628

- Cabin Fever Quilters Show
  (360) 379-0779

October
- Art Port Townsend
  (360) 437-9579

Lighthouse at Port Townsend

Manresa Castle

ATTRACTIONS: *Best architecture*

The Manresa Castle has a history dating to 1892, when it was built as a home for Charles and Kate Eisenbeis (the town's first mayor and his wife), resulting in the largest private residence ever built in the town. The Manresa Castle is a National Historic Site, the fourth permanent building ever built in the state of Washington. In 1928, Jesuit priests bought the home, added a wing and transformed it into a training castle. They named it Manresa Hall, after the town in Spain where Ignatius Loyola founded the order. The Jesuits left in 1963 and the building was converted into a hotel. Much work was done to renovate the building to modern standards while maintaining its Victorian elegance. There are rumors afoot that certain rooms

in the castle are haunted, but management cannot honestly say anyone has ever seen a ghost, although they say some guests do enjoy ghost hunting. Most guests simply enjoy the beauty and elegance of the Manresa Castle, and the breathtaking Olympic Peninsula. Join in the adventure by reserving a room of your own.

**7th and Sheridan,
Port Townsend WA
(360) 385-5750 or (800) 732-1281**
www.manresacastle.com

Pacific Traditions Gallery

GALLERIES: *Best gallery of Native art*

An eclectic collection featuring local and nationally recognized Native artists is displayed at Pacific Traditions Gallery. The works embody generations of tradition, as well as contemporary visions of Native art. Among the tribes represented are the Coast Salish, Cowichan, Nuu-Chah-Nulth, Tlingit and Haida, as well as tribes from across the nation. Proprietor Mary Hewitt was gifted the gallery from the Jamestown S'Klallam Tribe in 2000. She is honored that the tribes

have trust in her insight about Native art and their traditions. Mary strives to maintain a relaxed atmosphere, so you feel no pressure in the Gallery, allowing you to enjoy the history, stories and ambience of Native art. Past exhibits in the Gallery included a Wolf headdress by Micah McCarty, a member of the Makah Nation; carved cedar plaques by Leonard Sylvester, Penelkut from the Kuper Island Reserve; and traditional reproductions crafted by Gary Buckman of the Oglala Lakota tribe. Visit this Gallery to experience insights into the unique cultural significance and history of Native art and artists.

**637 Water Street, Port Townsend WA
(360) 385-4770**
www.pacifictraditions.com

Port of Port Townsend

ATTRACTIONS:
Best place to watch boats

Wooden boats on the water–and their crews–find every service they'll need at the Port of Port Townsend. Here, at the place where Puget Sound was discovered by Captain George Vancouver, is one of only four Victorian seaports in the U.S. This town was intended to be what Seattle is today, but railroads were unable to bring their trains this way at the time. Big mansions built back then are used as bed and breakfasts today. Many people who stay in the rooms bring their boats in for repairs and maintenance at the many marine firms who specialize in wooden boats of all eras. Over 200 maritime traders that specialize in wooden boat restoration are here. Whatever your maritime needs, you'll be able to have them met here. Come for the annual Wooden Boat Festival. Or come for the many recreation facilities. Stay at one of the Bed & Breakfasts, or one of the many RV parks. From the Hudson Bay Marina, it's an easy walk to town. The craftspeople, the festivals and various recreation opportunities all await you.

**333 Benedict Street, Port Townsend WA
(360) 385-0656**
www.portofpt.com

Williams Gallery

GALLERIES:
Best gallery in Port Townsend

The term *gallery* might normally bring to mind a sterile environment filled with

encased artifacts and track lighting. At William's Gallery in Port Townsend, strolling through the doors is like walking through a rainbow. Bold colors, sensuous designs and textures create a feast of artistic appreciation. William's Gallery has every nook and cranny filled with gorgeous displays of ceramics, jewelry, wood, textiles, photography, paintings and much more. Balancing a colorful, lively atmosphere with a homey yet pristine structure, owners Bill and Wendi Metzer boast an authentic gallery full of regional and worldwide art. Wendi, a recognized and well respected jeweler, has been nationally featured in magazines for her vast and exquisite line of jewelry. While their gallery is fairly young, both Bill and Wendi have extensive experience in business and art. In a shorter time than most, they have created a thriving hot spot in the community of Port Townsend.

914 Water Street, Port Townsend WA
(360) 385-3630
www.williams-gallery.com

FINS Coastal Cuisine

RESTAURANTS & CAFÉS: *Best seafood*

East meets West at FINS Coastal Cuisine in Port Townsend, where Douglas Seaver, co-owner and chef, mixes New England-style food preparation with Northwest ingredients. The result? The best chowder you'll ever have. A cod special that is outstanding. Pork medallions to make you weep. It's enough to make Doug and his co-owner, Joann Saul, blush. Both Doug and Joann have been in the restaurant business since the age of 15. Doug has more than two decades of experience as a chef. Recently the Peninsula Daily News and People's Choice both awarded FINS the honor of Best Seafood in Jefferson County. The Daily News also called FINS the Best Romantic Dinner in the county. FINS provides a warm and comfortable atmosphere, looking over Port Townsend Bay with a great view of the Olympic Mountains. An outdoor dining deck has steps leading down to the beach, just in case you want to wiggle your toes in the water after dessert. FINS Coastal Cuisine is not to be missed.

1019 Water Street, Port Townsend WA
(360) 379-FISH (3474)
www.finscoastalcuisine.com

Port Townsend Brewing Co.

RESTAURANTS & CAFÉS: *Best brewing company*

In Port Townsend, you can't keep a good brewery down. The Port Townsend Brewing Co., established in 1905, was one of the largest breweries of its time until Prohibition forced its closure in 1916. But 81 years later, along came Guy and Kim Sands to reopen the business and start locals' mouths watering again. When they opened the doors in 1997, they offered two beers, the Port Townsend Pale Ale and The Port Townsend Brown Porter. Today they brew 10 ales, including

Reel Amber, Port Townsend Winter Ale, Brown Porter, Pale Ale, Hop Diggidy, Peeping Peater Scottish Ale and Bitter End India Pale Ale. They also make a barley wine. Flavors range from light and refreshing (Chet's Gold) to intense-but-smooth (Strait Stout). As their production has increased, so has their community involvement. Port Townsend Brewing sponsors many events in Port Townsend. The largest is The Wooden Boat Festival, held the second weekend in September, which provides one of the largest shows of wooden boats in the country. They also sponsor the Centrum Arts-Blues Festival in August, the Port Townsend Film Festival in September and The Kinetic Skulpture Race in October. Guy and Kim have come a long way in a short time. Visit the Port Townsend Brewing Co. and see how they've done it.

330 C 10th Street, Port Townsend WA
(360) 385-9967
www.porttownsendbrewing.com

Macadoo's Barbeque
RESTAURANTS & CAFÉS:
Best Southern barbeque

Jeff Crumpton, chef and manager of Macadoo's Barbecue in Port Townsend, wants you to know that his barbecue cooking has specific roots: Tennessee Southern with some Georgia, to be exact. The menu features pulled-pork sandwiches, smoked beef brisket, ribs, salmon and chicken, slow cooked and smoked with 100-percent pesticide-free Eastern Washington apple wood. Macadoo's is a fun, high-energy, hopping kind of place with a theme of good food for good people. There's a dog in the story, too. The name Macadoo belongs to Jeff's dog. The pooch started out as Max, after being adopted at the Jefferson County Animal Shelter. Max evolved into Macadoo. One day, Jeff and his friends were sitting on the porch eating ribs and occasionally throwing Macadoo a bone. Jeff says, "We thought, what a great idea for [the dog] to have his own restaurant. The rest, as they say, is history." Jeff and Macadoo invite you to try their beef, pork and poultry after it's been brined for 24 hours, then slow-smoked for up to 32 hours. "It's a long process, but you'll find that kind of love in everything we do here," Jeff says. You have Macadoo's woof for it.

600 W Sims Way, Port Townsend WA
(360) 379-1619

Otter Crossing Café
RESTAURANTS & CAFÉS:
Best family-style dining

When you own a restaurant in Port Townsend and you get repeat business from Connecticut, you know you're doing something right. Heather Polizzi and her father David Hoppe had a dream of starting a restaurant together. Their desire was to open a family-friendly, homestyle place that served creative food. The Otter Crossing, with creative family-style dining, is the result. Among the house specialties is smoked salmon hash with toast. It includes sautéed garlic, shallots, tomato, spinach, red potatoes, capers, lemon zest, and dill, all smothered in smoked mozzarella and topped with two poached eggs. See what they mean by creative? Enjoy all of it with locally baked European style breads and locally roasted coffee. The food comes with a scenic view, as well. The Otter Crossing sits on the point of Hudson Marina with a view of Port Townsend Bay, the Olympic Mountains and Mount Rainier.

130 Hudson, Port Townsend WA
(360) 379-0592

Fountain Café
RESTAURANTS & CAFÉS:
Best paella and vegetarian penne

The amazing, high quality flavors of the food at Fountain Café are what set this restaurant apart. A vegetarian dish, the roasted walnut and Gorgonzola penne, is probably the Fountain Café's most popular dish, but Paella, Cioppino and Zuppa de Pesce are close behind, highlighting the fresh local shellfish which the Café is known for. The Fountain Café prides itself on supporting Port Townsend growers by using locally grown vegetables. The Café has been a local hot spot for 23 years. Kristen Nelson has owned it for the past six years. "It is a cozy, fun and enchanting place where you can come and get an amazing meal, and a great glass of wine from a charismatic and friendly staff," she says. The atmosphere at the Fountain Café is lively with world beat and blues music playing, an open kitchen where you can watch the chefs toss flames (and your dinner) on the stove, and a room filled with displays, each with a story. All of this is packed into a cute little Victorian building right in the heart of downtown. Open for lunch and dinner daily.

920 Washington Street, Port Townsend WA
(360) 385-1364

Sirens
RESTAURANTS & CAFÉS: *Best pub*

Sirens is an irresistible pub of distinction, located upstairs in the historic Bartlett Building. A breathtaking view of the Hudson Bay will delight you the moment you enter the Pub. Owned by Kristen Nelson, Sirens is a charming, old-fashioned pub which is truly one of a kind. They feature an extensive wine list, 11 beers on tap, a progressive martini roster and a diverse menu of appetizers, seafood, burgers, pizzas and pastas. Their customers' favorite food choices are the wild coho salmon sandwich, Gorgonzola burger, crab cakes and the Puget Sound *cioppino*. As for drinks, they are known for their muddled then shaken margaritas and mojitos. Open for lunch and dinner, Sirens' great staff invite you to enjoy their gigantic waterfront deck and live music.

823 Water Street, Port Townsend WA
(360) 379-1100
www.sirenspt.com

Silverwater Café
RESTAURANTS & CAFÉS: *Best use of spices*

The Silverwater Café started life in 1989 as a little café with a staff of 10. The business has grown over the years, and now supports a staff of up to 55 during the busy season. They have catered more than 100 weddings, dozens of private parties, office parties, anniversaries, graduations, engagements, retirements, and holiday extravaganzas. Owners Alison and David Hero love what they do. Their philosophy is that in a world of constant change, there must be places that feel like going home... places to re-charge, where you can duck out for a moment, relax, eat a great meal, capture a smile and remember to take a deep breath. Silverwater Café is that kind of place. Alison has been cooking professionally since she was 12. She oversees the kitchen and the production for catering. David is the lead baker, baking all of the wedding cakes and desserts for the restaurant. Their first cookbook, *Golden Moments at the Silverwater Café*, was published in 1999. It contains more 125 of their most popular recipes, plus entertaining stories about the staff and customers. Because of popular demand, the Silverwater sells a line of spice blends originally developed for use in the kitchen. Visit the Silverwater Café and discover a new home.

237 Taylor Street, Port Townsend WA
(360) 385-6448
www.silverwatercafe.com

FairWinds Winery

WINERIES: *Most friendly winery*

Situated on the outskirts of historic Port Townsend, FairWinds Winery draws on the maritime flavor of this Victorian seaport for its label and décor. Whether you have a sophisticated palate or you just like good wine, you will be welcomed and treated to a great experience at FairWinds Winery. It is a small winery, so you can take a tour and see the entire winemaking process with minimal walking. Owners Michael and Judy Cavett are proud that patrons say they are treated as guests rather than customers. FairWinds Winery relies on some of the best growers in the Yakima Valley to provide top quality fruits which are hand-picked, transported to the winery, fermented in small lots and made into FairWinds award-winning wines. Their reds are bottled without filtration and both reds and whites are given the minimum amount of sulfites needed to ensure freshness and longevity. Their average production is about 1,000 cases per year. Their wines are available at the winery, through a few local outlets, through their wine club, and on their website. Visit FairWind Winery. You will be treated like a friend.

1984 Hastings Avenue W, Port Townsend WA
(360) 385-6899
www.fairwindswinery.com

Water Street Brewing

RESTAURANTS & CAFÉS: *Best brew pub*

There's energy flowing in Port Townsend and you can soak it up at Water Street Brewing. Owners Mark Burr, Nina Law and Skip Madsen think of their establishment as an extended living room for local residents, with a wide open door for visitors, as well. Vibrant or artsy, pick your description of the atmosphere and find it at this eclectic and comfortable brewery and ale house. They are known for many things, including handcrafted ales and lagers made on premises by Brewmaster Skip. He's been brewing since 1992 and has won numerous medals at the Great American Beer Festival and other prestigious competitions. If fantastic brews aren't your game, fresh-squeezed juice cocktails are the talk of the town. As you might imagine, the cuisine caters to the seafood lover's palate. They support local fishermen and farmers, and buy baked goods from a local bakery, Pane D'Amore, which uses the brewery's spent grain to make their house bread. Wild, line-caught salmon and fresh halibut are among the varieties of seafood that accent the upscale pub fare. With live music and variety shows in the evening, a family dining room where kids are always welcome, and a deck on the water with bay and mountain views, you are sure to enjoy yourself in this historic building in beautiful Port Townsend.

639 Water Street, Port Townsend WA
(360) 379-6438
www.waterstreetbrewing.com

QUINAULT

With a population of just 160 people, Quinault isn't a town so much as it is a natural phenomenon. The only temperate rain forest in the northern hemisphere includes the glacial carved Quinault Valley, which sits on the Olympic Peninsula at the north end of Grays Harbor County. The Quinault Rain Forest is one of four rich temperate rain forest canopies that lie within the west side of the Olympic Mountains. It begins in the Mount Anderson drainage to the east and the Low Divide drainage to the northwest. The forest follows the paths of the north and east forks of the Quinault River, which flow through the valley and merge into the Quinault River, which empties into Lake Quinault. The Quinault Rain Forest completely surrounds Lake Quinault. In the Valley of the Rainforest Giants you can hike a loop trail that takes you past six trees that are recognized as the largest specimens of their types (Sitka spruce, Western red cedar, Douglas Fir, yellow cedar, mountain hemlock and Western hemlock).

PLACES TO GO

- Locke's Landing 9-hole golf course
  South shore of Lake Quinault

- Quinault Rain Forest
  (360) 288-0571

- Quinault Rain Forest Loop Drive

- Valley of the Giants Loop Trail

- Olympic National Park
  (360) 565-3130

THINGS TO DO

March
- Roosevelt Elk Festival
  Quinault Rain Forest, Lake Quinault Lodge

Lake Quinault Lodge
ACCOMMODATIONS: *Best lodge*

Lake Quinault Lodge, listed on the National Register of Historic Places, is the perfect place to leave the cares of the world behind. Rejuvenate your spirit under a multi-storied canopy of towering trees or enjoy delicious local cuisine in the panoramic Lakeview dining room. Breathe the fresh air and exercise by hiking, canoeing, kayaking or fishing. Built in 1926, in the tradition of the Old Faithful Inn in Yellowstone and the Sun Valley Lodge in Idaho, the Lake Quinault Lodge reflects the spirit of a bygone era. Period wicker and overstuffed furniture, a massive brick fireplace and ceiling beams decorated with Native American designs contribute to the ambience of the Lodge. As far back as the 1880s, Olympic Peninsula travelers gathered near Lake Quinault at the Log Hotel for lodging, meals and good times. When improved roads provided easier access, crowds from Grays Harbor gathered there on weekends to dance and socialize. On August 28, 1924, a fire consumed the structure, but supporters soon made plans to build a new, better hotel. The area's finest artisans and craftsmen were assembled and a mere 53 days later, a new resort hotel was unveiled: Lake Quinault Lodge. Visit Lake Quinault Lodge and see the amazing results of that artistic labor.

345 S Shore Road, Quinault WA
(360) 288-2900 or (800) 562-6672
www.visitlakequinault.com

SEQUIM

Sequim lies in the Dungeness Valley between the Olympic Mountains and the Strait of Juan de Fuca. Sequim, pronounced S'kwim, means quiet waters in the language of the S'Klallam tribe. Many farms and gardens here are open for tours, kayakers flock to the town, and history buffs are drawn to Sequim's museums. Sequim is located in the center of the North Olympic Peninsula, minutes from Port Townsend and a short drive from Port Angeles.

PLACES TO GO

- Dungeness River Audubon Center
  2151 West Hendrickson Road

- Railroad Bridge Park
  2151 West Hendrickson Road

- Rainshadow Natural Science Foundation
  2151 West Hendrickson Road

- Reuse Demonstration Park
  Next to the Carrie Blake Park

- Sequim Bay State Park
  Three miles southeast of Sequim on Highway 101

- Sequim Museum & Arts Center
  175 W Cedar

THINGS TO DO

April
- North Olympic Bird Festival
  www.dungenessrivercenter.org

- Olympic Chocolate Festival
  (360) 683-5774

May
- Bonsai Show
  (360) 683-2726

- Irrigation Festival Arts & Craft Fair
  (360) 683-6197

June
- North Olympic Discovery Marathon
  (360) 417-1301

September
- Dungeness River Festival
  (360) 681-4076

Sunset on Strait of Juan de Fuca from the shores of Dungeness Beach

Dungeness Golf Course
ATTRACTIONS: *Best golf course*

You're in Western Washington, it's wet, and you'd love a round of golf. What to do? Sequim gets a mere 13 inches of annual rainfall, compared to the 35 or so inches most everywhere else in Western Washington, and it is home to the Dungeness Golf Course. It's the driest golf course in the western part of the state, and also the most player-friendly and simultaneously challenging. The course is rated Four Stars by *Golf Digest*. "Our goal," says pro Bill Shea, "is to promote golf and player enjoyment in a friendly, relaxed atmosphere." The course is 18 holes, over 6,456 yards. While playing, try to avoid being distracted by the great views of the Olympic Mountains. When you're finished with the game, dine at the Greenside Grill and enjoy panoramic course views with your breakfast, lunch or dinner. The course is walkable. Call to reserve a cart and a tee time up to 30 days ahead. If you want to stay a while, golf packages are available at every hotel, motel, and bed and breakfast in Sequim and Port Angeles. When calling, let them know whether you want a green-fee-only package, or a Deluxe Package that includes the green fee, cart, range and five-percent golf shop merchandise discount.

1965 Woodcock Road, Sequim WA
(360) 683-6344 or (800) 447-6826
www.dungenessgolf.com

Seven Cedars Casino
ATTRACTIONS: *Best casino*

When you are near Sequim, head for the Seven Cedars Casino, where the Jamestown S'Klallam Tribe offers all the action and excitement of Las Vegas or Reno in a setting that rivals the finest Northwest resort. There are slots, roulette, craps, Let It Ride, bingo, blackjack, keno, poker, video poker, pull tabs and Mega Mania, as well as off-track betting. Smoking and non-smoking slots are available. When you've had your fill of fun at gaming, there is world-class entertainment, including live music and comedy. Three restaurants and lounges and an impressive gallery of Native American treasures add to your enjoyment. In the Salish Room Restaurant, try the elegant buffet of International delicacies and regional favorites like salmon, oysters and clams. In the art gallery, you'll find fine artwork and gift items among the treasures of Northwest Native Expressions. Housed in a traditional Indian Longhouse, this unique gallery represents nearly 200 Native American artists, including silversmiths, weavers, woodworkers, print makers and jewelers. Prices are reasonable and the quality is exceptional. Seven tall totem poles greet you at the door, serving as staunch sentries for the casino on Washington's North Olympic Peninsula.

270756 Highway 101, Sequim WA
(360) 683-7777
www.7cedarscasino.com

Olympic Game Farm
ATTRACTIONS: *Best wildlife park*

Just north of Sequim is the Olympic Game Farm, founded by Lloyd and Katherine Beebe. Though you might not recognize the name Lloyd Beebe, he is a legend in the world of wildlife documentaries. A native of the Pacific Northwest, Lloyd has always had a knack for training wild animals. In 1945, he began making movies as a hobby, filming his children and the animals on his ranch: a cougar, a fawn, and a bear cub. When he heard that Walt Disney Studios was producing a new series called *True Life Adventures*, he wrote to tell them about his footage. So began his career for Disney that took him across the world. He visited Antarctica with Admiral Byrd, filmed jaguars in Brazil, and even went to Point Barrow in Alaska to help polar bears suffering from stage fright. Disney provided additional camera equipment and a soundstage for Lloyd's ranch that became known as the Disney Wild Animal Ranch. In 1972, while taking a temporary break from Disney, Lloyd decided to open the ranch to the public. It was an immediate success and Disney agreed to let him keep it open. Today people come to see the bison, elk, Kodiak bears, timber wolves, zebras and llamas. Lloyd's son Ken and his sister-in-law Alice Beebe now run the farm, keeping Lloyd's dream alive. The Olympic Game Farm is open year round for driving tours. Guides give walking tours during the summer.

1423 Ward Road, Sequim WA
(360) 683-4295 or (800) 778-4295
www.olygamefarm.com

Snohomish & Skagit Valley

Tulip Festival

Snohomish & Skagit

Snohomish and Skagit

A series of fascinating cities line the shore between Puget Sound and the Straight of Georgia. South of Everett, Mukilteo derives its name from an Indian word meaning good camping place. It was at Mukilteo that the Point Elliott Treaty was signed with the chiefs of 22 Puget Sound tribes, opening the region for European settlement. The Mukilteo waterfront is popular among divers due to the diverse sea life.

Inland, Snohomish bills itself as the antique capital of the Northwest. Everett, the major city of Snohomish County, is home to Boeing's assembly plant for the 747, 767, 777 and 787. It is the largest building in the world by volume. Tours are available from the tour center in Mukilteo. Naval Station Everett is the Navy's most modern facility and the homeport for a US Navy Battle Group based on the USS Abraham Lincoln aircraft carrier.

To the north in Skagit County, Mount Vernon holds a famous Tulip Festival. Many bulbs are shipped from here to the Netherlands and sold as Holland tulips. Further north, Whatcom County produces more than half the nation's supply of raspberries. Bellingham serves as the southern terminus of the Alaska Marine Highway, which provides passenger and car ferry service to Alaska ports. To the east is Mount Baker, which in 1999 set a world record for snow—1,124 inches. As you might guess, the Mount Baker Ski Area is acclaimed as one of the best places to ski in the country.

© Steve K. Marl

BELLINGHAM

On Bellingham Bay with Mt. Baker as its backdrop, Bellingham is the last major city before the Washington coastline meets the Canadian border. Bellingham has an active waterfront that supports fishing, shipping and marina operations. Squalicum Harbor is the second largest in Puget Sound. Bellingham is home to Western Washington University on Sehome Hill, from which you have a sweeping view across the bay to the San Juan Islands.

PLACES TO GO

- American Museum of Radio and Electricity
  1312 Bay Street
  (360) 738-3886

- Bellingham Railway Museum
  1320 Commercial Street (360) 393-7540

- Mindport
  210 W Holly Street (360) 647-5614

- Whatcom Museum of History and Art
  121 Prospect Street (360) 676-6981

- Lake Paddan Park
  4882 Samish Way

- Larrabee State Park and Clayton Beach
  Chuckanut Drive

- Whatcom Falls Park
  1401 Electric Avenue

THINGS TO DO

May
- Ski to Sea Race and Festival
  (360) 734-1330

August
- Ferndale Street Festival
  (360) 384-3042

September
- Sand in the City
  Squalicum Harbor (360) 676-2500

October
- Whatcom Artist Studio Tour
  (360) 966-5148

November
- Really Big Weekend
  Western Washington University (360) 650-3846

- Fall Art Festival
  Blodel-Donovan Park Community Center (360) 398-1411

Creek in the Nooksack region

Chrysalis Inn & Spa
ACCOMMODATIONS: *Best in & spa*

At a breathtakingly beautiful location on Bellingham's waterfront, the Chrysalis Inn & Spa is a premier place to stay when you're visiting northern Washington. With 34 deluxe rooms and nine luxury suites, guests can delight in views and amenities that include gas fireplaces, Internet access, down comforters and complimentary breakfast buffets. Be sure to visit the spa, too. A warm ambience is created by natural wood, slate floors and custom lighting. Enjoy one of the many treatments available, including massages, facials and hydrotherapy. When you're ready for a meal, Fino Wine Bar at the Chrysalis Inn provides casual dining with classic European-style cuisine and a rich selection of premium vintages. The Chrysalis Inn arose from a personal vision to capture the essence of the Northwest and savor it as a holistic experience. It is a wonderful place for individuals or couples to relax and get away from everyday stress, as well as providing accommodations for groups. With state-of-the-art meeting facilities for up to 50 people and catering from Fino's, you can have a meeting to remember.

804 10th Street, Bellingham WA
(360) 756-1005 or (888) 808-0005
www.thechrysalisinn.com

Super Supplements
HEALTH & BEAUTY: *Best independent retail chain in the nation*

Science learns something new every day about the ways vitamins, herbs and nutritional supplements enhance health. Keeping up with all that cutting-edge information would be overwhelming without the help of experts. Super Supplements is a privately owned chain of 13 discount vitamin stores in western Washington. It was started in 1994 by John Wurts and bills itself as having some of the most knowledgeable staff members in the industry. John brings more than 18 years of experience in

the vitamin industry to his operation, which was voted 2004 Best Retail Chain in the Nation by *Vitamin Retailer* magazine. The stores feature wide, inviting aisles, a vast array of supplements, sports nutrition, herbs, body care and homeopathic products, plus a well educated staff prepared to provide the most up-to-date and accurate product information available. Bring your questions to university students, naturopathic doctors or herbalists, or take advantage of Healthnotes, a touchscreen information system that retrieves research on natural remedies, illnesses and potential drug interactions from vitamin, herb and food combinations. You'll get 10 to 70-percent discounts on products at Super Supplements locations from Bellingham to Lakewood. The same great service and more than 30,000 products are available on the website. Visit Super Supplements to begin your journey to a healthier life.

1300 Ellis Street, Bellingham WA (360) 676-9922
4031 Colby Avenue, Everett WA (425) 293-0373
Mail Order: (800) 249-9394
www.supersup.com

Du Jour Bistro & Vines Wine Shop
RESTAURANTS & CAFÉS:
Best wine café in Bellingham

Michael and Becki Petersen invite anyone who delights in the perfect pairing of food and wine to visit their bistro in the heart of downtown Bellingham. Enjoy food made with fresh local and seasonal products, pick out an accompanying wine at the wine shop, pay retail price for it and enjoy it with your meal for a small corkage fee. On Tuesday night the corkage fee is waived. The menu changes daily with availability of various ingredients, but on any given day you'll find a selection of appetizers, antipasti, cheese platters, exotic calzones, entrées and desserts. Entrées feature fresh local seafood, such as Dungeness crab. For dessert, try vanilla bean crème brûlée or other fantastic confections. The food alone would make this a must, but don't miss out on the wine. The Vines offers an extensive selection of Washington State and other Pacific Northwest specialties, including limited editions not readily available elsewhere. Join the Wine of the Month Club to keep up on special events, such as wine tastings and appearances by visiting experts. Reservations are recommended at the Du Jour Bistro & The Vines Wine Shop.

1319 Cornwall Avenue, Suite 102, Bellingham WA
(360) 714-1161
www.thevinesdujour.com

BLAINE

Blaine's greatest distinction is its location in the extreme northwest corner of the lower 48 states. Much of the modern-day economy is based on trade with Canada. The Peace Arch, on the waterfront at the border, commemorates almost two centuries of peace between the United States and Canada. Blaine's marina is popular with recreational boaters, and the wealth of birds in the area have made it famous among bird watchers.

PLACES TO GO

- MV Plover Foot Passenger Ferry
  Blaine Marina
  (360) 332-5742

- Semiahmoo Park Maritime Museum
  1218 4th Street
  (360) 332-5742

- Marine Park
  Marine Drive

- Peace Arch State Park
  2nd Street

THINGS TO DO

June
- Hands across the Border
  Peace Arch State Park
  (360) 332-1421

July
- Free Jazz Concert & Street Fair
  (360) 332-6484

August
- Wood on Water Boating Festival
  (360) 332-4544

September
- Peace Arch Dedication Days
  (360) 332-7165

Blaine-Peace Arch State Park

Semiahmoo Resort

ACCOMMODATIONS: *Best golf and spa resort*

Semiahmoo Resort lies just south of the U.S.-Canadian border. The AAA Four-Diamond, 198-room ocean front resort showcases a full-service European-style spa. A full-service exercise facility, complete with indoor/outdoor pool, offers an invigorating indoor fitness option. Fine dining is offered at Stars. Lunch and light meals are served daily at Packer's Lounge and Oyster Bar. The Blue Heron offers great pub fare with golf course views. Guests and visitors can golf year round at two of *Golf Digest's* Top 100 public play courses: the Arnold Palmer-designed Semiahmoo Golf & Country Club, and the Graham Cook-designed Loomis Trail Golf Club. Kayaking, hiking, biking, tennis, rollerblading, sailing, horseback riding, salmon fishing and whale watching are all available locally. The Resort is home to a 300-slip, privately-operated saltwater marina. The Resort offers more than 35,000 square feet of flexible conference and meeting space. As part of Washington's Premier Resort Group, Semiahmoo is affiliated with Skagit Valley Casino Resort. The site was once home to the Semiahmoo band of Native Americans and later served as the largest sockeye salmon cannery in the United States.

9565 Semiahmoo Parkway, Blaine WA
(360) 318-2000 or (800) 770-7992
www.semiahmoo.com

BOW

A small town overlooking Samish Bay, Bow was originally known as Brownsville, after its founder, William J. Brown. When the railroad arrived, Brown suggested the new name of Bow, after a large railway station in London, England.

PLACES TO GO

- Bow Lake Watersports
  18055 Bow Lake Lane
  (877) 754-2287

- Karma Place Japanese Garden
  3533 Chuckanut Drive
  (360) 766-6716

- Bay View State Park
  Bay View-Edison Road

Skagit Valley Casino Resort
ATTRACTIONS: *Best casino resort*

Skagit Valley Casino Resort has emerged as one of the region's leading entertainment and hospitality destinations. The only full-service casino resort on Washington's Interstate 5 corridor, this glittering, tastefully-appointed complex features a resort-style hotel, conference center, Las Vegas-style gaming, headline entertainment and fine dining. Each suite in the 103-room hotel has all of the modern comforts and amenities, including an indoor swimming pool, sauna, fitness room and hot tub. Guests can play more than 670 slot machines, video poker, bingo, keno and table games. The intimate, 450-seat Pacific Showroom spotlights year round entertainment. The Winners Lounge offers live music and dancing Friday and Saturday nights, and comedians every second and fourth Thursday. Fine dining takes center stage at The Skagit's award-winning Moon Beach Restaurant, featuring choice steaks, seafood and Northwest specialties in an intimate atmosphere. Casual dining alternatives include the Market Buffet and the Northern Lights Deli. The resort also offers more than 14,000 square feet of flexible meeting space. Its enviable location provides an excellent home base for day trips that could include a ferry ride on Puget Sound.

5984 N Darrk Lane, Bow WA
(360) 724-7777 or (877) 275-2448
www.theskagit.com

The Oyster Bar on Chuckanut Drive
RESTAURANTS & CAFÉS: *Best oyster bar*

The Oyster Bar was originally built as a shack to sell fresh shellfish on Washington State's first scenic highway, Chuckanut Drive. The shack gradually expanded into a restaurant and in 1946 Otto Amos bought it and renamed it The Oyster Bar. Otto and his wife coined the slogan The oysters that we serve today slept last night in Samish Bay. The restaurant has changed hands several times since, but all owners, including Guy and Linda Colbert, who now run The Oyster Bar, have given the noble oyster its due. Under the guidance of the Colberts, The Oyster Bar has become a premier dining destination. People come for the ambience as well as the food, enjoying romantic candlelit dinners while gazing out at the spectacular views of the San Juan Islands. Samish Bay oysters are still on the menu, as well as other local shellfish from Washington and British Columbia. You can also get wild game, such as Alaskan caribou, or Morro Bay abalone and other sumptuous dishes. At The Oyster Bar, even a grilled cheese sandwich for lunch is a delicacy, prepared with taleggio cheese, tomato, basil and red onions on sourdough. With its award-winning wine cellar and fabulous desserts, The Oyster Bar is a treat not to be missed.

2578 Chuckanut Drive, Bow WA
(360) 766-6185
www.theoysterbaronchuckanutdrive.com

EVERETT

Once a mill town built on wood-based industries, Everett now has a labor force employed in technology, aerospace and service-based industries. With 97,500 people, it is the largest Washington city north of Seattle and the hub of the Snohomish-Skagit region. Everett's marina is the second-largest on the West Coast

PLACES TO GO

- Evergreen Arboretum and Gardens
  145 Alverson Boulevard (425) 257-8597

- Imagine Children's Museum
  1502 Wall Street (425) 258-1006

- Museum of Snohomish County History
  1913 Hewitt Avenue (425) 259-2022

- Narbeck Wetland Sanctuary
  6921 Seaway Boulevard (425) 355-9112

- Forest Park
  802 E Mukilteo Boulevard

- Langus Riverfront Park
  400 Smith Island Road

- Thornton A. Sullivan Park
  11405 Silver Lake Road

- Walter E. Hall Park
  1226 SW Casino Road

THINGS TO DO

March
- Spring Music Festival
  Downtown (425) 303-1848

June
- Everett Kite Festival
  Biringer Farm (425) 339-9334

July
- Nubian Jam
  Forest Park (425) 257-8300

August
- Dahlia Show
  Floral Hall (360) 659-8687

- Fresh Paint Festival of Artists at Work
  Everett Marina (425) 257-7380

October
- Everett Sausage Festival
  (425) 349-7014

Gaylord House Bed & Breakfast

ACCOMMODATIONS: *Best bed and breakfast in Everett*

Life takes on the nostalgic qualities of another era at Gaylord House Bed & Breakfast in Everett, located between the Cascade Mountains and Puget Sound. Gaylord House sits on a maple-lined avenue with other turn-of-the-century homes. This AAA-rated establishment and member of the Washington Bed & Breakfast Guild belongs to Craig and Kay Zimmel. They provide a gourmet, award-winning breakfast to their guests and can arrange an early continental breakfast or special diet on request. Guests can relax on a covered porch or catch the morning sun on the back deck. A library full of books, games and videos is available for their pleasure. The five rooms at this delightful establishment set several distinct moods. Choose from the Commodore's Quarters, with its nautical appointments and view of the Cascades, or the tranquil Lotus Room with its double-headed shower and touches of Indonesian whimsy. Lady Anne's Chamber features a queen-size four-poster bed and old-fashioned claw-foot tub, while the Mediterranean Sunrise mimics southern Italy with a dreamy sleigh bed, private balcony, whirlpool, fireplace and marble-topped bedside tables. The fifth room, called the Garden Terrace, is the newest and most private. Located downstairs, removed from the other guest rooms, it features a private entrance from inside or out, king-size bed, jetted tub, and a private patio that overlooks the Cascades. Everett makes a great vacation destination. It's home to one of the largest marinas on the West Coast, boasts 28 parks and gardens, and two golf courses. Your hosts can arrange for sailing, fishing or whale-watching day trips or direct you to hiking, skiing, galleries and more. Put the modern world on hold and relax at Gaylord House Bed & Breakfast.

3301 Grand Avenue, Everett WA
(425) 339-9153 or (888) 507-7177
www.gaylordhouse.com

Everett Events Center

ATTRACTIONS: *Best event and conference venue*

The city-owned Everett Events Center hosts a myriad of events, including concerts, ice skating and family shows. The center is home to the Everett Silvertips of the Western Hockey League and the Everett Hawks of the Arena Football League 2. Other sporting events include basketball, volleyball, wrestling and gymnastics. Depending on the configuration, the Everett Events Center can seat anywhere from 3,500 to 10,000 people. Set up for a trade show, the center and its neighboring facilities can provide as much as 69,000 square feet of exhibition space. The center was built in 2003. *Venues Today* ranked the Everett Events Center 11th in the world for sales and eighth for attendance in the mid-sized arena category. The Edward D. Hansen Conference Center, located in the Events Center, hosts hundreds of events annually, including meetings, banquets and consumer shows. The conference center includes three 900-square-foot meeting rooms and a 12,000-square-foot ballroom, which can be arranged in a number of configurations. The Comcast Community Ice Rink, an NHL regulation rink immediately next to the Everett Events Center, is used for public skating, local hockey leagues and other events. The Everett Events Center is in downtown Everett just blocks from Interstate 5. Whether you are planning an event or simply attending one, you will find the center to be a most attractive facility.

2000 Hewitt Avenue, Everett WA
(425) 322-2600
www.everetteventscenter.com

Everett Silvertips

ATTRACTIONS: *Best bang for the buck in Everett*

It's standing room only when the Everett Silvertips take to the ice at Everett Events Center. The center debuted in 2003, and so did the all-new hockey team, setting just about every conceivable record for an expansion team. The hard-driving teenagers who power this junior team have won the hearts of Everett with their feisty style and passionate play. They are also responsible for introducing this sports-loving town to hockey, and what an introduction it has been. The 'Tips first season saw 35 wins, a U.S. Division title and a series win in the Western Hockey League finals. Many of the team members are Canadians who live with area families during the hockey season; some attend the local high school. Perhaps it's the speed and action of the game that has caught the attention of the fans, or the new events center, but what keeps the fans coming as the seasons stack up is the hard-driving spirit of the players under the leadership of head coach Kevin Constantine. The Everett Silvertips, entering their fourth season, inspire smiles as wide as skates when they make themselves available to the community for autograph signing, speaking events and hospital visits. Find out what is firing Everett with a visit to a Silvertips' home game at the Everett Events Center.

2000 Hewitt Avenue, Everett WA
(425) 252-5100
www.everettsilvertips.com

BreCyn Salon
HEALTH & BEAUTY: *Best salon*

Everyone who visits a hairdresser knows that the choice of a hairdresser is every bit as important as the choice of a hairstyle. First, there is the understanding that develops between you and the stylist; then there is the way that understanding translates into a style that matches your expectations. The clients who visit Cynthia Mitchell's BreCyn Salon in Everett enjoy a soothing atmosphere, massage services, and the thoughtful, creative work of stylists with international training. Cynthia opened the salon in 1989 and named it after herself and her daughter Breana. She is a bit of a celebrity in Snohomish County, thanks to her unparalleled services and loyal clients who rely on BreCyn Salon for their knowledge of the latest trends in hair care. The salon welcomes men, women and children. Visit BreCyn Salon for a difference you can see and feel. BreCyn invites you to indulge yourself in excellence.

8300 Beverly Boulevard, Everett WA
(425) 348-9288

Everett Vacuum Sales & Service

HOME: *Best place to buy vacuum cleaners in Everett*

Most people go to an expert when they want something done right. When the subject is vacuum cleaners, whether new, used or reconditioned, you should go to Laurie and Mary Steinberg of Everett Vacuum. Laurie has worked at Everett Vacuum for nearly 40 years and is only the third owner of the shop, started in 1944 when Ted Hagen, a door-to-door vacuum cleaner salesman, needed a storefront to sell his accumulated trade-ins. He moved his inventory and family into the 1896 Broadway building. By 1963, when son Dan took over the business, space had gotten so tight the family was forced to seek living quarters elsewhere. Everett performs warranty work on all major brands and can meet your needs with a selection of upright, canister and backpack-style vacuums. For top-of-the-line performance, try the electronically controlled Sebo-X series with hospital-grade filtration. An RV or a house full of stairs might best be served with an eight-pound Riccar Supralite. Look also for bagless models by Hoover, Eureka and Dirt Devil. People come from as far away as Bellingham, Port Townsend and Tacoma to shop here. Everett Vacuum also repairs sewing machines and sells parts for Coleman stoves and lanterns. Mention the Everett Vacuum website to earn a discount on your purchase.

2318 Broadway, Everett WA
(425) 252-4355 *www.everettvacuum.com*

Founder Ted Hagen and cohort, 1946

Wicked Cellars

WINES: *Best wine shop in Everett*

If you think fine wine is only for the wealthy or that you have to spend a decade learning the nuances of nose and bouquet to fully appreciate the ancient beverage, think again and head to Wicked Cellars for a memorable lesson you will thoroughly enjoy. Wine aficionado Kevin Nasr and his wife Bonnie purchased the existing wine shop in October 2004 and have since brought it to new heights in popularity by offering a whimsical atmosphere that's free of pretension. Wicked Cellars features a terrific array of wine from all over the world, including numerous vintages from the boutique wineries of Washington. Kevin and Bonnie choose the 2,000 labels they house from more than 60,000 varied selections. They also offer an assortment of specialty beers and ales. Kevin and Bonnie host four wine tasting events weekly, on Tuesday, Wednesday, Friday and Saturday. The tastings are ideal occasions for discovering your own preferences and the world of wine in general. The shop offers a members wine club and a delightful array of wine-related gifts and accessories, such as furniture, artwork and accessories. Discover for yourself why wine should breathe and the importance of decanting, while you search for new favorites with a visit to Wicked Cellars.

2616 Colby Avenue, Everett WA
(425) 258-3117
www.wickedcellars.com

Skagit River
Photo by Jim Poth

LA CONNER

The oldest community in Skagit County, La Conner is a small town near the coast. Nationally known artists have long settled here. Author Tom Robbins, a long-time resident, has set some of his stories here. The town is also famous for its many wild turkeys, the official town bird. La Conner is immediately adjacent to the Swinomish Indian Reservation.

PLACES TO GO

- Museum of Northwest Art
  121 S 1st Street (360) 466-4446

- Skagit County Historical Museum
  501 S 4th Street (360) 466-3365

THINGS TO DO

May
- Skagit River Poetry Festival
  (800) 804-8406

June
- La Conner Arts Festival
  (888)-642-9284

September
- La Conner Classic Yacht and Car Show
  (360) 466-4778

- Native American Day
  (360) 466-4778

LaConner Tulip Farm
Photo by Nancy McClain

Museum of Northwest Art

ATTRACTIONS: *Best museum of regional art*

Welcome to MoNA. The Museum of Northwest Art in La Conner opened in 1981 as a small regional museum devoted to major Pacific Northwest artists. After outgrowing its original home, the second floor of the historical Gaches Mansion, a fundraising drive enabled the acquisition of a new 12,000-foot space in downtown. The new space, open in 1995, allowed MoNA to redefine their

original vision to include a permanent collection and provide exhibition opportunities for up-and-coming artists, as well as established names. The only museum in the world devoted exclusively to art from the Pacific Northwest, the museum celebrates the work of artists who founded the Northwest school, such as Guy Anderson, Kenneth Callahan, Morris Graves and Mark Tobey. Many others, including celebrated glass artist Dale Chihuly, Sherrill Van Cott, Helmi Juvonen, are also shown. One exhibit paid tribute to 12 women artists who pioneered modernism in the Northwest. The admission fee is waived on the first Tuesday of every month. Be sure to visit the Museum of Northwest Art.

121 S First Street, La Conner WA
(360) 466-4446
www.museumofnwart.org

Bunnies By The Bay

SHOPPING: *Best bunny collectibles and baby gifts*

Bunnies By The Bay has been known for its collectible bunnies that have brought delightful dreams into homes and hearts since 1986. But it's not just bunnies anymore. Come visit this beautiful new shop to see, feel, touch, taste and smell all the great things they are designing and creating exclusively for the General Store. Their new Bunnies By The Bay baby gift line is simply adorable. Soft bunny Cuddle Coats, funny Flipper Slippers, fuzzy Quacker Jackets and froggy Croak Coats are some of the endearing gifts for wee ones. Take a hop, skip and a jump across the garden path to

the old green house next door known as the Hareytale Museum. Take a peek inside for handcrafted, one-of-a-kind bunnies, or cheer up your favorite friend with the gift of Haremones. Plan a scrumptious tea party, or birthday celebration, and learn the true story of the Bunnies By The Bay. To see the complete line of Bunnies By The Bay gifts visit their website.

Hareytale Museum: 617 Morris Street
General Store: 623 Morris Street,
La Conner WA
(360) 293-8037 ext 221
www.bunniesbythebay.com

Viking Cruises

ATTRACTIONS: *Best cruises*

For an exciting and informative cruise around the San Juan Islands, from bird and whale watching to overnight excursions, visit Viking Cruises in La Conner. This company offers cruises ranging from an hour to five days and four nights. Cruises include informative nature tours, cracked crab feasts or catered meals, family reunions, corporate functions, weddings and memorials. "We thrive upon the variety of cruises and the opportunity to show off this incredible part of the world," say owners Marci and Bob Plank. The off-season (November-March) is a favorite time to view migratory bird populations, including waterfowl, seabirds, shorebirds and raptors. It is common to see bald eagles, kingfishers, great blue herons, loons, cormorants and many varieties of ducks, seabirds and shorebirds. Nearby is the March Point Heronry, which is one of the largest rookeries in the continental United States with close to 600 active nests. People on board can observe from the large foredeck outside, inside the wheelhouse with the skipper or in the cabin below. With 32 large windows on the Viking Star, everyone has a great view. So dress warmly, bring your binoculars and camera, and head for Viking Cruises. Remember, there is always hot coffee, tea or chocolate available onboard.

109 N First Street, La Conner WA
(360) 466-2639 or (888) 207-2333
www.vikingcruises.com

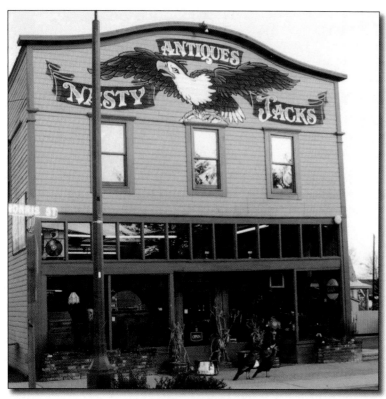

Nasty Jack's Antiques

HOME: *Best antiques in La Conner*

With a name like Nasty Jack's, you mighty expect...what? What you will find at Nasty Jack's Antiques in La Conner are the finest American and European antiques in western Washington. Okay, let's deal with the name first. In 1972, the business was established by Nasty Jack Wilkins and his partner, Diamond Jim Reynolds. Jim left the business some time later, but Nasty Jack ran the business until he died in 1994. Present owners are Marlo and Gary Frank, daughter and son-in-law of Jack. "Who says antiques can't be fun?" asks Marlo, who gets a warm feeling when she is finds something that a customer can't find anywhere else. A sample of offerings includes a large selection of early American pieces, such as fireplace mantles, church pews, tables, chairs, dressers, hall trees, parlor tables and bookcases.

Every month, Nasty Jack's receives 40-foot containers from England with draw leaf and drop leaf tables, chairs, dressing tables, buffets, tea carts, occasional tables, stained glass windows, garden gates and more. Nasty Jack's invites you to contact them via phone or their website with your requests. If they do not have what you are looking for, they will keep your request in their want file. They deliver from Tacoma to the Canadian border and will make shipping arrangements for out-of-state sales.

103 E Morris Street, La Conner WA
(360) 466-3209
www.nastyjacksantiques.com

View of Skagit Valley
Photo by Levy Sheckler

MILL CREEK

Incorporated in 1983, Mill Creek is one of the state's youngest cities. Mill Creek is a master-planned community, complete with a high school, middle school and an 18-hole golf course. The newest major project in Mill Creek, the Mill Creek Town Center, adds a retail heart to the to city.

PLACES TO GO

- Library Park
  15429 Bothell-Everett Highway

- McCollum County Park
  600 128th Street SE

- Nickel Creek Park
  1900 164th Street SE

- North Creek County Park
  1011 183rd Street SE

House of Bread

BAKERIES, COFFEE & TEA: *Best bread bakery*

The House of Bread in Mill Creek holds the Guinness World Record for the largest cinnamon roll. Clearly, owners Wayne and Anita Warren are creative bakers. Still, the House of Bread is best known for its breads. The store makes natural breads of the highest quality, because Wayne and Anita believe that bread should not just hold a sandwich together; bread should taste good all by itself. The House of Bread uses only Prairie Gold, a chemical-free high protein wheat from Montana. The wheat is milled cold, and the flour is used within the week. Much of the bread is fat free and is made with honey. The bakery is arranged so visitors can watch the bakers as they knead individual loaves by hand. While he does not recommend it to others, Wayne once tried living only on his own bread. At the end of a month, he had lost 10 pounds and was in perfect health. The House of Bread makes 25 premium breads, including Grandma's White and honey whole wheat. Look for an assortment of intriguing ingredients in the specialty breads, including basil and parmesan, garlic and cheddar, and jalapeño and jack. A lunch menu at House of Bread features soup and sandwiches made with house breads. Scones, sweet goods and espresso are available, too. Visit House of Bread, where good taste comes naturally.

15224 Main Street, Suite 105, Mill Creek WA
(425) 385-8553
www.houseofbreadwa.com

Zinnia
RESTAURANTS & CAFÉS: *Best casual fine dining*

You know you are about to receive great service when you learn that your maître d' is one of the owners. Owners and maître d's Matthew Bregar or Christopher Giusto may greet you when you enter Zinnia. Meanwhile, Owners and chefs Joseph Bounds and Kimberly Bregar are busy in the kitchen. These fearless restaurateurs provide fresh fusion fare, casual dining at its best. At lunch, you can choose from soups, sandwiches or huge salads with fresh greens, fruits and cheeses. Try a panini, such as the innovative bacon, cheddar and pear combination. At dinner, patrons in tuxes or athletic attire are equally comfortable. Appetizers include mushroom ravioli, grilled jumbo prawns and seared scallops. The fried ravioli appetizer stars on the sophisticated children's menu. Entrées feature rack of New Zealand lamb, basil crab halibut and Hawaiian ahi, all with zestful sauces. Zinnia is known for game, including venison and elk sausages. Venison lovers flock to Zinnia. Desserts are made in-house by pastry chef Kimberly, known for her signature sweet, coconut layer cake with a batter of pecans and buttermilk. A wine café, Zinnia stocks more than 73 labels. The *Seattle Times* and Everett newspapers have repeatedly given Zinnia glowing reviews. For some of the best dining in southern Snohomish County, don't miss Zinnia.

15130 Main Street, Mill Creek WA
(425) 357-0512
www.zinniawa.com

Nest Home & Gifts
SHOPPING: *Best home décor gifts*

Give your home a fresh look each season with irresistible décor from Nest Home & Gifts, where casual elegance with European flair is the order of the day. This popular boutique is owned and operated by Susan Stone, the author of the special occasion book *Memories in Moments*. She offers a spectacular array of fine gifts, décor, custom furniture and home products. Nest Home & Gifts offers a choice array of hand-selected, high quality products that are artfully arranged in such a way as to allow the customer to imagine how a piece would look in their own home. Visitors are delighted by the boutique's individualized vignettes, which magnificently display complementary items, such as candles, cookbooks and accessories. The shop also carries spa lotions, soaps and bath products, as well as bedding, pajamas, pillows and a slew of other décor and accent pieces that will add whimsical finishing touches to your favorite rooms. In addition to the shop, Susan and her colleagues also offer Nest—At Home, a home accessories consulting service. They will work with you to develop a design plan and budget, and ultimately transform your current space into a dream room. Enjoy great service and a fabulous shopping experience at Nest Home & Gifts, where friendliness and fun are always in style.

15217 Main Street, Mill Creek WA
(425) 357-6901

MOUNT VERNON

Mount Vernon is the largest city and the commercial hub of Skagit County, yet with about 30,000 people, it retains a small-town charm. Mount Vernon is close to some of nature's most scenic islands, snow-capped mountains and fields of glorious flowers. Its Tulip Festival is world-famous.

PLACES TO GO

- The Lincoln Theatre
  712 S 1st Street (360) 336-8955

- Bakerview Park
  3101 E Fir Street

- Edgewater Park
  600 Behrens Millett Road

- Hillcrest Park
  1717 S 13th Street

- Little Mountain Park
  300 Little Mountain Park

THINGS TO DO

April
- Skagit Valley Tulip Festival
  (360) 428-5959

July
- The Highland Games
  Edgewater Park (360) 416-4934

August
- Skagit County Fair
  Fairgrounds (360) 336-9453

- Shakespeare Northwest
  Edgewater Park (877) 754-6284

Skagit Valley Gardens

GARDENS, PLANTS & FLOWERS: *Best garden center*

Located on 25 acres, Skagit Valley Gardens offers a wonderful experience, whether you are in the market for serious gardening advice and plants, or are on a light-hearted search for the perfect gift. In spring and summer, the 16,000-square-foot retail area is filled to the brim with an abundance of colorful annuals, perennials, harvest baskets and more. When fall comes, the Gardens are transformed into a Christmas wonderland with theme trees, ornaments and unique gifts. For the past 22 years, the staff at Skagit Valley Gardens has been providing customers with distinctive plants and top-notch service. Take a walk through the display gardens and you will find a wealth of inspiration created by Skagit Valley Gardens' owner, horticulturalist Gary Lorenz. In the center of Skagit Valley Gardens, you'll find the Garden Café, serving coffee, soups, salads, sandwiches, desserts and many other delightful treats. The Rooster Coop features great outdoor furniture and accessories, while in the Gift Barn you'll find specialty items for that hard-to-shop-for person. These are among the many amenities that make a visit to Skagit Valley Gardens fruitful.

18923 Peter Johnson Road, Mount Vernon WA
(360) 424-6760
www.skagitvalleygardens.com

MUKILTEO

Mukilteo was settled by Europeans in 1858 and was the county seat of Snohomish County from 1861 to 1867. The Federal government built a lighthouse in 1906 that still stands today. The town also had a lumber mill, a brewery and a gunpowder plant. Powder Mill Gulch, named for the gunpowder plant, provides rail access from the Mukilteo waterfront to Paine Field. Home of the Boeing wide-body plant, Paine Field lies between Mukilteo and Everett. Visitors access the tour office and the Future of Flight attraction from the Mukilteo side.

PLACES TO GO

- Boeing Tour and Future of Flight Museum
  8415 Paine Field Boulevard
  (360) 756-0086

- 92nd Street Park
  4800 92nd Street SW

- Centennial Park
  1126 5th Street

- Mukilteo Lighthouse Park
  609 Front Street

- Picnic Point Ravine
  13000 43rd Avenue W

THINGS TO DO

May
- General Aviation Day and Taste of Mukilteo
  Paine Field
  (425) 353-2110 ext. 5000

September
- Mukilteo Lighthouse Festival
  (425) 353-5516

- Microbrew & Wine Tasting Garden
  Rosehill Tennis Courts
  (425) 347-1456

Four Seasons Gallery

GALLERIES: *Best gallery in Mukilteo*

Yumi Hines never refers to patrons of her Four Seasons Gallery in Mukilteo as customers. They are guests. The pace of the gallery is unhurried, and many folks drop by just to chat. Four paintings of the sky, one for each season, grace the ceiling and greatly enhance the cozy, boutique feel of the gallery. The emphasis here is on an environment designed to make visitors feel both at peace and at one with nature. Yumi supports local artists and likes to think she is helping to make them famous. She rotates featured artwork every two months to give many artists the opportunity for exposure and to constantly refresh the gallery's look with a new wave of paintings, jewelry and cards. Dear to Yumi are those items that reflect her Japanese heritage. Yumi carries *kai-wase* (intricately painted shells), *chirimen* (floral-shaped textile headbands) and *jinbei* (casual pants sets). Her goal is to nurture the spirit by introducing her guests to artistic variety. Yumi came to the United States in 1994. She brought with her secrets of style and emotional health that she learned from the most elegant women in Okinawa and from her 108-year-old grandmother. Her gallery is her guesthouse and classroom. Any season is a great time to come by and see Yumi at Four Seasons.

413 Lincoln Avenue, Mukilteo WA
(425) 423-8284

Maia Skin

HEALTH & BEAUTY: *Best cosmetic services*

Dr. Warren Magnus, DO, has been studying cosmetic services and techniques since graduating from medical school in 1996. The owner of Maia Skin in Mukilteo, he is noted for his individual approach. Everybody has their own comfort level when dealing with issues of appearance and aging. Dr. Magnus understands and respects that reality by providing honest yet discreet counseling for people with questions about the best techniques for maintaining a youthful appearance. Although Maia Skin offers many of the treatments available at conventional day spas, Dr. Magnus's techniques go beyond the spa and into the realm of cosmetic dermatology, without the clinical interface of a surgeon's office. Maia Skin offers Thermage®, laser hair removal, spider vein reduction and treatments for rosacea. They can address problems such as psoriasis and port wine birthmarks. The photodynamic therapy is ideal for acne, sun-damaged skin and abnormal cells too small to see. Chemical peels are physician-grade, and Botox is available. At Maia Skin, you can receive a free consultation to discuss your aesthetic goals and treatment options. Dr. Magnus and his staff strive to gain your trust so you can be confident that your journey to healthy skin is successful and comfortable.

631 Fifth Street, Suite 100, Mukilteo WA
(425) 355-1000
www.maiaskin.com

Riley's Pizza & Brewhaus

RESTAURANTS & CAFÉS: *Best New York-style pizza*

Michael Hopkins has been cranking out pizzas and calzones at Riley's Pizza & Brewhaus in Mukilteo for 14 years. With the help of his mother, Teri, who is a certified calzone expert, they've built a reputation as one of the best eateries in the North Sound region. At Riley's, the focus is on homemade dough, fresh ingredients, and ultra thin New York-style pizzas. Former New York residents have rated Riley's the best New York-style pizza in Washington state. They also happen to be craft brewers through their Eagle Brewing Company, which turns out microbrews, including amber, Irish red, porter and IPA. Jeff Matheson, the brewmaster for Eagle Brewing Company, turns out a premium root beer, as well. This laid-back, comfortable eatery is a favorite with locals. You'll often find the pilots who are training on the latest Boeing aircraft eating here, alongside the local high school hockey team. Besides the pizzas and calzones, which are most definitely the focus here, you can order an entrée-sized, not-so-chopped salad served either vegetarian style, or with chicken or salami. The vinaigrette is homemade. When you want a true Italian-style calzone or a premium, locally produced microbrew, check out Riley's Pizza & Brewhaus.

625 4th Street, Mukilteo WA
(425) 348-8088 *www.eaglebrewhaus.netfirms.com*

ROCKPORT

An hour east of I-5 on State Highway 20, Rockport and neighboring Concrete are the gateway to the Ross Lake National Recreation Area in the Cascades. North Cascades National Park, which lies to the north and south of Ross Lake Recreation Area, is more remote. The area contains a number of peaceful resorts from which you can easily view wildlife. Rabbits are amazingly tame. Guides offer whitewater rafting on the upper Skagit River. The Bald Eagle Interpretive Center in Rockport is open selected days December through February in the run-up to the Bald Eagle Festival.

PLACES TO GO

- Skagit River Bald Eagle Interpretive Center
  Fire Hall, Alfred Street, Rockport
  (360) 853-7626

- Rockport State Park
  51905 State Route 20

- Ross Lake National Recreation Area
  Newhalem Creek Road, Newhalem

THINGS TO DO

February
- Upper Skagit Bald Eagle Festival
  Concrete School Complex
  (360) 853-7283

Cascadian Farm

MARKETS: *Best organic farm market*

Three miles east of Rockport, you can find the best organic produce at Cascadian Farm, birthplace of Cascadian Farm brand organic foods now sold worldwide. The roadside stand is open daily from May through October and features fresh organic berries, vegetables, homemade ice cream, shakes and shortcakes, as wells as espresso, snacks, jams, pickles and salsas. All fruits and vegetables are picked fully ripe for peak flavor and nutrition. Managers Jim and Harlyn Meyer state their philosophy this way: "Organic farming is farming in harmony with nature. At Cascadian, we take our role as stewards of the land seriously. We use crop rotation, composting and cover crops to build the soil, which feeds the crops. We encourage Mother Nature's pest management program by creating habitats for beneficial insects that help us control the harmful ones." Enjoy fresh strawberries in June, raspberries in July, blueberries in July and August, a pumpkin patch in October and frozen berries all year. Be sure to stop by the first week in October for the Harvest Festival. Come to Cascadian Farm and see for yourself what great organic farming can do for your eating enjoyment.

55749 S.R. 20, Rockport WA
(360) 853-8173
www.cfarm.com

Snohomish Sky
Photo by Rob West

SNOHOMISH

Known for its antique shops, Snohomish prides itself in its historic downtown. Many houses throughout the town are historic landmarks. Snohomish is a top day-trip destination for visitors from throughout the Puget Sound region and beyond.

PLACES TO GO

- Blackman House Museum
  118 Avenue B (360) 568-5235

- Ferguson Park
  1330 Ferguson Park Road

- Hill Park
  1610 Park Avenue

- Pilchuck Park
  169 Cypress Avenue

THINGS TO DO

May
- Classic Motor Cycle Show
  (360) 568-7820

July
- Kla Ha Ya Days
  (360) 568-7076

- Snohomish Garden Tour
  (360) 568-2526

August
- Summer Festival
  (360) 568-2168

- Harvey Corn Roast and Fly-In
  Harvey Airfield
  (360) 568-1541

September
- Historical Society Home Tour
  (360) 568-5235

- Classic Car & Hot Rod Display
  Downtown
  (360) 568-2526

October
- Autumn Fest
  Downtown
  (360) 568-2526

- Juried Art Show
  Arts of Snohomish Gallery
  (360) 568-8648

Airial Balloon Company

ATTRACTIONS: *Best view*

For a little adventure and a lot of fun, Airial Balloon Company in Snohomish is the perfect place for a unique view of the area. You'll skim over the waters of Snohomish Valley and glide through the surrounding lowlands. View the Cascades, including Mount Baker and Mount Rainier, for a wide, sweeping picture of some of the most beautiful landscape in Washington. Because Airial Balloon Company offers three different packages seven days a week to fit any occasion, all ending with a toast of a sparking beverage and a personalized French certificate. If you prefer crisp, beautiful mornings, the Traditional Flight leaves just before daybreak and allows you to witness the spectacular colors of sunrise, traveling through the scenery so that you may watch the dew melt along your journey. You'll be greeted on the ground with a continental breakfast. The Sunset Flight offers the awe-inspiring imagery of farmlands and mountain ranges cast in the setting sun, as well as a full-course dinner prepared by chefs after your flight. The third flight is called Romance Aloft, and is strictly for couples wanting to share a breathtaking view and an unforgettable experience of the sun disappearing below the horizon, followed by a dozen long stemmed roses and a toast. To preserve your memorable experience on their hot air balloons, Airial Balloon Company features a gift shop open seven days a week, where you can purchase everything from t-shirts to jewelry. Come and be swept away at Airial Balloon Company.

10123 Airport Way, Snohomish WA
(360) 568–3025
www.airialballoon.com

Skydive Snohomish

ATTRACTIONS: *Most exhilirating attraction*

The most exciting way to take in the breathtaking views of Western Washington is to skydive in Snohomish. Skydive Snohomish has a perfect safety record and provides first class skydiving experiences year round. Located at historic Harvey Field 20 miles north of Seattle, this drop zone has a convenient location and exciting atmosphere for accommodating jumpers and spectators in groups of any size. Beginners can choose to make a tandem or static line jump. The most popular is the tandem skydive. After 30 minutes of training and a 20-minute scenic flight, you will experience the exhilaration of 30 to 60 seconds of freefall while securely harnessed to an instructor. Freefall is followed by a four to five-minute parachute descent featuring a gorgeous, 4,000-foot high panoramic view. Skydive Snohomish is located between the Cascade and Olympic Mountain ranges, overlooking the Puget Sound and San Juan Islands, and has a birds-eye view of the Seattle skyline, Mt. Rainier, Mt. St. Helens and Mt. Baker. Skydiving is a unique extreme sport in that a first-time jumper can embark on the same invigorating venture into human flight as an experienced skydiver. Although there is a weight and age limit, most everyone can live life at 120 miles per hour feeling comfortable and confident at Skydive Snohomish.

9912 Airport Way, Snohomish WA
(360) 569-7703 or (866) 759-JUMP (5867)
www.SkydiveSnohomish.com

Abri Counseling Services

HEALTH: *Best counseling services*

Abri Counseling Services and its affiliated clinicians are a caring team of healthcare professionals offering a holistic approach to health. Abri's mental health providers Maryalyce Stamatiou, RN and MA, Deborah Seidel, MN and ARNP, and Cherri Mann, MEd, offer individual, group, couples and family counseling for adults, adolescents and children. Stress management, mental health assessment, diagnosis and medication management are provided. Nutritional counseling and planning services are managed by Anne Dottai, MS, RD, of Serenity Nutritional Services. Lena Littler, LMP offers massage therapy and Linda Munson, LAc, MTCM, MA performs acupuncture. The clinicians at Abri Counseling Services are committed to providing affordable, high quality mental health and collaborative services to the people of Snohomish County.

602 Maple Avenue, Suites 201 & 202 (The Maple Building), Snohomish WA
(360) 568-2988
ABRIcs@msn.com

Comserv Copies & More

BUSINESS: *Best copying and printing*

With 35 years in the printing business, Barbara King can turn around a printed piece of paper with amazing speed. She opened Comserv Copies & More 22 years ago, and now, together with her "right and left hands" Mary Douglas and Todd Elvis, her business offers comprehensive printing services for all your needs. Whether you need do-it-yourself copies in a hurry, or full-service color and black-and-white digital copying for high-quality brochures and professional-looking books, Comserv can do it for you. They do architectural and engineering designs, photo reprints, reproductions, black-and-white or color photo enlargements, and artwork. They also offer any and every kind of binding and finishing option you can imagine. If you need invitations for weddings, baptisms, confirmations, openings, closings, or parties, they can help. Barbara and her team can

help you choose the perfect theme and tone for your invitations. In addition, they can meet your business needs for cards, brochures, and flyers. Whether you're creating business stationery and business cards, advertising layouts, newsletters, or résumés, Barbara can work with you to create high-impact professional and promotional materials. She'll work with you to get your initial design in 48 hours. So remember, if you need paper and print, this is where to come.

1030 Avenue D # 3, Snohomish
(360) 568-1644
www.comservcopies.com

HomeStar Lending

BUSINESS: *Best loan team*

One question that perplexes many prospective homebuyers is whether to go to a mortgage broker or a mortgage banker, because not many of us know the difference. HomeStar Lending makes it easy because it is both a mortgage banker and a mortgage broker, with a track record of success and a reputation to match. Since Richard Henke opened HomeStar Lending in 1995, his team of financial experts has underwritten more than 9,000 loans totaling more than 1.5 billion dollars. The reason is simple. At the heart of the firm are its twin goals of giving every customer an excellent experience and of making a positive impact on every life they touch. President Rich Henke and vice president Lisa Britton are committed to creating a business based on honesty,

integrity, caring, and knowledge of the mortgage market. They believe in the importance of balance and fulfilling personal values both for their clients and their employees. The result is a dedicated crew of top financing experts. Making the move into home ownership is a huge life decision. For solid advice and experience you can trust, consider HomeStar Lending. They will help you put together the puzzle and make the process simple.

209 Avenue D, Snohomish WA
(360) 568-6603 or (866) 568-6603
www.hsl.bz

Inside Out Home & Garden

HOME: *Best vintage home décor and more*

Inside Out Home & Garden in Snohomish offers heirlooms in a 100-year-old haunted house. Owners Alison Olsen and Jackie Kiter treat each vintage item like the special thing that it is. They select each piece not only for its beauty, but for the story behind it. Even the newer items they carry for your home or garden are chosen for their timeless and unique appeal. Inside Out has gifts for your most celebrated moments, such as weddings, baby arrivals and graduations. Among the exciting mix of items, you are bound to find ideas for decorating a college dorm, new business or guest room. This shop is rich in atmosphere. The counter is French and exquisite. The

front stained glass panels date from the 1700s. The chandeliers bathe you in light and make you feel like a movie star. As for the resident ghost, she is friendly, though a tad mischievous. She has been known to turn fans off and on, slide a broom across the room or rearrange the antique dolls. Be sure to ask for her when you drop by Inside Out Home & Garden, a store full of things you don't yet know you need, but can't possibly live without.

115 Avenue A, Snohomish WA
(360) 563-0767
www.einsideout.com

Star Center Antiques Mall

HOME: *Best antiques mall*

Snohomish has long been the antiques capital of the Northwest, and Star Center Antiques Mall was, and still is, one of the premier reasons. The historic Snohomish Armory was built in 1926, and in 1982, Star Center Mall opened in the building with 27 antiques dealers on the first floor. Tim and Holly Regan, the second generation of their family in the antiques business, have now expanded to cover all five floors and 25,000 square feet of the old Armory. More than 200 of the finest dealers in the country specialize in all things no longer new, including, but not limited to, art glass, Depression glass, pottery, Flow Blue china, vintage books and toys, old advertising, prints, sports memorabilia, silver and flatware, estate jewelry, and furniture. Each of the private dealers

guarantees authenticity and condition and they will ship anywhere in the country. If you would like to research an item, stop at the Collectors Reference Bookstore. With more than 10,000 reference books, they have information and history on any precious item you are considering. Whether you are an antiques novice or an expert, come lose yourself in treasures from days gone by at Star Center Antiques. But be warned: it may take two days to cover all five floors.

829 Second Street, Snohomish WA
(360) 568-2131
www.myantiquemall.com

Antique Rose Farm

GARDENS, PLANTS & FLOWERS:
Best place for antique roses

To qualify as a horticultural antique, a rose must have origins that date back to at least 1863. Antique Rose Farm has some antique roses that date back thousands of years. Antique Rose Farm, originally a dairy farm, has a breathtaking array of colors, shapes and fragrances of roses. The flowers they specialize in grow well in the Northwest. They are also disease resistant and hardy. Some of the varieties they carry are hybrid teas, floribundas, bourbons, gallicas, mosses, damasks and English. Their rugosa roses are resilient and easy to grow, with an abundance of blooms. The owners of Antique Rose Farm can advise you on the best varieties for your particular circumstances. They have a large selection of perennials and 5,000 square feet of furniture and other antiques in a charming barn, featuring folk art, gifts, rose books and more. The Antique Rose Farm gives classes on the care of roses, as well. This is a wonderful day trip, just three quarters of an hour from Seattle. They are open all year. Plan to visit during the first two weeks in June to enjoy the Farm's annual Rose Festival.

12220 Springhetti Road, Snohomish WA
(360) 568-1919

Way Out West

HOME: *Best Western furnishings*

As the name implies, Way Out West is about as far out west as you can get. The lodge and Western furnishings store, located in the heart of historic downtown Snohomish, was opened by Connie and Art Brediger in 1999. They have preserved the building's original pressed tin ceiling and restored the floors with reclaimed lumber stained in warm, rich tones. Way Out West features moderate to upper-end rustic, yet elegant, furnishings to complete that cozy cabin or western look. They feature hickory, log, and upholstered, handcrafted furniture, along with antler lighting, bed and bath, hide rugs, pillows, and wooden signs, plus a complete line of kitchenware and accessories. In addition, they offer vintage snowshoes, skis, canoes and authentic wagon wheels. They always look for something new after an item sells out so they do not buy the same merchandise over and over. They offer catalogs from more than 100 vendors and a library of more than 1,000 fabrics and leathers. You don't have to be a cowboy and you don't need a log home to enjoy the feel of the old ranch or the warmth of the family cabin. All you need is an appreciation of the look and the lifestyle. It seems that the more advanced our society becomes, the more we long to return to a time when life seemed less complicated. Let Way Out West take you back. Listen to the music of the old west, make yourself at home, and stay a while.

1116 First Street, Snohomish WA
(360) 563-6565
www.shopwayoutwest.com

Sunrise of Snohomish

LIFESTYLE DESTINATIONS: *Best assisted living*

Sunrise of Snohomish is situated in a quiet residential area, set on its own beautifully landscaped five-acre grounds with covered walkways, a gazebo and patio areas with country-style gardens to enjoy. Since 1993, Sunrise Senior Living of Snohomish has been providing care and services to champion the quality of life for seniors. The result is resident-centered model that focuses on each unique person and his or her needs and preferences. This approach embraces and helps preserve a resident's individuality. The cottage-style arrangement creates an intimate home-style environment in a neighborhood setting. Sunrise of Snohomish specializes in assisted living and caring for seniors with dementia in the Reminiscence neighborhood. Many of the residents of the Sunrise community have been life-long neighbors and some of their families were the original homesteaders within Snohomish County. Visit Sunrise Senior Living of Snohomish for the opportunity to upgrade your quality of life as a senior in the community.

1124 Pine Avenue, Snohomish WA
(360) 568-1900
www.sunriseseniorliving.com

Collector's Choice Restaurant

RESTAURANTS & CAFÉS: *Best place to eat while you antique*

Family owned and operated for 23 years, Collector's Choice Restaurant offers a warm and friendly atmosphere within the Star Center Antiques Mall. Owners John and Donna Hager strive to provide antique shoppers, locals and tourists with unique and comfortable meals. Collector's Choice has a lounge as well as an open restaurant. Serving breakfast, lunch and dinner, this is a full service restaurant complete with a private banquet facility and catering for private parties. Collector's Choice has a large open air patio for dining in good weather. Although the restaurant and lounge are non-smoking areas, smoking is allowed on the patio. This restaurant has many enticing menu choices, including certified Angus beef, outstanding seafood, and their signature entrée of seafood fettuccini. When you need to take a break from shopping, or if you're just looking for a good place to dine out, stop by Collector's Choice Restaurant for delicious food prepared well.

120 Glen Avenue, Snohomish WA
(360) 568-1277

Kitsap Peninsula

Kitsap Peninsula

Norwegian style home

THE KITSAP PENINSULA is drenched in rustic allure and romantic vistas. The entire area is known for extraordinary farmer's markets.

Bainbridge Island has been named by Money magazine as the second best place to live in the United States. The city has its own Performing Arts Center and an Arts and Crafts Gallery that promotes regional artists. Historic Winslow, Bainbridge Island's downtown, is dotted with cafés and island shops. Old Man House Park, owned by the Suquamish tribe, contains the largest longhouse on Puget Sound and was home to Chief Seattle and Chief Kitsap.

Norwegians developed the town of Poulsbo. For years, only Norwegian was spoken here and it still carries a Scandinavian ambience. Each year, the town hosts a Viking Fest, Scandia Midsommarfest and Yule Fest. Rosemale-pattern storefronts and outdoor murals decorate the town.

Bremerton is the population center of the peninsula. Ferry riders disembark onto a flower-lined boardwalk. To the south, across the Narrows Bridge from Tacoma, Gig Harbor has the feel of a peaceful fishing village. Waterfront walks, downtown shopping and expertly crafted artisan gardens dress the harbor.

On the mainland side of the Hood Canal, Hoodsport produces award-winning wines, clams, oysters and shrimp. Union is nestled amid groves of alder, evergreen and cedar. Small shops and gourmet restaurants are surrounded by spectacular scenery. The entire Kitsap Peninsula is an oasis of historical and natural charm.

Elandan Gardens
Courtesy of Kitsap Peninsula Visitor & Convention Bureau
Photo by Jean Boyle

Bainbridge Island

As you approach Bainbridge Island, glimpse the quiet harbors and homes along the rocky shoreline and the densely forested hills. The municipality of Bainbridge Island came into existence in 1990, when islanders voted to let the city of Winslow annex the rest of the island. Bainbridge has a wealth of gardens, such as the Bloedel Reserve. *Bicycling Magazine* has named the Chilly Hilly bicycle ride as one of four classic rides in the nation.

PLACES TO GO

- Bainbridge Island Historical Museum
  7650 High School Road NE

- Bainbridge Island Wine Museum
  8989 E Day Road

- The Bloedel Reserve
  7571 NE Dolphin Drive

- Battle Point Park
  11299 Arrow Point Drive NE

- Fay Bainbridge State Park
  Sunrise Drive NE

- Fort Ward State Park
  Fort Ward Hill Road NE

- Strawberry Hill
  7666 NE High School Road

THINGS TO DO

February
- Chilly Hilly Bicycle Ride
  (206) 522-BIKE (3222)

July
- Bainbridge in Bloom
  (206) 842-7901

- Bainbridge Bluegrass Festival
  Battle Point Park
  bainbridgebluegrassfestival.com

August
- Bainbridge Island Summer Studio Tour
  (206) 855-2924

- 'Round Bainbridge on the Virginia V
  (206) 842-2773

Photo by Liz Lawley

SpringRidge Gardens Bed and Breakfast
ACCOMMODATIONS: *Most romantic bed and breakfast*

At SpringRidge Gardens Bed and Breakfast on Bainbridge Island, the key word is simple: Romance. Host Wendy Burroughs strives to keep this romantic getaway a place where couples can kindle their relationships. This is the place for married couples to remember why they are married. Nestled in a spectacular garden setting on five peaceful acres, everything here revolves around romance. Even the DVDs and movies for guest use are romantic. Wendy maintains two private suites here: the Pensione and the Courtyard Suite. The European-inspired Pensione has

a full kitchen, queen and full beds, private bath, Tuscan Summer lighting and beautiful garden views. You'll feel like you're relaxing in a grown-up playhouse. The Courtyard Suite has a large living room with a fireplace adorned by a handcrafted antique mahogany mantel, baby grand piano, down sofa, kitchenette and private hot tub. There's a separate bedroom with a queen bed, antique writing desk and private bath. When you step out of either room, you step into Wendy's gardens, which have been featured in *Better Homes and Gardens, Pacific Magazine*, and *Water Gardening* magazine. It's impossible to stay here and not feel the romance.

7686 Springridge Road NE, Bainbridge Island WA
(206) 855-9763
www.springridgegardens.com

Bainbridge Gardens
GARDENS, PLANTS & FLOWERS: *Best nursery*

A family's 90-year history is rooted in the natural beauty of Bainbridge Gardens on Bainbridge Island. Zenhichi Harui, who came to America from Japan in 1908, is the creator of Bainbridge Gardens. By the 1930s, many would travel to see the magnificent sculptured trees and sunken gardens and fountains. Sadly, Zenhichi and his family were forced to leave with thousands of other Japanese Americans during World War II. When they returned, they found the nursery beyond restoration. In 1989, Junkoh Harui, one of Zenhichi's sons who had operated his own nursery business on the island for more than 40 years, decided to redevelop Bainbridge Gardens. Today, the seven-acre retail nursery honors the Harui family's living legacy. Japanese red pine trees that the elder Mr. Harui started from seeds he brought from Japan grace the grounds and nature trail. The Harui Memorial Garden features an old pear tree that Zenhichi Harui grafted into an exquisite shape. The Serenity Garden showcases Junkoh Harui's blend of Northwest and Japanese garden design. The onsite café serves lunch and espresso. Bainbridge Gardens offers a wide selection of trees and shrubs, perennials, bonsai, garden statuary and gifts for the home and garden. Visit the website for information about special events, classes and guest speakers.

9415 Miller Road NE, Bainbridge Island WA
(206) 842-5888 *www.bainbridgegardens.com*

Roby King Galleries
GALLERIES: *Best island gallery*

Wes King and Andrea Roby-King, residents of Bainbridge Island for 27 years, opened the Roby King Galleries in 1990. With educations in fine art, they spent their years prior to owning the gallery as potters, and created a small but nationally recognized line of pottery. The Kings' passion for art fills their lives both personally and professionally, and "since our early days as painters and potters, we have sought to promote and give venue to work that inspires us." Roby King Galleries exhibits representational art, from classical realism and Russian impressionism to contemporary. They represent more than two dozen artists, primarily oil painters, although the roster also includes watercolor and pastel painters, as well as textile, sculpture and mixed media artists. Many of the artists are Bainbridge Island residents or from the greater Northwest region. Others, such as nationally recognized oil painter Cheri Christensen, now of Santa Fe, were one-time residents of the Island who maintain their ties with Roby King Galleries. At their website you can view works by such notable artists as Diane Ainsworth, Mary Carlton, Hidde Van Duym, Phyllis Ceratto Evans, Pamela Fermanis, Pam Ingalls, Faye Judson, Louise Lamontagne, Patty Rogers, Frank Samuelson, David Turner, Lael Weyenberg, and Tatiana Zaits, but nothing is more enjoyable than going into the gallery to see it all in person.

176 Winslow Way E,
Bainbridge Island, WA
(206) 842-2063
www.robykinggalleries.com

Exotic Aquatics
RECREATION: *Best scuba and kayak shop*

Pam Auxier has a love for the water and all it can offer. Living on Bainbridge Island, she realized there was no dive or kayak shop to fuel her passion. In 1991, she opened Exotic Aquatics as a full-service SCUBA store and added a kayak operation in 1994 to provide everything you need both on and under the water. Pam and her professional staff arrange kayak tours and dives, sell or rent the necessary gear, and provide a comprehensive instruction program. The island is a close-knit community, and Exotic Aquatics is well known for its outstanding safety and service, its support of the community and catering to family fun. For example, if you are a diver, you can sample some world-class diving in and around the Bainbridge waters and perhaps see the resident giant Pacific octopus. For kayakers, local destinations include Eagle Harbor, historic Blakely Harbor and a picnic on Blakely Rocks, shooting the Agate Pass currents, or relaxing with a moonlight paddle while watching the distant lights of the Seattle skyline. While only a scenic 35-minute ferry ride from Seattle, Bainbridge Island seems like a different world. There are views of Mt. Rainier, bald eagles and osprey, harbor seals, and the migratory birds that frequent the shores and bays. Under water, Puget Sound hosts one of the most diverse marine environments on earth. For anyone who likes the water, Exotic Aquatics can fill your desires.

146 Winslow Way W, Bainbridge Island WA
(206) 842-1980 or (866) 842-1980
www.exoticaquaticsscuba.com www.exoticaquaticskayaking.com

The Harbour Public House
RESTAURANTS & CAFÉS: *Best English-style pub*

Jim Evans, Englishman and retired professor, dreamed of an English-style pub where islanders could congregate on the waterfront. That is what he has created with the help of his wife, Judy, daughter Jocelyn, and son-in-law Jeff Waite. Remodeled from an historic farm house, the Harbour Public House has no television or video games. It's a great place to talk, build relationships, and have a wonderful time with your friends and loved ones. It's also a great place to visit if you are passing through Bainbridge Island. They are famous for their fish and chips, as well as serving up delectable burgers and large green salads. The Harbour Public House serves mostly Washington microbrews, and supports local vendors. They handmake most of their menu items using free-range and organic products. They even squeeze the fruit juice they use in cocktails and drinks. The pub overlooks the Harbour Marina, which enables you to arrive by boat as well as land. You can enjoy phenomenal views of the Seattle skyline and Puget Sound while you eat. The *Bainbridge Island Review* has dubbed the Harbour Public House as the best in seven different categories, including best beer selection and best wait staff.

231 Parfitt Way SW, Bainbridge Island WA
(206) 842-0969 *www.harbourpub.com*

Eagle Harbor Book Company
SHOPPING: *Best independent booksellers*

Eagle Harbor Book Company, a locally owned and proudly independent bookstore, has been an integral part of the Bainbridge and Kitsap communities for more than 35 years. This mid-sized store of approximately 5,000 square feet presents a warm, intimate atmosphere and is open daily. They stock a diverse selection of more than 30,000 new and used titles, plus hard-to-find magazines, bargain books, and a large selection of gifts and calendars in season. They are known locally for excellence in customer service provided by a staff of experienced booksellers who love to share their enthusiasm for books and reading. They have been recognized nationally as winner of the Lucile Panell Award for Excellence in Children's Programming, as well as having been nominated for the 2002 *Publishers Weekly* Bookseller of the Year award.

157 Winslow Way E, Bainbridge Island WA
(206) 842-5332
www.eagleharborbooks.com

Skookum Clothing Company
SHOPPING: *Best historical Native American museum*

Owners Jack and Randi Morgan have created a store where the sale is secondary to caring about the customer. Skookum Clothing Company is known for personal service geared toward helping women create a look that is individual and exciting. The staff is knowledgeable and caring, and most have been with the store since its inception in 1994. The owners and staff have created a safe space. No matter your size or background, once you walk into the store, you become special and Skookum will treat you that way. Randi feels that too many stores just want to make a sale. At Skookum they want you to have a great experience and leave feeling wonderful about who you are and how you look. The clothes at Skookum are designed to flatter a woman's shape and to move with you. The goal is to provide unconditional comfort all day. To complement their clothes, Jack and Randi have chosen special body products and lingerie, in short, all the *stuff* that makes you feel good. They also carry fabulous children's clothes, newborn to size seven. Visit Skookum and discover why we love it so.

126 Winslow Way W, Bainbridge Island WA
(206) 842-0681

BREMERTON

Connected to downtown Seattle by a 60-minute ferry ride, Bremerton is home to Puget Sound Naval Shipyard. The shipyard dates back more than 100 years. The city today has a population of about 40,000, but during World War II shipbuilding swelled the numbers to more than 80,000. Today, the redeveloped downtown Bremerton Arts District includes museums, music venues and restaurants. *Reader's Digest* and *Money Magazine* have both recognized Bremerton as a great place to live.

PLACES TO GO

- Naval Memorial Museum of the Pacific
  402 Pacific Avenue (360) 479-SHIP (7447)

- Elandan Gardens
  3050 W State Route 16 (360) 373-8260

- USS *Turner Joy*
  300 Washington Beach Avenue
  (360) 792-2457

- Eastpark
  Magnuson Way and Homer Jones Drive

- Forest Ridge Park
  110 Summit Avenue

- Illahee State Park
  3540 NE Bahia Vista Drive

- Kitsap Lake Park
  1978 Price Road

THINGS TO DO

May
- Spring Tea & Fashion Show
  Bremer Building (360) 536-3656

August
- Kitsap County Fair & Stampede
  Fairgrounds (360) 337-5376

September
- Blackberry Festival
  Downtown
  (360) 377-3041

November
- Seattle International Stand-Up Comedy
  Competition
  Admiral Theatre
  (360) 373-6743

Bloedel Reserve Manor House is part of the 150-acre display gardens near Bremerton
Courtesy of Kitsap Peninsula Visitor & Convention Bureau
Photo by Jean Boyle

Gold Mountain Golf Club

ATTRACTIONS: *Best public golf complex*

At the Gold Mountain golf complex, you will fall in love with the greens and the surroundings. Be assured that the beauty you see will always be preserved the way you found it. That's because the complex is owned by the City of Bremerton. The City has created a full-service golf facility with two courses, while preserving important wildlife habitats and a community watershed for future generations to enjoy. Gold Mountain has received awards and accolades from numerous publications, including *Golfweek Magazine*, which rated it the best public course in Washington four years in a row. All that's left is for you to load up your clubs and head to Bremerton to prove it to yourself. After golfing, visit Tucker's Restaurant for casual dinning, good service and pristine views of the Olympic Mountains. The facilities include the Cascade Room, which provides an excellent meeting room for conferences and small corporate retreats, and the Olympic Pavilion, which can accommodate up to 300 people for banquets, weddings and other special events.

7263 W Belfair Valley Road, Bremerton WA
(360) 415-5432
www.goldmt.com

Photography of Gold Mountain Golf Complex
2005 John R. Johnson / Johnson Design Golf Marketing

Naval Undersea Museum

ATTRACTIONS: *Best submarine museum*

Every kid has imitated the submarine alarm: "Ah-oogah! Ah-oogah! Dive! Dive!" You can learn the true story of submarines at the Naval Undersea Museum, the largest collection of undersea technology in the country. Deep submersibles *Trieste II* and *Deep Quest* are on display outside. The *Trieste II* is a rebuilt version of the *Trieste* that took two passengers to the bottom of the Marianna Trench, the deepest spot on earth. Inside, exhibits include a manned Japanese kamikaze torpedo, a Confederate mine from the Civil War and a pressure-crushed Styrofoam cup. You can see torpedoes from the earliest days, modern weapons, and torpedo tubes from the submarine *USS Tecumseh*. Enter a simulation of the control room of the submarine *USS Greenling* and learn about mines, the weapons that wait. Exhibits also describe the oceans where submariners live and work. Hands-on displays teach about properties of the oceans, such as pressure, heat transfer and salinity. A microscope with slides of sea creatures, such as starfish and diatoms, lets children and adults see some of the fascinating creatures of the sea. See a video of the mysterious volcanic black smokers and tube worms from the Juan de Fuca Ridge 300 miles off the Washington coast. The museum has collections for researchers and a museum shop. Come to the Naval Undersea Museum, and let the Navy entertain you.

610 Dowell Street, Keyport WA
(360) 396-4148 ext. 220
http://naval.undersea.museum

The Kitsap Peninsula teems with migrating shore birds, such as Killdeer

GIG HARBOR

Gig Harbor, in the Pierce County bit of the Kitsap Peninsula, is noted for its beautiful harbor and many marinas. Gig Harbor is a major tourist attraction, and the historic waterfront offers boutiques and fine dining. The town celebrates festivals all through the spring and summer. The part of Kitsap on which Gig Harbor is located is called the Key Peninsula.

PLACES TO GO

- Gig Harbor Peninsula Historical Museum
  4218 Harborview Drive

- Sunrise Beach County Park
  10293 Sunrise Beach Drive NW

- Sehmel Homestead Park
  78th Avenue NW and Sehmel Drive NW

THINGS TO DO

April
- Arbor Day: Celebrate Our Earth
  City Hall (253) 851-8136

May
- Gig Harbor Juried Arts Exhibition
  (253) 853-3623

June
- Maritime Gig Festival
  (253) 851-6865

July
- Gig Harbor Summer Art Festival
  Downtown (253) 265-8313

- Key Peninsula Community Fair
  Fairgrounds (253) 884-4FUN (4386)

August
- Olalla Bluegrass Festival
  Olalla WA (253) 857-5650

September
- Gig Harbor Folk Festival
  (253) 265-1240

- Gig Harbor Quilt Festival
  (253) 857-2427

- Gig Harbor Chowder Cook-Off
  (253) 884-9672

December
- Tidefest Art Fair
  (253) 851-6131

Fisherman's Memorial in Jeresich Pa
Photo courtesy City of Gig Harb

The Maritime Inn

ACCOMMODATIONS: *Best small hotel in Gig Harbor*

The Maritime Inn, with graciously appointed rooms, fireplaces and harbor views, is the area's most distinctive small hotel. This European boutique-style hotel is situated in an area of pristine natural beauty that was once the original home and fishing grounds of a small band of Nisqually Indians. Now a bustling village, this postcard perfect area offers many recreational opportunities, including fishing, hiking and world-class golf. The Inn is ideally located within

walking distance to the harbor's finest restaurants, art galleries, thriving retail district and beautiful marinas. Graciously appointed rooms await guests with friendly staff, cozy fireplaces, charming Northwest interiors and views of the harbor. The Maritime Inn is truly the perfect small hotel. It's a glorious place to stay.

3212 Harborview Drive, Gig Harbor WA
(253) 858-1818 or
(888) 506-3580
www.maritimeinn.com

Waterfront Inn

ACCOMMODATIONS: *Best boutique inn*

Located at the head of Gig Harbor Bay and just steps from shops and restaurants, the Waterfront Inn offers luxurious accommodations. The Waterfront Inn offers three intimate suites just 20 feet from the water's edge, each with a private entrance and patio. They also have two spacious and sophisticated suites with king-size beds and sitting areas. The Lookout Room features a large fireplace and amazing water view. The Wheelhouse is bright, airy and dramatically furnished. These rooms share a peaceful living and dining area which serves as an excellent meeting room for small groups. All of the rooms have large private baths with a jacuzzi tub. Owners Steve and Janis Denton bought an old fisherman's home and renovated it into a beautiful boutique inn. They are known for providing privacy in their peaceful surroundings. Breakfast is brought right

to your door. You may enjoy the incredible view from the privacy of your room or from the huge deck over the water. Watch birds, ducks, seals, otters and the activity of boats on the bay. You may use their kayaks for exploring the bay, relax on the pier, walk around town or explore nearby trails. The Dentons can also arrange for charter trips through their company, Westerly Marine, featured on the next page.

9017 N Harborview Drive, Gig Harbor WA
(253) 857-0770
www.waterfront-inn.com

Westerly Marine

RECREATION: *Best charters*

Steve and Janis Denton, owners of Gig Harbor's Waterfront Inn, manage two fully crewed luxury charter yachts. The Amazing Grace is a 58-foot Topsail Schooner which was launched in 1990 to replicate an early 1800s Privateer. It looks like it came right off the movie set of *Master and Commander*. It has an overall spar length of 83 feet and more than 1,800 square feet of working sails. When you step below decks, the interior is breathtaking, with mahogany and old growth fir accented by 14 brass lanterns. Two guest staterooms are stunning, each with a double berth and their own toilet and sink. Allow the crew to serve you as you relax, or put your hand to the task of learning to sail and navigate. Adventuresome guests may string a hammock between the ratlines and sleep attached to a safety line suspended from the rigging. Week-long charters will tour the South Puget Sound, the San Juan Islands and Canadian Gulf Islands, or the famous Chatter Box Falls in Princess Louisa Inlet of British Columbia. Amazing Grace was featured in the Tall Ships Festival of Tacoma in July 2005, and The Victory is a fully restored 1974 Daytona 58 classic motor yacht with similar accommodations to the Amazing Grace. Both boats can be chartered together for a dinner cruise or a week-long trip. Both vessels hail from the Waterfront Inn in Gig Harbor.

9017 N Harborview Drive, Gig Harbor WA
(253) 857-0770
www.amazinggracetallship.com

HOODSPORT

Hoodsport Winery is the number-one industry in tiny Hoodsport, on the mainland near the Kitsap Peninsula. From the winery, you have a majestic view of the Hood Canal and the Olympic Mountains. A pioneer in the Washington State wine industry, Hoodsport Winery was founded in 1978 when there were only 16 wineries. The Skokomish Indian Reservation is immediately to the south.

PLACES TO GO

- Potlatch State Park
  21020 N U.S. Route 101, Skokomish Nation WA

THINGS TO DO

April
- Spring Barrel Tasting
  Hoodsport Winery (360) 877-9894

- Hood Canal Oyster Bite
  (360) 877-5301

May
- Memorial Day Barrel Tasting
  Hoodsport Winery (360) 877-9894

July
- Celebrate Hoodsport
  (360) 877-5301

November
- Hoodsport Chum Fishing Derby
  (360) 877-5301

Hood Canal Bridge connecting the Kitsap and Olympic Peninsulas is the world's largest floating bridge over saltwater.
Courtesy Kitsap Peninsula Visitor & Convention Bureau
Photo by Jean Boyle

Great Egret

Hoodsport Winery

WINERIES: *Best winery*

It all started long ago with Dick Patterson's hobby of making wine at home. Now his expertise and years of experience have been recognized by awards from around the world. Hoodsport Winery's 1994 Cabernet Sauvignon took the gold at France's 1996 Challenge International du Vin. Other award-winners include the Gewurztraminer and Hoodsport's unique Island Belle wine, made from a Puget Sound hybrid grape that originated in the mid-1800s and is now used by no other winemaker. When Dick and his wife Peggy moved from Montana in 1978 and founded Hoodsport Winery, it was one of only 16 wineries in Washington (there are now more than 300). Hoodsport is now incorporated, but it is still in many ways a family business. The Pattersons' daughter Ann now works in the marketing department. Dick shares the task of winemaking with Brent Trela, who has earned an international reputation for his knowledge of wines. Visit the winery and gift shop, where you'll not only find great wine and an invigorating view of the Olympic Mountains, but also a few surprises in the form of their special chocolate wine truffles, gourmet coffees and specialty fruit wines, featuring raspberry, cranberry and loganberry. The Hoodsport Winery is open daily.

N 23501 Highway 101, Hoodsport WA
(360) 877-9894
or (800) 580-9894
www.hoodsport.com

POULSBO

Poulsbo was settled by Nordic immigrants, principally from Norway and Finland. In fact, Poulsbo residents spoke Norwegian more often than English until war workers arrived during World War II. Downtown Poulsbo, a popular tourist destination, maintains a Scandinavian theme in its shops and restaurants. One local product, Poulsbo bread, is now available worldwide. The Port of Poulsbo guest marina is open 365 days a year and has 130 visitor slips. Easy access to shops and restaurants makes this a popular boating destination.

PLACES TO GO

- Island Lake County Park
  1087 NW Island Lake Road

- Liberty Bay (Waterfront) Park
  King Olav Vei

- Nelson Park
  317 NW Lindvig Way

THINGS TO DO

May
- Viking Fest
  (360) 697-2273

June
- St. Hans Midsommer Fest 2006
  Liberty Bay Park (360) 779-5208

August
- Poulsbo Arts Festival
  Liberty Bay Park (360) 779-2098

- Pawsbo Dog Days
  Verksted Gallery (360) 697-4470

October
- Annual Lutefisk & Lefse Dinner
  First Lutheran Church (360) 779-2622

November
- North Kitsap Holiday Arts Fest
  (360) 598-8403

December
- Scandinavian Yule Fest & Bazaar
  Liberty Bay Park (360) 779-5209

Poulsbo Kiana Lodge
Photo by Jan Tik

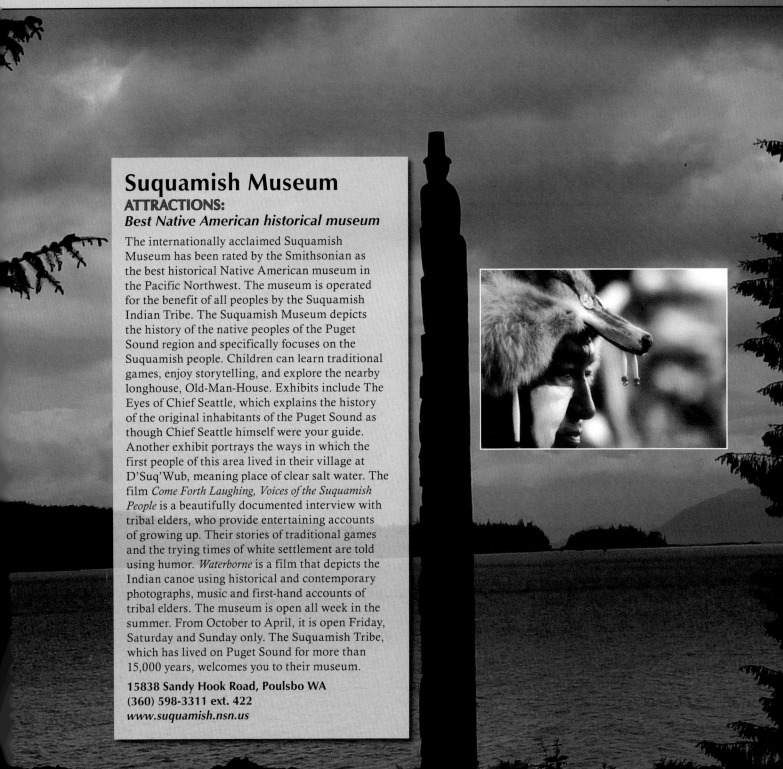

Suquamish Museum

ATTRACTIONS:

Best Native American historical museum

The internationally acclaimed Suquamish Museum has been rated by the Smithsonian as the best historical Native American museum in the Pacific Northwest. The museum is operated for the benefit of all peoples by the Suquamish Indian Tribe. The Suquamish Museum depicts the history of the native peoples of the Puget Sound region and specifically focuses on the Suquamish people. Children can learn traditional games, enjoy storytelling, and explore the nearby longhouse, Old-Man-House. Exhibits include The Eyes of Chief Seattle, which explains the history of the original inhabitants of the Puget Sound as though Chief Seattle himself were your guide. Another exhibit portrays the ways in which the first people of this area lived in their village at D'Suq'Wub, meaning place of clear salt water. The film *Come Forth Laughing, Voices of the Suquamish People* is a beautifully documented interview with tribal elders, who provide entertaining accounts of growing up. Their stories of traditional games and the trying times of white settlement are told using humor. *Waterborne* is a film that depicts the Indian canoe using historical and contemporary photographs, music and first-hand accounts of tribal elders. The museum is open all week in the summer. From October to April, it is open Friday, Saturday and Sunday only. The Suquamish Tribe, which has lived on Puget Sound for more than 15,000 years, welcomes you to their museum.

15838 Sandy Hook Road, Poulsbo WA
(360) 598-3311 ext. 422
www.suquamish.nsn.us

Liberty Bay Books

SHOPPING: *Best bookstore in Poulsbo*

Liberty Bay is not your conventional bookstore. The ambience generated here reflects the personality of its owner, Suzanne Droppert. Suzanne has always loved books and people. When this quaint, old-fashioned, independent bookstore became available, she jumped at the chance to become the new owner. The store is full of energy; it's a fun place to relax. The lounge area and espresso stand open early and close late. Liberty Bay is a general interest bookstore. Of particular interest are titles that are imported from Norway. Most are beautiful coffeetable books that are often carried home by Norwegian visitors. There is a great selection of Native American books, children's books and CDs. Interior design books are especially popular. Fiction and non-fiction selections are plentiful. Nautical books are one of their specialties. All of their staff love to read and enthusiastically share their favorite picks. Many books are discounted. Order from their website and they'll send books anywhere. Liberty Bay Books may not be the biggest bookstore you've ever been in, but it may be the liveliest.

18881 D Front Street, Poulsbo WA
(360) 779-5909
www.libertybaybooks.com

Raven Blues
GALLERIES: *Best gallery of local artisans*

Ravens are intelligent birds attracted to bright and shiny objects, just the sort of magnetic attraction you'll feel when you arrive at Raven Blues. Peggy Fiorini and Larry Girardi have assembled an eclectic mix of wonderful decorative items from fine art, handmade furniture and art glass to exquisite jewelry and women's *Art to Wear* apparel. Feather your nest with work by some of the most talented craftsmen from Washington and throughout the country, as well as celebrity artists. Examples include Angela Cartwright's photography for *Daddy* and *Lost in Space*, and whimsical sculpture by Robert Shields of Shields & Yarnell mime and television fame. Dare to wear a stylish statement with some of the finest women's jewelry and apparel available, including the collectible Double D Ranchwear line of clothing and accessories. At Raven Blues, there is definitely a lot to crow about.

18827 Front Street NE, Poulsbo WA
(360) 779-5662

Higuera Imports
SHOPPING: *Best Mediterranean imports*

When you walk into Higuera Imports, you feel like you've stepped into a colorful Mediterranean marketplace. Their Majolica ceramic items imported from Italy are stunning. The town of Deruta (a small hilltop town in Umbria) has made high-quality Majolica ceramics for centuries and has become known worldwide as the best source for these artistic objects. Deruta also is known for its unique tables. Higuera Imports offers tables that are handmade in the Old World ways with travertine antique terra-cotta and solid volcanic stone tables. The travertine tables are made of materials from ancient farmhouses and villas throughout Tuscany and Umbria estimated to be from 300 to 600 years old. Both types of tables are ice proof, heat proof and sun resistant. Higuera Imports decided to dedicate the flooring division solely to high quality bamboo products because of the benefits to the environment. Although the market share of bamboo flooring is currently less then 3.5 percent of the entire flooring industry, Higuera Imports sees a bright and unlimited future for their A-grade bamboo flooring. Higuera Imports also brings you the latest innovative designs in teak furniture. The owners of Higuera Imports spent time living in Europe and traveled all over the world for many years before opening their store. Ruth and Joe's experiences abroad not only educated them on quality but also opened the door for many important personal relationships with their sources abroad. The results is an outstanding selection of exceptional quality and affordable imported items.

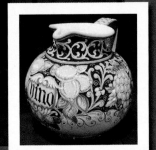

19006 Front Street, Poulsbo WA
(360) 779-4050 or (888) 300-2059
www.higueraimports.com

UNION

Union is on the south shore of Hood Canal, one of the warmest bodies of salt water in Puget Sound. Small shops, gourmet restaurants and lodging facilities are open to serve you. Alderbrook Resort, a popular destination for visitors, completed a major renovation with a grand re-opening in 2004.

PLACES TO GO

• Twanoh State Park
  12400 E State Route 106

THINGS TO DO

August
• SummerFest
  Harmony Hill Retreat (360) 898-2363

October
• Pumpkin Patch & Hayrides
  Hunter Farms (360) 426-2222

Great Blue Heron

Alderbrook Resort & Spa
ACCOMMODATIONS: *Best resort*

Hood Canal is one of Washington's natural wonders, a glacier-sculpted fjord more than 60 miles long, renowned for its sparkling waters and unique ecosystem. Located right on the water in Union, Alderbrook Resort & Spa is the perfect place to stay while enjoying the natural wonders of Hood Canal and the Olympic National Park just a few miles away. Alderbrook offers a PGA golf course and marina with more than 1,500 feet of docking space. Having undergone almost two years of renovations, Alderbrook offers state-of-the-art lodging and conference facilities. Warm earth tones and windows offering spectacular views highlight not only the beautifully designed guest rooms, but also the Restaurant at Alderbrook. You are invited to enjoy a sumptuous menu featuring the freshest local seafood and a world-class selection of wines. With 7,000 square feet of meeting space and a location just two hours from Seattle, Alderbrook is a perfect place for business conferences and family gatherings alike, and the natural beauty makes an unforgettably beautiful backdrop for open-air weddings. The cherry on the sundae is Alderbrook Spa, offering a full range of soothing and revitalizing body treatments in an incomparable setting.

10 E Alderbrook Drive, Union WA
(360) 898-2200 or (800) 622-9370
www.alderbrookresort.com

Washington Coast

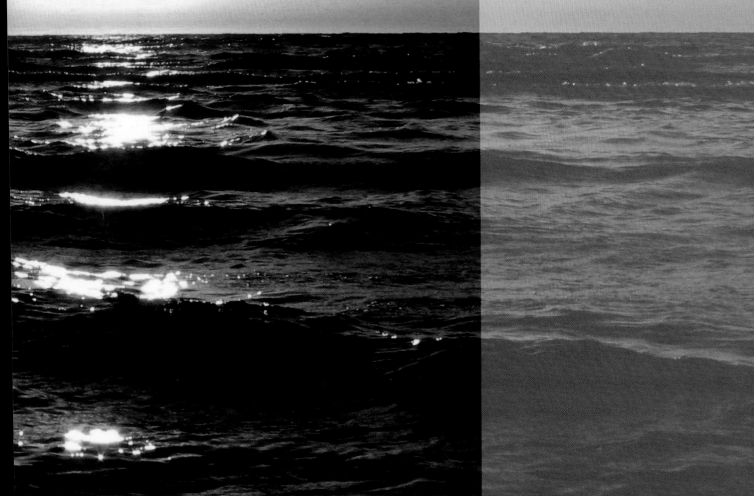

Washington Coast

THE WASHINGTON COAST shoreline is second to none. On Long Beach Peninsula, the beach stretches 28 miles without interruption, making it one of the longest beaches in the United States. While tourism is the number-one activity here, fishing, crabbing, oyster farming and cranberry farming are very important. History is ever-present, as well.

At the southern tip of the coast is Cape Disappointment, the western terminus of the Lewis and Clark expedition. William Clark walked the shore as far as the town of Long Beach. His path, today called the Discovery Trail, is lined with bronze sculptures of wildlife. Many visitors compare Long Beach Peninsula to Cape Cod.

Local fish and shellfish, berries and wild mushrooms define the Northwest Coastal Cuisine. Chefs work to upstage each other during the Wild Mushroom Festival in the fall. Another popular attraction is the Long Beach Kite Festival in August, when 5,000 kites fly in the Pacific winds.

The entire town of Oysterville is on the National Register of Historic Places. Further north on the coast is Ocean Shores, a six-mile beach peninsula that protects Grays Harbor from the sea. Ocean Shores offers more than 1,200 guest rooms and opportunities for bird watching, horseback riding and golf.

At the top of Grays Harbor is Aberdeen, the largest city in this region. You can tour the Broadway Hill historic homes or view birdcages downtown that contain metal replicas of endangered species.

LONG BEACH PENINSULA

The Long Beach Peninsula is an uncommon pencil of land stretched along the Pacific Ocean. Here, the shoreline provides vistas of the sea, starkly beautiful and imposing. Locals organize a range of activities to take advantage of the changeable weather. The wind is often ideal for kites, so a renowned Kite Festival takes place in August. The peninsula also is the home of the World Kite Museum, which holds 1,500 kites, including 400 kites from Japan and 300 from China and Malaysia. The museum gives six hands-on workshops through the year, and a kiting Hall of Fame honors outstanding kiting events in history. An indoor Windless Kite Festival takes place in January. Beachgoers can whale-watch in December and March and join in the Razor Clam digs January through April. July events include a rodeo, a sand-sculpture competition and FinnFest USA. For a little local history, visit the Willapa Bay Interpretive Center, an oyster station replica housed in a natural wooden building on the breakwater at Nahcotta. Inside, a 20-foot mural of the bay lines a wall. The center gives visitors the 150-year history of oyster growing in the bay. The Cranberry Museum offers a chance to walk through a cranberry bog and displays colorful photographs and artifacts. Don't miss the Cranberrian Fair in October. For a lighter note, try Marsh's Free Museum, which contains such oddities as a stuffed two-headed calf, petrified dinosaur dung and an authentic shrunken head. After many happy hours of experiencing Long Beach Peninsula, you can wrap up your days bathed in the glow of a coastal sunset.

Photo by Levy Sheckler

ABERDEEN

Aberdeen is the largest city on Washington's Pacific Coast and is the gateway to the western Olympic Peninsula. The city's economy was long based on lumber and fishing, but tourism and retail businesses are becoming ever more important. Aberdeen is the home port of the tall ship Lady Washington and the Hawaiian Chieftain. These ships sail up and down the coast, distributing romance with every stop. The Lady Washington portrayed HMS Interceptor in The Curse of the Black Pearl. The late musician Kurt Cobain was an Aberdeen native. The neighboring cities of Hoquiam and Cosmopolis are also part of the Grays Harbor urban area.

PLACES TO GO

- Grays Harbor Historical Seaport and Learning Center
  712 Hagara Street (360) 532-8611

- Grays Harbor National Wildlife Refuge
  Airport Way, Hoquiam (800) 303-8498

- Benn Park
  300 Hanna Avenue

- Morrison Riverfront Park
  1401 Sergeant Boulevard

- Pioneer Park
  214 S Tilden Street

- Stewart's Memorial Park
  2331 North B Street

THINGS TO DO

April
- Grays Harbor Shorebird Festival
  Hoquiam (800) 303-8498

July
- Art Walk & Downtown Celebration
  Aberdeen (360) 537-5755

- Hoquiam River Festival
  (360) 532-5700 ext. 244

September
- Hoquiam Logger's Playday
  (360) 532-5700 ext. 244

October
- Gray's Harbor Historical Seaport Anniversary
  Aberdeen (800) 200-LADY (5239)

Aberdeen Mansion

ACCOMMODATIONS: *Best coastal bed and breakfast*

Aberdeen Mansion has stood tall and proud for more than a century. The present owners, Al and Joan Waters, preside over an acre of beautiful grounds and a building that has maintained its grace, charm and elegance. In 1905, this building was home to the nine-member family of lumberman Edward Hulbert. In 1903, the Hulberts had lost their home to a fire that destroyed downtown Aberdeen. When Hulbert decided to rebuild, he chose the growing Broadway District. The new Queen Anne/Victorian-style home was erected using materials from the Aberdeen area. Local workers used native woods, setting them on a foundation of stone from a nearby quarry. Hulbert spared no expense on the three-story, 10,000-square-foot mansion, with its circular tower, imposing dormers and octagonal reception hall. Though outhouses were the norm at the time, the Hulbert mansion had four indoor bathrooms. Edward Hulbert died in 1918 and the home has changed ownership only four times since 1939, when his widow Laura died. This spectacular home was converted to a bed and breakfast in 1994. The Waters bought it in 1997 and it has become a popular destination for people looking for elegant accommodations and gourmet food.

807 North M Street, Aberdeen WA
(360) 533-7079 or (888) 533-7079
www.aberdeenmansionbb.com

MOCLIPS

Moclips is on the southern border of the Quinault Indian Reservation, and the members of the Quinault Tribe are the area's oldest residents. In 1905, Dr. Edward Lycan built the first of two fabulous resort hotels at Moclips. The first hotel burned almost immediately and the second was washed away by storms by 1913. Tourism returned after World War II with the construction of the Ocean Crest Resort. Moclip's neighbors to the south include Pacific Beach and the new planned community of Seabrook.

PLACES TO GO

• Museum of the North Beach
  4658 State Route 109 (360) 276-4441

• Quinault Indian Nation
  Fishing guides and tour services
  http://209.206.175.157

• Pacific Beach State Park
  2nd Street S, Pacific Beach

THINGS TO DO

September
• Shake Rat & Kelpers Festival
  Moclips and Pacific Beach (800) 286-4552

To Be Announced
• Razor clam digs
  (360) 249-4628

Ocean Crest Resort

ACCOMMODATIONS: *Best coastal resort*

Nestled in the trees on a 100-foot bluff overlooking the crashing waves of the Pacific Ocean, Ocean Crest Resort in Moclips is recognized by *Frommer's* as having "the most spectacular setting of any lodging on the Washington Coast." A beautiful staircase meanders through a wooded ravine to miles of open sandy beach where boating, clamming, crabbing, horseback riding, kite flying, and beachcombing are among your choices for a delightful afternoon. The resort has accommodations in all sizes, from studios to two-bedroom apartments, many with wood-burning fireplaces and all with full amenities. Enjoy world-class dining in their award-winning restaurant. The health club provides an indoor pool, hot tub, sauna, tanning, exercise room, and massage therapy. The conference facilities offer an unforgettable business retreat or meeting. Relax and enjoy at the Ocean Crest Resort.

4651 SR 109, Moclips WA
(360) 276-4465 or (800) 684-8439
www.oceancrestresort.com

Ocean Crest Resort Restaurant

RESTAURANTS & CAFÉS: *Best restaurant in Moclips*

Breathtaking views, award-winning regional cuisine and hospitality are just a few of the features that make the Ocean Crest Resort Restaurant so good. The restaurant at Ocean Crest Resort is recognized by Frommer's as having the best food in the region. The Curtright family started the resort in 1953 with three cabins and lots of enthusiasm. The restaurant followed in 1963, with founder Barbara Curtright Topete doing the cooking. The chef today turns out a full menu with an emphasis on local, fresh, seasonal ingredients. The restaurant, which has been written about in *Gourmet* and *Bon Appetit*, is gaining recognition for its extensive wine cellar. More than half the wines are produced in Washington and the others are almost exclusively from boutique wineries in the Pacific Northwest. It received *Wine Spectator's* Award of Excellence in 2004 and made *Wine Press Northwest's* Outstanding NW Wine List. For fine dining in a peerless setting, visit Ocean Crest Resort Restaurant.

4651 SR 109, Moclips WA
(360) 276-4465 or (800) 684-8439
www.oceancrestresort.com

NAHCOTTA

Since the coming of the Europeans, the various small communities in the northern part of Long Beach Peninsula have vied for prominence. Nahcotta was actually formed from two rival communities. It had the best moorage at what is now the Port of Peninsula, and in 1889 local boomers completed a small railway into the area. They founded two feuding towns at the north end of the railway, Nahcotta and Sealand. The towns thrived by shipping logs and oysters. Nahcotta eventually absorbed Sealand. The town burned down in 1915, however, and Ocean Park, on the Pacific side, became the new center. Today, it is the lure of the Pacific that pulls people to the peninsula.

PLACES TO GO

- Willapa Bay Interpretive Center
  Port of Peninsula (360) 665-4547

- Leadbetter Point State Park
  State Route 103

- Pacific Pines State Park
  Vernon Avenue and Joe Johns Road

THINGS TO DO

January
- Windless Kite Festival
  Ocean Park School (360) 642-4020

May
- Willapa Bay Seafood Festival
  Port of Peninsula (360) 665-4547

June
- Garlic Festival
  Sheldon Field, Ocean Park (800) 451-2542

July
- Independence Day in the Park
  Sheldon Field, Ocean Park (800) 451-2542

August
- Jazz and Oysters in Oysterville
  (360) 665-4466

September
- Rod Run to the End of the World
  Ocean Park (360) 665-3565

Ark Restaurant & Bakery

RESTAURANTS & CAFÉS:
Best restaurant in Nahcotta

The Ark Restaurant & Bakery has been a Willapa Bay institution since 1950. As you might expect from a bayfront restaurant originally founded by a fisherman, the sea's bounty is a feature attraction here. People come from far and wide to enjoy specialties such as pan-fried oysters fresh from Willapa Bay and pan-seared halibut in a shiitake mushroom crust served with dungeness crab. The bakery at the Ark provides homemade rolls that accompany every entrée, and the delicious and decadent desserts that have been singled out for praise by many reviewers. A special seasonal favorite is the blackberry cobbler, using fresh wild berries grown in the nearby hills. The Ark has been acclaimed in *Newsweek, Town and Country, Food and Wine, The New York Times* and in numerous television and radio spots. It overlooks Willapa Bay, the largest unpolluted estuary in the United States and features its own organic herb and edible flower gardens. Don't pass up a chance to dine in fine style at the Ark.

3310 273rd Street, Nahcotta WA
(360) 665-4133
www.arkrestaurant.com

OCEAN SHORES

Once you pass through the stones pillars that welcome you into this small tourist community, you will understand why it was voted Best of Western Washington five years in a row. This six-mile-long peninsula is surrounded by Grays Harbor and the Pacific and is threaded with 26 miles of interlocking fresh water lakes. The town constantly puts on special events, and you can watch wildlife anytime.

PLACES TO GO

- Environmental Interpretive Center
  1013 Catala Avenue SE (360) 289-4617

- Damon Point State Park
  Marine View Drive SE

- Ocean City State Park
  148 State Route 115

- Oyhut Wildlife Recreation Area
  Tonquin Avenue SW

THINGS TO DO

February
- Antique & Collectible Show
  (360) 289-5632

March
- Beachcombers Fun Fair
  (360) 289-4457

April
- Photo & Fine Arts Show
  (800) 76-BEACH (762-3224)

May
- Country Music Jam
  (360) 289-4411

June
- Kite Challenge
  (800) 76-BEACH (762-3224)

- Sand and Sawdust Festival
  360-289-5632

September
- Arts & Crafts Bazaar
  (800) 76-BEACH (762-3224)

October
- Whale of a Quilt Show
  (800) 76-BEACH (762-3224)

November
- Winter Fanta-Sea Arts and Craft Show
  (800) 874-6737

Photo by Jan Tik

The Polynesian Resort

ACCOMMODATIONS: *Best Ocean Shores resort*

Professionally managed by Vacation Villages of America, the oceanfront Polynesian Resort complex strives to meet all of its visitors' needs. Accommodations include 1,600-square-foot penthouses; 1,100-square-foot, two-bedroom family suites; condos; single rooms; studios with kitchenettes; and conference and banquet facilities. Generously stocked, full-sized bedrooms tout wood-burning fireplaces. Continental breakfast is served every weekday morning in a cozy room that later provides space for puzzles, reading, board games, and television. If you want special treatment enjoy the luxuriously appointed spa, sauna and indoor pool. Exclusive to the Polynesian Resort is their private park with a sport facility for basketball, volleyball, playground, picnic areas and barbeques. Mariah's is the onsite, award-winning restaurant. There are nightly specials, daily happy hours, and a fabulous Sunday brunch. Mariah's is very popular with the locals, a telltale sign of great food and atmosphere. Package deals and discount programs are available at this family and pet friendly resort.

**615 Ocean Shores Boulevard NW,
Ocean Shores WA
(360) 289-3361 or (800) 562-4836**
www.thepolynesian.com

Quinault Beach Resort & Casino
ACCOMMODATIONS: *Best coastal casino resort*

Owned by the Quinault Indian Nation, Quinault Beach Resort & Casino is ready to provide a Native American experience that can transform your visit from the common to the extraordinary. Located directly on the beach at Ocean Shores, Quinault Beach Resort is Washington's premier coastal destination. With broad vistas of the Pacific Ocean and 200 acres of protected wetlands in every direction, the Resort blends nature, architecture and technology to create an unsurpassed destination for vacationers and business gatherings. The 150 Northwest décor, oversized guestrooms feature French balconies, fireplaces and sweeping views. You can be pampered and renewed in the full service spa, swimming pool and fitness facility. The Activity Center offers educational and recreational opportunities. The Resort features 16,090 square feet of state-of-the-art function space for meetings, banquets and special events. Emily's Restaurant satisfies the palate as well as the spirit with fresh Northwest cuisine and views of the Pacific Ocean. There is live entertainment and high energy in the Cabaret and quiet relaxation in the Lobby Lounge. The only thing left to chance is their international-style casino that features the latest electronic gaming machines and a complete array of table games. Quinault Indian tribal members entertain and inform you through traditional music, dance and song.

78 State Route 115, Ocean Shores WA
(360) 289-9466 or (888) 461-2214
www.quinaultbchresort.com

First Cabin
SHOPPING: *Best nautical gifts*

First Cabin is not a gallery, and they are not stuffy, even though they are POSH. First Cabin is a nautical term meaning "the best, the front of the ship, view of the shore." POSH means Port Out, Starboard Home, the best that can be offered. Owners Brenda Love-Loveland and Al Loveland offer quality merchandise from more than 400 vendors. Before making a decision to carry an item, Brenda and Al ask themselves, "Is it First Cabin?" You will find extraordinary accessories for Captain, Crew and Quarters. In addition to nautically-themed gifts, First Cabin carries jewelry, paintings, glassware, nautical textiles, pewter, lamps and weather-related instruments. They have been selling amber for 14 years and are known for the best pricing of amber jewelry on the West Coast. First Cabin prides itself on above-board customer service, which includes free gift wrapping. Special orders are welcome and they will ship anywhere.

698 Ocean Shores Boulevard NW, Ocean Shores WA
(360) 289-9070

McCurdy's Celtic Marketplace

SHOPPING: *Best Celtic merchandise*

Food, teas, hand-knit sweaters, hats, woolens, linens, Belleek Parian China, Guinness Licensed Products, plus the art of Vettriano and Montague Dawson: These are just a few of the fine imports you will find in McCurdy's Celtic Marketplace. Owners Jim and Colleen Earp gather the best of Ireland, England, Scotland, Wales, and lesser-known Celtic countries in this charming shop. It was named after Colleen's grandmother, Lulu B. McCurdy (the family immigrated from a fine little whiskey town called Bushmills). Their goal is to bring a bit of Ireland and other Celtic cultures to Ocean Shores. Among the beautiful handcrafts, porcelain, art and jewelry you will find many surprises, including Beatles memorabilia and a silk Irish chain quilt from the 1700s. The shop is a bit of the old and some contemporary mixed with traditional Celtic wares. The teapot is always on at McCurdy's, so you can take pleasure in a cup while you are enjoying the inviting atmosphere.

114 E Chance a la Mer NE Boulevard, #107, Ocean Shores WA
(360) 289-3955

Raining Cats & Dogs

SHOPPING: *Best gifts for pets and their owners*

When you enter Raining Cats & Dogs, you feel like you have stepped into a world of extravagance. The shop has designer clothing and gourmet food for the discriminating dog and cat—and for their discriminating humans, too. Cool stuff for dogs and cats and their owners, what could be more fun? Jim and Colleen Earp run the store, but the real owner is Abigale Earp, the seven-pound Maltese who lives in the shop. It is very easy to while away the time in the charming and luxurious atmosphere with a European flair. The Earps have mood CDs, unusual chess sets, great framed prints, jazzy little martini glasses, and great bath and body products. Do not forget the home party items and fun entertainment pieces for that special house guest. Raining Cats & Dogs is a twist on everyday accessories and entertainment. Go in to enjoy.

698 Ocean Shores Boulevard SW, Ocean Shores WA
(360) 289-4100

SEAVIEW

Seaview, Long Beach and Ilwaco make up the southern end of the Long Beach Peninsula. This area is rich in tradition, raw beauty and award-winning lodging and dining. Surrounded by the Pacific Ocean, Columbia River and Willapa Bay, the peninsula is a refuge for migrating birds. The beach extends a full 28 miles. Thousand-year-old western red cedars thrive on Long Island in Willapa Bay.

PLACES TO GO

- Cranberry Museum
  2907 Pioneer Road, Long Beach

- Ilwaco Heritage Museum
  115 SE Lake Street, Ilwaco

- Lewis & Clark Interpretive Center
  Cape Disappointment State Park 8

- World Kite Museum
  303 Sid Snyder Drive, Long Beach

- Cape Disappointment State Park
  244 Robert Gray Drive, Ilwaco

- Willapa National Wildlife Refuge
  3888 State Route 101, Ilwaco

THINGS TO DO

January–February
- Asian New Year Kite Event
  (360) 642-4020

March
- Peninsula Quilt Guild Show
  Ilwaco Heritage Museum (360) 642-3446

- Long Beach Bluegrass Festival
  (360) 446-3645

April
- Black Lake Fishing Derby *(360) 642-3145*

May
- Loyalty Day Celebration *(360) 642-4441*

July
- SandSations Sandcastle Competition
  (800) 451-2542

August
- Kite Festival *(360) 642-4020*

October
- Cranberrian Fair *(360) 642-3446*

- Wild Mushroom Festival *(800) 451-2542*

The Shelburne Inn Bed & Breakfast

ACCOMMODATIONS: *Best bed & breakfast in Seaview*

The Shelburne Inn in Seaview is to breakfast what the Louvre is to art. So wrote a reviewer from the *St. Louis Post Dispatch*. This is another way of saying that the cuisine and service at this inn are internationally acclaimed. The gourmet breakfast is complimentary, and the Shoalwater Restaurant and Heron & Beaver Pub/Café are right on the premises. The Inn is a relaxing retreat for city dwellers and a sanctuary for nature lovers. All rooms are furnished in antiques and have private baths, and most have private decks. Wrote *Northwest Palate* magazine, "It is the human touch that keeps Shelburne's devoted regulars coming back: a hand-braided rug on the floor by an exquisite four-poster bed… or an antique vase filled with flowers to bring all the fragrance and color of the Shelburne's English side garden indoors." The Shelburne Inn, established in 1896 and listed on the National Historic Register, retains that intimacy and charm of yesteryear rarely found in our modern world. It has offered travelers warm hospitality, wonderful food and comfortable shelter for more than a century. Overnight guests delight in breakfast, lunch and dinner here, which feature an abundance of fresh, local ingredients lovingly prepared.

4415 Pacific Highway, Seaview WA
(360) 642-2442 or (800) INN-1896
www.theshelburneinn.com

The Shoalwater Restaurant and The Heron & Beaver Pub

RESTAURANTS & CAFÉS: *Best regional cuisine on the Peninsula*

The Shoalwater Restaurant is located in Seaview's historic Shelburne Inn, along with its sister establishment, The Heron & Beaver Pub. Both eateries have been owned and operated since 1981 by Tony and Ann Kischner, who moved to the Long Beach Peninsula from Seattle. East Coast-trained chef Lynne Pelletier has been in charge of the kitchen since 1998 and has continued The Shoalwater's long tradition of awards and rave reviews. The excellent menu changes seasonally and utilizes all manner of local products in imaginative ways, from an abundance of fresh seafood, such as oysters, crab, clams and salmon, to Peninsula cranberries and a wide variety of wild mushrooms, berries and greens. Many delicious condiments are made in-house from local products. They are used in The Shoalwater's cooking and are also available for sale. Ann bakes wonderful home-style breads and desserts on the premises. Superb lunches and dinners are served daily from the same kitchen in the The Shoalwater's elegant dining room and in the more informal Heron & Beaver Pub. The Pub is named after the ubiquitous local bird and Charles Beaver, who built The Shelburne Inn in 1896. Tony manages the dining room, as well as a stellar cellar of 450-plus mostly-regional wines. He stocks the Pub with a full complement of fine liquors including 18 single-malt Scotches and 40-plus domestic and imported beers, including many local craft brews.

4415 Pacific Highway, Seaview WA
(360) 642-4142
www.shoalwater.com

The Depot Restaurant

RESTAURANTS & CAFÉS: *The Peninsula's only display kitchen*

Built 100 years ago, the historic Clamshell Railroad Station in Seaview is now home to The Depot Restaurant. The restaurant houses the only display kitchen on the Long Beach Peninsula. Owners Michael Lalewicz and Nancy Gorshe invite you to make a reservation for the special Chef's Table event, where you can watch Michael (also the chef) and sous-chef Cleveland Graham as they whip up the amazing theme dinners that bring people back to The Depot time after time. Michael has traveled and cooked around the world. After coming to the Pacific Northwest, he developed the Greek kitchen at Portland's premier jazz club, Jimmy Mak's, and served as sous chef of Portland's Tolouse Restaurant before pulling in to The Depot. Cleveland Graham is a Northeast native who honed his cooking skills at such venues as Earth and Ocean at Seattle's famous W Hotel. Together they've created a menu that merges international cooking styles with the finest local ingredients, with signature dishes such as Willapa Bay Clam Chowder and Northwest Crab Bucatini. The food alone is more than enough reason to book your table at The Depot, but bear in mind that the restaurant also offers casual elegance with a superb selection of wines from around the world, microbrew beer on tap, and a heated outdoor deck.

1208 38th Place & L, Seaview WA
(360) 642-7880
www.depotrestaurantdining.com

Whale Skull on the beach in Seaview
Photo by Janet Dancer

The Islands

The Islands

Man fishing along the bank

THE ISLANDS, a paradise for lovers of boating, fishing and whale watching, contains dozens of federal, state and local parks. The islands lie in the state's most northwesterly waters, south of the Straight of Georgia and north of Puget Sound. They include the San Juan islands, plus Fidalgo, Whidbey and Camano islands. These last three are accessible by road, but the San Juan islands can be reached only by boat or air.

Each of the San Juan islands has its own individual character. Lopez Island, the first one you reach on the ferry from Anacortes, is rural and friendly. Everyone waves on the roads. It is the flattest island, and is great for bicycling. On Orcas Island, hamlets are filled with art galleries. The view from 2,409-foot Mount Constitution is considered one of the best in the world. Friday Harbor on San Juan Island, the commercial center of the islands, makes an excellent base for exploration.

These islands were once in dispute between Britain and the United States. In 1859, an American farmer shot a British pig rooting in his garden, setting off the Pig War in which thousands of British and Americans faced off against each other. No shots were fired, however, and the dispute was settled peaceably.

Further south, Fidalgo Island is the home of Anacortes, where the Washington State Ferries dock. Whidbey Island is tied to the mainland by Deception Pass Bridge, one of the most spectacular spans anywhere, high over a turbulent saltwater channel. Camano Island, the part of the region closest to Seattle is ideal for beachcombing and bird watching.

ANACORTES

Anacortes is the crown jewel of Fidalgo Island, easternmost of the San Juan Islands and gateway to the rest of the world-renowned archipelago. Anacortes is home to the Washington State Ferry terminal, serving the rest of the San Juans and Victoria, British Columbia. Fidalgo is a drive-to island, set off from the mainland by the narrow Swinomish Channel. It is also connected to Whidbey Island by a spectacular bridge over Deception Pass. Anacortes boasts a myriad of recreational activities. You can watch whales or birds at Washington Park. You can enjoy boating, fishing or diving. On land, you can hike, mountain bike on Mount Erie or beach comb.

PLACES TO GO

- Anacortes History Museum
  1305 8th Street (360) 293-1915

- Deception Pass State Park
  State Route 20

- Mount Erie Park
  Heart Lake Road

- Washington Park
  6300 Sunset Avenue

THINGS TO DO

May
- Anacortes Waterfront Festival
  (360) 293-7911

August
- Anacortes Arts Festival
  (360) 293-6211

September
- Anacortes Jazz Festival
  Curtis Wharf (360) 293-3832

Deception Pass State Park
Photo by Pavel Rybin

SeaBear Smokehouse

MARKETS: *Best smoked salmon*

When you visit Anacortes, follow your nose to 30th Street and you will find yourself at SeaBear Smokehouse, home of wild salmon fillets and smoked salmon. SeaBear started in 1957 as Specialty Seafoods, a backyard smokehouse built by Anacortes fisherman Tom Savidge and his wife, Marie. Tom smoked salmon for the local taverns. When tavern owners asked him how to preserve the salmon longer, Tom (who loves to tinker) blended canning technology with flexible packaging material to create the Gold Seal pouch, which preserved the salmon naturally, without refrigeration. Specialty Seafoods was awarded a patent on this new idea and a direct mail smoked salmon business was born. Today SeaBear remains a small custom-built smokehouse dedicated to the same principles upon which the company was founded. SeaBear uses only the best of the best, 100-percent wild salmon, caught from the abundant runs of Alaska. Less than one percent of wild Alaskan salmon meet SeaBear's strict standards. Every SeaBear salmon is hand filleted for quality and taste. SeaBear salmon is smoked using centuries-old traditions of the Northwest, over slow burning native alder. Make it a point to visit the outlet store. While there, take a tour to view the whole process of smoking salmon or have your picture taken with a huge King salmon.

605 30th Street, Anacortes WA
(360) 293-4661 or (800) 645-FISH (3474)
www.seabear.com

Anacortes Kayak Tours

RECREATION: *Best way to see The Islands*

If you want a Pacific Northwest kayak tour that is off the beaten path, visit Anacortes Kayak Tours. It's the only kayak operation that does not require you to take a long ferry ride to get into the San Juan Islands. Says the staff, "Our hand-picked sea-kayaking trip locations allow you to explore the least-developed shorelines in the San Juan Islands. Off the beaten path, we are free to enjoy some of the most incredible scenery that the Pacific Northwest has to offer without having to worry about crowded beaches, noisy yacht traffic and hordes of other kayak tour groups." You will be comfortable and entertained as their expert staff guides you through the peaceful side of the San Juans. Owners Megan and Erik Schorr traveled the world, paddled on five continents and can say with confidence that the best sea kayaking on the planet is "right here in the San Juan Islands." Both were born and raised on the shores of this magnificent location, and they feel fortunate to be able to share what they love, such as Cypress Island. "This is the postcard location for kayaking in the San Juans. It boasts the longest stretch of undeveloped shoreline in the archipelago. Wildlife abounds here, particularly in the Cone Islands, with a cluster of National Wildlife Refuges just offshore. We paddle here for close encounters with seals, porpoise and bald eagles. From Cypress Island we have stunning views of Mt. Baker and the Cascade Mountains. With pocket beaches, hidden bays, island clusters and amazing views around every corner, Cypress Island is the premier destination for kayaking in Washington State." Bring a hat, sunscreen, layered clothing and shoes appropriate for the beach.

1801 Commercial Avenue, Anacortes WA
(360) 588-1117 or (800) 992-1801
www.anacorteskayaktours.com

CAMANO ISLAND AND STANWOOD

Camano Island has it all, thousands of acres of unspoiled hills and miles of uncrowded Puget Sound shoreline. It is easily accessible by bridge—no waiting for ferries here. Camano Island is a quiet, bucolic place that attracts many artisans. Alpacas de la Patagonia, with hundreds of alpacas, is a farm across from Camano Plaza. Camano Island and the city of Stanwood in Snohomish County share many amenities, including Stanwood–Camano School District. Stanwood is immediately across from Camano Island in the Islands region. Islanders do much of their shopping in Stanwood. The town is also the center of an agricultural district known for its seeds and vegetables.

PLACES TO GO

• Camano Island State Park
2269 S Lowell Point Road

• D. O. Pearson House Museum
27108 102nd Avenue NW, Stanwood
(360) 629-6110

• Heritage Park
276th Street NW, Stanwood

• Church Creek Park
72nd Avenue NW, Stanwood

THINGS TO DO

May
• Out on a Limb Orchids Open House
(360) 387-2341

• Serenity Herb Gardens Open House
(360) 387-0727

June
• Pilchuck Glass School Exhibition and Sale
Gala Opening   (360) 387-5225

August
• Stanwood-Camano Fair
Stanwood Camano Fairgrounds
(360) 629-4121

Inn at Barnum Point

ACCOMMODATIONS: *Best beachfront bed and breakfast*

Barnum Point was a remote spot on Camano Island when the Barnum family settled here in 1904. Even today it feels far away from the modern world. The Inn at Barnum Point, a bed-and-breakfast, is one of seven family homes on the original 110 acres of unspoiled beachfront. Proprietor Carolin Barnum Dilorenzo is the sole operator of the year round inn. She keeps the place clean and well maintained, serves big heartwarming breakfasts each morning and provides the link between Barnum Point's past and present. She tells of rum runners who came to the area in their fast boats during Prohibition. She recalls the days when the Barnums found a mammoth tusk on a cliff, and how years before, when it was legal, they kept a pet seal named Philip. Guests at the inn can choose from three rooms, the Heron, the Eagle, or the Shorebird suite, each with queen-sized beds, a fireplace and its own bathroom. Port Susan Bay, home to seals, river otters and an abundance of birds, including Eagles and Herons, is right outside your window. On clear days, the inn offers breathtaking views of Mount Rainier and the Cascades. Guests stay active combing the beach and hiking nearby old growth forest trails. A golf course is close by, as well as art studios scattered about the island. Of course, you may choose to do nothing but melt your worries away. Come and let Carolin help you unwind at the Inn at Barnum Point.

464 S Barnum Road, Camano Island WA
(360) 387-2256 or (800) 910-2256
www.innatbarnumpoint.com

Photos © Steve K. Marl

Ready Mortgage

BUSINESS: *Best mortgage loans for your home purchase*

When securing a mortgage appears difficult, improbable or downright impossible, turn to Ready Mortgage in Stanwood. Branch manager Kathy Ready and her team specialize in the difficult. Certainly, they can help someone with good income, manageable debt and great credit, but it's the tough cases that have earned them their reputation for tenacity. Kathy hails from Los Angeles and moved herself and her daughters to Stanwood in 1990 for a better life. She opened Ready Mortgage in 1999 and has been earning the loyalty of the community ever since. She has more than 20 years experience in the mortgage and banking industries, and a team of loan officers who work with hundreds of lenders and keep abreast of every loan program and payment system out there, from fixed and adjustable rate mortgage loans to sub-prime loans for people who lenders generally view as high risks, due to circumstances like no verifiable income, recent bankruptcies or poor or non-existent credit. When you work with Ready Mortgage, you can count on the savvy to find you the best rate from among hundreds of lenders. Because Ready is not limited to specific financing sources or programs, the company usually offers better mortgage rates than banks. Whatever your circumstance, visit Ready Mortgage when you want results.

26915 98th Drive NW, Stanwood WA
(360) 629-6001 or (888) 457-5299
www.readymortgage.net

Camano Properties

BUSINESS: *Best homegrown Camano Island property experts*

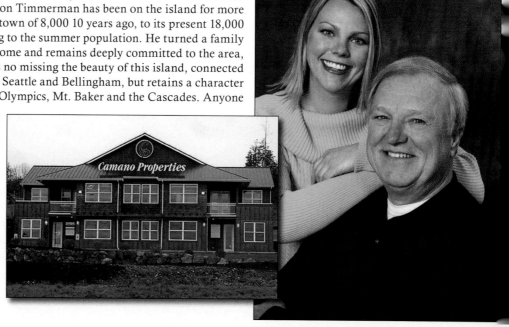

There's not much that Camano Properties and its agents can't tell you about Camano Island and the surrounding area. As one of three owners, co-owner Don Timmerman has been on the island for more than 50 years and has watched it grow from a sleepy town of 8,000 10 years ago, to its present 18,000 permanent residents with a swell of snowbirds adding to the summer population. He turned a family beach house at Driftwood Shores into a permanent home and remains deeply committed to the area, also co-owning nearby Stanwood Properties. There's no missing the beauty of this island, connected by land bridge to the mainland. It's relatively close to Seattle and Bellingham, but retains a character all its own with wonderful beaches and views of the Olympics, Mt. Baker and the Cascades. Anyone seeking property here or in Snohomish, Skagit or Island Counties should call Camano Properties. These insiders know most everybody and make sure their knowledge benefits you. If you're taking your first look around the area, be sure to stop by their new professional center at Terry's Corner. They'll treat you to a free map of Camano Island and Stanwood. A real estate purchase affects your life. Let the experts at Camano Properties help with the details.

811 N Sunrise Boulevard, Suite A,
Camano Island WA
(360) 387-7999 or (866) 387-7999
www.camanoproperties.com

Rustic Impressions

HOME: *Best home decorating*

Great business ideas often evolve through acquaintances, and that's just how Rustic Impressions in Stanwood got its start. Pat Powell and Becky Tiland, owners of Rustic Impressions, met at volunteer school events 11 years ago when their sons were both in first grade. Today, their three-room store takes customers on a pleasant tour of European country-inspired home décor and furnishings. Rustic Impressions stocks a surprising assortment of items that run the gamut from primitive to contemporary. You can special-order Rowe and Four Seasons furniture with upholstery to match your tastes, purchase a new armoire or bedroom suite, or find just the right framed print, Tuscan pitcher or ceramic piece to bring a room to life. Decorative accents for country kitchens are always popular, and the choices at Rustic Impressions are fresh and fun. Pat and Becky seek to provide upscale décor without the upscale prices. Their good taste, knowledge and friendliness make Rustic Impressions a favorite destination. If you are visiting Rustic Impressions from out of town, you can easily make a day of it in downtown Stanwood with interesting local shops, restaurants and a Scandinavian bakery. When you want to make a lasting impression, start with a visit to Rustic Impressions.

8620 271st Street NW, Stanwood WA
(360) 629-6997

Camaloch Golf Course

RECREATION: *Best golf course in The Islands*

Camaloch Golf Course on scenic Camano Island is a wonderful place for golf lovers. Catering to both beginners and seasoned players, this is more than a golf course, it's a golfing community, open to the public. Homeowners at Camaloch enjoy unlimited free golf, swimming pool privileges and bass fishing at the well stocked lake. Golfers love the smooth, consistent greens and the surprisingly sunny weather. Camaloch is located in Puget Sound's sun belt, protected from the legendary rains of the Washington Coast by the towering Olympic Mountains. The friendly, knowledgeable staff helps to guarantee customer satisfaction at Camaloch. General manager Gary Schopf brings knowledge and experience gained as a PGA professional and puts it to good use. Camaloch offers golfers an exciting challenge, with narrow fairways lined by huge evergreens, heavily-bunkered greens and water hazards. With help always at hand, this par-72 course is a great place to learn the ins and outs of golf. There's a Pro Shop where the staff will help you find the equipment you need, a deli to refresh you before or after the game, and many fine amenities at this unique course.

326 NE Camano Drive, Camano Island WA
(360) 387-3084 or (800) 628-0469
www.camalochnews.org

La Hacienda Mexican Restaurant

RESTAURANTS & CAFÉS: *Voted best food four consecutive years*

Walk in the door of La Hacienda Mexican Restaurant in Stanwood, and you'll think you've traveled a few thousand miles south to enjoy authentic Mexican food and atmosphere. No wonder the restaurant has been so popular for 14 years and has received an award for best food for 5 years running from the Stanwood Chamber of Commerce. Co-owners Hector Guitron and Pedro Hernandez know what people want and seek to increase quality and service every day with their great ideas, direct from Mexico, and plenty of customer input. Their loyal staff includes one of the restaurant's original chefs, Carlos DeDios. The partners have worked together in the restaurant business since 1982 and also own the popular Los Hermanos Taqueria in Bellingham. You'll find convenient free parking, an assortment of live special events, and a big screen television in the bar for enjoying your favorite game. La Hacienda is also a favorite place to host a meeting, party of reunion. The owners of this beloved restaurant are active in the community and support many school and charity events. When you want a wonderful margarita or some award winning carne asada, enchiladas or tacos, visit La Hacienda Mexican Restaurant.

9200 271st Street, Stanwood WA
(360) 629-3563
www.lahaciendarest.com/stanwood
www.dosreales.com

Brindles Marketplace
SHOPPING: *Best place to shop*

Brindles Marketplace puts the necessities and pleasures of life under one roof for Camano Island residents. You'll find quality products and a commons area for music, art fairs and other special events that draw the community together. Bonnie and Don Brindle of Brindles Market are at the heart of this enterprise. The market specializes in the best premium meat and wild-caught seafood. Family-owned ranches and farms provide much of the natural and organic meat, turkey and chicken. Meats are cut-to-order. Don's seafood expertise assures selections from Canadian rivers and pristine Alaskan waters. The Brindles also provide recipes to assure your triumphs. A visit to Great Blue Heron Wine Cellars promises that your meal will have the very best accompaniments with wine tastings every Friday, Saturday and Sunday. The market's bistro creates specialties such as fish 'n chips from halibut or cod, and salmon seafood chowder. They also cater. The attractions continue with Bonnie Z's Place for island living and special occasion women's clothing. Also included is the Gallery in the Loft for artwork by Camano Island artists. The Snow Goose Bookstore carries a selection of books to suite every reader; Island Custard & Gelato will keep you refreshed with frozen desserts; and Camano Island Coffee Roasters will treat you to the best shade-grown, organic coffee in the world. Karen's Kitchen will also supply all of your gift needs in and out of the kitchen. To complete the marketplace atmosphere, local musicians provide entertainment on Friday and Saturday nights. Next time you need it all, visit Brindles Marketplace at Camano Commons, the gateway to Camano Island.

848 N Sunrise Boulevard, Camano Island WA
(360) 722-7480
www.brindlesmarket.com

Karen's Kitchen & Gifts

SHOPPING: *Best kitchen & gifts store*

No one in the greater Stanwood/Camano Island vicinity has any excuse not to cook gourmet meals or give great gifts since Karen's Kitchen & Gifts opened in 2004. It's the only store of its kind in the area, and what a store it is. Karen's Kitchen, owned by Karen and Stan Malmin, is stocked with cookware, bakeware, appliances, gadgets and specialty items that bring gourmet capability to the everyday kitchen. It carries some of the best brand names in the industry, competitively priced, including All Clad, Cuisinart, Emile Henry, La Creuset and Viking. Kitchen and household gifts bring added popularity to this Camano Plaza shop, with Polish pottery, tableware and collectibles. You'll even find bath products, children and baby gifts, as well as something for dad. The bridal registry is popular and complimentary gift wrapping comes with any purchase. For the art lover, the store has a large collection of local artwork. Karen's Kitchen has been named Best Gift Shop three years in a row in the annual Stanwood/Camano news poll. Next time you need to cook a gourmet meal, give a special gift, or are just in the mood to browse, visit Karen's Kitchen & Gifts.

370 N East Camano Drive, Camano Island WA
(360) 387-1609
www.karenskitchenandgifts.com

COUPEVILLE

Coupeville features well preserved Victorian mansions built by wealthy sea captains who took advantage of the abundance of oak and pine trees to make their fortunes in the timber trade. Many of these are now luxurious bed & breakfasts. Take a stroll along Front Street at the Penn Cove waterfront with its quaint gift shops, galleries and restaurants. Here you can take in the great skeleton of Rosie the Whale.

PLACES TO GO

- Coupeville Arts Center
  15 NW Birch Street
  (866) 678-3396

- Ebey's Landing National Historical Reserve
  162 Cemetery Road
  (360) 678-6084

- Island County Historical Society Museum
  908 NW Alexander Street
  (360) 678-3310

- Fort Casey State Park
  1280 Engle Road

- Fort Ebey State Park
  395 Fort Ebey Road

THINGS TO DO

March
- Penn Cove Mussel Festival
  (360) 678-1100

May
- Penn Cove Water Festival
  www.penncovewaterfestival.com

August
- Historic Coupeville Arts & Crafts Festival
  (360) 678-5116

Coupeville's historic pier

Fort Casey Inn

ACCOMMODATIONS: *Best Whidbey Island getaway*

The Fort Casey Inn on Whidbey Island is perfect for a romantic weekend getaway or a family outing. The Inn's charming Georgian Revival cottages have two bedrooms apiece and each comes with a bath, living room and fully-equipped kitchen. They were built nearly a 100 years ago for one of the three U.S. Army forts guarding Admiralty Inlet and originally served as officers' residences. Large groups can rent Garrison Hall for special events. The buildings that make up the Inn were sold at public auction in 1956 and opened as public accommodations after being lovingly restored. In 2001, Seattle Pacific University acquired the property and now operates both the Inn and the nearby Camp Casey Conference Center. Guests of the Inn have access to board games, picnic tables, hiking trails and the beach. The former grounds of Fort Casey, beyond the officers' quarters, are now Fort Casey State Park, a 467-acre public park with a lighthouse, bunkers, 10-inch disappearing guns and other fascinating reminders of Whidbey Island's military history. Other attractions include the bird sanctuary at Crockett Lake and the shops of historic Coupeville, just a few minutes away by car.

1124 S Engle Road, Coupeville WA
(360) 678-5050 or (866) 661-6604
www.fortcaseyinn.com

FRIDAY HARBOR

On the east side of San Juan Island is the town of Friday Harbor, the San Juan County seat. A quaint seaport, Friday Harbor rises from the ferry landing and public marina to the town's parks, restaurants and shops. Whale watching is a major tourist activity on here. For orca sightings, try Lime Kiln Point State Park on the west side of the island. The British Camp and American Camp of San Juan Island National Historical Park commemorate the two sides of the Pig War of 1859. Fortunately, the only casualty in this war was the pig.

PLACES TO GO

- Island Museum of Art
  314 Spring Street (360) 370-5050

- Westcott Bay Sculpture Park
  Roche Harbor Road (360) 370-5050

- The Whale Museum
  62 1st Street N (360) 378-4710

- Lime Kiln Point State Park
  Westside Road S

- San Juan Island National Historical Park:
  American Camp
  Cattle Point Road

- San Juan Island National Historical Park:
  British Camp
  W Valley Road

THINGS TO DO

May
- San Juan Island Orca Fest
  (888) 468-3701

July
- Pelindaba Lavender Harvest Festival
  (866) 819 1911

- Summer Arts Fair
  (360) 378-5240

November–December
- San Juan Northern Lights Fest
  (360) 378-5240

- Lighted Boat Parade
  (360) 378-5240

Best Western Friday Harbor Suites

ACCOMMODATIONS:
Best hotel in Friday Harbor

Best isn't just a word in the title of Best Western Friday Harbor Suites. It's a promise of the quality and comfort you will find in this outstanding lodging facility. Owner Don Jang has gone out of his way to create luxurious accommodations in his newly remodeled, spacious and stylish suites. One and two-bedroom units beckon you to relax in cozy living rooms with gas fireplaces and your own private balcony or deck. Amenities include plush pillow-top mattresses, ceiling fans, 27-inch color televisions and high-speed Internet connections. Efficient kitchens include china, glass and silverware. The friendly and helpful staff will be happy to assist you and answer your questions. Complimentary deluxe breakfasts, an outdoor Jacuzzi, fitness room, free parking and shuttle service add to this Best Western's overall appeal. Friday Harbor Suites puts you near all the best of San Juan Island. Imagine ferryboats gliding among emerald isles with white-capped Mt. Baker in the distance. World-class museums, gardens, galleries and outdoor destinations provide some of the most exciting opportunities for sightseeing in the Northwest. For more interactive thrills, try sea kayaking, hiking, bicycling and whale watching. Tour the island and discover incredible shorelines and breathtaking views. When you're ready for an outstanding meal and some relaxation, take a seat at the Best Western's Peppermill Restaurant and Lounge. Plan your dream family vacation, romantic getaway or corporate retreat in the San Juan Islands with Best Western Friday Harbor Suites.

680 Spring Street, Friday Harbor WA
(800) 752-5752
www.fridayharborsuites.com

Horseshu Hacienda

ACCOMMODATIONS:
Best place to stay on San Juan Island

Horseshu Hacienda owner Roxanne Christensen loves horses, nature and being around happy, peaceful people. Guests at the large, private house are the number one priority, from protecting your privacy to working with you scheduling activities at the Ranch or around the island. The Hacienda is a well kept modern Ranch Home with three bedrooms, including a master suite with a private bath and a whirlpool tub. The open floor plan provides ample room for group entertaining or business meetings. Abundant amenities include wireless Internet and satellite television. You can also gather fresh eggs from the chicken coop, located only a few steps away. The home features a woodstove and a large deck, perfect for barbecues. You can enjoy outdoor dining with spectacular sunsets and views across the San Juan Valley. Kick back and sip refreshments while having a birds-eye view of the open pastureland, horse barns and riding arena, or go on down and participate in the fun. If you are interested in horses and riding, ranch manager Jessica Colling will gladly accommodate horse riders of all ages. She can help you learn basic safe riding within a short period of time, or get you comfortable on a gentle saddle horse for a leisurely stroll around the Ranch Grounds. Contingent on the weather reservations at the Hacienda include a 30-minute complimentary ranch tour on horseback for two guests. You can arrange for private or group lessons. Small groups of experienced riders can reserve a two-hour trail ride through the island forest. Youngsters enjoy Giddy-Up Little Cowpoke Rides with lead-line ponies. Open year round, you can experience San Juan Island from the comfort of Horseshu Hacienda and its many pleasures.

131 Gilbert Lane, Friday Harbor WA
(360) 378-2298
www.horseshu.com

Lakedale Resort

ACCOMMODATIONS: *Best resort*

Location, location, location is at the heart of Lakedale Resort. "When you come here you know you have come to someplace different and very, very special," says Columbia Hospitality's Lakedale manager, Craig Fischer. This special locale is nestled between Roche Harbor and Friday Harbor on San Juan Island. Situated on 82 gorgeous acres with three spring-fed lakes, this resort is an ideal San Juan Island getaway with three different accommodation options. Couples looking for a romantic retreat will enjoy the 10-room lodge, named one of the Top 10 Romantic Getaways in the country by *Fine Living*. Each of the log cabins makes a perfect family retreat with opportunities for swimming, fishing and canoeing. For the outdoor enthusiast, Lakedale's award-winning campground features an abundance of beautifully situated campsites. Hiking, biking and watching otters and eagles in their natural habitats are some of the favorite outdoor activities here. You may want to rent a paddleboat, rowboat or canoe to explore the nooks and crannies of the beautiful lakes. If you are looking for an ideal wedding location, Lakedale offers an unparalleled site for a wedding and reception. The beautiful event room overlooking Neva Lake provides a warm reception atmosphere and the resort's experienced staff will be happy to assist you with menu selections, set-up and event coordination. For getaways to suit every taste and first-class service guaranteed to please the most discriminating guests, visit Lakedale Resort.

4313 Roche Harbor Road, Friday Harbor WA
(360) 378-2350
www.lakedale.com

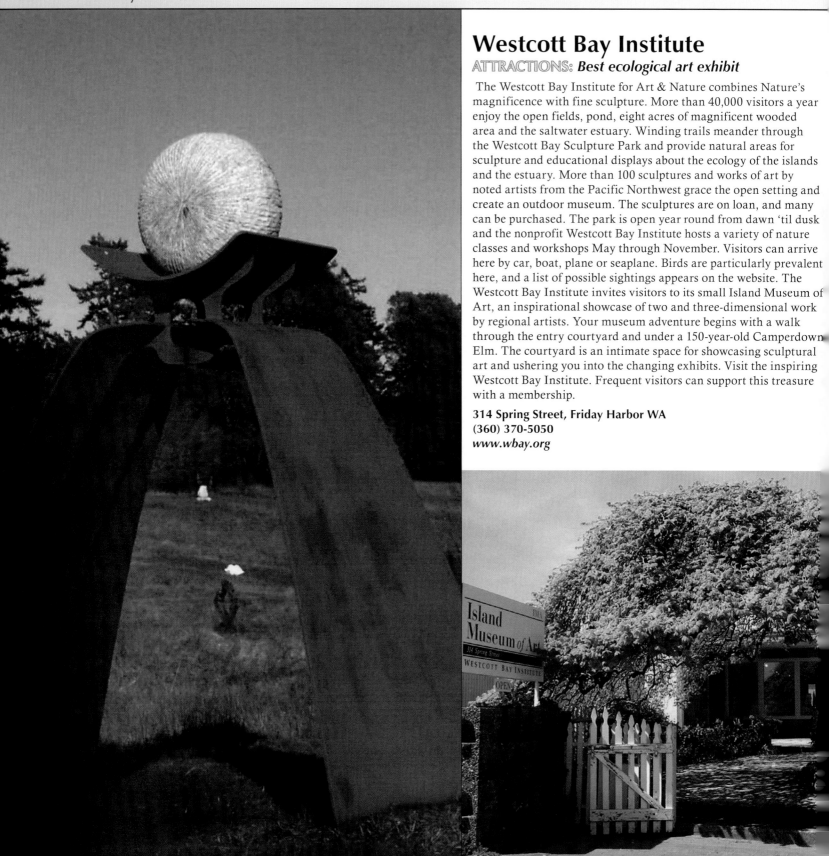

Westcott Bay Institute

ATTRACTIONS: *Best ecological art exhibit*

The Westcott Bay Institute for Art & Nature combines Nature's magnificence with fine sculpture. More than 40,000 visitors a year enjoy the open fields, pond, eight acres of magnificent wooded area and the saltwater estuary. Winding trails meander through the Westcott Bay Sculpture Park and provide natural areas for sculpture and educational displays about the ecology of the islands and the estuary. More than 100 sculptures and works of art by noted artists from the Pacific Northwest grace the open setting and create an outdoor museum. The sculptures are on loan, and many can be purchased. The park is open year round from dawn 'til dusk and the nonprofit Westcott Bay Institute hosts a variety of nature classes and workshops May through November. Visitors can arrive here by car, boat, plane or seaplane. Birds are particularly prevalent here, and a list of possible sightings appears on the website. The Westcott Bay Institute invites visitors to its small Island Museum of Art, an inspirational showcase of two and three-dimensional work by regional artists. Your museum adventure begins with a walk through the entry courtyard and under a 150-year-old Camperdown Elm. The courtyard is an intimate space for showcasing sculptural art and ushering you into the changing exhibits. Visit the inspiring Westcott Bay Institute. Frequent visitors can support this treasure with a membership.

314 Spring Street, Friday Harbor WA
(360) 370-5050
www.wbay.org

Bella Luna

RESTAURANTS & CAFÉS:
Best Italian cuisine

Combine the atmosphere of The Islands with authentic Italian cuisine, and you'll have a night to remember at Bella Luna Ristorante in Friday Harbor. Classy touches abound, from crystal bottles of olive oil on glass-topped tables to the light and subtle flavors of the vinaigrette on the fresh tossed salads. The ambience refined and casual, with tapestries and grapevines gracing the interior, and a bar featuring a black-lit aquarium. You'll start your repast with fresh bread served with an olive oil and minced garlic spread. The enchanting entrées have caught the attention of the reviewers for their fresh approach to old classics. Look for such favorites as spaghetti carbonara with prosciutto and a wonderful Italian sausage. Bring a Roman appetite, because servings here are very generous. The restaurant features live blues and jazz on Sundays and Wednesdays. It also offers catering on and off premises. Bella Luna opened in 1999 and is one of several local eateries owned by Charles Thomas. Charles invites you and your family to sample the tastes of Italy at Bella Luna, where memorable food and generous proportions promise a night of Roman pleasure.

175 First Street, Friday Harbor WA
(360) 378-4118

China Pearl

RESTAURANTS & CAFÉS:
Best Chinese food

Sometimes you can have it all: reasonably priced Chinese food, live entertainment and game choices in a picturesque vacationland. That's the promise of China Pearl in downtown Friday Harbor. Charles Thomas owns this special lunch and dinner location, known for its combination platters and seafood, served in Mandarin, Cantonese and Szechwan styles. Like Peppermill and Bella Luna, other Friday Harbor restaurants he owns, China Pearl features the affordable prices families appreciate. The upstairs lounge brings in live music every weekend and keeps it lively during the week with a Wednesday ladies night and a Thursday open mike. You'll find a dance floor and plenty of game options, including pool tables, pinball, video games and an Internet jukebox. The happy hour is seven hours long and starts at noon. Next time you want Chinese food, Island-style, or the chance to extend your evening in a lively lounge, visit China Pearl.

51 Spring Street, Friday Harbor WA
(360) 378-5254
or (360) 378-5551 (lounge)

Peppermill Seafood & Steakhouse

RESTAURANTS & CAFÉS:
Best surf and turf

For casual fine dining in the San Juan Islands, turn to Peppermill Seafood & Steakhouse. This two-year-old restaurant, one of Charles Thomas's dining establishments, is located inside the Best Western Friday Harbor Suites. It joins a restful atmosphere and attentive service with in-season seafood choices, tender steaks, a lounge and martini bar. An outdoor, heated patio extends your dining options. Choose from live lobster, Pacific salmon or grilled prawns. Steak lovers are sure to appreciate the Nebraska corn-fed beef and grilled baby back ribs. Expect a creative wine list and a full complement of mixed drinks and cocktails, including martinis in many flavors and colors. On weeknights, the two-hour happy hour features special prices on appetizers. Every night includes a festive martini happy hour from 10 pm to midnight. Peppermill is also the place Friday Harbor turns for catered events. A catering staff will attend to every detail of your menu, whether your event takes place at Friday Harbor Suites or elsewhere on the island. For a restaurant with well prepared food and drink, visit Peppermill Seafood & Steakhouse.

680 Spring Street, Friday Harbor WA
(360) 378-7060
www.peppermillsanjuan.com

Mystical Mermaid
SHOPPING: *Best gift gallery*

If you can't have fun what's the point? That is the motivation that drives Rick Thompson and Wendy Beckler, owners of Mystical Mermaid, an enchanting gift gallery with an eclectic mix of treasures from around the world. The gallery showcases everything from coffee mugs to artistic bronze sculptures and is one of the few stores in town where you can buy a gift for under $20. Rick and Wendy have chosen exquisite jewelry and clothing that is both artful and utilitarian. Candles and bath luxuries tempt your romantic leanings. Art glass and incense add an exotic touch to any interior space. Rocks, crystals and fantasy items abound. Rick and Wendy meticulously choose the shop's artwork for its universal appeal and ability to add character and a bit of fun to any surrounding. You'll find everything having to do with mermaids here, including whimsical mermaid yard art, bird feeders and luminaries for outdoor settings. Explore mermaid bronzes, mermaids for the bath and kitchen, and mermaids for children. Wendy and Rick promise that if you can imagine it, they probably have it. Venture over the threshold of Mystical Mermaid, and discover a bit of enchantment.

65 Spring Street, Friday Harbor WA
(360) 378-2617
www.mysticalmermaid.com

Herb's Tavern

RESTAURANTS & CAFÉS: *Best tavern*

If you are feeling like a game of pool, a draft beer and a great burger while you are in The Islands, head to Herb's Tavern in Friday Harbor. Charles Thomas and Shelley Borahan, who have launched several successful eateries in Friday Harbor, are co-owners of this quintessential American pub, where you can choose from 18 draft beers, including microbrews, domestics and imported selections, while you watch sports, and play pool or pinball. You can also relax over a good, ground chuck burger with an assortment of toppings, or try the beer-battered cod or chili dogs. Munchies, like fries or hot wings, are popular choices. This comfortable neighborhood bar has been going strong since 1943, thanks to its neighborhood feel and mix of food and fun. The staff at Herb's welcomes your visit and promises a convivial setting, great cocktails, beers to satisfy every palate and some of America's favorite pub fare.

80 1st Street, Friday Harbor WA
(360) 378-7076
www.herbstavern.com

GREENBANK

Greenbank has a population of just around 250 folks who call themselves Bankers. Greenbank Farm, a living-history farm, winery, recreation site and community center, is a major attraction. Another is the Meerkerk Rhododendron Gardens, located in the 43-acre Meerkerk Woodland Preserve. South of Greenbank is Freeland, inhabited by Freelanders and surrounded by two of Whidbey Island's best parks.

PLACES TO GO

- Greenbank Farm
  Wonn Road and State Route 525
  (360) 678-7700
- Meerkerk Rhododendron Gardens
  3531 Meerkerk Lane (360) 678-1912
- Double Bluff Beach & Dog Park
  Double Bluff Road, Freeland
- South Whidbey Island State Park
  4128 S Smugglers Cove Road, Freeland

THINGS TO DO

July
- Loganberry Festival
  Greenbank Farm (360) 678-7700

August
- Highland Games
  Greenbank Farm (360) 331-4688

September
- Whidbey Island Open Studio Tour
  www.widbeyopenstudiotour.org

Whidbey Pies Café at Greenbank Farm

BAKERIES, COFFEE & TEA: *Best artisan pies*

When was the last time you took a bite of loganberry pie, full of that plump, ruby colored berry, a cross between a blackberry and a raspberry? Head for the Greenbank Farm on Whidbey Island and the Whidbey Pies Café. There, owner Jan Gunn proudly sells buttery crusted loganberry pies, homemade soups, including salmon chowder, and sandwiches. Besides loganberry, pies include apple, marionberry, blueberry and cherry. Says Jan in explaining her baking and business philosophy, "Make the best product possible. Make sure it meets your own high standards. Whatever you do, be sure you can be proud of it. We have devoted ourselves to the lost art of artisan pie making since 1986. Each pie is a unique and intimate experience. With every pie the pastry is tender and rich; the berries dense and not too sweet. When you have perfect fruit you don't need lots of sugar. Whidbey Pies are made with a light touch from the finest ingredients, plump fruit, sweet unsalted butter, cane sugar and unbleached flour." Jan and staff use no preservatives or artificial flavors in their pies. Best of all, they sell pie frozen and ready to bake, so when you get it home you can say, "I baked it myself."

765 Wonn Road, Greenbank WA
(360) 678-7700
www.greenbankfarm.com

Priest River
Photo by Nancy McClain

Eastern Washington

Eastern Washington

North Cascades National Park

EASTERN WASHINGTON provides abundant recreational and cultural opportunities in a bountiful natural environment that extends from the Cascades to Idaho. Wenatchee, just east of the Cascades, is a center for mountain adventures. Northwest Washington contains Lake Roosevelt, a ribbon of blue running through ponderosa pine that features houseboats for rent and plenty of space to water ski, swim and fish. Lake Roosevelt was created by the Grand Coulee Dam.

The scope and size of the dam are hard to comprehend. It is almost a mile long and more than twice as tall as Niagara Falls. When completed in 1941, it was the largest dam in the world. The Palouse prairie that extends from the southeast up past Spokane is one of the world's most productive agricultural regions. Whitman County in particular produces more barley, wheat, dry peas and lentils than any other in the U.S.

Spokane means Children of the Sun in the Salishan Indian language. Spokane is a city of parks. Riverfront Park downtown was the site of the environmentally themed Expo '74, which made Spokane the smallest city to ever host a World's Fair. Spokane has been named the host of the 2007 U.S. Figure Skating Championships.

Pullman, in Southeast Washington, is home to Washington State University. The school has fostered an expanding high-tech economy in Pullman. Further south, ocean-going vessels stop at the port of Clarkston on the Snake River. The port's marina also serves boats that travel through nearby Hells Canyon.

Priest River
Photo by Nancy McClain

CHELAN

Chelan lies at the tip of Lake Chelan in the heart of Washington's apple and wine country. This resort community offers boating, fishing, golfing and bicycle rentals. There is also plenty of swimming and hiking, wine tasting and shopping to be had in the area. Don't miss the 100-year-old log church and the historical museum right in the heart of downtown. Take time to view the 14 featured murals in and around the downtown area; in each one look for the hidden form in the shape of an apple. The city's year round population runs around 3,500, but the area is popular with visitors and part time residents. During the summer months, the Northern Lights put on a spectacular show.

PLACES TO GO

- Lady of the Lake boat tours
  1418 W Woodin Avenue
  (509) 682-2224

- Lake Chelan Historical Museum
  204 E Woodin Avenue
  (509) 682-5644

- Lakeshore City Park
  Downtown Chelan

THINGS TO DO

January
- Winterfest—Fire & Ice on the Lake
  (800) 424-3526

February
- Red Wine and Chocolate
  (866) 455-9463

April
- Earth Day Celebration (fair & flea market)
  (509) 682-5756

May
- Annual Manson Apple Blossom Festival
  (509) 687-3833

September
- Lake Chelan Sailing Regatta
  (509) 682-2544

- *River Daze Arts & Crafts Festival*
  (800) 424-3526

August
- Riverwalk Fine Arts
  (800) 424-3526

Lake Chelan and the Lady of the Lake

ATTRACTIONS: *One of the most remote places in America*

Lake Chelan lies within the deepest gorge in North America, deeper than the Grand Canyon. Roads extend less than halfway up the 80-mile glacial valley, so the up-lake communities of Stehekin and Holden Village are accessible only by boat or air. From the shores of the upper lake, rugged snowcapped peaks rise 7,000 feet or more, and dark evergreens cover the mountainsides. You can tour Lake Chelan on the Lady of the Lake II or the Lady Express, vessels run by the Lake Chelan Boat Company. On either boat, the captain speaks on folklore and points of interest. In the winter, the Lady Express runs alone, four days a week. This excursion is known world-wide—the *National Geographic*, the *New York Times* and *Sunset Magazine* have featured it. The 70 year-round residents of Stehekin rely on these boats to bring them groceries and supplies, building materials and, of course, tourists. The community has a single pay telephone near the North Cascade Stehekin Lodge. A shuttle bus runs a further 11 miles up the valley, allowing views of the spectacular Rainbow Falls. The community of Holden Village, inland from the port of Lucerne, is not quite as far up-lake as Stehekin, but is even more remote. Holden Village is a year-round retreat center affiliated with the Lutheran Church, but is open to everyone. It has no phones at all. Both Stehekin and Holden Village are surrounded by designated wilderness areas. If you would like to visit some of the most isolated areas in the lower 48 states, Lake Chelan and the Lady of the Lake Cruise are for you.

1418 W Woodin Avenue, Chelan WA (Lady of the Lake)
(509) 682-2224 or (509) 682-4584
www.ladyofthelake.com
www.cometothelake.com

Grand Coulee Dam

Grand Coulee Dam, the largest concrete structure in the United States, is an awesome sight. When it was completed in 1941, it was the largest dam in the world. It has since been surpassed, but the sheer size of the dam is still hard to grasp. All the pyramids at Giza could easily fit within the base of the dam. Like many of the world's great dams, Grand Coulee had a cultural impact to match its physical size. It was built during the Great Depression of the 1930s, and in those hard times, Americans were eager for proof that they were still capable of great things. Grand Coulee appeared to provide that proof. As Woody Guthrie sang, "Now the world holds seven wonders that the travelers always tell, some gardens and some towers, I guess you know them well. But now the greatest wonder is in Uncle Sam's fair land, it's the big Columbia River and the big Grand Coulee Dam." The Grand Coulee was originally envisioned as a source of irrigation water. It was completed right before World War II, however, and hydroelectricity suddenly became more important. The dam provided power to smelt aluminum for the war effort. It also powered the Hanford Nuclear Site, part of the Manhattan Project. In 1951, the dam finally began to provide the water that would eventually flow to most of the farms in eastern Washington. A good place to view the dam is from Crown Point State Park. Tours in the summer include a ride down the face of the dam in a glass-enclosed elevator. In the evening, a laser light show is projected onto the dam wall. Come marvel at Grand Coulee Dam.

Grand Coulee WA
(509) 633-9501
www.grandcouleedam.org

Sage Grouse
Photo courtesy of U.S. Fish and Wildlife

SPOKANE

The second largest city in the state, Spokane lies in the heart of the Inland Northwest and is home to 201,600 residents. The Spokane River runs through downtown with spectacular falls on the western end of the city. The town's nexus is Riverfront Park, which sprawls over two islands in the middle of the river. Be sure to see the charming, hand-carved, 1909 Looff Carousel.

PLACES TO GO

- Northwest Museum of Arts and Culture
  2316 W 1st Avenue (509) 456-3931

- Manito Park
  S Grand at 18th Avenue

- Riverfront Park
  808 W Spokane Falls Boulevard

- Mount Spokane State Park
  State Route 206

- Riverside State Park
  9711 W Charles Road

THINGS TO DO

February
- Northwest Bach Festival
  (509) 325-7321

May
- Lilac Festival
  (509) 535-4554

June
- Spokane Dixieland Jazz Festival
  (509) 922-7800

July
- American Music Festival
  (509) 625-6685

- Cherry Festival
  (509) 238-6970

August
- Peach Festival
  (509) 238-6970

September
- Spokane County Interstate Fair
  (509) 535-1766

- Apple Festival
  (509) 238-6970

Spokane Clocktower

Hotel Lusso
ACCOMMODATIONS:
Best small luxury hotel

Hotel Lusso is a fountain of luxury. Choose from the 48 extravagantly appointed oversized guest rooms that are waiting for you at Spokane's finest hotel. Originally built in 1890, Hotel Lusso is a member of the highly acclaimed "Small Luxury Hotels of the World." *Lusso* actually means luxury in Italian, which aptly describes the elegant Italian-style décor. The 14-foot ceilings and generous use of marble, archways and detailed scrollwork in each room make you feel as though you've landed in your own little palace. Standing between the Cascade Mountain Range and the Rockies, Spokane is known as the heart of the inland Northwest. Hotel Lusso is next to one of the nation's largest sky-walks, linking River Park Square's upscale shops, excellent restaurants and exceptional entertainment. The Spokane Opera House is just five blocks away and Riverfront City Park, Theme Park and Big Easy Concert Hall are nearby. For the more adventuresome, easily accessible snow-capped mountains and roaring white waters beg to be challenged. Nearby Coeur d'Alene's pristine lakes provide a peaceful interlude after the excitement of skiing and rafting. The Mediterranean theme is carried through the intimate and contemporary Cavallino Lounge, as well as the award winning Fugazzi Restaurant that features outstanding steak and seafood. A visit to the Hotel Lusso will be one of your favorite memories.

North One Post, Spokane WA
(509) 747-9750 or (800) 215-2167

Riverside State Park

ATTRACTIONS: *15 miles of freshwater marshes and beauty*

A visit to Riverside State Park is a great way to get in touch with nature. The park is more than 15 square miles of freshwater marshes and beautiful countryside along the Spokane and Little Spokane rivers northwest of Spokane. The 37-mile paved Spokane River Centennial Trail starts at the north end of the park. The Bowl and Pitcher area of the park, the most popular scenic attraction, contains large basaltic knobs like oversized lumps of sugar along the edges of the Spokane River. A swinging suspension footbridge crosses the river here. The Bowl and Pitcher offers 16 standard campsites, 16 utility hookup sites and a group area with 13 utility hookups and two large spots for tents. Riverside State Park provides a 600-acre off-road vehicle area for dirt bikes and snowmobiles. Miles of trails are available for horseback riding. A kayak or canoe trip on the Little Spokane River is a fabulous way to get intimate with wildlife. The Deep Creek area of the park has 100-foot vertical rocks for climbers. Some routes have bolted anchors installed. The park is open year round. Winter activities include cross-country skiing, snowmobiling and sledding. The park contains the oldest building in Spokane County, a log hay shed. The Spokane House Interpretive Center tells the history of the early fur trade and its effects on the local American Indians. The center is open weekends from Memorial Day to Labor Day. Spokane folk love the outdoors, and a visit to Riverside State Park will show you why.

9711 W Charles Road, Nine Mile Falls WA
(509) 465-5064
www.riversidestatepark.org

Riverside State Park, Bowl and Pitcher
Photo by Nancy McClain

Spokane River Centennial Trail

ATTRACTIONS: *Rated number one attraction in the area*

The Spokane River Centennial Trail, a paved path that starts at the north end of Riverside State Park, is great for hiking, biking and in-line skating. *TripAdvisor* members have rated it the number-one attraction in the Spokane area. The Centennial Trail runs 37 miles along the Spokane River from Nine Mile Falls through downtown Spokane and east to the Idaho state line. In Idaho, it continues on as the North Idaho Centennial Trail. You can hike or bike, ride horseback in designated areas, or simply enjoy the natural beauty. Athletes can traverse the entire course of the trail, while casual visitors can take a short stroll on the sections that run through town. You can picnic on the river's edge, launch a canoe, or sit and contemplate the rhythmic flow of the river. The trail is designed for use by people of all ages and physical capabilities. Specifically, the trail is wheelchair-accessible. This community asset is maintained and operated by the Washington State Parks and Recreation Commission in cooperation with Spokane City Parks, Spokane County Parks, and the Friends of the Centennial Trail. Come enjoy the Spokane River Centennial Trail, a pathway that has something for everyone.

9711 W Charles Road, Nine Mile Falls WA
(509) 624-7188
www.spokanecentennialtrail.org

The Davenport Hotel

ATTRACTIONS: *One of America's most beautiful hotels*

Spokane was built by great men—that is what the businessmen who built the Davenport Hotel almost a century ago wanted to articulate. Indeed, when the Davenport opened in 1914, it was one of the grandest hotels anywhere in the world. It was among the very first to be air-conditioned throughout. It had the largest private telephone exchange in the Northwest. It also contained the largest plumbing system, with 30-miles of pipes delivering hot, cold and drinking water to every one of its 405 rooms. Gold leaf and crystal decorated the public spaces. Coins were washed and bills ironed before they were handed out as change. In the years that followed, almost every celebrity in the country visited the hotel. Decline set in after World War II. The hotel closed in 1985 and demolition was considered. In 2000, however, local developers Walt and Karen Worthy purchased the hotel and devoted almost all of their substantial personal fortunes to a complete restoration. Today, the glory of the past is restored. *Expedia* has named the Davenport one of the top 10 hotels in the nation. AAA gives it four diamonds. Guests rave not only about the beauty and comfort of the hotel, but about the extraordinarily polite and welcoming staff. The Palm Court Grille and the Peacock Room provide fine dining. Spokane society once again gathers in the Hall of the Doges and the Marie Antoinette Ballroom. Join them with a stay at the Davenport Hotel, one of Spokane's greatest treasures.

10 S Post Street, Spokane WA (509) 455-8888 or (800) 899-1482 *www.thedavenporthotel.com*

The Bing Crosby Memorabilia Room

ATTRACTIONS: *Best exhibit at Gonzaga University*

Today's younger generation rarely understands how enormously important Bing Crosby was to the development of American popular culture. Whatever your age, you can learn more about this American icon at the Bing Crosby Memorabilia Room at Gonzaga University. Bing attended Gonzaga and contributed generously to the school all his life. His boyhood home is actually on the campus. Gonzaga now has the largest public collection of Crosby-bilia in the world. The collection includes photographs, recordings of Bing's songs and radio shows, and Bing's own paintings and artwork. You can see Bing Crosby ice cream cartons and coloring books. Researchers can access Crosby's correspondence, often with other greats, such as Bob Hope and Rosemary Clooney. Other research material includes clippings, files and a collection of fan club periodicals. Bing, who lived from 1903 to 1977, had an impact on popular music rivaled only by Elvis Presley and The Beatles. He created the style of singing later adopted by Frank Sinatra, Dean Martin and others. From 1934 to 1954 he dominated recorded music, radio and motion pictures. He was the first performer in the world to pre-record his radio shows and master his commercial recordings on magnetic tape. His gift of an early tape recorder to musician Les Paul led directly to Paul's invention of multi-track recording. Come celebrate Bing Crosby's life and work at the Bing Crosby Memorabilia Room at Gonzaga University.

502 E Boone Avenue, Spokane WA
(509) 328-4220 ext. 4097
guweb2.gonzaga.edu/bing

Mobius Kids

ATTRACTIONS: *Best hands-on discovery museum for kids*

Children and their families have a new place to learn about the world. Mobius Kids, a hands-on discovery museum, debuted in River Park Square in 2005. Permanent installations include *Bayanihan*, which means community spirit in the Tagalog language of the Philippines. Here you can bargain at the *sari-sari* (variety) store, shop at the local fish market, and husk rice in the *bahay kubo* (single-room dwelling). The Geotopia exhibit, which features the Spokane River and aquifer, tells the story of water and soil conservation and habitat protection. Removable panels let visitors change water currents. Live insects and arachnids include a Rosehair Tarantula named Leggy Peggy. Cooper's Corner promotes safety with a tour of a miniature city. Here you can take control of city traffic signals, fit a bicycle helmet and meet a crash test dummy. In the Enchanted Forest, infants and toddlers can crawl, climb and romp their way through a tree slide, a foam pond and woodland-animal puppets. The Globe Theater gives children an opportunity to perform, and the Out-of-Hand Art Gallery displays their creations. Mobius Kids is the result of the merger of SciTech and the Children's Museum of Spokane. The Mobius Science Center, intended for older children, will be built on the north bank of Riverfront Park in 2007. Mobius Kids is available for birthday parties and special events, and is the site for summer camps and school programs. Let your little ones roam free at Mobius Kids.

808 W Main Avenue, Spokane WA
(509) 624-5437
www.mobiusspokane.org

Riverfront Park

ATTRACTIONS: *100 acres of fun in downtown Spokane*

Riverfront Park is 100 acres of fun in the heart of downtown Spokane. Built on the site of the Expo '74 World's Fair, the park features dozens of rides, activities and entertainment. The brand new aerial Skyride offers a spectacular view of the Spokane Falls and Gorge. The IMAX Theatre, located in the Expo '74 United States Pavilion, seats 385 and features a 53-by-69-foot screen. Amusement rides include the Dragon Coaster, Ferris wheel, bumper cars and a half-dozen others. These rides close in the winter, but in their place you can enjoy the Ice Palace, recognized as one of the best outdoor ice-skating rinks in the nation. Spokane's famous Looff Carrousel, a National Historical Landmark built in 1909, is one of America's most beautiful and well preserved wooden carrousels. It includes 54 carved horses, a giraffe, a tiger and two Chinese dragon chairs. The new Rotary interactive fountain is located near the carrousel. Enchanted Forest mini-golf is another traditional pleasure. Riverfront Park is home to many fascinating large-scale sculptures, such as the Red Wagon, a 12-foot high, 26-ton reinforced concrete replica of an old-fashioned Radio Flyer wagon. The Red Wagon is across a street from the Garbage Goat, which can vacuum up any trash you offer it. More than a dozen other sculptures include the Vietnam Veteran's Memorial and the Place Where Ghosts of Salmon Jump. For a great time, bring your kids—or your inner child—to Riverfront Park in Spokane.

808 W Spokane Falls Boulevard, Spokane WA
(509) 625-6600 or (800) 336-PARK (7275)
www.spokaneriverfrontpark.com

Spokane River
Photo by Nancy McClain

Super Supplements

HEALTH: *Voted best independent retail chain in the nation*

Science learns something new every day about the ways vitamins, herbs and nutritional supplements enhance health. Keeping up  with all that cutting-edge information would be overwhelming without the help of experts. Super Supplements is a privately owned chain of 13 discount vitamin stores in western Washington. It was started in 1994 by John Wurts and bills itself as having some of the most knowledgeable staff members in the industry. John brings more than 18 years of experience in the vitamin industry to his operation, which was voted 2004 Best Retail Chain in the Nation by *Vitamin Retailer* magazine. The stores feature wide, inviting aisles, a vast array of supplements, sports nutrition, herbs, body care and homeopathic products, plus a well educated staff prepared to provide the most up-to-date and accurate product information available. Bring your questions to university students, naturopathic doctors or herbalists, or take advantage of Healthnotes, a touchscreen information system that retrieves research on natural remedies, illnesses and potential drug interactions from vitamin, herb and food combinations. You'll get 10 to 70-percent discounts on products at Super Supplements locations from Bellingham to Lakewood. The same great service and more than 30,000 products are available on the website. Visit Super Supplements to begin your journey to a healthier life.

2525 N Ruby Street, Spokane WA
(509) 326-8505
6630 E Sprague Avenue, Spokane Valley WA
(509) 456-3660
Mail Order: (800) 249-9394
www.supersup.com

WENATCHEE

With four distinct seasons, 300 sunshine-filled days a year, a river running through town and mountains so close you can touch them, your stay in Wenatchee will be memorable. You can take in the Art on the Avenues sculpture tour, experience the Wenatchee Valley Symphony, visit local award-winning wineries or attend a performance at one of Wenatchee's theaters. Wenatchee is known as the Apple Capital of the World for the valley's many orchards, which produce apples enjoyed around the world. Although the first settlers of this area migrated during the last ice age, the city was officially founded in 1893 by Don Carlos Corber, who named it after the Indian Chief Wenatchee.

PLACES TO GO

- Ohme Gardens
  3327 Ohme Road
  (509) 662-5785

- Rocky Reach Dam Park
  U.S. Highway 97A
  (509) 663-5722

- Wenatchee Valley Museum & Cultural Center
  127 S Mission
  (509) 664-3340

- Horan Natural Area
  Wenatchee Confluence State Park
  (800) 572-7753

THINGS TO DO

April
- Ridge 2 River Relay
  www.r2r.org

May
- Washington State Apple Blossom Festival
  (509) 662-3616

September
- Tour de Vine Bike and Wine Tour
  (800) 572-7753

November
- Wenatchee Festival of Trees
  (509) 663-ARTS

Wenatchee Lake State Park
Photo by Steve Andersen

Wenatchee River
Photo by Jim Poth

Wenatchee Valley Museum and Cultural Center

ATTRACTIONS:
Exhibits go back 12,000 years

People have lived in Wenatchee a very long time. Archeological digs have uncovered artifacts dating back almost 12,000 years, proving that members of the ancient Clovis culture settled at Wenatchee in the last ice age. You can see these artifacts and much more at the Wenatchee Valley Museum and Cultural Center. The museum was founded in 1939 by members of the local archaeological society, who wanted a place to display their private collections of Native American artifacts. Indian artifacts on display today include petroglyphs from Rock Island and beadwork. From the 1800s, Wenatchee's existence depended on transportation. A coin-operated HO gauge diorama sends a model train chugging along narrow tracks, over trestles and through replicas of historic Cascade tunnels. The apple industry is celebrated by an operational vintage apple packing line with an apple wiper, a sorting table and a catapult sizing machine. A wall display showcases hundreds of vintage apple box labels. A farm shop, Victorian house and an extensive Main Street portray life of a century ago. A key exhibit illustrates the career of aviation pioneer and Chelan County native Clyde Pangborn, who completed the first-ever non-stop, trans-Pacific flight with a landing in Wenatchee. Children enjoy Coyote's Corner, which introduces three eco-systems in the valley. An art gallery displays local paintings and photography. The Wenatchee Valley Museum and Cultural Center is one of the area's most engaging attractions. Be sure to see it.

127 S Mission Street, Wenatchee WA
(509) 664-3340
www.wenatcheevalleymuseum.com

Wenatchee National Forest

ATTRACTIONS: *Largest recreational resource in the north Cascades*

Some people consider the Wenatchee National Forest to be the best recreational resource in the north Cascades. It is certainly the largest, covering an area about 40 miles wide and 140 miles long, from Lake Chelan in the north to the Yakama Indian Reservation in the south. The vegetation varies from sagebrush and pine at 2,000 feet, to alpine fir and huckleberry higher up, to the crest of the Cascades where vegetation is sparse. About two-fifths of the forest is wilderness area, where foot travel is the only method of transportation allowed. Elsewhere, more than 100 campgrounds and picnic sites can support 13,000 people at a time. Some campgrounds are for tents, others for RVs and some are especially designed for horse folk. About 5,000 miles of forest roads provide access to campgrounds, trailheads and scenic vistas. Hikers, bicyclists and horse riders can make use of about 2,500 miles of trails. In the winter, snow-covered roads support cross-country skiing, snowshoeing and snowmobiling. Woodcutting, berry picking and rockhounding are popular. Those who fish will discover that streams and lakes are home to several varieties of trout, salmon and steelhead. Thousands of hunters pursue deer, elk, bear and grouse in the fall. Some of the best rock climbing in the Northwest is in the Leavenworth Ranger District, and hundreds of peaks offer alpine climbers some of the best mountaineering anywhere. If you seek the great outdoors, you will find it in the Wenatchee National Forest.

215 Melody Lane, Wenatchee WA
(509) 664 9200
www.fs.fed.us/r6/wenatchee

Ohme Gardens

ATTRACTIONS: *One of America's most famous Alpine gardens*

Ohme Gardens, on a high rocky bluff north of Wenatchee, is one of the most famous alpine gardens in America. Just 75 years ago, this site was a barren hillside of sagebrush. The Ohme family spent years moving rock, watering and pulling weeds, and the result is one of America's most acclaimed gardens. The garden appears natural, but in fact is highly sculptured. The alpine scenery includes evergreens, grass, ponds and waterfalls that blend with the existing rock. Over 100 wildflower species are on display. The garden overlooks the Wenatchee Valley, the Cascades and the Columbia River. Stone paths lead through forest and wildflowers to hidden pools and panoramic views. Stone benches suddenly appear under trees and beside little ponds where you can stop and sit. The site is a cool reprieve during the scorching Wenatchee summers. The grounds include irregularly shaped lawns, rustic shelters and a wishing well. Herman and Ruth Ohme began the garden as a private family retreat in 1929, their own big backyard. The growing patch of green was easily visible from the valley below, and locals flocked to see it. In 1939, the Ohmes bowed to the pleas of their friends and admirers by opening the gardens to the public. Herman and Ruth's son Gordon took over in 1953 and expanded the garden to its present nine acres. Today, Ohme Gardens is owned by the state and run by the county as a park. Whether you visit for an hour or a day, you will always remember the Ohme Gardens.

3327 Ohme Road, Wenatchee WA
(509) 662-5785
www.ohmegardens.com

TWIN POOLS

Ohme Gardens
Photo by Levy Sheckler

Photo by Thorin Nielson

Columbia Gorge & Tri-Cities

Gorge & Tri Cities

Water running through the woods

THE COLOMBIA RIVER GORGE AND TRI-CITIES regions are defined by their rivers. To the west, the stunning Columbia River Gorge National Scenic Area extends for 80 miles. Windsurfers and kite boarders regularly perform on the water, and hiking, hunting and fishing are also popular.

East of the Cascades, the landscape is open prairie dotted with brush and the occasional juniper tree. More sheltered areas contain ponderosa pine and oak savannahs. This is the Wine Country, one of the greatest tourist draws in Washington. The Tri-Cities of Richland, Kennewick and Pasco, with 160,000 metro residents, form the largest urban area in southeastern Washington.

The Tri-Cities were founded on irrigation-based agriculture, and the vast number of high-quality wineries that have opened in recent years carry on that tradition. The Tri-Cities are also a historic site for another reason—the Federal government established the Hanford Nuclear Site here as part of the Manhattan Project. Today, parts of the Hanford Site have been turned into a wildlife refuge where visitors in shallow boats drift past pelicans, herons, deer and other creatures. The Tri-Cities continue to serve as a high-tech center, now specializing in energy and the environment.

Further east is Walla Walla, center of the Walla Walla appellation and more than 65 boutique wineries. In 2005, Sunset Magazine named the town the Wine Destination of the Year. The county is also home to the famous Walla Walla Sweet Onion, the best tasting onion in the world. Whitman College in Walla Walla is one of the most distinguished liberal arts schools in the Northwest.

Columbia River at Sunrise
Photo by David Smigelski

BENTON CITY

Benton City is a small town with a big wine industry. A dozen excellent vineyards, wineries or cellars offer tastings. Benton City even has its own appellation, Red Mountain, Washington's smallest. This 5.6-square-mile district consists of sloping lands beneath the broad Red Mountain overlooking Benton City. Annual rainfall is only about six inches, and irrigation is usually provided for a few months into the growing season. Wines made from Red Mountain fruit express great strength and richness, while maintaining exceptional balance of fruit, acidity and tannin. German immigrants founded the community, which was once known as Giezentanner. It incorporated as Benton City in 1945.

THINGS TO DO

April
• Benton City Spring Opener
  Car and Bike Show
  (509) 588-3251

July
• July 4th Celebration
  Benton City Park

Cañon De Sol

WINERIES: *Best boutique winery*

Victor Cruz broke into new territory as the first Latino to own a winery in Washington. The extraordinary quality of his wines and the reception the wines receive at contest time adds to Victor's list of boundary breaking achievements. Cañon De Sol is a boutique winery that produces small quantities of ultra-premium, mostly red, handcrafted wines. Cañon de Sol's 2000 Syrah won Best of Show against over 700 other entries at the 2002 Northwest Wine Summit. The 1999 Merlot, made in Cañon De Sol's first year of production, received a bronze, and the awards continue to pile up. The winery is the result of a childhood friendship between Victor Cruz and Charlie Hoppes. Victor, whose parents were farm laborers, grew up to become an engineer with Westinghouse and a successful investor. Charlie grew up to become a top winemaker. Wine Press Northwest has called Charlie "perhaps the finest winemaker in Washington." After early retirement, Victor opened the winery with Charlie's help. Victor arranged the necessary investment, and Charlie designed the wines. Today, Victor is a working owner, dressed these days in jeans rather than a suit. Charlie is a consultant to Cañon de Sol and several other successful boutique wineries. The Cañon de Sol barrel room is open for tasting by appointment and open to the general public for special events during the second weekend of March, the fourth weekend of June and the last weekend of September. Schedule a visit to Cañon De Sol Winery.

46415 E Badger Road, Benton City WA
(509) 588-6311
www.canondesol.com

Yellow Rose Nursery

GARDENS, PLANTS & FLOWERS:
Best water and demonstration gardens

Garden designer Lou Gannon can help you put together a garden or landscape with a theme that expresses your sense of style. Lou, who owns Yellow Rose Nursery with his wife, Teresa, has traveled extensively and studied the gardens of the world, from the magnificent gardens of Japan and Europe to those of India's Taj Mahal. He holds a bachelor of science in landscape architecture, is a licensed landscape architect and has 30 years of practical experience helping gardeners attain their goals. The nursery can help you design water gardens, from simple koi ponds to more elaborate gardens that incorporate streams and waterfalls. Various themed garden displays, such as Pacific Northwest, English and Mediterranean, show plants in their natural settings to allow you to see how different plants can be used to achieve the look you want. The Gannons are especially proud of the Tree of Life display. Ground cover plants are available, as are trees and water plants. Yellow Rose stocks many varieties of rocks, soils and fertilizers for completing and maintaining your garden. Hanging baskets make perfect gifts for nearly anyone. The Yellow Rose stocks Smith and Hawken gardening tools and furniture to make working and relaxing in your garden distinct pleasures. Lou and Teresa believe in going the extra mile for their clients, so in addition to design and plant sales, Yellow Rose provides complete installation services. Stop by the Yellow Rose Nursery and enjoy the landscape.

600 Merlot Drive, Prosser WA
(509) 786-3304

ELTOPIA

Amidst irrigated circles of wheat and dry ravines you will find Eltopia. Supposedly the name comes from the time when railroad workers were building the town and the railroad. A storm washed out most of the work that had been done. A Cockney worker than said, "There will be hell to pay." The name stuck. Eltopia is a prime hunting ground. It is located under a major flyway for geese and ducks, and the area's farmland provides plenty of cover for the local populations of pheasants, quail and chukkars.

PLACES TO GO

- Juniper Dunes Wilderness
  Peterson Road off Pasco-Kahlotus Road
  (509) 536-1200

THINGS TO DO

October
- Washington Cutting Horse Association
  Finals Show
  Bonina Ranch
  (509) 297-4480

November
- St. Paul's Dinner Auction
  (509) 297-4371

Middleton Orchards
GARDENS, PLANTS & FLOWERS:
Best organic orchards

Middleton Orchards is a family-owned orchard that produces premium organic fruit. For owner Gary Middleton, a third-generation grower, farming is a passion. He once had the largest carrot farm in the Northwest and later grew substantial quantities of asparagus. Starting in 1995, he committed to the development of an entirely organic orchard. His orchard currently includes Gala, Golden and Granny Smith apples. Cherry types are Bing, Van and Black Republican. The farm grows blueberries, too. Middleton Orchards uses natural fertilizers, such as manure and compost, and beneficial insects to help control pests. Instead of herbicides, the staff weeds by hand or with mechanical methods. All of the apple blocks are certified organic. Some of the cherries are certified and some are transitional, which means they have been grown organically, but have not yet undergone the three-year qualifying period. A key staff member is orchard manager Juan Delgado, who has been farming with Gary for 20 years. Middleton Orchards markets through local farmers markets. It also has a rare Euro Gap certification that allows sales in Europe. Middleton Orchards believes that its organic fruit has more flavor than conventional fruit. Schedule a visit to Middleton Orchards and taste the quality of organically grown fruit for yourself while exploring the benefits of organic farming.

4293 Eltopia W Road, Eltopia WA
(509) 297-4441
www.middletonorchards.com

GOLDENDALE

Goldendale is named for John Golden, an early homesteader. The Little Klickitat River and Bloodgood Creek, a spring-fed water source, run through the town. Both sport rainbow trout and host waterfowl such as ducks and the great blue heron. Flowers and green meadows and prairies make Goldendale a particularly beautiful site in the spring. North of town is Goldendale Observatory State Park, which contains four telescopes, including the largest telescope in the United States that is available to the general public. This instrument, a 24.5-inch reflecting telescope, was the work of four amateur astronomers. It was originally intended for Clark College in Vancouver, Washington, but was donated to the town of Goldendale instead. In the town of Maryhill, just to the south on the Columbia River, you can find one of the nation's best small museums, with the largest stationary Rodin sculpture exhibit in the United States, as well as other sculptures, paintings and Native American artifacts.

PLACES TO GO

- The Golden Art Gallery
  103 E Main Street
  (509) 773-5100

- Goldendale Observatory State Park
  1602 Observatory Drive
  (509) 773-3141

- Maryhill Museum of Art
  35 Maryhill Museum Drive
  (509) 773-3733

THINGS TO DO

May
- Maryhill Winery Anniversary Celebration
  (877) 627-9445

August
- Klikitat County Fair and Rodeo
  (509) 364-3526

September
- Maryhill Arts Festival
  Maryhill Museum (509) 773-3733

- Concours de Maryhill Car Show I
  Maryhill Museum (509) 773-3733

Maryhill Winery

WINERIES: *Most scenic winery*

Maryhill Winery began as a partnership between four wine enthusiasts: Craig and Vicki Leuthold, Donald Leuthold and Cherie Brooks. In 2000, the four broke ground on a site adjacent to the Maryhill Museum of Art with sweeping views of the Columbia River Gorge and Mt. Hood. Maryhill Winery focuses on producing premium red wines, with special attention to Zinfandel and Sangiovese. The vineyards include the largest planting of Zinfandel in Washington State, as well as Viognier, Cabernet Sauvignon and Merlot. John Haw, a 25-year industry veteran, is Maryhill Winery's winemaker. John produces many complex blends and wines that are ready to drink upon bottling. In competitions, the wines have won too many gold, silver and bronze medals to mention. Visitors to the winery find their attention split between the stunning views and the massive carved-wood tasting bar. Samplers can take a glass onto the deck or grounds. Maryhill Winery also has a 4,000-seat outdoor amphitheater, which is a major concert venue. The 2005 season included Bob Dylan, B. B. King and ZZ Top. The audience has panoramic views of the stage, the river and Mount Hood. Guests can bring blankets or chairs for the grass-terraced general admission area or purchase reserved seats. The 2006 season was suspended due to construction, but a full schedule returns in 2007. Maryhill Winery offers an experience you will want to repeat.

9774 Highway 14, Goldendale WA
(877) 627-9445
www.maryhillwinery.com

PLACES TO GO

- East Benton County Historical Museum
  205 Keewaydin Drive
  (509) 582-7704

- Nine Canyon Wind Farm
  Nine Canyon Road, Finley
  (509) 585-3677

- Civic Center Complex Park
  209 W 6th Avenue

- Columbia Park
  Columbia Park Trail

- Grange Park
  1600 S Union Street

THINGS TO DO

April
- Cowboy Get Together
  Fairgrounds
  (509) 947-5785

July
- River of Fire Festival (4th of July)
  Columbia Park
  (509) 736-0510

- Tri-Cities Water Follies and Hydroplane Race
  Colombia Park
  (877) 73-HYDRO (734-9376)

August
- Benton Franklin Fair & Rodeo
  Fairgrounds (509) 586-9211 Ext. 3

- Ye Old Car Club Antique Car Showcase
  (509) 586-5633

September
- Grapefest
  Downtown
  (509) 582-7221

- Fiesta de la Independencia Mexicana
  Fairgrounds (509) 542-0933

October
- Tri-Cities Antique Show
  Fairgrounds (509) 586-9211

November
- Christmas Memories
  Three Rivers Convention Center
  (800) 762-1101

December
- Christmas Lighted Boats Parade
  (509) 737-1166

KENNEWICK

The name Kennewick comes from an Indian word meaning grassy place. With more than 60,000 people, Kennewick is the largest of the Tri-Cities. People from all over southeastern Washington come to shop in the city's commercial district, which includes the Columbia Center Mall. Two bridges link Kennewick to Pasco across the Columbia River: the Blue Bridge and the Cable Bridge, one of the longest cable-stayed bridges in the world. In the summer, the Water Follies puts on hydroplane racing on the Columbia River. It was during one of these races that a spectator discovered the 8,400-year-old remains of Kennewick Man. The relationship of this prehistoric individual to modern Indians is a major question. Kennewick is the host city of the Tri-City Americans of the Western Hockey League, as well as of the 2005 National Indoor Football League champions, the Tri-Cities Fever.

Nine Canyon Wind Project

Guesthouse International Suites

ACCOMMODATIONS:
Best family accommodations

After a busy day of sightseeing, golfing or wine tasting along the Columbia River Gorge, you'll want a comfortable place to call home for the night. Guesthouse International Suites in Kennewick offers comfort and attractive amenities in an environment that welcomes families and business travelers. Kids under 18 years old stay free in rooms with their parents, and high-speed Internet is available in select rooms. You'll find a fitness center, a business center and laundry facilities. Owner Joo Kim and his crew are dedicated to making your stay a pleasurable experience. They can accommodate guests with pets, with handicaps and with nonsmoking preferences. The spacious mini-suites come equipped with microwaves, refrigerators and coffeemakers. Hairdryers and irons add to your convenience, while cable television with HBO adds to your entertainment. A free Continental breakfast each morning will have you raring to explore nearby attractions, which include Bateman Island and Hanford Reach National Monument. Guesthouse International Suites offers daily and weekly rates and discounts to seniors and members of AAA, AARP and Qualified Corporate. Joo Kim also owns Clarion Hotel, a second site in the Tri-Cities area, located just off George Washington Way in Richland, not far from the airport. Visit Guesthouse International Suites or Clarion Hotel, your jumping off spots for business or pleasure in the Upper Columbia River Gorge.

5616 W Clearwater Avenue, Kennewick WA
(509) 735-2242 or (800) 424-1145
www.ghsuites.com

Tri-Cities Fever Football
ATTRACTIONS:
National Indoor Football League's Bowl V Champs

Indoor football has taken the Tri-Cities area by storm, thanks to the Tri-Cities Fever. In its 2005 inaugural season, the Tri-Cities Fever won the National Indoor Football League's Indoor Bowl V, making the Fever the first professional indoor football team to best two unbeaten teams on the way to a national championship. Team owners and partners Randy Schillinger and Teri Carr, along with Head Coach Dan Whitsett, are proving to be a winning combination. Not only can they deliver a championship team, but one that's fast becoming beloved by the Tri-Cities communities. The precocious Fever football team is a proud member of the NIFL, formed in 2001 from 18 franchises across the United States. The League's vision is to provide inexpensive family entertainment and quality football action. In 2002, the League jumped from 18 to 21 teams; in 2003, it expanded from 21 to 24 teams; and in 2004, it grew to 26 teams. Fever owners and managers live and work in the Tri-Cities area, and have a strong loyalty to their community and a dedication to providing affordable family entertainment close to home. Fans are showing an equal loyalty as they hitch their wagons to this rising star. For riveting action from a championship team, catch the Tri-Cities Fever at the Toyota Center.

7016 W Grandridge Boulevard, Kennewick WA
(509) 222-2215
www.tricitiesfever.com

Tri-City Americans
ATTRACTIONS: *Western Hockey League stars for 18 Years*

When it comes to hockey, Tri-Citians are passionate about their beloved Americans. Millions of fans have attended Americans home games over the team's 18 seasons. The Americans, part of the 21-team Western Hockey League, recruits 16- to 20-year-old players who take pride in serving as role models for the youth of the area. Americans fans have witnessed the athleticism and competitive spirit of several Tri-City players who have gone on to play in the National Hockey League, including Olaf Kolzig, Stu Barnes, Daymond Langkow and Scott Gomez; as well as visiting players such as Mike Modano, Scott Neidermayer and Jarome Iginla. In April 2005, former Tri-City Americans (and current NHL standouts) Kolzig and Barnes, along with Kennewick accountant Dennis Loman and longtime WHL general manager Bob Tory, purchased the Americans to ensure that the franchise continued to provide affordable, high-quality family entertainment to the region. In October 2005, the City of Kennewick and Compass Facilities Management partnered with Toyota of Tri-Cities and renamed the Americans home venue the Toyota Center. The owners, sponsors and community agree that the Tri-City Americans are Here to Play, Here to Stay.

7000 W Grandridge Boulevard, Kennewick WA
(509) 736-0606, ext 283
www.amshockey.com

Toyota Center

ATTRACTIONS: *Best sports venue in the Tri-cities*

The Toyota Center hosts more than 150 events every year. Many great names in music have played the center, which is also the home of the Western Hockey League's Tri-City Americans, and the Tri-City Fever of the National Indoor Football League. The center hosts trade shows, banquets and meetings of all kinds, and comfortably seats from 5,000 to 7,000 in six configurations. A flexible floor allows the stage to be moved freely for the best viewing and listening. An ice sheet is available for hockey and ice shows. For trade shows, the floor transforms into a 27,000-square-foot exhibit hall. A banquet area at the top of the center can accommodate groups from five to 250. The Toyota Center is in the heart of Kennewick on the Three Rivers Campus, owned by the City of Kennewick. The campus also holds the Toyota Arena and the Three Rivers Convention Center. The Toyota Arena provides 17,000 square feet of space that can be configured with an ice sheet for skating or a hard surface for meetings and trade shows. When not reserved, the arena is open for public skating. The beautiful Three Rivers Convention Center offers more than 50,000 square feet of meeting and exhibit space. It has wireless high-speed Internet throughout the building, as well as advanced lighting and audio/visual technology. Whether you are a promoter, business executive or a fan, the Toyota Center and the Three Rivers Campus have something for you.

7016 Grandridge Boulevard, Kennewick WA
(509) 735-9400
www.yourtoyotacenter.com
www.threeriversconventioncenter.com

Rocky Mountain Chocolate Factory

FUN FOODS: *Best chocolate*

One visit to any of the Rocky Mountain Chocolate Factory branches and you will discover why this store is such an attraction for chocolate lovers. The shop carries 15 varieties of rich, creamy, handmade fudge, freshly dipped huge strawberries and 20 varieties of caramel apples. You can also find hand-dipped clusters and truffles, barks, hard ice cream and many other delights. Rocky Mountain has low-carb chocolates and a huge assortment of sugar-free items approved for diabetics. You can watch as the staff dips crisp apples in thick, bubbling caramel from a traditional copper kettle. The caramel apple is then rolled in a rainbow of tasty toppings to complete your old-fashioned treat. A signature item is the humongous Pecan Bear Apple, which is dipped in caramel, rolled in roasted pecans, coated with milk or dark chocolate and drizzled with a white confection. Linger awhile longer and learn how fudge is made. Staff members fashion a creamy fudge loaf on a traditional marble slab, the old-fashioned way, right before your eyes. Everyone gets a free sample. Do not leave without picking up a gift of fine chocolate to share your experience. Gifts are elegantly crafted and beautifully packaged in boxes, tins and baskets. Stop in at Rocky Mountain Chocolate Factory, where they keep the kettle cooking for you.

1321 Columbia Center Boulevard, Suite 393, Kennewick WA
(509) 735-7187
or (800) 454-RMCF (7623)

1419 1st Avenue, Seattle WA
(206) 262-9581 or (877) 276-0482

401 NE Northgate Way, Suite 2020, Seattle WA
(206) 363-1399

99 Yesler Way, Seattle WA
(206) 405-2872

www.rmcf.com

Tri-City Court Club

HEALTH & BEAUTY:
Best athletic club

The goal of Tri-City Court Club is to entertain, enlighten and energize your life. Everything offered at the club focuses on at least one of these three Es. A recent remodeling of the club upgraded equipment and added to the club's overall ambience. Among the changes are new upstairs studios, one set up for personal training and the other for group exercise and cycling. Both studios add variety to your workout with high-tech lighting effects, theater quality surround sound and big-screen digital video displays. The club offers individual and group personal training sessions, plus more than 100 group classes. Consider yoga, indoor cycling, water aerobics or programs like Boot Camp, an intense military-style cardio and weight training class. Beginners and those looking for gentler programs will appreciate beginning Pilates, low impact aerobics or a stretching class for releasing tight muscles through breathing and relaxation. The club offers classes for every age and conditioning level. Kids and teens have opportunities to start fitness habits early, while seniors find power in specialized workouts, like Nice and Easy, where you move to music. Popular teen and adult weight loss programs help guarantee success with education and motivation. Exercise is infectious, and one class soon leads to another. Consider tai chi, kickboxing or track running. Jazzercise and NIA (Neuromuscular Integrative Action) are popular disciplines, while the Ab Lab will put your abdominal muscles in high gear. Try a class at Tri-City Court Club, and prepare to experience a renewed enthusiasm for life.

1350 N Grant Street, Kennewick WA
(509) 783-5465
www.tricitycourtclub.com

Escape Body Care Studio

HEALTH & BEAUTY:
Best beauty care and gift shop combination

Soothe, relax and rejuvenate at Escape Body Care Studio and Ideal Jewelry & Gallery, two businesses sharing one great space in Kennewick. From the moment you enter the door, you are enveloped in warmth and loving attention. Imagine a soothing pedicure easing away tensions of the day or a manicure suited for your special occasion. Consider waxing services that leave your whole body smooth. Owner Lisa Allen offers a variety of body care treatments.

Ideal Jewelry & Gallery

FASHION: *Best jewelry*

This gallery specializes in quality Sterling Silver jewelry and gemstones from around the world. Owner and designer Tami Davenport strives for that double "wow" response: The first because you are amazed by how beautiful and unique the jewelry is, and the second because you are impressed by the great value. Ideal Jewelry is your passport to gemstones from around the world.

8390 W Gage Boulevard, #105, Kennewick WA
Escape: (509) 783-7111
Ideal Jewelry & Gallery:
(509) 366-1873
www.idealjewelry.citymaker.com

Mirage Pool 'n' Spa
HOME: *Best pool & spa company*

Mirage Pool 'n' Spa offers a complete line of services and top-of-the-line products for every pool and spa. From start to finish, Mirage Pool 'n' Spa gives individualized service and attention to detail. Mirage can help you realize dreams and make your backyard a success with custom-designed pools and spas built to your exact specifications and needs. Mirage also features stunning gazebos, wet bars and grills in the latest styles and fashions. The store's extravagant outdoor kitchens feature upscale stainless steel appliances. On-site and in-store services are available for your convenience. Experienced service technicians keep everything in tip-top shape with seasonal pool services, in-store water analysis, liner installation, equipment replumbing, leak detection and repair. With 30 years of experience, Mirage Pool 'n' Spa is a leader in the industry. Owner and manager Chad Simmonds, along with partners Jon Rettig, Diehl Rettig, Frank Armijo and Bill Lampson, believe in integrity and going the extra mile for every customer. Chad grew up in the pool business and knew this was his future. He worked many years with his father and early on gained a loyal following of customers who are still with him to this day. Chad and his partners invite you to start your backyard fun by visiting Mirage Pool 'n' Spa.

7422 W Clearwater Avenue, Kennewick WA
(509) 735-2000
www.miragepoolnspa.com

Inca Mexican Restaurant
RESTAURANTS & CAFÉS: *Best Mexican food*

Friendly service and an authentic hacienda-style décor are just the beginning of a superb dining experience at Inca Mexican Restaurant. Freshly prepared foods and a full-service bar are big reasons to choose Inca for meals with family and friends. You can try two convenient Tri-Cities locations—in Kennewick and Richland. Sizzling fajitas and succulent *arroz con pollo* are favorites on a menu loaded with authentic Mexican specialties. Owner Javier Rodriguez adds flare and creativity with original dishes created especially for the two restaurants. Javier started out as a busboy at a Mexican restaurant in Seattle in 1985 and, within five short years, became cook and bartender. In 1989, he and his brother, José Rodriguez, opened Inca Mexican Restaurant in Kennewick. Their cook, Antonio Mendoza, eventually joined the Rodriguez brothers as a partner. Together they give the Tri-Cities area a reason to get out of the house and eat Mexican food. They feel a strong loyalty to their community and donate to many local charities. As Inca's popularity continues to spread, Javier, José and Antonio look toward expanding to new locations. For a great meal with south-of-the-border flavor and charm, visit Inca Mexican Restaurant, where quality and service always come first.

3600 W Clearwater Avenue, Kennewick WA
(509) 735-6098
1813 Leslie Road, Richland WA
(509) 628-1070

Fun 2 Learn

SHOPPING: *Best educational resource store*

Fun 2 Learn is an educational resource store with a mission. Owners Mary Peterson and Val Donovan value young minds and recognize the importance of providing quality products for the classroom, home or anywhere children want to learn. Teachers, parents, friends and relatives find top quality instructional tools, games and toys at Fun 2 Learn. The merchandise reflects a philosophy of endorsing products that stimulate and nurture the intellect versus the usual mass market items found in other venues. The original store opened in Kennewick 10 years ago, and another store opened in Yakima in 1998 to excellent reviews. Teachers shop here on weekends, and parents come throughout the week for special educational books, games or toys. Teachers have been known to come into the store and pay out of their own pocket for a learning tool they know will make a difference in one child's ability to learn. The store carries the full line of Carson-Dellosa and Dianne J. Hook clip art on disk for an artful touch to stationery, reports and decorations. Prepare today's young people for the challenges and opportunities of tomorrow by shopping at Fun 2 Learn.

5215 W Clearwater Avenue, Kennewick WA
(509) 736-1581
5611 Summitview Avenue, Yakima WA
(509) 457-2707

PLACES TO GO

- Columbia Basin College Esvelt Gallery
  2600 N 20th Avenue
  (509) 547-0511

- McNary National Wildlife Refuge
  500 E Maple Street, Burbank
  (509) 547-4942

- Kurtzman Park
  S Wehe Avenue and E Alton Street

- Memorial Park
  N 14th Avenue and W Shoshone Street

- Sacagawea State Park
  and Interpretive Center
  2503 Sacajawea Park Road

THINGS TO DO

May
- Cinco de Mayo Celebration
  Downtown
  (509) 545-9776

- Untapped Blues Festival
  TRAC Center
  (509) 585-6387

June
- Lewis and Clark Bluegrass Festival
  Sacajawea State Park
  (509) 366-7995

July
- Penny Carnival
  Memorial Park
  (509) 545-3456

September
- Pasco Fiery Foods Festival
  Downtown
  (509) 545-0738

- Hands around the World
  TRAC Center
  (509) 546-0365

October
- Lewis and Clark Heritage Days
  Sacajawea State Park
  (509) 492-1555

- Tri-Cities Women's Expo
  TRAC Center
  (509) 366-9243

PASCO

The Lewis and Clark expedition stopped near Pasco, at what is now Sacagawea State Park. The Franklin County seat, Pasco is the oldest of the Tri-Cities and the area's transportation hub. Formerly it was a rail center; today it hosts the airport. Pasco is one of the fastest-growing cities in Washington. The population is 56 percent Hispanic, compared to 15 percent in Kennewick and less than 5 percent in Richland. As a result, Pasco's bustling downtown has an interesting Mexican flavor, with myriad small Hispanic-owned businesses and restaurants. Pasco is home to the Tri-City Dust Devils of the Northwest baseball league.

Best Western Pasco Inn & Suites

ACCOMMODATIONS:

Quality and comfort near all of Pasco's attractions

Many folks stay at the Best Western Pasco Inn & Suites in Pasco because of its convenient location next to the Sun Willows Golf Course. Others like being close to the airport, to wineries or to the large event center known as TRAC. Whatever your reason, you will find the quality and comfort you have come to expect from Best Western, the world's largest hotel chain. Built to meet the demands of the modern traveler and businessperson, the hotel features Douglas fir double-wall construction to ensure privacy. Every room comes well equipped with a refrigerator, microwave, hair dryer and iron. Free high speed fiber optic hard-wired internet access is available in each room. Whirlpool rooms are also available. A business center provides computers, fax and copier. Guests have access to a 24-hour indoor heated pool, spa and fitness center. A hot and cold breakfast buffet is free. They also offer a complimentary airport shuttle. Best Western knows how hard it is to feel at home while traveling, that's why the Pasco Inn & Suites includes such extras as free morning *USA Today* and *Seattle Times* newspapers and freshly baked cookies every evening. Make the Best Western Pasco Inn & Suites your home away from home.

2811 N 20th Avenue, Pasco WA
(509) 543-7722 or (800) 780-7234
www.bestwestern.com

Crazy Moose Casino

ATTRACTIONS: *Eastern Washington's best casino*

The Crazy Moose Casino is the Tri-Cities' entertainment haven, offering Las Vegas-style gaming, live comedy and sports viewing on a state-of-the-art satellite system. The biggest card room in eastern Washington attracts those ready to test their luck and skills at Texas Hold 'em, Black Jack, three and four-card Poker, and many other popular games. You will find 15 tables at the Crazy Moose, the maximum allowed by the state of Washington. The billiards room offers first-class tables on an hourly basis. Thursday, Friday and Saturday are comedy nights, featuring some of the hottest and funniest acts on the national and regional scene. Every night is sports night, as the Crazy Moose connects the sports enthusiast with the vast world of sports. The 10 different satellite links guarantee that you will never miss a single pitch or punt of the big game. Screens are perfectly placed to deliver clear, sharp programming no matter where you are in the casino. The kitchen serves food and spirits until the wee morning hours. The dynamic Crazy Moose Casino is doing its best to make sure that nobody in the Tri-Cities area ever gets bored. Whether your goal is to play, laugh or root for your favorite team, let the Crazy Moose be your destination.

510 S 20th Avenue, Pasco WA
(509) 542-8580
www.casinocity.com/us/wa/pasco/crzymoos

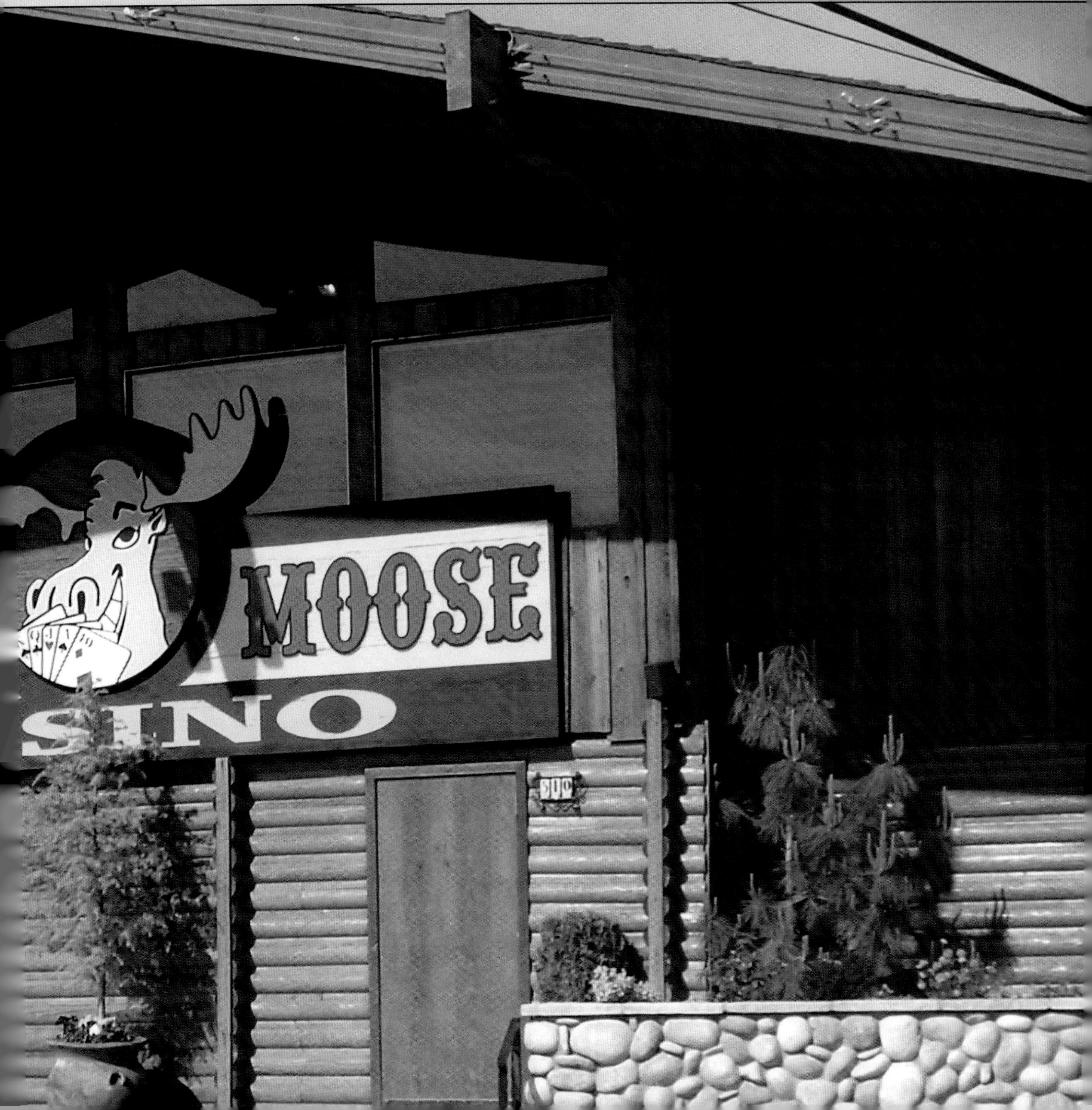
MOOSE
SINO

PLACES TO GO

- Columbia River Exhibition of History, Science & Technology
  95 Lee Boulevard
  (877) 789-9935

- Hanford Reach Jet Boat Tour
  Howard Amon Park (888) 486-9119

- LIGO Hanford Observatory tours
  (509) 372-8106

- Badger Mountain Centennial Preserve
  (509) 943-3992

- Badger Mountain Park
  Keene Road west of Gage Boulevard

- Colombia Park West
  1776 Columbia Park Trail

- Howard Amon Park
  Amon Park Drive

- Leslie Groves Park
  Hains Avenue and River Road

THINGS TO DO

February
- Red Wine and Chocolate
  (800) 258-7270

March
- Amon Basin Wildlands Day
  (509) 627-0950

May
- National Astronomy Day @ LIGO
  (509) 372-8106

June
- FingerFest
  Howard Amon Park (509) 521-9850

- Cool Desert Nights Car Show
  (509) 736-0510

July
- Sidewalk Art Show
  Howard Amon Park (509) 521-9677

- Hot Jazzy Nightz Jazz & Wine Festival
  John Dam Plaza
  (509) 430-5862

August
- Tumbleweed Music Festival
  (509) 528-2215

October
- Savor the Art Wine Yakima Valley
  (800) 258-7270

RICHLAND

At the start of World War II, Richland was a sleepy farm town of 300 people. When the war ended, its population was 25,000. During the war, the U.S. Army purchased 640 square miles—half the size of Rhode Island—for the Manhattan Project that built the atom bomb. Much of Richland was planned by the Army Corps of Engineers, and many of the streets are named after famous engineers. With the shutdown of the last production reactor at the Hanford site in 1987, environmental technology became a major industry. Richland is the home of Pacific Northwest National Laboratory. One of two Laser Interferometer Gravitational-wave Observatory (LIGO) sites is located in the old Hanford site. Many small high technology businesses and consultancies have grown up around the Richland technology center. Richland is also a center of the Wine Region, and many fine wineries are located within the city.

An arm of the beamtube housing the interferometers at LIGO Hanford Observatory stretching out over the desert towards Rattlesnake Ridge.
Photo by Tobin Fricke

Hot Shotz Xtreme Laser Tag

RECREATION:
Best laser tag and video arcade

Hot Shotz Xtreme Laser Tag is the fun place to meet for memorable family entertainment, birthday parties and youth group activities. Family-owned and operated, Hot Shotz is the only laser tag facility in the area surrounding Richland. Owner Bob Foerderer and co-owner Michael Griffen take pride in providing enjoyable activities at affordable prices. A 5,000-square-foot darkened arena with swirling smoke, Halo 2 music and other game soundtracks provide the ultimate laser tag experience. Up to 30 people can play simultaneously for added excitement. Closed circuit television allows parents and spectators to view games in progress. In addition to laser tag, you'll find 18 amusing arcade games. Large-screen televisions show MTV videos and football games. A spacious party room is an inviting location for large or small gatherings. The staff can order pizza and drinks for your special event. Bob and Michael have created the family destination spot of their dreams and invite you to enjoy it along with them. Hot Shotz offers safe, clean family fun in a nonsmoking, air-conditioned environment. Located next to The Jungle and Chuck E. Cheese, Hot Shotz Xtreme Laser Tag is a popular spot for kids of all ages.

2630 N Columbine Center Boulevard, Richland WA
(509) 735-4438
www.hotshotzxtremelazertag.net

Club Paradise

RESTAURANTS & CAFÉS:
*Best live entertainment and
global cuisine*

Dance to live bands and enjoy world-inspired cuisine at festive Club Paradise. Housed in Richland's historic movie theater, this building has been transformed into an entertainment hot spot, featuring live entertainment and national acts along with Music Television and Country Music Television. Club Paradise is a great place to kick up your heels to many music styles. It received the Best Salsa Dance award for three years in a row, and offers lessons in Latin and ballroom-style dancing. The restaurant promises a multicultural feast with a menu of Caribbean, Chinese-American, Italian, Mexican and Russian dishes. You can count on an acclaimed chef to prepare superb meals, just one of the reasons why wedding banquets are a Club Paradise specialty. A full bar complements the dining and dancing experience. Club Paradise supports the local community by donating space for fundraisers and contributes to such youth organizations as the Boy Scouts and Girl Scouts. The club is located to serve travelers, who will find nearby lodging, and anyone living in the Tri-Cities area. Owners Raul Nava and Ana Cuevas invite you to Club Paradise, where you can count on a night of dining and dancing in paradise.

**2588 N Columbia Center Boulevard,
Richland WA
(509) 737-0020**

Rattlesnake Mountain Brewing Company

RESTAURANTS & CAFÉS: *Best brewpub*

Kimo Von Oelhoffen is considered one of the NFL's gentle giants. He started for the Pittsburgh Steelers against the Seattle Seahawks in Super Bowl XL. Kimo lives in Washington, where he owns Kimo's Sports Deli, located inside Rattlesnake Mountain Brewing Company. During the season, Steelers fans dominate the establishment early in the day when Pittsburgh plays back East. Later in the day, Seahawks fans take over to watch the home team in the West on one of the 19-inch, high-definition flat-screen televisions. In the off-season, Kimo stops by two or three times a week. He's always willing to sign autographs or talk to customers. He was quoted during the playoffs as calling his restaurant, "an island of certainty in a sea of wishful thinking." Kimo's caters to sports enthusiasts of all ages with good times, great beer and food. Entertainment goes beyond the games to include pool tables, a game room and live jazz, blues and rock 'n' roll. Large stainless steel holding tanks and fermentation tanks behind glass walls house Rattlesnake Mountain's naturally brewed beer, including Helluva Hefe, an American-style wheat ale. Guests can enjoy a brew while sitting on the patio overlooking the beautiful Columbia River. The company also operates R. F. McDougall's, a cozy Irish pub on West Columbia Park Trail, a tradition in the Tri-Cities since 1979. When you want a friendly hangout, a local brew and good food, head to Kimo's and the Rattlesnake Mountain Brewing Company, or visit R. F. McDougall's.

**2696 N Columbia Center Boulevard,
Richland WA
(509) 783-5747**

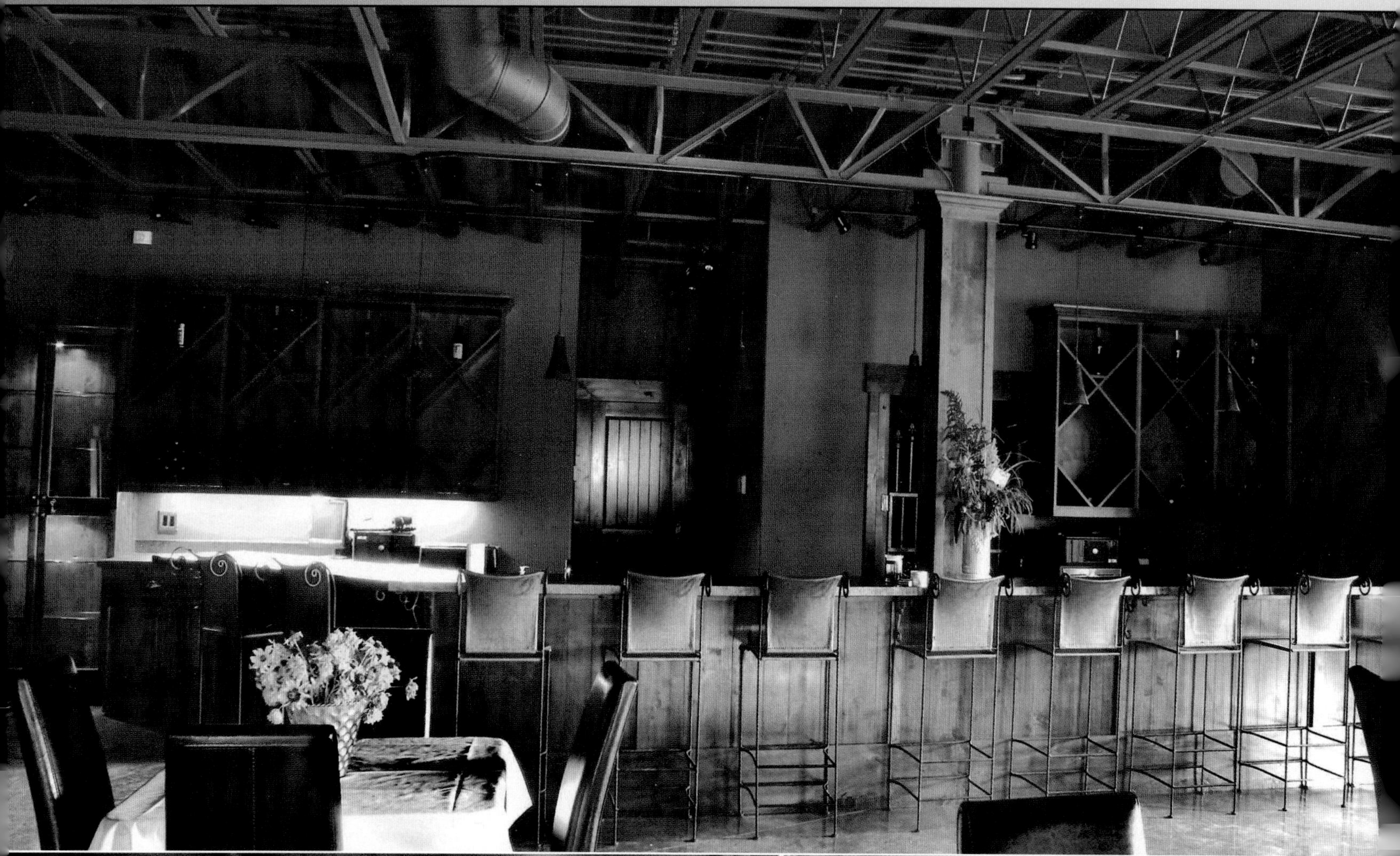

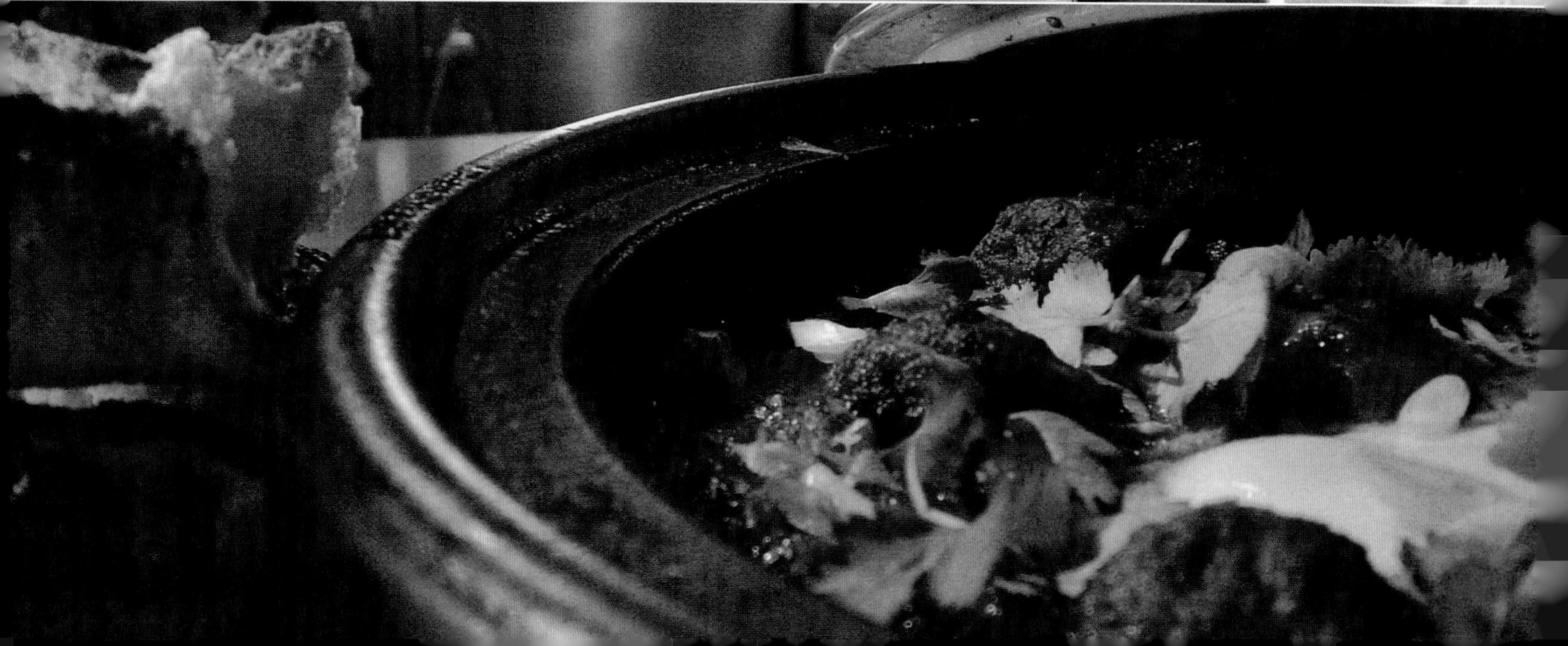

Tagaris Winery
WINERIES: *Best Richland winery*

Visitors to Tagaris Winery can sample fine wines in the tasting room, in front of a cozy fireplace, on the veranda or over a meal served in an intimate bistro. Michael Taggares founded the winery in 1987, returning his family name to the proper Greek spelling. Michael is the third generation in his family to grow grapes in the Columbia River Valley. This winery produces both white and red wines from old-vine vineyards, located in microclimates where conditions support wines with big, bold fruit flavors. The vineyards span 200 acres and produce 16 varieties of wine. The Taverna at Tagaris rounds out your experience of the best things in life with Mediterranean-inspired cuisine served in an inviting space with large tables, a wine bar and a lounge. For intimate, private gatherings, inquire about the Estate Room, which opens onto a private balcony. Summertime brings open-air dining and light fare created at the Patio Kouzina, the winery's outdoor Greek kitchen. The large veranda features a 33-foot fountain, an outdoor fireplace, two firepits and live music. This beautiful establishment is thoughtfully designed and makes a splendid showcase for fine food and incomparable wine. Chef Chris Ainsworth creates seasonal menus that feature Pacific Northwest meats and seafoods and local fruits and vegetables. Visit Tagaris Winery, where food and wine receive the respect and attention Mediterranean cultures have always reserved for the staples of life.

844 Tulip Lane, Richland WA
(509) 628-0020
www.tagariswines.com

PLACES TO GO

- Bonneville Dam Washington Shore Visitor Complex
  Milepost 40, State Route 14
  (541) 374-8820

- Columbia Gorge Interpretive Center
  990 SW Rock Creek Drive
  (800) 991-2338

- Beacon Rock State Park
  State Route 14, Skamania

THINGS TO DO

June
- Brews, Blues and Barbecues
  Waterfront, Stevenson
  (800) 989-9178

- Carson Fish Hatchery Open House
  (509) 427-5905

July
- Red, Wine and Blues & Art Too!
  Columbia Gorge Interpretive Center
  (800) 991-2338

- Gorge Days in North Bonneville
  (509) 427-8182

- Skamania Folk Festival
  Fairgrounds, Stevenson
  (509) 427-3980

- Adventure Bluegrass Festival
  Fairgrounds
  (509) 427-3980

August
- Skamania County Fair
  Fairgrounds
  (509) 427-3979

September
- Beacon Rock Heritage Days
  North Bonneville
  (509) 427-5383

- Hoptoberfest
  (509) 427-5520

- Spring Creek Fish Hatchery Open House
  (509) 493-1730

October
- Woodland Fairy Fall Weekend
  Bonneville Hot Springs Resort
  (800) 989-9178

STEVENSON

Stevenson is the seat of Skamania County, almost all of which is taken up by the Gifford Pinchot National Forest and the Cascades. Hiking, mountain climbing and camping are popular. Mount St. Helens is inside the northwest corner of Skamania County, though it is accessed from the east. Mount Adams is just outside the northeast corner. Much of the action in the county, however, is in the Columbia River Gorge to the south, which is dominated by the mighty Bonneville Locks and Dam.

Skamania Lodge

ACCOMMODATIONS:
Best lodge-style resort

Skamania Lodge, conference center and rustic mountain resort destination is surrounded by the waterfalls, peaks, forests and canyons of the majestic Columbia River Gorge. The warmth of the Lodge is characterized by Native American-inspired rugs, original stone rubbings, warm woolen fabrics and Mission-style wood furnishings, along with some of the most spectacular scenic views in the world. Guestrooms include forest view rooms, river view rooms and one-bedroom parlor suites. The amenities are numerous. The Lodge, member of the International Association of Conference Centers, offers 22,000 square feet of meeting, exhibition and banquet space. Onsite audio/visual equipment and technical support are provided. The Cascade Room at Dolce Skamania Lodge features casual fine dining, serving breakfast, lunch and dinner with an incredible view of the Columbia River and the Cascade Mountain Range. Their menu features hearty, Northwest seasonal cuisine that is centered around a wood-fired oven. Inspired by the great National Park lodges of the Northwest, the dining room has an open, festive feeling with wood and iron décor and a floor that dates back more than 200 years. The Kamania Golf Center features a beautiful and challenging 18-hole, par-70 golf course. The indoor Fitness Center includes a 20-yard swimming pool, sun deck and spa. There are also tennis courts, sand volleyball court and more than four miles of hiking or biking paths. Visit Skamania Lodge and enjoy.

1131 Skamania Lodge Way, Stevenson WA
(509) 427-7700 or (800) 221-7117
www.skamania.com

Bonneville Lock and Dam

ATTRACTIONS: *Best place to see migrating salmon*

The Visitor Centers at Bonneville Lock and Dam are located at Bradford Island for the Oregon side and at Washington Shore for the Washington side. Visitors on the Oregon side will find a five-level facility with an observation deck, interior exhibits, a large theater and panoramic views of the Columbia River Gorge, drawing hundreds of thousands of visitors a year to the Dam and Locks. Just a walk away is the viewing area inside the first Powerhouse. Visitors can also watch the navigation lock in operation on the Oregon shore. On the Washington side, visitors will enjoy one of the world's most accessible views of a powerhouse. Inside the powerhouse, visitors will see generators from 85 feet above the powerhouse floor, get close-up views of a generator and can examine a rotating turbine shaft through special viewing windows. Visitors can also enjoy fish ladder viewing from this location. Learn about alternative transportation modes, why river transport is an important ecological choice and how power is managed. Learn to identify the local fish types, which are endangered and what is the best time of year to view each type. Educational centers provide films and displays about hydropower, river navigation and the history of this significant area. The Visitors Centers at Bonneville Lock and Dam can be reached by taking Interstate 84 to exit 40 or Washington State Highway 14 to milepost 40. The Bridge of the Gods, located about 2 miles upstream from the Dam, links Oregon and Washington.

(541) 374-8820
www.nwp.usace.army.mil/op/b/

PLACES TO GO

- Carnegie Art Center
  109 S Palouse Street
  (509) 525-4270

- Children's Museum of Walla Walla
  77 Wainwright Place
  (509) 526-PLAY (7529)

- Fort Walla Walla Museum
  755 Myra Road
  (509) 525-7703

- Kirkman House Museum
  214 N Colville Street
  (509) 529-4373

- Pioneer Park Aviary
  Whitman Street and S Division Street
  (509) 527-4403

- Whitman Mission National Historic Site
  U.S. Highway 12
  (509) 529-2761

- Fort Walla Walla Park
  Dalles Military Road and NE Myra Road

- Pioneer Park
  E Alder Street and S Division Street

THINGS TO DO

April
- Whitman College Renaissance Faire
  (509) 527-5111

May
- Hot Air Balloon Stampede
  Fairgrounds (877) WWVISIT (998-4748)

June
- Lewis and Clark Days
  Fort Walla Walla Museum
  (509) 525-7703

- Art Promenade
  (509) 301-0185

July
- Walla Walla Sweet Onion Festival
  Fairgrounds
  (509) 525-1031

August
- Taste of Walla Walla
  Main Street
  (509) 529-8755

- Walla Walla Fair and Frontier Days
  Fairgrounds
  (509)527-3247

WALLA WALLA

The Walla Walla Valley was one of the first areas between the Rockies and Cascades to be permanently settled. Explorers discovered gold in 1860, and Walla Walla quickly became a commercial, banking and manufacturing center, the largest city in Washington Territory. After the gold rush ended, farming anchored the community. Agriculture remains vital. As a group, Walla Walla County's farms are the oldest in the state. More than half of the county's 47 centennial farms were established before 1875. Peas, wheat, sweet onions and similar crops remain important, but the wine grape is today's agricultural treasure. The Walla Walla wine appellation is one of the most highly esteemed in the nation.

Tucker Inn Guest House

ACCOMMODATIONS: *Best private accommodations*

For vacation lodging that is a bit out of the ordinary, how about renting an entire house? In Walla Walla, the Tucker Inn Guest House can be rented for visitors who want to feel at home. This appealing inn has three bedrooms and two baths. The three bedrooms hold roomy queen-size beds, and the living room contains a comfortable hide-away bed. The house can easily quarter six people, or eight with one couple staying in the Cranberry bedroom on the lower level. Even if only two couples share the building, the house is surprisingly affordable. Rates do go up during certain peak weekends scattered throughout the year. The Tucker Inn provides digital cable TV, a computer with broadband Internet and wireless Internet for those who bring a laptop. The kitchen is equipped with a gas range, electric convection oven and all of the necessary equipment. Wine enthusiasts will enjoy drinking out of Riedel Vinum glasses. The dining room table expands to accommodate eight diners. Quality linens are found throughout the home. A washer and dryer are available in the utility room. The backyard features a gas barbecue, table and chairs. Tucker Inn is emphatically pet friendly. Dogs are warmly welcomed, and so are children. The backyard is fenced for Fido's safety. The guest house is located conveniently near downtown. Rea and Todd Tucker invite you to Tucker Inn Guest House, and will do whatever they can to help make your stay a pleasure.

1134 S Howard Street, Walla Walla WA
(888) 399-2308
www.tuckerinnww.com

City Slickers Salon & Spa

HEALTH & BEAUTY:
Best Aveda salon

City Slickers Salon & Spa is an Aveda concept salon that offers the complete product line, including hair care, color and retexturing services. For the past six years, owner Sandra LeFore has worked to earn the recognition and support of the prestigious Aveda Company. The all-natural, plant based products provide some of the most beautiful colors in the world. The staff at City Slickers Salon & Spa engage in advanced training to introduce and support cutting-edge trends in hairstyling, cut and color, as well as innovative new products and concepts in botanical science and aromatherapy. Setting the standard for beauty and environmental leadership, Aveda Salons have a worldwide network with headquarters around the globe. Every season Aveda stylists rock the runways during Fashion Week in New York, London and Milan. The staff of City Slickers takes joy in providing customers with personalized attention and products that they will love. The stylists will enhance your well-being from roots to ends. The colorists are artists with the ability to make your color truly yours. They take special care of the fried and the flipped, the over-dyed and the dull, as they inspire the uninspired. City Slickers does it all with pure flower and plant ingredients, allowing nature's beauty to naturally enhance yours. Make time to free your hair, your body and your mind with Aveda. Make your life even better than it already is at City Slickers Salon & Spa.

14 W Main Street, Walla Walla WA
(509) 529-2108

Walla Walla Valley Wine Alliance

WINERIES: *Wine growers working together*

With more than 1,200 acres of vineyards, the Walla Walla Valley is quickly taking its place as one of the top wine producing regions in the world. The Walla Walla Valley Wine Alliance is a group of area wineries and growers committed to working together toward the success of local wines. Well known for its red wines, particularly Cabernet Sauvignon and Merlot, the Walla Walla Valley is an ideal location for growing grapes, thanks to long, warm summer days, cool evenings and limited rainfall. The Alliance offers many special events that involve the wineries, such as the Vintage Walla Walla Tasting in early June. This tasting features older vintages and rare wines, as well as new releases from the Valley's wineries. With its newly revitalized downtown and the stunning Blue Mountains in the background, Walla Walla abounds with places to enjoy a glass of Syrah or another regional wine. This vineyard-dotted valley is one of the reasons that Wine Enthusiast Magazine named Washington State the Wine Region of the Year in 2001. Contact the Walla Walla Valley Wine Alliance for a calendar of wine-related events and detailed information on local wines.

128 N 2nd Avenue, Suite 219, Walla Walla WA (509) 526-3117 *www.wallawallawine.com*

Photos by Hans Matschukat

Yakima Valley

Yakima Valley

Lush green field

THE YAKIMA VALLEY is the gateway to Washington's Wine Country. The Valley, extending east past Prosser, contains three of Washington's most important wine appellations—Yakima Valley, Red Mountain and Rattlesnake Hills. Many of the wineries are open to the public, and wine tours are an increasingly popular activity.

Yakima County is Washington's most productive agricultural county and the sixteenth most productive county in the entire United States. It leads the nation in apples, winter pears, hops and mint. Mount Adams, in the far southwest of Yakima County, is the second highest mountain in the state. It can be seen from viewpoints throughout the valley and serves as a local emblem.

The city of Yakima is the anchor of the region and is an excellent base for exploring the valley. The Yakama Indian Reservation lies south of the city of Yakima and stretches west to Mount Adams.

East of Yakima, each of the towns along the Yakima River offers its own attractions. Toppenish, a city of murals and museums, is within the reservation and is the headquarters of the Yakama nation.

Zillah is a center for the Rattlesnake Hills appellation. Sunnyside sponsors the states' largest Cinco de Mayo celebration, which honors the many immigrants from Mexico drawn to the valley's agricultural bounty. Wineries surround Prosser, a town noted for its many festivals. The largest, on the fourth full weekend of September, includes the Grea Prosser Balloon Rally, the harvest festival and a street painting festival. Come visit the Yakima Valley, a land of fruit and honey.

GRANDVIEW

Grandview's economy is based on agriculture, with apples, cherries, hops and other fruit and vegetable production supported by processing plants and cold storage facilities. Of course, there are grapes and wineries. The community's grand view is both of snow capped Mount Rainier and Mount Adams dominating the horizon to the west and of the Rattlesnake Hills and Horse Heaven Hills to the north and south. The Yakima Valley enjoys an average of 300 days of sunshine per year.

PLACES TO GO

- Ray E. Powell Museum
  311 Division Street
  (509) 882-9238

- Country Park
  812 Wallace Way

THINGS TO DO

February
- Red Wine and Chocolate
  (800) 258-7270

April
- Spring Fling
  (509) 882-2100

August
- Yakima Valley Fair and Rodeo
  Country Park (509) 786-8250

September
- Grandview Grape Stomp
  (509) 882-2100

Ashley's Catering
BUSINESS: *Best catering*

For more than 35 years, Ashley's Catering has provided the Yakima Valley with creative cuisine, flawless event organizing and unparalleled customer service. Ruth Ashley and her husband, Charles, created Ashley's Catering in 1970. Ruth continues to maintain an advisor role, but the Ashleys' grandson, Bradley Charvet, now manages the business on a day-to-day basis. Event planning begins when the customer meets with an experienced and attentive event consultant, who custom designs the menu and coordinates décor and presentation to ensure a spectacular result. Weddings are one of the many specialties at Ashley's Catering. Class and family reunions and corporate functions are also handled here. Ashley's is not limited to providing delicious, fresh food. Its consultants can provide a one-of-a-kind outdoor site loaded with beautiful waterfalls and water gardens containing numerous Koi and Goldfish. They can advise on standard wedding customs or one-of-a-kind variations to make your event that much more special. In addition to the wedding itself, Ashley's can help with bridal luncheons, showers, post-wedding receptions and a host of other gatherings. Business catering has become a mainstay at Ashley's Catering. Ashley's Express is a menu designed for corporate clients. Whether your team is working late or preparing to host a critical meeting, Ashley's can bring fresh, healthful food to your door. Ashley's menus can be formal or casual. Cuisines can include Mexican, Italian or barbecue. Innovative menus are available for breakfasts, luncheons and receptions. If you have a reason to celebrate, Ashley's Catering can help you experience the moment.

1641 Grandridge Road, Grandview WA
(509) 882-1457
www.ashleys-catering.com

Karen's Floral
GARDENS, PLANTS & FLOWERS:
Best floral arrangements

Karen's Floral is a genuine Grandview tradition. Karen Homer's mother founded the family flower business 25 years ago, and three generations of the family have worked at the shop. Designer Betty Trevino has been with Karen's Floral for 15 years. Specialties of the store include fresh and silk arrangements, accessories and balloons. Karen's Floral was one of the first florists in the Yakima Valley to carry fresh roses from Ecuador. Weddings and funerals always receive Karen's exceptional personalized service, which on occasion has meant being available 24 hours a day. Needless to say, Karen's Floral delivers. Karen's Floral also offers gourmet gift baskets that combine flowers with Yakima Valley products, such as the region's acclaimed wines. Customer satisfaction is Karen's number-one concern, and 100-percent satisfaction is guaranteed. Karen's Floral participates in major florist alliances, such as FTD. For any occasion that calls for flowers, visit or contact Karen's Floral.

802 W Wine Country Road, Grandview WA
(509) 882-1026
www.ftdfloristsonline.com/karenswa

The Lawns at Hollow Way Meadows
RECREATION: *Best place for lawn sports*

The Lawns at Hollow Way Meadows is a lawn sports park, located in the beautiful Yakima Valley and owned by Merle and Dorothy Cohu. Hollow Way Meadows promotes the lawn sports of croquet, lawn bowling and bocce ball, as well as the socializing that accompanies the games. The park also provides facilities for volleyball, badminton and horseshoes. Memberships are available by the year or the month, but the park is a public facility, and drop-by players are always welcome. Hollow Way Meadows offers the opportunity to join a local United States Croquet Association Club, the Hollow Way Meadows Croquet Club. You can also join the national associations for lawn bowling or bocce ball. The park even has a pro shop. Hollow Way Meadows makes special provisions for children visiting in grade school groups or through the summer YMCA program. Group rates are available, but the park asks that groups make reservations. Hollow Way Meadows offers light refreshments, such as iced tea, and groups may organize their own catering. The lovely lawns and many activities make the Lawns a pleasant choice for a birthday party or wedding. Step out of the world into a personal, green getaway at the Lawns at Hollow Way Meadows. The playing season lasts from March 15 to November 1. Come visit once, and you may find yourself hooked on hitting the lawn.

1017 S Euclid Road, Grandview WA
(509) 882-3150

Dykstra House Restaurant, Gifts & Antiques
RESTAURANTS & CAFÉS: *Best out-of-the-way restaurant*

The Dykstra House Restaurant and Gift Shop is a leading Grandview restaurant with a notable ambience and food selections that have gained the attention of the press and the public. A visit here will demonstrate why Dykstra House earned a place in *Northwest Best Places*, and readers of *Pacific Northwest* magazine named it Best Out-of-the-Way Restaurant. The romantic setting is a 1914 Craftsman-style house of brick and stucco, formerly owned by a Grandview mayor. The house has been named a National Historic Site. Owner Linda Hartshorn first purchased it for her picture framing business before turning it into a fine food restaurant in 1984. Guests can enjoy three fireplaces, rich antique furniture and fine dining. The fireplace located in the main dining area is the Hearthside Dreams, designed by Ernest Batchelder. The restaurant offers Northwest cuisine with regional wines and beers. The homemade asparagus and gazpacho soups are famous, and the restaurant's recipe for raspberry vinaigrette has appeared in *Sunset* magazine. Breads are made from hand-ground, locally grown wheat. Lunch features fresh salads, sandwiches and daily specials. Friday night is Italian night, and Saturday night dinners feature chicken, beef or fish. Upstairs rooms are available for private luncheons or dinners. Catering is also available. The gift shop offers cards, crafts and other treasures. Dykstra House Restaurant and Gift Shop is a place for all seasons.

114 Birch Avenue, Grandview WA
(509) 882-2082

Garcia's Drive-Thru Restaurant
RESTAURANTS & CAFÉS: *Best Tex-Mex food*

Paul Garcia wanted it all—to live in the Yakima Valley and bring the favorite foods from his Texas youth to this wine country. The authentic Tex-Mex food at Garcia's Drive-Thru Restaurant in Grandview is the culmination of that dream. Years ago, owner Paul Garcia came up from Texas to the Yakima Valley to visit his aunt and fell in love with the area. He worked for several years as a medical interpreter before finding the opportunity to start his family business in 2001. The result is Garcia's Drive-Thru Restaurant, where the Tex-Mex meals are fast, authentic and homemade. The restaurant quickly became a hit. Paul's best-selling items are tamales, fajitas and tacos. Garcia's uses only certified Angus beef, assuring a high quality meal. Be sure to try the monster burritos. Paul also specializes in custom orders. Festive music plays while you sit at the covered outdoor tables. People from Seattle to Spokane stop at Exit 73 on Interstate 82 for a satisfying taste experience. Next time you are in Washington wine country, visit Garcia's Drive-Thru Restaurant and sample the flavors Paul missed most when he left Texas.

1027 W Wine Country Road, Grandview WA
(509) 882-0239

PROSSER

Prosser, the Birthplace of Washington's wine industry, is a must-stop on any wine tour. Wineries sponsor special tasting events throughout the year. The Prosser Wine and Food Park sponsors many of these. The park is a 90-acre site that houses wineries and other businesses. Downtown Prosser is known for its distinctive character, historic design and relaxing appeal. Prosser is also the seat of Benton County.

PLACES TO GO

- City Park
  7th Street, Memorial and Sommers Avenue

- E. J. Miller Park
  Park Avenue and Kinney Way

- Crawford Riverfront Park
  W Byron Road

THINGS TO DO

February
- Red Wine and Chocolate
  800) 258-7270

March
- Sweet Retreat tastings
  (509) 786-3177

April
- Spring Fling
  (800) 408-1517

May
- Wine Country Spring Fair
  (509) 375-3060

June
- Prosser Scottish Fest
  (509) 375-3060

July
- Gallery Walk & Wine Gala
  (800) 408-1517

September
- Great Prosser Balloon Rally
  (509) 786-4134

- Harvest and Street Painting Festivals
  (800) 408-1517

August
- Prosser Wine and Food Fair
  (800) 408-1517

The Barn Restaurant & Lounge, Motor Inn RV Park

ACCOMMODATIONS: *Wine Country lodgings and food*

There are not many places that everyone loves, but the Barn Restaurant & Lounge, Motor Inn RV Park is certainly such a place. As soon as you walk in, you will feel like you are visiting with old friends, so prepare to make yourself comfortable and stay a while. The Barn is located next to Prosser Airport and minutes from more than a dozen wineries. The lounge features a full bar, local wines and a cozy fireplace. The restaurant, which got its start in 1946, serves breakfast, lunch and dinner. An affable waitstaff serves hearty steak and seafood dinners, and Sunday brunch is so good that people have been known to fly into the nearby airport just for the meal. The Barn includes a 30-unit motel. It features an outdoor swimming pool, air-conditioned rooms and room service. If you happen to be driving through with your RV, you can pull into one of the 16 full-service RV parking sites. The Barn is a town landmark, built as a dairy barn in 1908. The surrounding countryside still supports dairy and beef cattle, and farmers here grow fruit, grapes and grains. Owners Duke and Linda Pappenheim are strong supporters of their community, and local organizations like Rotary Club, Kiwanis and Prosser Chamber of Commerce routinely meet in one of the Barn's banquet rooms. Whether you are coming from near or far, the Barn Motor Inn, Restaurant & Lounge is a destination certain to make you want to stay a while.

490 Wine Country Road, Prosser WA
(509) 786-2121 or (509) 786-1131
www.barnmotorinn.com

Best Western The Inn at Horse Heaven

ACCOMMODATIONS: *Best hotel in wine country*

The Inn at Horse Heaven has assembled a first-rate team of professionals to make your stay at this Best Western as comfortable as possible. General manager Don West, assistant manager Lilli Prieto and sales director Jacob Van Pelt and their staff make you feel right at home with quality service and true concern for your needs. The Inn at Horse Heaven places you in the heart of Washington wine country, with vineyard views from the lobby's expansive windows. You will find golfing, river sports and world-class wineries close at hand. Your room features a refrigerator, microwave and hair dryer. Amenities include free breakfast buffet, an exercise room and a heated outdoor pool with a tanning deck. Two spacious meeting rooms make the Inn at Horse Heaven a perfect place for businesses and organizations to convene. Computers, fax and Internet access are available. The inn is a proud jewel in the Best Western chain, serving the community through event sponsorship and the promoting of area tourism. Stay at the Inn at Horse Heaven, and feel what it is like to have a dedicated team working for you.

259 Merlot Drive, Prosser WA
(509) 786-7090 or (800) 688-2192
www.bestwestern.com

4 Seasons River Inn
ACCOMMODATIONS: *Best bed and breakfast*

The 4 Seasons River Inn is a special bed and breakfast that justifies a visit to the Yakima Valley all by itself. The Inn boasts a spectacular location right on the Yakima River in the heart of the wine country. Three bedrooms and a separate cottage are available. Not only is the setting serene, the amenities are exceptional for such a small inn. Guests enjoy a heated pool and spa, games like tennis and pool, and a fitness center. The elegant, modern house has several rooms in which guests can relax. The living room has a large rock fireplace. An intimate sitting area adjacent to the living room is an inviting place for board games, cards or conversation. The casual and comfortable family room has DVDs you can watch on the wide-screen television. A large deck sports an incredible view. By special request, guests can reserve the well equipped gourmet kitchen for their own culinary pursuits. Of course, your breakfast is prepared in this kitchen, as well. Your hosts are Les and Nancy Bender, who have lived in Europe, Central America and South Africa. They have made new acquaintances everywhere they have lived and traveled, and they have a wealth of fascinating stories. The guest rooms are thematically decorated and two have Sleep Number® Beds from Select Comfort®. Make your visit to the Yakima Valley complete with a stay at the 4 Seasons River Inn.

16202 S Griffin Road, Prosser WA
(509) 786-1694 or (509) 778-1695
www.4seasonsriverinn.com

Yellow Rose Nursery

GARDENS, PLANTS & FLOWERS:
Best water gardens and demonstration gardens

Garden designer Lou Gannon can help you put together a garden or landscape with a theme that expresses your sense of style. Lou, who owns Yellow Rose Nursery with his wife, Teresa, has traveled extensively and studied the gardens of the world, from the magnificent gardens of Japan and Europe to those of India's Taj Mahal. He holds a bachelor of science in landscape architecture, is a licensed landscape architect and has 30 years of practical experience helping gardeners attain their goals. The nursery can help you design water gardens, from simple koi ponds to more elaborate gardens that incorporate streams and waterfalls. Various themed garden displays, such as Pacific Northwest, English and Mediterranean, show plants in their natural settings to allow you to see how different plants can be used to achieve the look you want. The Gannons are especially proud of the Tree of Life display. Ground cover plants are available, as are trees and water plants. Yellow Rose stocks many varieties of rocks, soils and fertilizers for completing and maintaining your garden. Hanging baskets make perfect gifts for nearly anyone. The Yellow Rose stocks Smith and Hawken gardening tools and furniture to make working and relaxing in your garden distinct pleasures. Lou and Teresa believe in going the extra mile for their clients, so in addition to design and plant sales, Yellow Rose provides complete installation services. Stop by the Yellow Rose Nursery and enjoy the landscape.

600 Merlot Drive, Prosser WA
(509) 786-3304

Lower Valley Athletic Club
HEALTH & BEAUTY: *Best fitness club*

Whether you are a long-time fitness buff or just starting to work out, Lower Valley Athletic Club can be your partner as you strive to feel and look great. Owners Rodd and Peggy Buttars run a clean and bright facility with cutting-edge programs and cardio and weight equipment that's always in tip-top shape. They offer all of the high quality features you would expect from larger fitness clubs, including a swimming pool and spa, a climbing wall, and a supervised play room to keep children active and occupied while their parents work out.

The exercise classes are first rate, too, and feature BodyPump and BodyFlow exercise programs formulated by Les Mills International. BodyPump is an athletic workout using adjustable weights and upbeat music, and BodyFlow incorporates elements of tai chi, Pilates and yoga. Customer service is a number one priority at the club; a friendly and knowledgeable staff is always happy to explain equipment use or proper techniques. The staff wants you to feel welcome and comfortable, so you can make exercise a regular part of your lifestyle. Whatever your fitness needs, Lower Valley Athletic Club has the equipment and expertise to help you reach those goals.

1419 Sheridan Avenue, Prosser WA
(509) 786-4753
www.northwest-sports.com

Prosser's Family Fun Center
RECREATION: *Best family-friendly place to play*

When it comes to family fun, Prosser's Family Fun Center knows how to keep adults and kids entertained. Owners Paul and Wendy Paeschke and their three children all work together to make the center a safe, family-friendly place for kids to hang out. It is evident in the way they run the business that they truly care about the children that come in. The younger crowd loves roller skating here or trying for a new top score in the arcade. On the rink, they can play organized skate games like the popular Slimy Fish Catch. For the older set who no longer see the appeal in Slimy Fish Catch, Prosser's Family Fun Center offers an on-site espresso bar, where mom and dad can relax and enjoy a hot mocha while watching the skaters. For something a little more filling, try the Mustang Grill, named after the Prosser High School state champions. The grill serves up what local residents have been known to call the best burgers in town. For good clean fun for the whole family, come spend an evening at Prosser's Family Fun Center.

602 7th Street, Prosser WA
(509) 786-3515

World's Edge

RECREATION: *Best selection of skateboards and snowboards*

From skateboards and snowboards to paintball guns and accessories, World's Edge skate shop has got you covered. Twenty-four-year-old combat veteran William Peterson turned his dream of providing world-class sports equipment and clothing into reality with the opening of his shop in January 2006. He kept his dream firmly in mind while serving as an infantry medic in the Iraq war and in travels from coast to coast. He even managed to eye some boards while deployed in Bosnia. He's put his sports savvy to use to open the only paintball and skate shop in the Lower Valley. His large inventory includes such radical brand-name equipment as Flip Skateboards, Tech 9 Snowboards, Independent Trucks, Element Skateboards and Empire Paintball products. Located near Prosser's world-class skate park, World's Edge features gear and accessories for up-and-coming professional skaters, as well as local enthusiasts. William is a certified skateboard and snowboard technician who can keep your equipment in top shape for best performance. He thanks parents Mary and Bill Peterson and longtime friends Cooper Carter, Matt Bateman and Terri Clark for help in opening his downtown Prosser shop. Whether you're a kid, mom, skater or snowboarder, World's Edge can put excitement into your extreme play.

1207½ Meade Avenue, Prosser WA
(509) 786-7008
www.sk8worldsedge.com

Bern's Tavern
RESTAURANTS & CAFÉS:
Best old time saloon

Planet Prosser Pale Ale can be found at just one place, Bern's Tavern in Prosser. It is a perfect stop when traveling along I-82, about midway between Yakima and Tri-Cities. The original antique back bar is housed in a building dating back to the early 1900s. Bern's, owned by Darren and Carla Dodgson, is a landmark, one of the few remaining taverns in the State. Of nearly a dozen saloons from the past, it is the only one left in Prosser. Bern's is famous for its Bern's burger and other great pub foods, music and comedy. The museum-like décor represents 100 years of town history. Musical instruments are used as decorations, and many world-class entertainers pop in for the occasional hideaway gig. The environment is laid back, a place where everyone seems to know each other, but where visitors feel welcomed. Calling Bern's a *sports bar* would be an understatement. There is a television in each booth and many more placed throughout. You can have your privacy or socialize away. In true pub fashion there are pool tables, music, video games and the great fun of gambling pull-tabs. Bern's sells many microbrews and all your old favorites, as well as Washington Wines. Stop in, relax and be entertained, especially if Darren is there. Darren has beaten those drums professionally for 25 years. Bern's was his first gig, at the age of 14, in the late 1970s. Darren and Carla purchased the business from Carla's parents a decade ago, but her father, Carl Grimes, can still be seen helping out. Patrons insist old ghosts roam the city from the real Underground that once existed and partially remains. In Bern's Tavern, a persistent lone cowboy and a sailor in an old uniform, are often glimpsed. Stop in for some fun and great food at Bern's Tavern. See all there is to see, and maybe more.

618 6th Street, Prosser WA
(509) 786-1422

El Caporal Family Mexican Restaurant

RESTAURANTS & CAFÉS:
Best Mexican food and margaritas

There's a mutual admiration society in the Yakima Valley, and its headquarters is the El Caporal in Prosser. For years, the staff has been greeting guests with a hearty "Bienvenidos, Amigos" (Welcome, Friends), serving them cheerfully, and sending them home well fed. In return, folks keep coming back to this cozy and comfortable family-run restaurant. More than that, locals have bestowed award after award on El Caporal for its hospitality, service and food. This proud business has been voted Best Small Business of the Year in the valley, as well as the best place for Mexican food. Its margaritas, too, have been named the best in the area, making it the perfect way to begin your lunch or dinner. The full bar also features a fine selection of local wines. For your main course, the menu offers a seemingly endless list of tempting choices. Favorites include the fajitas, served on a sizzling platter, and *arroz con pollo*. One of El Caporal's legion of satisfied customers left this comment: "We love your smiles, great service and fabulous foods." Those sound like three great reasons to make El Caporal your dining choice.

624 6th Street, Prosser WA
(509) 786-4910

The Barn Restaurant & Lounge, Motor Inn RV Park

RESTAURANTS & CAFÉS: *Great casual eats*

There are not many places that everyone loves, but the Barn Restaurant & Lounge, Motor Inn RV Park is certainly such a place. As soon as you walk in, you will feel like you are visiting with old friends, so prepare to make yourself comfortable and stay a while. The Barn is located next to Prosser Airport and minutes from more than a dozen wineries. The lounge features a full bar, local wines and a cozy fireplace. The restaurant, which got its start in 1946, serves breakfast, lunch and dinner. An affable waitstaff serves hearty steak and seafood dinners, and Sunday brunch is so good that people have been known to fly into the nearby airport just for the meal. The Barn includes a 30-unit motel. It features an outdoor swimming pool, air-conditioned rooms and room service. If you happen to be driving through with your RV, you can pull into one of the 16 full-service RV parking sites. The Barn is a town landmark, built as a dairy barn in 1908. The surrounding countryside still supports dairy and beef cattle, and farmers here grow fruit, grapes and grains. Owners Duke and Linda Pappenheim are strong supporters of their community, and local organizations like Rotary Club, Kiwanis and Prosser Chamber of Commerce routinely meet in one of the Barn's banquet rooms. Whether you are coming from near or far, the Barn Motor Inn, Restaurant & Lounge is a destination certain to make you want to stay a while.

490 Wine Country Road, Prosser WA
(509) 786-2121 or (509) 786-1131
www.barnmotorinn.com

Sister to Sister
SHOPPING: *Best boutique*

Have you ever noticed that sometimes when you go to a friend's house, you walk in the door and instantly feel welcomed? Some houses just make you feel right at home, calling for you to curl up with a good book and a cup of tea. Sister to Sister is a great little boutique that can help give your house that welcoming touch. As soon as you walk in, you will want to stay and browse. The store is packed with all kinds of home accents, jewelry and gifts. The items found here are carefully chosen for their rarity and are not found at big chain stores. Owners Ken and M'liss Bierlink carefully select each item and encourage their customers to stop by to see what's new and to stay for a friendly chat. If you dread the idea of traipsing around a crowded mall filled with harried shoppers and never quite finding the right thing, a trip to Sister to Sister should be a fun and relaxing change of pace. You'll find gifts for weddings and babies and probably a little treat for yourself. The shop provides complimentary gift wrapping. Visit Sister to Sister, and as the store's motto proclaims, Make the Place You Live the Place You Love.

1211 Meade Avenue, Prosser WA
(509) 786-SHOP (7467)

Coyote Canyon Winery and Lounge
WINERIES: *Best winery & lounge*

Coming from third and fourth generations of farming in the Horse Heaven Hills, Matt Gray and his stepfather, Mike Andrews, have added a winery to the long list of their family's accomplishments. Coyote Canyon Winery and Lounge is located in historic downtown Prosser. They showcase their wines in a relaxed wine lounge atmosphere of comfy couches and seats, gallery-quality artwork and a rotating live music series. From fine dining and simple whole foods to café-style fare, Coyote Canyon Winery and Lounge offers a complete wine and food experience. Premier wines, exclusive desserts, and special-order, small-plate selections combine with the hippest atmosphere in Prosser for just about any event you can imagine. Coyote Canyon Winery and Lounge also offers wine composition classes, food and wine pairing courses, four seasonal events with several Yakima Valley area wineries, and live music during Yakima Valley's special event weekends. Matt is the winery co-owner and managing partner, while Mike is the co-owner of the winery and managing partner of Coyote Canyon Vineyard. The family started making wine from their 2004 harvest, and 2006 is the first year of winery/lounge operations. 2006 also marks Coyote Canyon Vineyard's 12th year of operation. Visit Coyote Canyon, where you will experience wines of quality and complexity in a setting that is... heavenly.

717 6th Street, Prosser WA
winery: (509) 786-7686
www.coyotecanyonwinery.com

Winery co-owner Matt Gray
All photos by Kathy Kongelbak

Coyote Canyon Vineyard
WINERIES: *Award-winning grape growers and vintners*

In 1994, Coyote Canyon Vineyard, located in the Horse Heaven Hills, began growing premium wine grapes to sell to Pacific Northwest wineries. Coyote Canyon Vineyard grows both well known varietals, such as Merlot, Cabernet Sauvignon and Chardonnay, and lesser known varietals like Barbera, Tempranillo and Marsanne. Pend O'Reille Winery, which was named 2003 Idaho Winery of the Year, uses Coyote Canyon Cabernet Sauvignon and Merlot for their award-winning wines, while Syncline Wine Cellars has released a beautiful Viognier straight from the Vineyard. This year Yakima Cellars contracted its first harvest with Coyote Canyon for several acres of Sangiovese. Starting this year Bergevin Lane will be using Coyote Canyon Roussanne and Viognier grapes. Coyote Canyon Vineyard's largest contractor is Columbia Crest Winery, located in Patterson.

Mike Andrews checking his grapes

Coyote Canyon Winery and Lounge is arty, casual and very hip.

Willow Crest Winery

WINERIES: *Recognized by the New York Times for its premium wines*

It all starts with the vines, say David and Mandy Minick, owners of the award-winning Willow Crest Winery in Prosser. They should know. David grew up with grapes. His family supplied Concord grapes to Welches for many years. Then times changed and in the 1980s they converted the family farm to wine grapes. In 1995 he fulfilled a dream by founding Willow Crest Winery. David wanted to take the love he had for raising grapes to the next level by making premium wine. David is a true wine professional who has been written about in the New York Times and other publications. David has the knowledge and ability to take the fruit from vine to wine. His background shows in the quality of Willow Crest's wines. Willow Crest started out small, but by 2001 they were producing 3,000 cases a year. In 2004 they reached 5,000. Varieties include Pinot Gris, Syrah, Mourvedre, Cabernet Franc, Syrah Port, and assorted late harvests and sparkling wines. They were one of the first wineries in Washington to produce Pinot Gris, and the first to do Syrah Port, Syrah Sparkling, and Mourvedre. Overlooking the Yakima Valley from a 1,300-foot elevation, six miles north of Prosser, Willow Crest features state-of-the-art equipment. Their tasting room is in a quintessentially classic farmhouse with great views of the vineyards. Willow Crest wine is smooth on the palate and lingers in the memory. Take tour of the winery and see for yourself. If you can't make it today, you can order Willow Crest wines on-line. QFC and other outlets statewide also stock Willow Crest wines.

590 Merlot Drive, Prosser WA
(509) 786-7999
www.willowcrestwinery.com

The Hogue Cellars

WINERIES: *One of the Columbia Valley's largest wine producers*

Farming has been a way if life for three generations in the Hogue family. In 1974, Mike Hogue planted the family's first wine grapes in the Yakima Valley. In 1982, Mike and Gary Hogue opened the Hogue Cellars. Today, the Hogue Cellars ships over half a million cases of wine a year, making Hogue one of the largest producers in the Columbia Valley. The winery is also one of the best. Wine & Spirits magazine has repeatedly named Hogue as one of its Wineries of the Year, most recently in 1998. The climate and soils of the Columbia Valley produce wines with ripe, zesty fruit flavors that make them ideal complements to a wide range of food. The valley contains several sub-regions, such as Horse Heaven Hills, Wahluke Slope and Walla Walla. Hogue takes its grapes from growers who have correctly matched grape varieties with the specific local soil and climate. The growers include Gary Hogue himself, who grows grapes as well as leading the cellar's marketing effort. Another key staff member is David Forsyth, general manager and director of winemaking. Like Hogue's other winemakers, David has academic training and long industry experience. You can experience Hogue wines at the cellar's tasting room in Prosser. Hogue Cellars also accepts Internet orders. Come taste the award winning wines at the Hogue Cellars tasting room.

2800 Lee Road, Prosser WA
(509) 786-4557 ext. 208 or (800) 565-9779
www.hoguecellars.com

Hinzerling Winery

WINERIES: *Oldest family-owned winery*

If you are interested in learning more about the art of winemaking, a visit to Hinzerling Winery will satisfy your curiosity. The Wallace family planted the first grapes here in 1972, making Hinzerling the oldest family-owned and operated winery in the Yakima Valley. Hinzerling Winery specializes in small lots of handcrafted, boldly flavored wines. The winery produces a dry Gerwurtzminer along with vintage ports, sherries, muscats and other dessert and late harvest wine styles. Mike Wallace, son of founder Jerry Wallace, is the winemaker here. Mike studied winemaking at the University of California at Davis graduate program in viticulture and enology. The winery is located in the center of Prosser and welcomes visitors to its working cellars for tastings. A family member is often on hand to pour samples and answer questions. Some guests have been known to take part in the picking and crushing of grapes. After learning about the craft of winemaking, you can relax and enjoy a picnic lunch under the grape arbors or make reservations at the Hinzerling Winery's fine dining restaurant, which features a seasonal six-course menu served family-style. In 2001, the family opened the Vintner's Inn next door to the winery. The bed-and-breakfast, a 1905 farmhouse that the family moved onto the property and restored, offers two guestrooms with private baths and a continental breakfast. You won't find televisions or ringing telephones here. For a hearty welcome and a glimpse into the world of winemaking, be sure to visit the Wallace family at Hinzerling Winery.

1520 Sheridan Avenue, Prosser WA
(509) 786-2163 or (800) 727-6702
www.hinzerling.com

Photo by
Kathy Kongelbak

SUNNYSIDE

Visit Sunnyside and you will experience
sunny rural America at its best, with golf,
hunting, fishing, and many other outdoor
activities. Taste Washington's finest wines,
partake of the abundance of the land and
access it all with ease from a central location
in the fertile Yakima Valley. The many dairies
in this small community make it easy to see
why Darigold built a milk and cheese factory
here. Don't miss the Sunnyside Cinco de
Mayo Celebration, one of the largest in the
state. The Lighted Farm Implement Parade
in December is actually an amazing event
that the A&E has named one of the best in
the nation.

PLACES TO GO

- Sunnyside Historical Museum
  4th Street and Grant Avenue
  (509) 837-6010

- Central Park
  559 S 4th Street

THINGS TO DO

February
- Red Wine and Chocolate
  (800) 258-7270

May
- Cinco de Mayo Celebration
  (800) 457-8089

- Mayfest
  (800) 457-8089

June
- Pioneer Picnic
  (800) 457-8089

August
- Guerra's Produce Pepper Festival
  (509) 837-8897

September
- Sunshine Days
  (800) 457-8089

December
- Lighted Farm Implement Parade
  (800) 457-8089

Darigold Dairy Fair

ATTRACTIONS: *World-famous cheese-making factory*

A fun and educational experience awaits you at the Darigold Dairy Fair in Sunnyside. Darigold is a cheese industry leader. The cheese manufacturing plant on the premises produces more than 155 million pounds of cheese a year. Milk arrives locally from the many dairies of the beautiful Yakima Valley. The upstairs features a viewing area overlooking the manufacturing plant. Guests can take a free self-guided tour to learn about the art of making cheese. The Sunnyside plant is one of the most modern of its kind in the world. After your tour, you will find a tasty array of cheeses, local gourmet foods and ice cream in the gift shop, while a selection of deli sandwiches and soups offer lunchtime possibilities. With so many cow gifts on display, who could resist the urge to moo in the aisle? The Dairy Fair can accommodate groups and is fully handicap accessible with an elevator to get guests to the upstairs viewing area. Plenty of parking for cars, motor coaches and recreational vehicles is available. Visitors have come from throughout the United States and from a number of foreign countries. The Darigold Dairy Fair invites you to be the next visitor.

400 Alexander Road, Sunnyside WA
(509) 837-4321
www.darigold.com

The Knot Hole Gallery
GALLERIES: *The art of Thomas Kinkade, Painter of Light*

The Knot Hole Gallery specializes in the work of Thomas Kinkade, America's most collected living artist. The gallery is the only Thomas Kinkade gallery in Eastern Washington and offers canvas reproductions, prints and lithographs of Kinkade's art. You can also find Kinkade calendars and such novelties as jigsaw puzzles. Kinkade's representational paintings emphasize simple pleasures and inspirational messages. As a devout Christian, Kinkade uses his gift to communicate life-affirming values and he is known as the Painter of Light. Kinkade's prints and paintings are distinguished by glowing light and vibrant pastel colors. Rendered in an impressionist style, his works often portray bucolic, idyllic settings, such as gardens, cabins, landscapes, cottages and picturesque main streets. He has also depicted many patriotic and Christian scenes. Master highlighters from Kinkade's studio have visited the Knot Hole to add glowing highlights of fresh paint to the canvas reproductions. Ellen and Lloyd Phinney, owners of the gallery, create a warm and welcoming atmosphere for guests in their quaint showroom. They also carry a variety of special products that are not part of the Kinkade line. Come to the Knot Hole Gallery and see the beloved artwork of Thomas Kinkade, which hangs in one of every 20 American homes.

327 Yakima Valley Highway, Sunnyside WA
(509) 837-4836
www.theKnotHoleGallery.com

Black Rock Creek Golf Club
RECREATION:
Best place to toast the game of golf

Black Rock Creek Golf Club is in the Lower Yakima Valley wine country, and it is an attractive destination for both the golfer and the wine connoisseur. The club's slogan is "toasting the game of golf," and Black Rock Creek promotes local vintages. Black Rock Creek Golf Club prides itself on its excellent championship course and its customer service. The club presents an enticing challenge to every skill level, from novice to advanced. The course is links-style with water at 14 of the 18 holes. Black Rock Creek has great practice facilities, with a driving range, practice bunker and putting green. Instruction is available. While the club is a membership organization, the general public is welcome, and children are also welcome with their parents. The Black Rock Creek Grille has a full menu, featuring homemade soups and pies. Kelley Bowen, the superintendent, and Jeffrey Bender, the head golf pro, have worked together for many years to make Black Rock Creek a success. They hope to see you on the first tee.

31 Ray Road, Sunnyside WA
(509) 837-5340
www.blackrockcreekgolfclub.com

Apex Cellars

WINERIES: *One of Washington's most respected wineries*

The goal of Apex Cellars is to produce the finest quality wines imaginable and in this they have succeeded. *Wine News* says, "Almost everything [Master Winemaker] Brian Carter touches turns to gold, silver or bronze... medals." Brian founded Apex with Harry Alhadeff, a successful wine retailer and now the company president. Apex owns Outlook Vineyard, its own source for grapes. In his search for the best possible results, however, Brian also uses grapes from other vineyards. The Apex line of wines, the winery's premier offering, is made in small lots to ensure top quality. A second line, Apex II, uses grapes and oak barrels that do not quite make the cut for the premium line. Apex II wines are still excellent and are sold at an attractive price. Brian uses oak with restraint to enhance rather than dominate the fruit. Every Apex wine displays harmony, balance and complexity. The wines are smooth when first released and age beautifully. Apex wines range from Merlot and Cabernet Sauvignon to Chardonnay. If you cannot find Apex or Apex II wines in your area, you can contact the winery for direct shipments. Apex Cellars also sponsors a wine club that ships three bottles of wine quarterly for you to sample and enjoy. Tours of the winery are available. Visit in late April and you can participate in the spring barrel tasting.

111 E Lincoln Avenue, Sunnyside WA
(509) 839-9463 or (800) 814-7004
www.apexcellars.com

TOPPENISH, CITY OF MURALS AND MUSEUMS

If you are looking for a glimpse of the Old West, you can find it in Toppenish. The pride of Toppenish is the 69 murals depicting historical events which are painted on walls and buildings all over town. From May through September you can jump on a horse-drawn wagon for a narrated tour. Stop by the Visitors Center any time and pick up a guide map for a do-it-yourself tour. In 1989, a dozen artists gathered to celebrate the Washington Centennial. They completed the mural *Clearing the Land* in one day and began a tradition. Every year on the first Saturday in June, artists create a new Mural-in-a-Day. The murals have won several awards, including the Governors Art Award and a national Prettiest Painted Places award. Toppenish is also a city of museums. Take in the American Hop Museum, the Yakima Valley Rail & Steam Museum and the Yakama Nation Cultural Center, which boasts one of the finest Native American museums anywhere. A restaurant serves authentic Indian cuisine and you can rent teepees. Enjoy full Vegas-style gaming at the Yakama Nation Legends Casino. South of town is the Toppenish National Wildlife Refuge, where you can view water fowl. Fort Simcoe, an old army fort, is 30 minutes to the south and a perfect place to picnic and play horseshoes. It provides a museum and a great view of majestic Mount Adams. In addition to Mural-in-a-Day, Toppenish celebrates Treaty Days the first weekend in June and the Toppenish Pow Wow and Rodeo on July 4. The Toppenish Western Art Show is the third weekend in August. Toppenish is a great place to shop for Pendleton blankets, Trail of the Painted Ponies items or Western art. Come to Toppenish, where the West still lives.

TOPPENISH

PLACES TO GO

- American Hop Museum
  22 South B Street
  (509) 865-HOPS (4677)

- Northern Pacific Railway Museum
  10 S Asotin Avenue
  (509) 865-1911

- Yakama Nation Cultural Heritage Center
  U.S. Highway 97 and Buster Road
  (509) 865-2800

- Toppenish National Wildlife Refuge
  U.S. Highway 97
  (509) 865-2405

- Fort Simcoe State Park
  5150 Fort Simcoe Road, White Swan

THINGS TO DO

March
- Spilyay Indian Market and Arts Fair
  (509) 877-3505

April
- Spring Fling
  (509) 865-3262

June
- Mural-in-a-Day
  (509) 865-6516

- Yakama Nation Treaty Days Pow Wow
  (509) 865-5121

July
- Toppenish Pow Wow and Rodeo
  (509) 865-5121

- Toppenish Rail and Western Art Show
  (509) 865-3262

- Whistlestop Music Festival
  (509) 865-3262

September
- Fiestas Patrias Celebration
  (509) 865-3262

- National Indian Days Pow Wow
  (509) 865-5121

December
- Toppenish Toy Train Christmas
  (509) 865-3263

Best Western Lincoln Inn

ACCOMMODATIONS:
Only hotel in Toppenish proper

Whether visiting for business or pleasure, enjoy the comforts of home at the Best Western Lincoln Inn. The Lincoln Inn is the only hotel located right in the city of Toppenish itself, and is minutes away from Legend's Casino and the Yakama Nation's Cultural Center Museum. The hotel has been recently remodeled and is fresh and pleasant. Free high-speed Internet and Wi-Fi are available throughout the building. All rooms have a microwave and refrigerator. Several two-room suites are available with kitchenettes or in-room whirlpool tubs. The Lincoln Inn has a 24-hour fitness center, spa and a kidney-shaped indoor pool. There is a business center and meeting facilities. Guests partake of a deluxe breakfast buffet and freshly baked cookies every evening. Visit the Best Western Lincoln Inn on your next trip through Eastern Washington. Their friendly, knowledgeable staff will make you feel right at home.

515 S Elm Street, Toppenish WA
(509) 865-7444 or (877) 509-7444
www.bestwesterntoppenish.com

Northern Pacific Railway Museum

ATTRACTIONS: *Best place to learn about railroads*

Railroads are romantic. For proof, consider the devotion of the rail fans who established the Northern Pacific Railway Museum in the old depot in Toppenish. For 50 years, the depot served as the transportation center of the community. In 1981, however, it was boarded up. In 1989, local residents formed the Yakima Valley Rail and Steam Museum Association to reopen the depot as a museum. The group's good fortune was to have a depot, engine and track all available for use. After many hours of volunteer work, the museum opened in 1992. The depot was restored to the ambience of the 1930s. Its exhibits include dining car china, a Pullman berth and the refurbished dispatcher's office. In 1993, the museum obtained a 1902 Northern Pacific engine. After many more hours of volunteer work, the once derelict locomotive will return to service in 2007. A 1930s vintage freight train is also being restored. Cars include an ice refrigerator, a gondola and a ballast spreader/snowplow. A 1908 wooden caboose provides rides on special occasions. The museum is open May through October, Wednesday through Sunday. Special festivals include the Spring Fling in late April and the Toppenish Rail and Western Art Show in late August. On Saturdays from Thanksgiving to Christmas, visitors can view toy trains and meet Santa Claus. To learn about the importance of the railroads to Western development, come to the Northern Pacific Railway Museum.

10 S Asotin Avenue, Toppenish WA
(509) 865-1911
www.nprymuseum.org

American Hop Museum

ATTRACTIONS: *Best place to learn about the hops industry*

The nation's only agricultural hop museum was born out of the dream of local growers and is dedicated to showcasing the history of the obscure perennial vine bearing the botanical name *Humulus lupulus*. Hops have more than 200 active essential oils in the lupulin glands that are used in the brewing process to provide beer with its taste, smell, foam, flavor and physical stability. They are also used in medicines, herbal remedies, skin creams and perfumes. The Museum's remarkable facade, designed and painted by nationally acclaimed artist Eric Grohe, features larger-than-life murals depicting a brief visual history of the local hop industry. The trompe l'oeil architecture, murals and text won second place in the Signs of the Times international mural competition. When you enter the museum you will have an opportunity to view a video depicting the planting, growing and harvesting of hops in the 1990s. Then you will step back in time where visitor's can view striking informative exhibits, historical industry specific implements, artifacts and photographs. The museum chronicles growing hops, beginning in the 1600s in the Northeast to its migration to the Northwest in the mid 1870s and beyond. The visitor may envision the arduous processes and various activities undertaken to grow, harvest, dry and bale hops while visiting the exhibit area. Exhibits range from the original pole yards to the current 18 foot trellis, from hand picking to the portable picking machines and from hand ratcheted bale presses to horse drawn bale presses. In addition, the tools and implements used in storage and testing hops, as well as a mock kiln drying floor, can be seen. The displays depict the very beginnings of change in hop growing linked with the arrival of new technologies of hop cultivation, machines and tools. The distinctive gift shop features Hop apparel, jewelry, soaps, paintings, home, office and garden décor. Visit the American Hop Museum to learn more about hops and their unique history in American agriculture. They are Located in the City of Museums and Murals.

22 South B Street, Toppenish WA
(509) 865-HOPS (4677)
director@americanhopmuseum.org
http://Americanhopmuseum.org

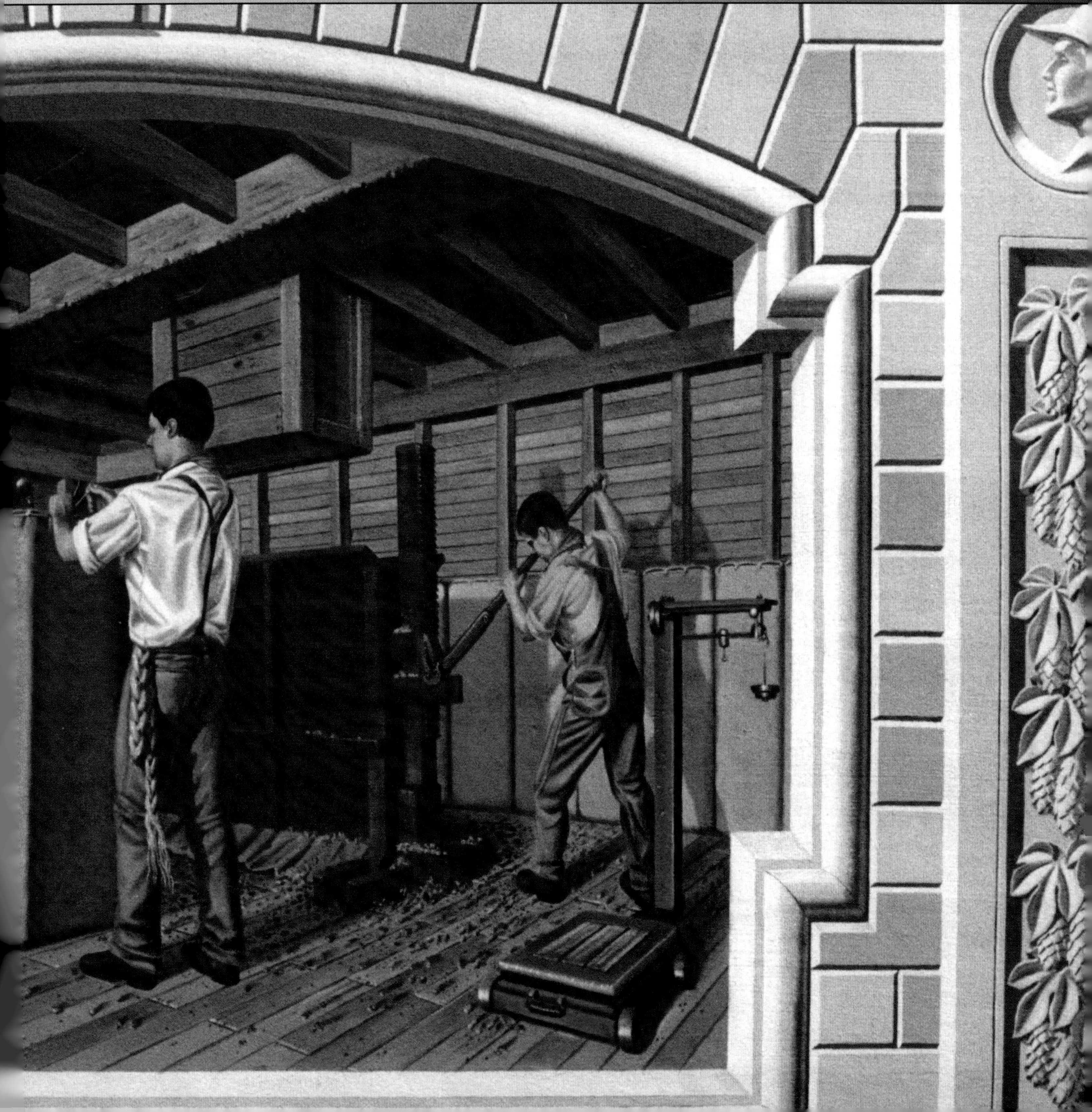

Gibbons Pharmacy

FUN FOODS: *Best soda fountain*

Once upon a time, the drug store soda fountain was the social center of every small town. Fountains like that are scarce today. In Toppenish, however, you can enjoy old-fashioned service at Gibbons Pharmacy and then go next door for a true old-time experience at Gibbons Soda Fountain. The Gibbons family has been serving Toppenish for more than 40 years. Everett and Mary Gibbons bought a pre-existing drug store in 1965, and today their son Greg Gibbons runs the business with his wife, Doris. In addition to their personalized service, the Gibbons display an impressive collection of old pharmacy artifacts. You can pick up gifts, souvenirs and collectibles. At the soda fountain, you can treat yourself with Tillamook ice cream, old-fashioned candies or caramel popcorn. The fountain can make milkshakes, sundaes and banana splits. The fountain serves a satisfying breakfast and has excellent hamburgers. In a concession to modernity, you can order espresso drinks or fruit smoothies. Toppenish is a city of museums and murals, and Greg gives back to the community by participating in this effort. For a great pharmacy and a fountain of memories, stop by Gibbons Pharmacy and Gibbons Soda Fountain.

117 S Toppenish Avenue, Toppenish WA (Pharmacy)
(509) 865-2722
113 S Toppenish Avenue, Toppenish WA (Soda fountain)
(509) 865-4688
www.goyakimavalley.com

We've Got Your Bag!!
SHOPPING: *Best designer handbags*

We've Got Your Bag!! is a gift shop that features unique handbags for unique people. The shop also carries the famous Trail of Painted Ponies horse figurines and is, in fact, the largest dealer of this art in the state. These figurines are replicas of the original life size statues from Santa Fe that are handcrafted with exquisite detail, each with an incredible story to tell. Mike and Vicki enjoy meeting people from all over the world and educating them about the products and the local history. This fun shop also carries many other novelty and gift items for all of your *retail therapy* needs. We've Got Your Bag!! is located in Toppenish, The City of Murals on the Yakama Indian reservation, and has a beautiful view of Mt. Adams. Plus you can stop in and say hello to Nacho, the store chihuahua.

202 W 1st Avenue, Toppenish WA
(509) 930-8030

PLACES TO GO

- Central Washington Agricultural Museum
  Union Gap
- McAllister Museum of Aviation
  2008 S 16th Avenue
- Yakima Area Arboretum
  1401 Arboretum Drive
- Yakima Valley Museum
  2105 Tieton Drive
- Chesterley Park
  N 40th Avenue and River Road
- Franklin Park
  S 21st Avenue and Tieton Drive
- Randall Park
  S 48th Avenue
- Painted Rocks State Park
  Powerhouse Road and Ackely Road
- Sarg Hubbard Park
  111 S 18th Street
- Yakima Sportsman State Park
  904 S 33rd Street

THINGS TO DO

April
- Spring Barrel Tasting
  (509) 965-5201

May
- Cinco de Mayo Fiesta Grande
  (509) 453-2050
- Yakima Live!
  (509) 453-2561

July
- Yakima Folklife Festival
  (509) 248-0747

August
- Vintiques Car Show
  (509) 454-3663

September
- Sunfair Parade
  (509) 452-7108
- Central Washington State Fair
  (509) 248-7160

October
- Fresh Hop Ale Festival
  (509) 966-0930

YAKIMA

Each year thousands of tourists come to the Yakima Valley for the sunshine, scenery, recreation and the abundance of attractions. During your stay in Yakima, take a step into history with a stroll along the boardwalk of Track 29 and visit unique shops located in authentic railroad cars. Visit the restored 1912 Northern Pacific Depot, which now houses a brew pub and one of the nation's first micro-breweries. You can see many other shops and attractions on North Front Street. Walk, ride a bike or in-line skate on the Yakima Greenway, a 10-mile paved path that follows the Yakima River and includes a string of parks, shady nooks, lakes and playgrounds. An unusual sight is the Indian painted rocks in a tiny state park just outside of town. The origin of these paintings is unknown to the current Indians of this region. Yakima is home to the Yakima Bears baseball team of the Northwest League. The Yakima Reds soccer team plays in the Premier Development League. The Yakima Mavericks football team is part of the Evergreen Football League.

Birchfield Manor Country Inn

ACCOMMODATIONS: *Best Inn*

If you stay or dine at Birchfield Manor Country Inn, you are traveling first class. This restaurant and inn has received too many awards and recommendations to list. One is the *Pacific Northwest Magazine's* Best of the Northwest. Birchfield Manor is the only Washington inn east of the Cascades in the Select Registry of Distinguished Inns of North America. The inn's setting is quiet and pastoral. The outdoor pool and park-like grounds are surrounded by pastures and hop fields. Wil Masset, a Swiss-trained chef and classical cooking instructor, bought the facility in 1979 with his wife Sandy and began serving Northwest cuisine with a continental twist. The menu changes seasonally. When available, try the salmon in puff pastry, one of the most famous entrees. Dinners are served Thursday through Saturday and sometimes on other evenings. Parties and receptions take place Sunday through Wednesday. The acclaimed wine cellar features local vintages—and you may find your favorite winemaker at the next table. Wil's son Brad is now the chef and manages the inn with his wife Erika. The inn has 11 rooms, five in the main building and six in the cottage building. Some rooms have fireplaces and many have two-person whirlpool tubs. An award-winning breakfast is included. The Massets can personalize a tour of the local wineries or provide a special package for honeymooners. Whether you seek a romantic getaway or a relaxed dinner with friends, stop at the Birchfield Manor Country Inn.

2018 Birchfield Road, Yakima WA
(509) 452-1960 or (800) 375-3420
www.birchfieldmanor.com

Hilton Garden Inn

ACCOMMODATIONS: *Most advanced hotel in the Tri-Cities*

The Hilton Garden Inn - Yakima, the city's newest first-class full-service hotel, is within walking distance of the new Yakima Convention Center. The Hilton Garden Inn builds on its exceptional guest service by offering the latest advanced technology and ergonomic comfort. For example, the Hilton Garden Inn provides more than a good bed. It has the trademarked Garden Sleep System that contours to your body and adjusts to your weight. Chairs are ergonomic Mira desk chairs by Herman Miller with 11 adjustable points. Naturally, all rooms have high-definition, flat-screen television sets. Even the alarm clocks in the rooms are high tech. They have jacks for your portable MP3 player so you can wake up to music of your own choice. The meeting rooms likewise have the latest technology. Rooms all have refrigerators and microwaves, and the lobby has a 24-hour convenience mart. The Great American Grill serves freshly prepared American favorites in a friendly setting. It is open for breakfast, lunch, dinner and offers room service.

Food and beverage director Peter Drobeck has helped open many fine restaurants throughout the Northwest, and sales director Sara Olson brings her award-winning experience to the hotel's goal of complete guest satisfaction. Along with general manager Randy Persinger, they invite you to stay at the Hilton Garden Inn - Yakima.

401 E Yakima Avenue, Yakima WA
(509) 454-1111
(877) STAYHGI (782-9444)
www.yakima.stayhgi.com

The Capitol Theatre
ATTRACTIONS: *A jewel of Yakima*

The Capitol Theatre has touched the lives of many people in Yakima. In the years since the restored theater was reopened in 1978, it has hosted Broadway productions, major speakers and a Christian concert series. It is the home of the Yakima Symphony Orchestra. It has even been used for weddings and baptisms. The Capitol Theatre first opened in 1920 as a grand vaudeville hall, the dream of Frederick Mercy. Renowned theater architect B. Marcus Pretica designed the building and A. B. (Tony) Heinsbergen created the decorative murals that graced the theater's interior. At that time, The Capitol Theatre was the largest theater in the Pacific Northwest. By the 1970s, however, it had fallen into disrepair. Fearing that it would be torn down, local residents rallied to save it. In 1975, the City of Yakima purchased the theater, which is now on the National Register of Historic Sites. Just days after the purchase, a fire gutted the building. The people of Yakima rallied to rebuild the structure and restore the grandeur of the 1920s. Heinsbergen came out of retirement to renew the murals, the last great project of his life. Some aspects of the building were improved rather than precisely restored. The orchestra seats have more foot room and better sight lines. The builders created a new lower level under the original building for offices and a reception room. Be sure to take a tour or see a show at The Capitol Theatre, Yakima's jewel box.

19 S 3rd Street, Yakima WA
(509) 853-8000
www.capitoltheatre.org

Yakima Valley Museum

Best regional history museum

History comes alive at the Yakima Valley Museum in Yakima's beautiful Franklin Park. The exhibits at this striking facility portray the valley's natural history, American Indian culture and pioneer life. Additional exhibits depict early city life and the roots and development of the valley's fruit industry. The museum features a superb collection of horse-drawn vehicles. It contains a reconstruction of the office of former Yakima resident and Supreme Court Justice William O. Douglas and is the repository for his personal belongings. The collections of the museum and its Sundquist Research Library include more than 38,000 objects and some 40,000 documents and photographs. In addition to permanent exhibits, the museum regularly hosts special shows. Programs and concerts take place throughout the year. Within the museum is the Children's Underground, an interactive center where children from five to 15 can learn while they play. A central courtyard contains the Neon Garden, a spectacular collection of neon advertising art from Yakima Valley's past. The Museum Soda Fountain is a functioning replica of a late 1930s Art Deco soda fountain that serves Green River soda, malts and phosphates. An Art Deco-style banquet and conference hall looks out on Franklin Park and is available for rent. The museum shop offers locally themed gifts plus one of the best available selections of books on Yakima culture, history and nature. For a true understanding of the Yakima area, come to Yakima Valley Museum.

2105 Tieton Drive, Yakima WA
(509) 248-0747
www.yakimavalleymuseum.org

The Seasons Performance Hall

ATTRACTIONS:

Yakima's premier music venue

The Seasons Performance Hall in Yakima is a 400-seat concert hall with unparalleled natural acoustics. Together with clear lines of sight from the tiered seating, the acoustics make the hall a perfect setting for live music. Jazz critic Doug Ramsey has called it a "listener's dream." The mission of Seasons is to nurture jazz and classical music, and since 2005, it has rapidly become a major venue for nationally recognized musicians, such as Mose Allison, Jessica Williams and David "Fathead" Newman. Donated by the Strosahl family, the hall was originally a Christian Science church and features the striking Renaissance/Romanesque architecture often favored by that denomination. At concert time, the doors open an hour early so that patrons can admire the grandeur of the hall, taste Washington wines and munch on desserts or appetizers. When the music is right, guests can dance on a floor in front of the stage.

The Seasons Music Festival puts on spring and fall programs, as well as weekly performances throughout the year. The hall is available for rent whenever the performance schedule permits, and local high schools and colleges often book the space for recitals. Every Friday at noon the Seasons sponsors a low-cost, brown bag concert with local and regional musicians. Here, you can see tomorrow's stars on the way up. Come visit the Seasons Performance Hall, a community gem that keep visitors returning to the Yakima Valley.

**101 N Naches Avenue,
Yakima WA
(509) 453-1888
or (888) 723-7660**
www.seasonsmusicfestival.com

Essencia Artisan Bakery and Chocolaterie

BAKERIES, COFFEE & TEA:
Best baked goods and chocolates

In pastry chef Ivone Petzinger's native Portuguese, *essencia* means essence. Essencia Artisan Bakery and Chocolaterie is home to the quintessential loaf of fresh baked bread, plus memorable pastries and chocolate confections. Pick up a baguette, croissant or ciabatta, then stay for breakfast, a lunchtime sandwich or pizza, along with a coffee or chocolate drink. Linger to use the Wi-Fi Internet access while enjoying the charm of this antique brick building. Essencia bakes bread in the artisan tradition, using a long fermentation process for rich, complex flavors. The loaves are shaped by hand and baked in a stone/steam oven to produce a crispy crust. The mouthwatering desserts and pastries include mousse cakes, tarts and muffins. Ivone's expertise with chocolate translates into killer brownies and Belgian truffles. Born in Brazil, Ivone is a culinary arts graduate of Johnson & Wells University. Essencia's professional team welcomes such special orders as wedding cakes. You'll get some of the best espresso drinks in town, all made with the café's house-brand coffee. The café also features its own fragrant version of chai tea and drinks that use chocolate essence, an intense mixture of high-quality chocolate made at the store. The shop hosts frequent dessert evenings, which pair specially prepared delicacies with wine. Ivone uses locally grown products, including wheat, whenever possible. Come sample the essential goodness of baked goods and chocolates at Essencia Artisan Bakery and Chocolaterie.

4 N 3rd Street, Yakima WA
(509) 575-5570
www.servalstudios.com/essencia

Yellow Rose Nursery

GARDENS, PLANTS & FLOWERS:
Best water gardens and demonstration gardens

Garden designer Lou Gannon can help you put together a garden or landscape with a theme that expresses your sense of style. Lou, who owns Yellow Rose Nursery with his wife, Teresa, has traveled extensively and studied the gardens of the world, from the magnificent gardens of Japan and Europe to those of India's Taj Mahal. He holds a bachelor of science in landscape architecture, is a licensed landscape architect and has 30 years of practical experience helping gardeners attain their goals. The nursery can help you design water gardens, from simple koi ponds to more elaborate gardens that incorporate streams and waterfalls. Various themed garden displays, such as Pacific Northwest, English and Mediterranean, show plants in their natural settings to allow you to see how different plants can be used to achieve the look you want. The Gannons are especially proud of the Tree of Life display. Ground cover plants are available, as are trees and water plants. Yellow Rose stocks many varieties of rocks, soils and fertilizers for completing and maintaining your garden. Hanging baskets make perfect gifts for nearly anyone. The Yellow Rose stocks Smith and Hawken gardening tools and furniture to make working and relaxing in your garden distinct pleasures. Lou and Teresa believe in going the extra mile for their clients, so in addition to design and plant sales, Yellow Rose provides complete installation services. Stop by the Yellow Rose Nursery and enjoy the landscape.

600 Merlot Drive, Prosser WA
(509) 786-3304

Yaktown's Finest Barber Shop
HEALTH & BEAUTY:
Voted top barbershop in the Yakima Valley

If the readers of the *Yakima Valley Business Times* can be believed, Yaktown's Finest Barber Shop is more than a name. It is a description. Micahn Carter, owner of the shop, started cutting hair when he was only 11 years old. He attended barber school in Seattle and worked there for two years, winning hair shows and contests. On the day he opened his Yakima shop, his first customers included the Yakima Sun Kings basketball team. Word of mouth did the rest. Barber J. D. Mares has since joined the shop, which recently moved to Nob Hill Boulevard. Many of the shop's customers are members of the younger set, aged from junior high to their early 30s. A shop specialty is the fade, a short cut that smoothly graduates almost from shaved skin to a longer length. Evidence of Micahn's talent with leading-edge styles is his ability to cut designs into hair. When the Seattle Seahawks made their first Super Bowl appearance, Micahn cut the Seahawks logo into the hair of two of his customers. He told the *Yakima Herald-Republic* that he sees hair-cutting as an art. "I just use the head like a canvas," he said. When not cutting hair, Micahn is a pastor at Morning Star Worship Center. He has mentored troubled youth and tries to uphold Christian values in business. If you are a gentleman who wants to look your best, you should visit Yaktown's Finest Barber Shop.

3609 W Nob Hill Boulevard, Yakima WA
(509) 469-2729

Meredith Furniture
HOME: *Best place for country-style furniture*

Meredith Furniture specializes in country furniture that is an extension of your lifestyle and personality. Look for sofas and recliners engineered for real comfort, including pieces featuring the good looks and luxurious feel of quality leather. Country bedroom suites at Meredith are sure to evoke sweet dreams. You'll find replicas of vintage styles and creative new expressions in rustic pine, oak and iron. For large spaces, the massive proportions of pieces by Randall Lee Dining set the tone for a warm country welcome. The Mission styling of Vintage Craft is always a tasteful choice. Meredith Furniture has been locally owned for more than 60 years, founded by Leo and Anna Meredith in 1946. In 1971, the Merediths sold the business to John Shuel, and John's son Mike became operations manager in 1977. The staff includes family members and longtime employees like warehouse manager Mike Andring, who has been with the company for 23 years. This Yakima institution gains more than 50 percent of its business from repeat customers, thanks to first-class customer service and top name brands like Lane, Howard Miller and Broyhill. The furniture experts at Meredith Furniture want you to know that your home is where their heart is. Whether you want comfortable pieces for cuddling up with the family to watch a movie or a bedroom reminiscent of a country manor, Meredith Furniture can enhance your lifestyle with pieces that will become family heirlooms. For a satisfying furniture shopping experience, visit Meredith Furniture.

2201 S First Street, Yakima WA
(509) 452-6221
www.meredithfurniture.com

Classic Events Catering

RESTAURANTS & CAFÉS: *Best catering*

Did the bride's mother forget to thaw the rolls? Donna Menard, owner of Classic Events Catering, has a solution. Donna understands that people hire catering services so the caterer can do the worrying and the client can enjoy the event. At a wedding, for example, the caterer should do the work, not the bride. Donna has been catering for more than 20 years and has handled events for up to 500 people. At first, it was a part-time job, but now business is booming. Today, Donna and general manager Lori Devitt sometimes handle three to four events in a weekend using multiple crews. Donna has an album of thank-you cards and long letters from grateful brides and their families. She earns this praise by doing everything possible to understand the needs and tastes of her customer well in advance of the event. On the day itself, "there's no situation I can't handle," says Donna. Classic Events can accommodate almost any menu request, but Donna has recipes of her own that are much in demand. These include her signature Wine Country Salmon and Baron of Beef. Donna has handled events at most of the local wineries, as well as fundraisers for Heritage University and the Yakima Symphony. She was vice president of the Washington Bridal Show for more than 15 years and has hosted a local public television show called *Best of Yakima Valley Cooking*. You can rely on Classic Events Catering for your next celebration. Don't just hope for the best, let Donna create it for you.

5453 Ashue Road, Wapato WA
(509) 961-7525

Miner's Drive-In Restaurant
RESTAURANTS & CAFÉS: *Best old-time burgers and shakes*

Miner's Drive-In Restaurant is an ode to the rock 'n' roll tradition of the great American drive-in restaurant. Ed and Irene Miner and their son, Lee, opened Miner's in 1948. Today the Miner's Drive-In empire includes Lee and his wife, Lois, their son and daughter, Gary and Renee, Gary's wife Diane, and their children Krystal, Rachael and David, otherwise known as Ed and Irene's great-grandchildren. Though it started with only three, Miner's now employees a dedicated staff of more than 70, some of whom have been with the business for more than 20 years. It takes teamwork to turn out the food at Miner's, because the food is never cooked ahead of time or pre-packaged. Everything's fresh or handmade, and they don't put a thing together until you've called in your order over the speakers. When was the last time a drive-in asked you how you wanted your burger done? Well, at Miner's, they cook it your way. In addition to the famous Big Miner burger, you can get many fabulous sandwiches, fish burgers and of course, that obligatory second-fiddle, hot dogs. A thick milkshake and crisp golden fries or onion rings add the finishing touches to a meal that'll have you humming golden oldies under your breath. The heart and care that goes into every Miner's burger is what has kept people coming back for more than 50 years. So come drive through and enjoy a great taste of our country's past.

2415 S First Street, Yakima WA
(509) 457-8194
www.minersdriveinnrestaurant.com

Russillo's Pizza & Gelato
RESTAURANTS & CAFÉS: *Best pizza and gelato*

In the beginning, Brandon Russell simply wanted a cute little ice cream parlor. With every step, though, his business plan grew larger and more Italian. Ice cream turned into gelato. Gourmet pizza became an absolute must. The result was Russillo's Pizza & Gelato, which takes the name of the original family patriarch. Russillo's charming décor reflects Brandon's Hollywood days. Brandon worked in the film industry for many years following his 1983 debut in *Bachelor Party*. If 12 blocks of Wilshire Boulevard can be recreated in a parking lot for *Volcano*, Brandon thought, we can surely rebuild Old World Italy in a little shop in Yakima. After Russillo's opened its doors in 2004, it quickly became a local favorite. Pizza built its reputation, but it is also the only gelaterie for miles around. Try the gourmet garlic chicken pizza or the Granitto Special with tomatoes and anchovies. Many claim that nothing beats a traditional Neopolitan with the thin Italian crust. If you want to branch out a bit, the Knuckle Sandwich is suspiciously like a calzone, and the Low-Carb Wrap is like a warm pizza burrito. Gelato powers the Italian sodas. Wines are exclusively from Italy or Washington State. Most nights feature live jazz, bluegrass or folk music. Come to Russillo's Pizza & Gelato, and enjoy what the *Yakima Valley Business Journal* has called the best pizza and ice cream in town.

1 W Yakima Avenue, Yakima WA
(509) 469-0516
www.russillospizza.com

Shopkeeper

Best boutiques for gifts, home décor and more

When Joe Simon began working part-time at the Shopkeeper in 1982, he never imagined that eight years later he would own it. In 1990, Joe and his business partner purchased Yakima's premier gift and floral shop, expanding its already impressive vendor list. They continued to build upon a reputation of providing excellent customer service, award winning floral designs and showrooms that spark the imagination. The Shopkeeper and the new Shopkeeper Downtown provide the most discerning buyer with unique, one-of-a-kind gift items and each of the 10 showrooms provides a stunning display of the finest home furnishings, from leather sofas to mahogany dining tables set with Baccarat crystal water and wine glasses and the finest imported china. Customer service, unique gifts, award-winning fresh floral and timeless silk arrangements have all helped to make the Shopkeeper a unique shopping experience, but the talk of the town and perhaps the Pacific Northwest, is the Shopkeeper Christmas Open House that happens each year on the last Sunday in October. The Shopkeeper's main Christmas showroom, secreted behind draped windows for weeks, is unveiled on Saturday evening and each year the Christmas Showroom is better than the year before. The Open House draws customers from all over the northwest for the spectacular viewing of more than 40 Christmas trees, each with a different holiday theme, from traditional to contemporary. Shopkeeper and Shopkeeper Downtown, located on Yakima Avenue next to the new Hilton Garden, are a must see for anyone visiting the Yakima Valley.

**3105 Summitview Avenue, Yakima WA
(509) 452-6646
Shopkeeper Downtown
399 E Yakima Avenue, Suite 180,
Yakima WA
(509) 457-8500**
www.shopkpr.com

Photos by Irene Pearcy

Fun 2 Learn

SHOPPING: *Best educational resource store*

Fun 2 Learn is an educational resource store with a mission. Owners Mary Peterson and Val Donovan value young minds and recognize the importance of providing quality products for the classroom, home or anywhere children want to learn. Teachers, parents, friends and relatives find top quality instructional tools, games and toys at Fun 2 Learn. The merchandise reflects a philosophy of endorsing products that stimulate and nurture the intellect versus the usual mass market items found in other venues. The original store opened in Kennewick 10 years ago, and another store opened in Yakima in 1998 to excellent reviews. Teachers shop on the weekends, and parents come throughout the week for special educational books, games or toys. Teachers have been known to come into the store and pay out of their own pocket for a learning tool they know will make a difference in one child's ability to learn. The store carries the full line of Carson-Dellosa and Dianne J. Hook clip art on disk for an artful touch to stationary, reports and decorations. Prepare today's young people for the challenges and opportunities of tomorrow by shopping at Fun 2 Learn.

5215 W Clearwater Avenue, Kennewick WA
(509) 736-1581
5611 Summitview Avenue, Yakima WA
(509) 457-2707

ZILLAH

Zillah is the business district of the Rattlesnake Hills wine appellation. Few places in the United States are surrounded by such a density of high-quality vineyards, wineries and cellars. Zillah and Toppenish are neighbors, incidentally. The trip from one downtown to the other takes seven minutes. Zillah has a number of unusual sights. One is the Teapot Dome gasoline station, shaped like a teapot. Built in the 1920s, it is one of the oldest functioning stations in the country, and is on the National Register of Historical Places. It was built to commemorate the Teapot Dome scandal of those years. Another sight is a 10-foot wire-and-pipe statue of Godzilla carrying a cross that was constructed by the Church of God, Zillah, which adopted the monster as a mascot.

PLACES TO GO

- Bonair Winery
  (509) 829-6027

- Claar Cellars
  (509) 829-6810

- Eaton Hills Winery
  (509) 854-2220

- Horizon's Edge Winery
  (509) 829-6401

- Hyatt Vineyards
  (509) 829-6333

- Maison de Padgett Winery
  (509) 829-6412

- Masset Winery
  (509) 877-6675

- Paradisos del Sol
  (509) 829-9000

- Piety Flats Winery
  (509) 877-3115

- Silver Lake at Roza Hills
  (509) 829-6235

- Tefft Cellars
  (509) 837-7651

- Two Mountain Winery
  (509) 829-3900

THINGS TO DO

February
- Red Wine and Chocolate   *(509) 829-5053*

May
- Zillah Community Days   *(509) 829-5151*

*Photo by
Kathy Kongelbak*

Hawk Haven

ACCOMMODATIONS: *Best guest house in wine country*

Hawk Haven Guest House does more than get you close to the wineries in and around Zillah. It is, in fact, nestled in the midst of the vineyards of several wineries. The house features two bedrooms with queen beds and a living room with a queen-size sofa bed, making it perfect for a weekend getaway for two or for several couples on a winery tour. Ten wineries host tastings within five minutes of your front door. You will enjoy sipping the wine of the day on Hawk Haven's 1,200-square-foot deck. The deck comes with barbecue grills and you can set the mood for the evening by selecting from the CD library. A Continental breakfast is served every morning. Six people can relax comfortably in the large hot tub. While conveniently located for a busy weekend of touring, the guesthouse is also popular with those seeking a quiet retreat. The grounds are lush and beautifully landscaped. Hawks and bald eagles frequently cruise the sky above the surrounding vineyards. A garden gazebo provides a serene spot for reading or contemplation. Whatever your mood, active or meditative, owners and innkeepers Chris and Susan Miller look forward to seeing you at the Hawk Haven.

2060 Bailey Road, Zillah WA
(509) 945-6455 or (509) 949-6001
www.thehawkhaven.com

Cozy Rose Inn Bed and Breakfast
ACCOMMODATIONS: *Best bed and breakfast*

Mark and Jennie Jackson go the extra mile to ensure that you will truly experience the luxury and privacy you are looking for in this beautiful country setting. After all, they are experts when it comes to knowing how travelers like to be treated. They have traveled around the world and have visited more than 400 inns and bed-and-breakfasts. From the moment you enter one of the five suites, you will feel like you have stepped into another country, perhaps France or Italy. The rooms catch the sunlight, while providing views of waterfalls and other lovely vistas. An air of freshness rises from the garden, where the Jacksons grow fruits and herbs for the inn's gourmet, intimate dinners in the beautiful new Tuscan-style dining room. The grounds are dotted with fruit trees and two acres of a lush green oasis of yards, flowers and gazebos. Stroll through the family vineyards and enjoy sweeping views of both grapes and hops. Modern amenities complement the Old World charm. Each room is very large with a private entry, large jetted or two-person soaking tub and shower. All suites host king-size beds, fireplaces, wireless Internet and satellite television. A candlelight breakfast can be delivered to your suite. An 18-hole golf course is located just five minutes away. With 50 wineries and breweries within 30 minutes of your door, the inn is perfectly located for tasting tours. *Bed and Breakfasts in the Northwest & California* awarded the Cozy Rose its highest five-star rating. It is the perfect balance of pampering and privacy. If you are ready to be pampered, let the Jacksons be your hosts. Wine and roses are available upon request.

1220 Forsell Road, Grandview WA
(509) 882-4669 or (800) 575-8381
www.cozyroseinn.com

Comfort Inn Zillah

ACCOMMODATIONS: *Best hotel in Zillah*

When you have driven or visited all day, it is a pleasure to stop at a hotel that does more than check you into a room. At the Comfort Inn Zillah, staff members bake fresh cookies every night and set them out with cold milk from 8 pm to 10 pm. They put on a crock pot of chili every day from 8 am to 12 pm, keep the coffee available 24 hours a day and have fresh fruit out all day. In the evening, you can pick up a book from a lending library with no required return, or rent one of more than 300 movies. The next day will be a new day, but tonight the Comfort Inn wants to live up to its name. An expanded hot breakfast is available, local calls are free and the entire hotel is a Wi-Fi hot spot. Most rooms are available with a refrigerator and microwave, 14 mini-suites have a sofa bed and two spa suites have in-room whirlpool baths. Naturally, the Comfort Inn has an exercise room, indoor heated pool and a spa. The Inn's conference room can accommodate 50 people and a variety of meeting equipment is on hand. Catering is available from several vendors. Put together the meeting room, catering and a spa suite, and the Comfort Inn becomes an excellent venue for a wedding reception and party. When visiting the wine country, relax and make the Comfort Inn Zillah your headquarters.

911 Vintage Valley Parkway, Zillah WA
(509) 829-3399 or (800) 501-5433
www.comfortinnzillah.com

Mount Adams

Oasis Spa Salon
HEALTH & BEAUTY: *Best spa and salon*

Located in the heart of the Yakima Valley's wine country you'll find Oasis Spa Salon. As you enter the doors to the relaxing aroma of lavender and chamomile or a hint of peppermint and other essential oils you can be assured that they create spa treatments just for your pleasure. Oasis Spa Salon caters to men and women, as well as those weary travelers looking to relax and rejuvenate away from their busy schedule. They offer a wide array of body, skin and hair services including spa parties that are exclusive to Oasis. Services are offered in beautiful indoor or outdoor surroundings, perfect for all occasions. Wine tours frequently begin and end at Oasis, so they also offer catering and limo services as options to spa parties and packages. Two popular party options are the Spa Pedi/Mani party and the Oasis Escape party. Call the spa director today to reserve your party or if you'd like to have a service provided by the talented staff. At Oasis Spa Salon you can enjoy holistic treatments and services for a totally relaxed and rejuvenated you.

505 1st Avenue, Zillah WA
(509) 829-6477

RATTLESNAKE HILLS WINE TRAIL

Eastern Washington State is one of the top five regions in the world for wine quality. The Yakima Valley is the heart of the wine region and Rattlesnake Hills is Yakima Valley's top fruit-growing area. Peaches and apricots grow here in one of the warmer parts of eastern Washington. Cherries are exported to Japan. The most highly regarded fruit, however, is now the grape. For 25 years, families and partnerships with a passion for wine have opened boutique wineries in Rattlesnake Hills. As a result, the area contains some of Washington's youngest and oldest wineries. As you meander among the 15 participating wineries of the Rattlesnake Hills Wine Trail, you will discover bold Merlot, elegant Gewürztraminer and luscious Port wines. Vineyards in the area successfully grow more than 30 grape varieties – all the varieties of Bordeaux and Burgundy plus top grape types from Germany, Italy, Croatia, and elsewhere. In the cozy tasting rooms of the wineries, you may cross paths with wine tourists from Europe, Asia, or anywhere else in the world. In 2006, the United States government named Rattlesnake Hills an American Viticultural Area (AVA), or appellation. The southern slopes of the Rattlesnake Hills, which make up the AVA, boast fertile soils and near-perfect growing

conditions. Fine, silt loam soils are left over from the last ice age. The Umtanum Ridge, the Yakima Ridge, and the Rattlesnake Hills ridge lines divert cold arctic air to the east, protecting the grapes. The southern exposure collects sunlight and warmth. Annual precipitation is less than eight inches, so there is plenty of sunshine for optimal growing. Irrigation comes, via canals, from the snows of the Cascade Mountains.

The best way to follow the wine trail through the rolling hillsides of the appellation is to buy a $5 passport (benefit card) from any of the tasting rooms. Start early. Most rooms are open daily. You will find wines ranging from Angelica to Zinfandel. Try new wines. Every vintage is a new experience. The wine type you thought was only so-so on an earlier trip may stun you today. Drink plenty of water between tastings. Let your hosts guide you and ask lots of questions. At many of the smaller wineries, the winemaker will be there in person at the tasting room. Special events take place frequently throughout the spring and summer. Take to the Rattlesnake Hills Wine Trail and enjoy palate-pleasing wines.

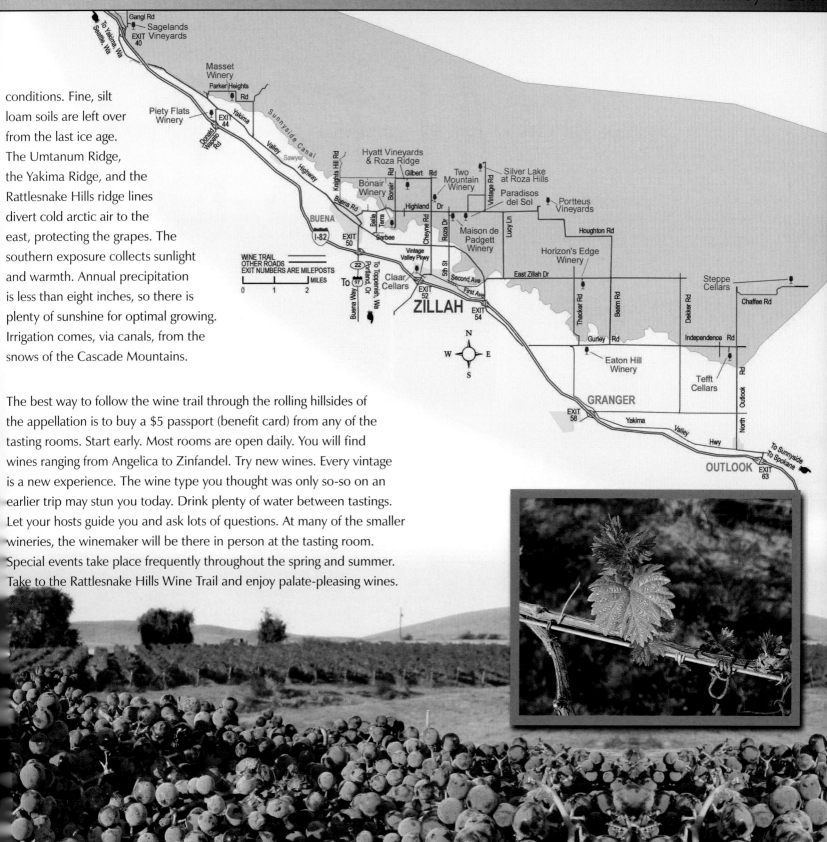

Map labels: Gangl Rd; Sagelands Vineyards; EXIT 40; To Yakima Wa; To Seattle, Wa; Masset Winery; Parker Heights Rd; Piety Flats Winery; EXIT 44; Yakima; Donald Wapato Rd; Sunnyside Canal; Valley; Sawyer; Highway; Knights Hill Rd; Buena Rd; Hyatt Vineyards & Roza Ridge; Gilbert Rd; Bonair Winery; Bonair Rd; Highland; Two Mountain Winery; Dr; Vintage Rd; Silver Lake at Roza Hills; Paradisos del Sol; Portteus Vineyards; BUENA; I-82; EXIT 50; Bella Terra; Barbee; Cheyne Rd; Roza Dr; Maison de Padgett Winery; Lucy Ln; Houghton Rd; WINE TRAIL; OTHER ROADS; EXIT NUMBERS ARE MILEPOSTS; MILES; 0 1 2; 22; To Toppenish, Wa; To Portland, Or; 97; Claar Cellars; Vintage Valley Pkwy; 5th St; Horizon's Edge Winery; East Zillah Dr; Steppe Cellars; Chaffee Rd; Buena Way; EXIT 52; Second Ave; First Ave; ZILLAH; EXIT 54; Thacker Rd; Beam Rd; Dekker Rd; Outlook Rd; N W E S; Gurley Rd; Independence Rd; Eaton Hill Winery; Tefft Cellars; GRANGER; EXIT 58; Yakima; Valley; Hwy; North; To Sunnyside; To Spokane; OUTLOOK; EXIT 63

Bonair Winery

The Puryear family invites you to visit Bonair Winery, their little hobby that got out of hand. The Puryears have been indulging their passion for winemaking since 1985. Bung the Wonder Dog will greet you when you come. You can taste buttery award-winning Chardonnays, elegant barrel-aged reds, fruity sipping wines and mead while admiring the art in the winery's gallery. Stroll through the vineyards and picnic by the koi pond. Bonair Winery is featured in the Best Places to Kiss in Washington.

500 S Bonair Road, Zillah WA
(509) 829-6027 or (800) 882-8939
www.bonairwine.com

Claar Winery

Claar Cellars is owned by the Claar family, who believe that wine is fun, healthy and an integral part of the good life. Members of the family have farmed the land since 1950. They planted the first grapes in 1980 and began making their own wine in 1997. Bruno Corneaux, the Claar Cellars winemaker, is a graduate of the University of Enology in Dijon and has made wine all over the world.

The winery has one of the more knowledgeable and friendly tasting room staffs in the valley. Be sure to try the Corneauxcopia, the Riesling and the Nouveau.

1001 Vintage Valley Parkway,
Zillah WA
(509) 829-6810
www.claarcellars.com

Top: Overlooking the Columbia River at the White Bluffs
Right: Claar Cellars' Tasting Room at Zillah on the Rattlesnake Hills Wine Trail
Background: Vineyards stretch toward the Columbia River

Eaton Hill Winery

Eaton Hill Winery invites you to taste its wines, handcrafted by winemaker Gary Rogers. Cabernet Sauvignon, Sun Glow and Orange Muscat are among the many varieties. Ed and JoAnn Stear own this historic Rattlesnake Hills property, formerly a fruit and vegetable cannery operated by the Rinehold family. The main building and the adjoining farmhouse are examples of the work of master builders in the early 1900s. The restoration of these historic buildings is an ongoing project. Eaton Hill Winery has a gift shop and a picnic area. RVs enjoy easy access and bicyclists are welcome.

530 Gurley Road, Granger WA
(509) 854-2220 or (866) EATONHILL (328-6644)

Horizon's Edge Winery

Horizon's Edge Winery is a real working winery where you can see the tanks and barrels at work. The winery's name originates in the panoramic view from the tasting room, which encompasses the Yakima Valley, Mt. Adams and Mt. Rainier. You can walk through 18 acres of prime vineyard and enjoy a picnic. All wines are produced in small batches. Varieties include Pinot Noir, Monster Chardonnay and Gewürztraminer. Have a sweet tooth? Try the Ice Wine, Nouveaux-Riche or Cream Sherry. Renowned winemaker Tom Campbell founded the winery in 1985, and David Padgett owns it today.

4530 E Zillah Drive, Zillah WA
(509) 829-6401

Hyatt Vineyards/Roza Ridge

Hyatt Vineyards is in the heart of the new Rattlesnake Hills appellation. From the start, Leland and Lynda Hyatt specialized in Merlot, which now accounts for half of the vineyard's production. Merlot was a fortunate choice because it has become very popular. In 2005, Hyatt added a Reserve tier of wines under the Roza Ridge label that has met with great success. Roza Ridge wines are mostly reds and include Cabernet Sauvignon and Syrah. Hyatt also produces Chardonnay, Riesling, dark Rosé from Black Muscat and—vintage permitting—a rare Ice Wine called Winter Harvest. The spacious tasting room overlooks a large picnic area with stunning views of Mt. Adams and Mt. Rainier.

2020 Gilbert Road, Zillah WA
(509) 829-6333
www.hyattvineyards.com

Maison de Padgett Winery

Maison de Padgett Winery, owned and operated by the Padgett family, specializes in good conversation and quality wine. Come explore the European gardens, relax on the shaded patio with your lunch or enjoy the panoramic view from the tasting room. Maison de Padgett wines are crafted with a twist that is reflected in the names on some of the labels, such as Risqué Chardonnay, Medusa Muscat, Singing Toad and End of the Road Red. Maison de Padgett Winery throws great parties. The winery has its own wedding chapel and banquet facilities are available.

2231 Roza Drive, Zillah WA
(509) 829-6412

Masset Winery

Masset Winery produces elegant wines to be enjoyed with dinner. The grapes come from established vineyards and are handled gently. The wines are aged in small French and American oak barrels. The winery's production includes Cabernet Sauvignon, Merlot and Syrah in small batches. The tasting room is located among beautiful orchards in an historic 1905 French-inspired farmstead, the home of Winemaker and Executive Chef Greg Masset and his wife Michaela, an artist. Masset Winery is the only non-California member of P.S. I Love You, a Petit Sirah advocacy group. The tasting room is open five days a week, so be sure to drop in.

620 E Parker Heights Road, Wapato WA
(509) 877-6675
www.massetwinery.com

Paradisos del Sol

Paul Vandenberg and Barbara Sherman of Paradisos del Sol drink more of their own wine than anyone else, so they want it to be healthful and nutritious. Paul says it must also be "wine that makes music in the glass." One of Washington's most experienced enologists, Paul has made a living from Washington wine since 1983. An organic farmer, he believes that great wine is grown, not made. The family-friendly Paradisos del Sol tasting room is in a '64 Rambler with chickens, cats, and dogs. Come taste the Rosé Paradiso, Angelica G, and Under 10 Buck Red. Come taste Paradise!

3230 Highland Drive, Zillah WA
(509) 829-9000 or (509) 829-5590
www.paradisosdelsol.com

Piety Flats Winery

Winemaker David Minick, Jim and Kris Russi, and partner Bryan Eglet produce distinctive wines at Piety Flats Winery. You can sample Syrah, Pinot Grigio/Chardonnay and Black Muscat, among others. The tasting room is in the charming 1911 Donald Fruit and Mercantile building, surrounded by other buildings from Wapato's early days—Piety Flats was the first part of the Yakima Valley to have irrigation. Enjoy a picnic with wine in the shady apple orchard next to the store, or sit on the winery's porch and enjoy a peach sundae. The kids will love the old-fashioned natural root beer.

2560 Donald-Wapato Road, Wapato WA
(509) 877-3115
www.pietyflatswinery.com

Left: Grape stomping contest at Silver Lake Winery's annual September Harvest Party in Zillah, Washington

Top right: William Ammons is Silver Lake Winery's winemaker

Background: The southern sloping Roza Bowl, as it is sometimes referred to, is situated between 900 and 1200 feet above sea level. Its protection gives grapes consistent ripeness and balance

Silver Lake at Roza Hills

Visit Silver Lake at Roza Hills and you can picnic on a spacious viniferanda with a dramatic view of the entire valley. The winery was founded by three professors at the University of Washington who shared a passion for wine. In the past 13 years, the winery has grown to become the seventh largest in Washington State. Roza Hills Vineyard, which underpins most of the wines produced by Silver Lake, produces outstanding red wines with intense varietal character. Silver Lake at Roza Hills has banquet facilities for everything from weddings to corporate meetings.

1500 Vintage Road, Zillah WA
(509) 829-6235
www.silverlakewinery.com

Tefft Cellars

You can stay overnight at Tefft Cellars, as well as enjoy the wine. In 2006, the winery reopened its completely renovated Outlook Inn Guest House. By hosting overnight visitors, the Teffts get to know their customers better. The Tefft family and their friendly staff produce small batches of premium wines. Wines handcrafted by Joel Tefft include award-winning Cabernet Sauvignon, Merlot and Italian varietals. The winery also makes ports, dessert and sparkling wines. The tasting room and picnic deck overlook the vineyard next to the guest house. A full-wall wine country mural decorates the patio and picnic area.

1320 Independence Road,
Outlook WA
(509) 837-7651 or (888) 549-7244
www.tefftcellars.com

Two Mountain Winery

The name of Two Mountain Winery was inspired by the breathtaking view of Mount Adams and Mount Rainier visible within a few steps of the tasting room. The Schmidt family produces award-winning wine in the shadow of these mountains. Phil Schmidt founded Schmidt Orchards in 1951 and three generations of Schmidts have established themselves in the heart of wine country. Matt Rawn, Phil's grandson, is vineyard manager and co-winemaker. Two Mountain Winery is known for its family friendly atmosphere and a place where you stop by to sip some wine and end up staying for dinner. Two Mountain Winery uses estate grown grapes to produce all of its wine, and has won awards in every competition entered.

2151 Cheyne Road, Zillah WA
(509) 829-3900
www.twomountainwinery.com

El Ranchito Restaurant

RESTAURANTS & CAFÉS:
Best Mexican restaurant

Tourists who regularly pass through Zillah have learned to schedule a stop at El Ranchito Restaurant. This family-owned establishment has been voted the region's number-one Mexican restaurant in *Northwest Best Places* six years in a row. As you might expect, customers rave about the authentic Mexican food. Walk through the doors and you enter Spanish America, decorated with piñatas and graced with *musica Mexicana*. Try the wonderful #2 enchiladas combination plate. As an alternative, consider the empanadas, small pies with a flaky crust and spicy filling. Seafood is another good choice. El Ranchito sports a casual, fun atmosphere, and it is a great place to bring the kids. The restaurant has a long beer and wine list and offers outdoor seating in season.

El Ranchito also has a Mexican bakery with the finest pastries made fresh daily. A grocery store and gift shop stock everything from *camales* (tortilla grills) and small Mexican pottery masks, to serapes. Banquet and meeting facilities seat up to 100 guests. Catering and takeout are available.

The restaurant grew out of an older business that manufactured tortillas for sale across the Northwest. El Ranchito Restaurant has been proudly serving the Northwest for more than half a century. Visit El Ranchito and discover why.

1319 1st Avenue, Zillah WA
(509) 829-5880

The Squeeze Steakhouse & Bar
RESTAURANTS & CAFÉS:
Best steakhouse

The Squeeze Steakhouse & Bar started life as the only soda, coffee and sandwich shop in Zillah when Thyri Bainter opened it 74 years ago. It had eight stools and the whole place was only nine feet wide. Thyri's son Ted took over the restaurant for her, and now Ted's son Rod works the family business, along with his wife Reneé. The name has changed, the restaurant has grown to 80 seats, and once prohibition was over the family got one of the first liquor licenses in town, but the fabulous food, terrific service and good times have stayed the same all these years. When a business has been around this long, it becomes a treasured part of the community. The minute you walk in the door you can feel the warm family atmosphere of the place. Fresh-cut, certified Angus steaks and prime rib are done to perfection here, with good old-fashioned side dishes that will make your mouth water. Seafood and pasta are also popular choices. You can find great wines from the area's local wineries here too, because the Bainters believe in supporting their own community. For three generations the Bainter family has been here, and those 80 seats have now been filled by three generations of regulars, so stop by and become part of the Squeeze Steakhouse family tradition.

611 1st Avenue, Zillah WA
(509) 829-6226

Index by Treasure

Index by City